THIS DAY IN
BASEBALL

THIS DAY IN
BASEBALL

A DAY-BY-DAY RECORD OF THE
EVENTS THAT SHAPED THE GAME

DAVID NEMEC AND SCOTT FLATOW

TAYLOR TRADE PUBLISHING
Lanham • New York • Boulder • Toronto • Plymouth, UK

Published by Taylor Trade Publishing
An imprint of The Rowman & Littlefield Publishing Group, Inc.
4501 Forbes Boulevard, Suite 200, Lanham, Maryland 20706
www.rlpgtrade.com

Distributed by NATIONAL BOOK NETWORK

Library of Congress Cataloging-in-Publication Data

Nemec, David.
    This day in baseball : a day-by-day record of the events that shaped the game / David Nemec and Scott Flatow.
        p.   cm.
    ISBN-13: 978-1-58979-380-4 (pbk. : alk. paper)
    ISBN-10: 1-58979-380-3 (pbk. : alk. paper)
    ISBN-13: 978-1-58979-407-8 (electronic)
    ISBN-10: 1-58979-407-9 (electronic)
    1. Baseball—United States—History—Chronology.   I. Flatow, Scott, 1966–
II. Title.
    GV863.A1N48   2009
    796.357—dc22   2008029012

♾ ™ The paper used in this publication meets the minimum requirements of American National Standard for Information Sciences—Permanence of Paper for Printed Library Materials, ANSI/NISO Z39.48-1992.

Manufactured in the United States of America.

Contents

Introduction

The history of our national pastime is so rich that books like *This Day in Baseball* could easily run to more than 1,000 pages and still not begin to cover every important event and development. It immediately becomes a practical matter of selecting only those moments in baseball lore that the authors judge to be the most interesting and significant. To a degree, it also becomes a matter of taste, and here that is certainly true. While we endeavor to include all the highlights and great achievements in the major leagues and minor leagues as well as many from Negro leagues, Japanese leagues, and the amateur scene, we also hope that even the most knowledgeable readers will find *This Day in Baseball* a trove of new information. Many of the entertaining nuggets we have included appear in a work of this nature for the first time.

Our decision to present our chronology of selections via the days in each month rather than the months in each year was done so as to more fully capture the flavor of how dramatically the game has changed since its inception. On January 5, 1916, for example, an entire major league team with an already long and successful history was sold for $500,000; 30 years later a single good but far from immortal player was sold for $175,000; and 55 years down the road a player who had yet to appear in his first major league game signed a pact for $14,000,000. Turning to Independence Day, we find that in 1873 a team leading 11–3 in the bottom of the 9th inning was nonetheless required by the rule at that time to take its last raps and scored 21 runs to win 32–3. In 1923 the rules were still in such a state of flux that the umpires permitted a player not on his team's active roster to participate in a game, but by 1985 the rules had been refined so that a pitcher with a .074 career batting average was forced to bat for himself in the bottom of the 18th inning because his team was out of substitutes—albeit with an unexpected result.

Along with providing a vivid sense of each era in baseball history, our aim is to supply famous firsts and lasts, the drama of pennant races, postseason action, and individual and team competitions and records. In addition to the major achievements and transitions both on and off the field, the low points, tragedies, and bizarre occurrences are also chronicled. All important trades, including many from the 19th century that have never appeared before in book form, are here, often with comment as to their ultimate impact. Likewise represented are free-agent signings, suspensions, and banishments from the game. We also feature key home run performances, perfect games, unique no-hitters, landmark seasons, and career milestones. However, we have not included every no-hitter, batter who hit for the cycle, .400 season, and microscopic ERA, but only those we deem the most significant. Our goal is to present a capsule history of the game rather than a record book.

For statistics, as our authority we use the current edition of *The ESPN Baseball Encyclopedia*, except in the rare instances where that reference conflicts with our own research findings. We differ more frequently, however, with *The ESPN Baseball Encyclopedia* and other reference works with respect to the names by which early players were most commonly known by their peers. Other primary sources consulted are *Sporting Life*, *The Sporting News*, many major newspapers, books similar to ours, our own notes from games we were spectators at, and figures in baseball we interviewed.

Significant points of demarcation for pitching and stolen base achievements are 1893, when the current pitching distance was established, and 1898, when the current rule for what constitutes a stolen base was established. Consequently, achievements in these areas are often prefaced with post- or pre-1892 and post- or pre-1897. We prefer these demarcations because they are more precise than the term "modern," which pertains to everything that happened after 1900 on the rare occasions when it appears in this book. Other demarcations we use are the Deadball Era (1901–1919), the Lively Ball Era (everything after 1919), and prewar and postwar (referring to World War II). We also advise readers that we recognize the National Association (1871–1875) as the first major league and hence have reported on several achievements in that loop as major league records and firsts.

There is a wealth of new information in this book, much of which we owe to fellow researchers and writers. In particular, we would like to thank David Ball for his seminal work on 19th-century trades and transactions, Dick Thompson, Al Blumkin, Dave Zeman, Frank Vaccaro, Peter Morris, Ross Adell, and Susan McNamara. Special thanks are owed to Cliff Blau for checking our feats, facts, and figures.

Throughout *This Day in Baseball*, we have used a number of abbreviations. Most will be familiar to baseball fans, and all are generally spelled out the first time or two they are encountered in the text. When a term like as batting average or a minor or major league like the International League or the National Association is mentioned for the first time, it is given in its complete form. After that it will usually be abbreviated as BA, IL, or NA, respectively. Postal abbreviations are used for states and sometimes for cities. For the sake of brevity, inning numbers are presented in numeral

Introduction

form (1st, 2nd, 3rd, and so forth); likewise, centuries are in numeral form: 19th, 20th, and 21st.

Abbreviations

AA	American Association (as both a major and minor league)
AB	at bats
AL	American League
ALCS	American League Championship Series
ALDS	American League Division Series
ALer	American leaguer
BA	batting average
BBWAA	Baseball Writers' Association of America
DBH	doubleheader
DH	designated hitter
ERA	earned run average
FA	Fielding Average
FL	Federal League
GM	general manager
HBP	hit by pitched balls
HOF	Hall of Fame
IA	International Association
IL	International League
IPHR	inside-the-park home run
KC	Kansas City
LA	Los Angeles
LCS	League Championship Series
LDS	League Division Series
ML	major league
MLB	Major League Baseball

MLer	major leaguer
MVP	most valuable player
NA	National Association or National Agreement, depending on context
NBA	National Basketball Association
NFL	National Football League
NL	National League
NLCS	National League Championship Series
NLDS	National League Division Series
NLer	National leaguer
NLRB	National Labor Relations Board
OB	Organized Baseball (referring to all major and minor leagues)
OBP	on-base percentage
OPS	on-base percentage plus slugging average
PA	plate appearances
PCL	Pacific Coast League
PL	Players League
RBI	runs batted in
TSN	*The Sporting News*
UA	Union Association

January

1

1894 Baltimore bilks Brooklyn out of future Hall of Famers Dan Brouthers and Willie Keeler in return for Billy Shindle and George Treadway.

1952 Puerto Rican hurler Hi Bithorn, an 18-game winner with the 1943 Cubs, dies in a Mexican hospital after being shot two days earlier by a police officer who is later imprisoned for his murder.

1974 Lee MacPhail succeeds Joe Cronin as American League president and holds the position until 1984, after which he joins his father, Larry, as the only father-son combo in the HOF.

1977 Danny Frisella, a reliever with five ML teams, dies at the age of 30 of injuries incurred in a dune buggy accident in Phoenix, AZ.

2

1888 Second baseman Fred Dunlap signs with Pittsburgh for $5,000, matching his 1884 Union Association salary with St. Louis and reputedly making him the highest-paid National League or American Association player to date.

1977 Ted Turner's tampering in the signing of free agent Gary Matthews leads Commissioner Bowie Kuhn to suspend the Braves owner for one year.

3

1923 The Yankees snare pitcher George Pipgras and infielder Harvey Hendrick from the Red Sox for catcher Al DeVormer and cash.

1946   The Red Sox get slugger Rudy York from Detroit for shortstop Eddie Lake.

1973   Great Lakes shipping mogul George Steinbrenner heads a limited partnership that purchases the Yankees from CBS for $12,000,000.

2005   Although not even located in a suburb of LA, the Anaheim Angels announce that their official new name will be the Los Angeles Angels of Anaheim.

4

1901   In recompense for jumping from the National League to the fledgling AL, John McGraw is given a chunk of the Baltimore AL franchise and appointed the team's player-manager.

1916   As part of the peace agreement between the Federal League and the two established major leagues, Phil Ball, the owner of the FL St. Louis Terriers, buys the AL St. Louis Browns for $500,000.

1932   The AL, in a Depression cost-cutting measure, reduces its staff of regular umpires from 11 to 10.

1942   Rogers Hornsby is the lone player named to the Hall of Fame in the year's balloting.

1957   The Dodgers are the first ML team to own its own source of transportation to away games when they buy a 44-passenger twin-engine airplane.

1977   Mary Shane is hired by the White Sox to be the first female television play-by-play announcer.

2005   Wade Boggs is elected to the HOF in his first year of eligibility.

2008   The House Committee on Oversight and Government Reform asks Roger Clemens and four other principals in the steroids scandal to testify under oath.

5

1893   Sokitaro Muriyakama, a Japanese college student attending school in the United States, throws a wrench into currently accredited stories of how baseball came to Japan when he tells the *Pittsburgh Dispatch* that a Professor Strange, an American educator at Tokyo High Academy, introduced baseball to Japan in the late 1870s.

1915   The FL sues organized baseball, calling it an illegal trust, and the case is assigned to Judge Kenesaw Mountain Landis, who deliberately waffles over his decision until the FL and its two rival major leagues make peace following the 1915 season.

1916   To shed disliked owner Charles Murphy, the NL arranges for his Cubs to be sold to Charles Weegham, owner of the FL Chicago Whales, for $500,000, and agrees to let Weegham relocate the Cubs in the Whales' Weegham Park, which was eventually renamed Wrigley Field.

1927   Judge Landis launches a public hearing to investigate charges instigated by former ML pitcher Hubert "Dutch" Leonard that Tris Speaker and Ty Cobb, among others, conspired to fix games in 1917.

1943   To comply with wartime travel restrictions, ML teams move their spring training sites to northern locales, inducing the Dodgers to train in Bear Mountain, NY, and the Yankees in Atlantic City, NJ.

1946   The Giants pay the Cardinals $175,000 for receiver Walker Cooper.

1963   HOF second baseman Rogers Hornsby escapes a second season as a coach with the hapless New York Mets by dying at the age of 66 of heart failure.

1975   Astros hurler Don Wilson dies in his Houston garage of carbon monoxide poisoning. Although police officially rule his death an accident, rumors circulate that it was suicide.

1999   Nolan Ryan, George Brett, and Robin Yount are elected to the HOF, the first trio to jointly make it in their initial year of eligibility, with Ryan bagging a record-tying 98.8% of the vote.

2001   Seven-time Japanese league batting titlist Ichiro Suzuki signs a three-year pact with the Mariners worth more than $14,000,000.

2005   After years of denial, Pete Rose admits on ABC's *Good Morning America* that he bet on baseball but continues to aver that he never wagered on or against his own Cincinnati club.

6

1877   Learning that a club can now assess a player $30 for his uniform and 50¢ a day to defray the cost of meals while the team is on the road, third baseman Joe Battin balks at signing a contract with St. Louis for the coming season but eventually complies.

1885   The NL allows Henry Lucas, the prime mover behind the UA, to replace the disbanding Cleveland NL franchise with his UA champion St. Louis Maroons.

1895   Chicago GM Jim Hart recommends that all players wear numbers on their uniform sleeves, as do polo players and bicycle riders, to help spectators identify them.

1896   John Ward, retired since 1894, takes legal issue with the New York Giants for continuing to carry him on their reserve list, but the practice of keeping retired players under reserve to prevent them from returning to the game with a different team lasts well into the 20th century.

1914   The National Commission grants several concessions to the Players Fraternity, organized the previous year by former ML outfielder Dave Fultz, specifically that clubs will pay players' travel expenses to spring training and will also notify them in writing whenever they are farmed out or released.

1920   Eleven days after the deal was actually made, the Yankees confirm they have purchased Babe Ruth from the Red Sox.

1942   Bob Feller is the second ML star to enlist in the military in preparation for World War II when he follows Hank Greenberg's lead and joins the navy.

1977   Angels shortstop Mike Miley is killed in a car accident in Baton Rouge, LA, at the age of 23.

2004   Paul Molitor and Dennis Eckersley join the HOF in their initial year of eligibility, with Molitor the first honoree who logged more than 1,000 games as a DH.

7

1890   After leaving the AA and joining the minor league Western Association, Kansas City sells one of its two rookie stars, Billy Hamilton, to Philadelphia of the NL for $6,000, and several days later peddles its other rookie sensation, shortstop Herman Long, to Boston of the NL for a similar sum.

1915   The Yankees get a bargain when they obtain first baseman Wally Pipp from Detroit on waivers.

1924   Cleveland sends catcher Steve O'Neill, second baseman Bill Wambsganss, pitcher Danny Boone, and outfielder Joe Connolly to the

Red Sox for first baseman George Burns, catcher Roxy Walters, and infielder Chick Fewster.

1933 As an example to players that all Americans must sacrifice during the Depression, Commissioner Kenesaw Mountain Landis cuts his own salary by 40%.

1962 Founded in 1901, one of the oldest and most venerated minor leagues, the Class B Three-I League (Illinois-Iowa-Indiana), folds when its teams are unable to compete with ML games televised into their areas.

1981 The Reds are the last ML team to test the free-agent market when they sign outfielder Larry Biittner, who hit just .213 during the season and was released a year later.

1985 Lou Brock is elected to Cooperstown in his initial appearance on the ballot and is joined by Hoyt Wilhelm, the first relief pitcher to earn admission.

1991 After serving five months for tax evasion, Pete Rose is released from federal prison in Marion, IL, and begins serving 1,000 hours of community service at Cincinnati inner-city schools.

1992 Rollie Fingers and Tom Seaver are elected to the HOF, with Seaver earning a then record 98.8% of the votes cast.

8

1898 NL president Nick Young outlines his plan for implementing an experimental two-umpire system for the coming season.

1916 Backed by banker friends, Harvard football coach Percy Houghton buys the Boston Braves for approximately $500,000.

1918 The Braves send second baseman Larry Doyle to the Giants along with pitcher Jesse Barnes for infielder Buck Herzog.

1944 Bill Terry quits as New York Giants manager to enter the cotton business.

1953 When St. Louis Browns owner Bill Veeck refuses to share the money he is paid to telecast the Browns' home night games, Cleveland refuses to schedule any night games at St. Louis.

2002 Defensive wizard Ozzie Smith earns Cooperstown induction with the lowest career batting average (.262) of any first-year-eligible, position-playing inductee.

2003 Slugger Eddie Murray and catcher Gary Carter join the HOF, with Murray among the growing number of first ballot selections in recent years.

9

1860 Frank Olin is born in a Vermont logging camp. Despite receiving little formal early education, he gives up a promising ML career in 1885 to become founder of the Olin Chemical Company, one of the world's largest makers of munitions. Possibly the game's first self-made multimillionaire who came from the playing ranks, Olin was worth more than $50,000,000 at the time of his death in 1951.

1893 Jack Cattanach, a former ML pitcher, steps into the ring at the Metropole in Boston, MA, and defeats heavily favored Jimmy Doherty in a 10-round light heavyweight bout.

1894 Charlie Bennett, one of the best catchers of the 19th century, loses both legs when he steps off a moving train and slips under its wheels.

1903 Following a series of talks at Cincinnati, the NL and AL reach a peace agreement that ends players' jumping between the two leagues, requires both loops to play under the same set of rules, and sets AL president Ban Johnson into motion to replace the ramshackle Baltimore franchise with a team in New York that will play in a park at 165th Street and Broadway at the highest elevation in Manhattan and appropriately be called the Highlanders.

1915 Overriding the protests of Pittsburgh owner Barney Dreyfuss, the National Commission declares University of Michigan pitching star George Sisler a free agent, enabling Sisler to sign with the Browns.

1927 The Giants get HOF pitcher Burleigh Grimes in a three-team trade with Brooklyn and Philadelphia in which they give up little.

1952 The Marines recall Ted Williams to active duty as an aviator in the Korean War.

1971 Former ML outfielder Elmer Flick dies in Bedford, OH, just two days shy of his 95th birthday, making him at the time the oldest member in the Hall of Fame's history.

1979 Hinkey Haines dies at the age of 80, 56 years after becoming the first man in sports history to play on two pro championship teams in the same season: the 1923 MLB Yankees and NFL New York Giants.

1980   Al Kaline earns Cooperstown on his first attempt while Duke Snider makes it in his 11th appearance on the ballot.

1989   Johnny Bench and Carl Yastrzemski are elected to the HOF in their first shot, with Bench the first catcher to earn membership in his initial try.

1990   On their first try, Jim Palmer and Joe Morgan are named to the HOF.

1995   Mike Schmidt makes the HOF in his first appearance on the ballot.

2007   First ballot candidates Cal Ripken Jr. and Tony Gwynn are voted into Cooperstown.

10

1835   Baseball pioneer and manager of the fabled 1869 Cincinnati Red Stockings Harry Wright is born in Sheffield, England.

1918   A's owner Connie Mack deals Stuffy McInnis, the last remaining member of the A's $100,000 infield, to the Red Sox, but for once Mack's goal is not cash, as he acquires two useful players in return, Tilly Walker and Larry Gardner.

1928   Never a fan of Rogers Hornsby, Giants owner Charles Stoneham sends Hornsby to the Braves for catcher Shanty Hogan and outfielder Jimmy Welsh.

1938   Willie McCovey is born 103 years to the day after Harry Wright. The two are currently the only pair of Hall of Famers born on the same day more than 100 years apart.

1991   The Orioles engineer a deal that will dog them for years by shipping Curt Schilling, Steve Finley, and Pete Harnisch to the Astros for Glenn Davis, who will play three injury-riddled seasons in Baltimore and hit .247 before exiting the bigs.

2006   Fireman Bruce Sutter is the first pitcher elected to the HOF without making a start in his career.

11

1901   Frank Brill, a pitcher with 1884 Detroit NL, wins the first ever American Bowling Congress individual championship of the United States in a meet in Chicago. Brill's reign as one of the top bowlers in the country will last for almost 40 years.

1958 Congressmen Kenneth Keating and Patrick Hillings reluctantly abandon their protracted efforts to make baseball conform to the nation's antitrust laws.

1971 Tigers lefty reliever John Hiller suffers a heart attack at the age of 27 but eventually returns to the diamond and sets a then season record in 1973 with 38 saves.

1973 In what is initially only a three-year trial, all 24 owners approve the AL's use of a DH.

2001 Hanshin Tigers star Tsuyoshi Shinjo is the first Japanese position player to sign a contract with a NL team when he inks a deal with the Mets.

12

1903 Shortly after being named Detroit's new player-manager, pitcher Win Mercer commits suicide in San Francisco while suspected of misappropriating gate receipts from California winter league games.

1920 After years of debate, the majors end the first-come-first-served system for drafting minor leaguers and vote for teams to draft in inverse order to the previous season's final standings.

1932 George Weiss resigns as GM of the Baltimore International League club to move to the Yankees front office.

1954 Organized Baseball comes to Cuba for the first time when Springfield, MA, of the IL is moved to Havana.

1983 Juan Marichal and Brooks Robinson earn Cooperstown enshrinement, with Robby being the initial third baseman selected for the honor in his first year of eligibility.

1994 Cooperstown taps Steve Carlton on his first try.

1999 Guernsey's Auction House in New York sells Mark McGwire's 70th home run ball for $2,700,000 to an anonymous buyer who is later revealed to be Todd McFarlane, creator of the comic book *Spawn*.

13

1883 The AA New York Mets and the new NL entry in New York— soon to be called the Giants—agree to schedule games simultaneously at their shared facility, the Polo Grounds, with their respective fields separated only by a wooden fence.

1922 Buck Weaver is the first of the eight banned Black Sox to apply unsuccessfully for reinstatement.

1939 Yankees owner Jake Ruppert dies at the age of 71 and is replaced as team president by GM Ed Barrow.

1954 The Phils trade pitcher Andy Hansen and infielder Lucky Lohrke to the Pirates for luckless Murry Dickson, who led the NL in losses in 1952 and 1953 and will lead again in 1954.

1972 When the New York Court of Appeals rules in favor of umpire Bernice Gera, mandating that OB hire her, in June she becomes a woman in blue in the New York–Pennsylvania League.

1978 HOF manager Joe McCarthy, who guided seven Yankees world championship teams, dies in Buffalo, NY, at the age of 90.

1982 Hank Aaron and Frank Robinson are both named to the HOF in their first year on the ballot.

14

1905 New York Giants owner John T. Brush, who joined with his manager, John McGraw, in refusing to play AL champion Boston in a World Series the previous fall, proposes a rule requiring the two pennant winners to meet in a postseason championship match at the conclusion of all future seasons.

1928 Al Reach, among the first players to openly admit to being paid a regular salary to play and later the founder of the A. J. Reach sporting goods empire, dies at the age of 87.

1940 Commissioner Landis condemns Detroit's mode of operation by declaring 91 players in the Tigers organization free agents.

1941 A dinner is held in New York City for baseball's leading concessionaire, Harry Stevens, and his four sons to celebrate the hot dog's 50th anniversary.

1949 Chicago sportswriter Fred Hayner, a star quarterback at Lake Forest College in the early 1890s and a one-game pitcher with Pittsburgh NL in 1890, dies in his Lake Forest home when the furnace explodes in the basement, where he went to rescue the family poodle after a fire breaks out on the upper floors. The circumstances are so suspicious that a coroner's inquest is held, but its findings are inconclusive.

1954 Former Yankees star Joe DiMaggio marries actress Marilyn Monroe in San Francisco, CA.

1981   When Frank Robinson is named manager of the Giants, he is the first NL African American pilot six years after breaking the same ground in the AL.

2000   The Arizona Diamondbacks sign journeyman pitcher Mike Morgan, enabling him to set a new record for playing with the most ML teams (12).

15

1885   The rebel UA disbands when only two teams send representatives to its winter meeting in Milwaukee, WI.

1888   The Texas League is organized but experiences numerous collapses and rebirths before attaining stability in the early 1900s.

1889   Former ML catcher Lew Brown dies in a Boston hospital of pneumonia exacerbated by a mental breakdown after learning that his leg would have to be amputated. The injury occurred during a scuffle with a crony at the Saracen Head saloon in which Brown's kneecap was shattered by a length of gas pipe wielded by a woman barkeep trying to separate the two combatants.

1934   As a sign of both the Depression and his fading skills, Babe Ruth has little choice but to accept the Yankees' offer of a $17,000 pay cut and sign for $35,000.

1936   When IRS figures are made public, to everyone's surprise the highest-paid figure in baseball is not any of the game's stars but Cards GM Branch Rickey at $49,470.

1942   In his famous "Green Light Letter," Commissioner Landis authorizes OB to continue play during World War II and encourages more night games so that war workers can attend, but the Cubs drop plans to install lights at Wrigley Field because the material can be better used in the war effort.

1958   The Yankees receive more than $1,000,000 to televise all but 14 of their road games in 1958.

1981   In his initial year of eligibility, Bob Gibson is the first African American pitcher elected to the HOF.

1990   Returning to the United States after a year in Japan, slugging behemoth Cecil Fielder signs with the Tigers and blasts 51 homers, the first big leaguer to top 50 since the Reds' George Foster in 1977.

16

1895   Pittsburgh sends pitcher Red Ehret and $3,500 to St. Louis for pitcher Pink Hawley.

1905   The Boston Americans trade future AL bat king George Stone to the Browns for former multiple-NL bat king Jesse Burkett, who quits after one dreary season in the Hub.

1916   A rookie sensation with the Cubs in 1910, pitcher King Cole dies at the age of 29 of testicular cancer.

1964   Charlie Finley's proposal to move his A's from KC to Louisville is rejected 9-1 by AL owners, and he is instructed to either sign a new lease in KC or lose his club.

1970   Cards All-Star outfielder Curt Flood files a civil lawsuit against MLB's reserve clause after announcing he will refuse to report to the Phillies, to whom he was traded three months earlier.

1974   Yankees teammates and long-standing friends Mickey Mantle and Whitey Ford make Cooperstown together, Mantle on his first try.

2001   In their first year on the ballot, Dave Winfield and Kirby Puckett are elected to the HOF.

2003   To increase incentive for participants in the annual All-Star Game, the owners endorse a proposal that the winning league in each contest will gain home-field advantage that fall in the World Series.

17

1916   The Giants win the bidding war for three elite FL players: two-time FL batting champ Benny Kauff, catcher Bill Rariden, and pitcher Fred Anderson.

1936   The Yankees acquire pitcher Bump Hadley and outfielder Roy Johnson from Washington for outfielder Jesse Hill and pitcher Jimmy DeShong.

1937   Cleveland sends homegrown outfielder Joe Vosmik to the Browns along with Bill Knickerbocker and Oral Hildebrand for outfielder Moose Solters, pitcher Ivy Andrews, and shortstop Lyn Lary.

1953   The Dodgers deal outfielder Andy Pafko, a major disappointment in Brooklyn, to the soon to be Milwaukee Braves for second baseman Roy Hartsfield and $50,000.

18

1938   Pete Alexander is the only new player named to the HOF.

1947   Unwilling to meet aging Hank Greenberg's salary demands, the Tigers sell the 1946 AL home run leader to the Pirates.

1950   After winning just 15 games the previous year, Cleveland's Bob Feller agrees to have his salary slashed by nearly a third, from $65,000 to $45,000.

1973   Orlando Cepeda signs with the Red Sox, making the former NL MVP the initial player inked by a club expressly to serve as a DH.

1995   Former flamboyant ML umpire Ron Luciano, known for his irreverent books about his days as an arbiter, is found dead of carbon monoxide poisoning in the garage of his home in Endicott, NY.

19

1900   After displaying the classic symptoms of a bipolar sufferer, Boston catcher Marty Bergen slays his wife and two children at the couple's Massachusetts farm and then takes his own life with a straight razor.

1931   Brooklyn purchases catcher Ernie Lombardi from Oakland of the Pacific Coast League.

1937   Nap Lajoie, Cy Young, and Tris Speaker are the second group of inductees to the HOF.

1938   After resigning his post with Cincinnati, Larry MacPhail accepts a position as the Dodgers' new GM.

1961   Cleveland releases Don Newcombe, freeing Newk to be the first former big league 20-game winner to try pro ball in Japan after he inks a deal the following year with the Chunichi Dragons.

1972   The baseball writers select Sandy Koufax, Yogi Berra, and Early Wynn for enshrinement, making first-timer Koufax, at the age of 36, the youngest member.

1977   Ernie Banks is the first shortstop to make the HOF in his initial year of eligibility.

2004   Retracting his retirement vows, 41-year-old Roger Clemens signs with the Astros and logs an 18-4 record, earning him an unprecedented seventh Cy Young Award.

20

1885 The AA abandons its one-year "expansion" experiment as a 12-team loop by dropping four franchises—Toledo, Virginia, Columbus, and Indianapolis—to again reduce the league eight clubs.

1930 Commissioner Landis forbids all pro baseball players from boxing as a sideline when White Sox first baseman Art "The Great" Shires challenges Cubs outfielder Hack Wilson to get into the ring.

1947 Josh Gibson, arguably the most renowned Negro league player apart from Satchel Paige, dies of a brain tumor at the age of 35.

1966 Ted Williams is the first AL position player selected for the HOF in his initial shot.

1984 The Mets again lose future HOF hurler Tom Seaver when they fail to protect him from a possible draft as the White Sox acquire him in compensation for losing free-agent chucker Dennis Lamp to the Blue Jays.

1997 Curt Flood, who challenged baseball's reserve system and ultimately made multimillion-dollar contracts a reality, dies at the age of 59 in LA.

21

1921 Kenesaw Mountain Landis officially takes office as baseball's first commissioner.

1947 Dodgers manager Leo Durocher marries actress Laraine Day, who becomes known as "the first lady of baseball" and writes a book after Durocher becomes manager of the New York Giants coyly titled *Day with the Giants.*

1953 The HOF snubs Joe DiMaggio in his first year of eligibility (the rule then required a player to be retired only one year) while selecting Dizzy Dean and Al Simmons.

1993 Tigers HOF second sacker and former GM Charlie Gehringer dies in Bloomfield Hills, MI, at the age of 89.

22

1857 The Knickerbockers orchestrate the first baseball convention in New York, with 16 clubs, all from Manhattan or Long Island, attending.

1913 The Giants grant the Yankees permission to share their Polo Grounds facility in 1913, a one-year concession that will be renewed each season until Yankee Stadium is built in 1923.

1918 The Yankees acquire pitcher Eddie Plank, second baseman Del Pratt, and $15,000 from the Browns for five players, including pitcher Urban Shocker and second baseman Joe Gedeon. When Plank opts to quit, the Browns receive the better deal.

1929 The Yankees announce that their players will wear numbered uniforms in 1929, with each of the first eight numbers corresponding to a player's spot in the batting order.

1943 The Yankees solve the first-base problem that has plagued them since Lou Gehrig's departure when they send the Phils $10,000 and four mediocre players for future AL home run king Nick Etten.

1960 Professing that he was overpaid in view of his poor perform-ance, Stan Musial, at his own request, is granted a salary cut from $100,000 to $80,000.

1969 Nine years to the day after raising eyebrows by requesting a pay cut, Stan Musial joins Roy Campanella in the HOF, with "The Man" earning the honors on his first go-around.

2003 The Red Sox launch a euphoric era in Fenway by signing Twins free-agent castoff David Ortiz for a mere $1,250,000.

23

1958 The Red Sox acquire infielder Pete Runnels from Washington for first baseman Norm Zauchin and the 1958 AL Rookie of the Year, Albie Pearson.

1962 The HOF elects Jackie Robinson and Bob Feller in their first year of eligibility.

1975 Pirates clubber Ralph Kiner is elected to the HOF by the scant margin of one vote.

1979 Willie Mays waltzes into the HOF, notching 94.7% of the vote in his first year on the ballot.

1993 By electing Reggie Jackson on his initial try, the HOF admits its first position player to total more career strikeouts than hits.

24

1939 Eddie Collins, George Sisler, and Willie Keeler are named to the HOF.

1962   The Southern Association, which was founded in 1885 as the Southern League and had remained in continuous operation since 1901, ceases operation.

1973   Pitcher Warren Spahn becomes a member of the HOF in his first year of eligibility. The mandatory five-year wait is lifted to allow the posthumous election of Pirates great Roberto Clemente.

1980   Publishing magnate Nelson Doubleday and Long Island businessman Fred Wilpon purchase the Mets for more than $21,000,000 from the Payson family.

25

1899   Baltimore trades shortstop Gene Demontreville to Chicago for shortstop Bill Dahlen, who joins Brooklyn in the spring when the syndicate ownership of Brooklyn and Baltimore opts to stock Brooklyn, the larger city of the two, with the cream of the players it jointly controls.

1934   In an interview, Giants manager Bill Terry jocularly inquires, "Is Brooklyn still in the league?" when asked about the Dodgers' chances in 1934, and the remark comes back to bite him when Brooklyn knocks the Giants out of the NL race in the closing days of the season.

1945   A group headed by Larry MacPhail, Dan Topping, and Del Webb purchases the Yankees from the estate of the late Jake Ruppert for $2,800,000.

1946   Five players in the Class D Evangeline League, including pitcher Bill Thomas, are banned for betting on 1946 playoff games, but Thomas, the all-time minor league win leader with 383, is reinstated in 1949.

1974   McDonald's mogul Ray Kroc buys the San Diego Padres for $12,000,000.

1978   The Padres trade lefty reliever Dave Tomlin plus an estimated $125,000 to the Rangers for an aging Gaylord Perry, who goes 21–6 and wins the NL Cy Young Award for the season.

26

1879   The NL admits Troy, NY, hiking the struggling loop to eight teams for the first time since 1876.

1901 Former gridiron teammate of University of Wisconsin great Pat O'Dea, Bert Husting, is the first hurler to defect from the NL to the fledgling AL when he abandons Pittsburgh to sign with Milwaukee. In Husting's case, the motive is not money but geography, as his grand-father, Solomon Juneau, was former mayor of Milwaukee, and Hust-ing later practices law in the city until Franklin Roosevelt appoints him U.S. District Attorney for eastern Wisconsin in 1933.

1931 Perennial minor league star Buzz Arlett finally gets his lone big league opportunity when Oakland of the PCL, which for years refused offers for him, sells him to the Phillies.

1932 Cubs owner William K. Wrigley, for whom the team's park is renamed Wrigley Field, dies, leaving both the Cubs and their minor league affiliate in LA to his son, Philip.

1963 The MLB Rules Committee, for reasons never explained, ex-pands the strike zone from the top of the shoulders to the bottom of the knees, resulting in a cumulative drop in batting average in the bigs of more than ten points and almost 300 fewer homers than the previ-ous year.

1990 The BoSox name Elaine Weddington assistant GM, making her the highest-ranking African American female executive in the majors.

27

1927 Commissioner Landis clears Ty Cobb and Tris Speaker, among others, of any wrongdoing in the 1917 game-fixing scandal, allowing both to sign as free agents with new teams; however, neither of them manages in the majors again.

1943 The Reds err when they sell aging Paul Derringer to the Cubs, who get three productive years from him, including 16 wins in his 1945 ML finale.

1944 A group headed by Lou Perini buys the Boston Braves and fires Casey Stengel as manager.

1953 The A's trade two-time AL batting champ Ferris Fain to the White Sox for shortstop Joe DeMaestri, first baseman Eddie Robinson, and outfielder Ed McGhee.

1982 In a swap that will haunt Phillies fans for the rest of the century, the Cubs ship shortstop Ivan DeJesus to the City of Brotherly Love for an aging Larry Bowa and future Hall of Famer Ryne Sandberg.

28

1847   George Wright, baseball pioneer and the game's first "King of Shortstops," is born in Yonkers, NY.

1901   The AL formally organizes as a rival major league, with the Baltimore Orioles, Washington Nationals (Senators), Philadelphia Athletics, and Boston Somersets (Red Sox) admitted to join the Cleveland Blues (Indians), Detroit Tigers, Milwaukee Brewers, and Chicago White Stockings, who were all members of the AL the previous year when it was still a minor league.

1953   Cards owner Fred Saigh is convicted of income-tax evasion and sentenced to 15 months in prison.

1980   Hank Aaron refuses Commissioner Bowie Kuhn's award honoring him for belting his 715th homer, citing baseball's neglect of retired Negro leaguers.

29

1949   The Cards sell pitcher Murry Dickson to the Pirates for $100,000, a transaction they come to regret when several of their young hurlers fail to develop while Dickson emerges as one of the NL's best pitchers in the early 1950s.

1951   The television and radio rights for the next six All-Star Games are sold for $1,000,000 per year.

1958   Only half a mile from his home in Glen Cove, NY, Roy Campanella crashes into a telephone pole in a rented Chevy sports sedan and sustains a broken neck that renders him paralyzed from the waist down for the rest of his life.

1970   Seattle Pilots rookie hurler Mickey Fuentes is shot to death during a barroom scuffle in his hometown of Loiza Aldea, PR.

1989   MLB drops the game-winning RBI as an official stat after nine years, assuring first baseman Keith Hernandez of forever being the career record holder with 129.

30

1923   The Yankees pick the Red Sox' pocket again by snatching future Hall of Famer Herb Pennock for three subs and $50,000.

1936 Anxious to change their team's image, the new owners of the Braves beg local newspaper reporters and fans to find a new nickname for the club. The consensus is Bees, which never captures public fancy.

1954 The Giants trade 1951 hero Bobby Thomson and catcher Sam Calderone to the Braves for pitcher Don Liddle, catcher Ebba St. Clair, and former "Bonus Baby" Johnny Antonelli, who will lead the NL in winning percentage and ERA in 1954.

1959 Cincinnati sends pitcher Harvey Haddix, catcher Smokey Burgess, and third baseman Don Hoak to Pittsburgh for pitcher Whammy Douglas; outfielders Jim Pendleton, Frank Thomas, and Johnny Powers; plus cash.

1994 Deion Sanders appears with the Dallas Cowboys in Super Bowl XXVIII at Atlanta's Georgia Dome, marking him the only athlete to date to play in the NFL's most esteemed contest and a big league World Series (1992 with the Braves).

31

1898 Cap Anson is unceremoniously fired after 19 years as player-manager of Chicago, and the Colts (nee White Stockings) are soon renamed the Orphans by the Windy City press.

1950 The Pirates make high school pitcher Paul Pettit baseball's first $100,000 "Bonus Baby."

1956 Cincinnati blunders by trading pitcher Brooks Lawrence and infielder Sonny Senerchia to the Cards for pitcher Jackie Collum.

1958 BoSox GM Joe Cronin signs a seven-year deal to replace retiring AL president Will Harridge.

1969 Minor league chieftains agree to introduce the DH in the International, Texas, Eastern, and New York–Pennsylvania leagues.

2000 Braves reliever John Rocker is slapped with a month's suspension by Commissioner Bud Selig for the bullpenner's racial and ethnic comments in a December *Sports Illustrated* article.

2001 A furor erupts after a piece in the *Wall Street Journal* quotes three members of the 1951 New York Giants confessing that the team conspired to steal opposing catchers' signs at their home park, the Polo Grounds, to aid the Giants' miraculous stretch drive to overtake the Dodgers for the pennant.

February

1

1911   After an outstanding rookie season in 1910, Cubs third baseman Jim Doyle dies at the age of 31 from complications following an appendectomy.

1913   Three-sport athlete Jim Thorpe is the first impact Indian player since Louis Sockalexis to sign with a ML team when he joins the New York Giants.

1926   Yankees first baseman Wally Pipp is sold to Cincinnati for $7,500 after losing his job to Lou Gehrig.

1957   ML club owners accept a new five-year player-pension plan proposed by the players but again reject their request to raise the minimum salary from $6,000 to $7,500.

1999   The Yankees deal third-base prospect Mike Lowell to the Marlins for three minor league pitchers who prove forgettable while Lowell launches an All-Star career in Florida.

2

1876   To help legitimize his coup that lured four star members of the Boston National Association champs to his Chicago club, William Hulbert effectively destroys the NA by organizing the National League at a meeting in New York that brings all of the NA's top teams aboard his new loop.

1919   The Giants acquire nefarious first baseman Hal Chase from Cincinnati for catcher Bill Rariden and first baseman Walter Holke.

1925   The NL celebrates the coming of its 50th season by staging its spring meeting in the same room in New York's Broadway Central

Hotel that hosted the initial loop meeting on February 2, 1876, and inviting all living players who participated in the NL's inaugural season.

1936 The baseball writers select the first entrees to the new Baseball Hall of Fame in Cooperstown, NY, with Ty Cobb, Babe Ruth, Honus Wagner, Christy Mathewson, and Walter Johnson being the initial choices.

1944 MLB agrees to count military service as playing time if a pension plan is ever implemented.

1949 The DeWitt brothers, Bill and Charlie, acquire a controlling interest in the St. Louis Browns for approximately $1,000,000.

1976 The Veterans Committee elects Roger Connor, Freddie Lindstrom, and umpire Cal Hubbard to Cooperstown, making Hubbard the first man elected to both the Football HOF and Baseball HOF.

1977 The Special Committee on Negro leagues elects Martin Dihigo, the first Cuban-born Hall of Famer, and shortstop John Henry "Pop" Lloyd, who was dubbed the "Black Wagner."

1989 When former All-Star first baseman Bill White replaces Bart Giamatti as president of the NL, he becomes the highest-ranking African American official in U.S. pro sports.

2005 The Cubs sever ties with slugger Sammy Sosa by shipping him to the Orioles for infielder Mike Fontenot, second baseman Jerry Hairston, and pitcher Dave Crouthers.

3

1898 Louisville makes its best trade during its eight-year tenure in the NL, sending pitcher Bill Hill to Cincinnati for outfielder Dummy Hoy, infielder Claude Ritchey, and pitcher Red Ehret.

1914 One of the last significant rule changes is adopted, making it an automatic out if a base coach makes contact with a base runner even if it is not his intent to impede or assist the runner.

1915 The AL bans the "emery" ball, first introduced to effect by Russ Ford in 1910.

1933 In response to the Depression and declining attendance figures, both the Cardinals and the Browns opt to discontinue broadcasting their home games from Sportsman's Park.

1979   The Twins swap Rod Carew to the Angels for outfielder Ken Landreaux and three others.

4

1901   Pittsburgh outfielder Tom O'Brien dies of consumption, which he reportedly contracted when a teammate convinced him on a voyage to Cuba that the best way to combat seasickness was to drink ocean water.

1909   HOF pitcher John Clarkson dies at the age of 47 in a psychiatric facility in Belmont, MA.

1938   The Reds acquire second baseman Lonnie Frey, a linchpin on their 1939 and 1940 pennant winners, from the Cubs for slightly more than the waiver price.

1950   The IL announces that it will make its first franchise shift in 13 years with the Newark club moving to Springfield, MA.

1958   The HOF fails to elect any new members for the first time since 1950.

1969   In a unanimous vote, team owners elect attorney Bowie Kuhn the fifth commissioner of baseball.

1976   Arbitrator Peter Seitz's decision to grant free agency to pitchers Andy Messersmith and Dave McNally is upheld by federal judge John W. Oliver, unleashing a flood of skyrocketing player salaries.

1990   The St. Petersburg Pelicans trounce the West Palm Beach Tropics 12–4 to win the championship of the Senior Professional Baseball Association in the lone full season it remains in operation as a haven for retired players.

1991   The Hall of Fame's Board of Directors votes unanimously to bar Pete Rose from the ballot, but Rose still garners 41 write-in votes in 1992, his first year of eligibility.

5

1880   Worcester is accepted into the NL, replacing Syracuse, the last NL club to fail to complete its schedule when it folded the previous season on September 10.

1905   Under suspicion after boasting that he made more money in losing the 1903 Chicago city series than he would have made in winning it, Cards pitcher Jack Taylor is spared expulsion by the NL Board of Directors when they render a verdict of "not proven" to the charge that he threw games.

1941 Planning to convert second baseman Joe Gordon to a first sacker, the Yankees sell Babe Dahlgren, Lou Gehrig's replacement in 1939, to the Braves.

1942 Without a first baseman after Johnny Sturm, the interim solution when the 1941 Joe Gordon experiment failed, enters the military, the Yankees make another ill-conceived deal, swapping minor league outfielder Tommy Holmes to the Braves for first sacker Buddy Hassett (like Sturm, a solution for only one year) and outfielder Gene Moore.

1956 ML owners reject the players' bid to raise the minimum ML salary from $6,000 to $7,000.

1999 MLB announces that it will give each circuit's best all-around hitter an annual Hank Aaron Award.

6

1935 Reigning NL MVP Dizzy Dean avers that he will not play for a penny less than $25,000, only to sign with the Cardinals the following day for $19,500.

1956 Brooklyn owner Walter O'Malley pledges to buy $4,000,000 in bonds to support the bill proposed by New York mayor Robert Wagner and Brooklyn borough president Frank Cashmere to build a $30,000,000 sports center in downtown Brooklyn that will include a new stadium to house the Dodgers.

1958 Some eight days after the Cards sign Stan Musial for $100,000, a new NL high, Ted Williams signs with the Red Sox for a reported $135,000, the highest ML salary to date.

1976 Headed by an investment group that features comedy film star Danny Kaye, Seattle is granted a franchise by the AL and debuts the following year as the Mariners.

7

1899 Now under syndicate ownership, Brooklyn and Baltimore stage a series of mock player trades that bring most of Baltimore's best players north to Brooklyn, including Willie Keeler, Joe Kelley, and Hughie Jennings, along with manager Ned Hanlon.

1908 Weary of his zany southpaw, Rube Waddell, Philadelphia A's GM/manager Connie Mack sells him to the St. Louis Browns for $5,000.

1942 The Reds sell the 1939 NL MVP, catcher Ernie Lombardi, to Boston, where he wins his second NL batting title for the season.

1949 Joe DiMaggio is the recipient of the first six-figure salary in ML history when the Yankees sign him for $100,000.

1950 Ted Williams is the new highest-paid player in ML history when the Red Sox ink him for a reported $125,000.

1959 Bill Veeck orchestrates a deal with White Sox president Dorothy Comiskey Rigney to buy the Pale Hose for $2,700,000, an agreement finalized on March 10.

1979 The Twins send Jesse Orosco to the Mets as the player to be named later in exchange for veteran lefty Jerry Koosman. Orosco eventually logs more games (1,252) than any other pitcher in ML history.

1994 NBA legend Michael Jordan switches from hoops to the diamond, signing a minor league contract with the Chicago White Sox Double A affiliate Birmingham Barons in the Southern League.

8

1891 Some 10 days after purchasing second baseman Cupid Childs from the disbanding Syracuse AA franchise, Boston's new AA entry trades Childs to Cleveland of the NL for infielder Cub Stricker and outfielder Paul Radford.

1897 Fleury Sullivan, loser of 35 games in 1884, his lone ML season with Pittsburgh, dies from a bullet wound inflicted the previous day by James Enright, a court bailiff, during a heated political argument.

1901 News leaks out that Nap Lajoie, one of the NL's elite performers, has jumped from the Phillies to the new Philadelphia AL club, along with two teammates, pitchers Chick Fraser and Bill Bernhard.

1927 In one of their few unsuccessful trades in the 1920s, the Yankees send career 200-game winner Sad Sam Jones to the Browns for Joe Giard and Cedric Durst.

1956 Connie Mack dies at the age of 93.

1972 Cooperstown welcomes Homestead Grays stars Josh Gibson and Buck Leonard, making them the first position players from the Negro leagues to receive HOF honors.

1982 The Dodgers ship second baseman Davey Lopes to the A's, breaking up LA's infield of Lopes, first baseman Steve Garvey, shortstop Bill Russell, and third baseman Ron Cey, a union that had remained intact for a record eight years.

1999 Elizabeth Neumeier, the first woman to hear an arbitration case since the process began in 1974, denies Red Sox outfielder Midre Cummings his salary request.

9

1914 Luckless Buster Brown, owner of the worst career winning percentage (.331) among ML pitchers in a minimum of 150 decisions, dies at the age of 32 of lymphoma.

1920 The Joint Rules Commission bans pitchers from applying foreign substances to the ball or altering it in any way, but a special provision allows established ML spitballers to use their pet pitch for one more season, although it is later revised to exempt them for the remainder of their careers.

1943 The Phils sink so low that bankrupt owner Gerry Nugent surrenders his majority ownership to the NL, which pays a meager $10 a share.

1949 When Danny Gardella's suit against OB for having banned him is sent by a federal appeals court to a lower court for trial, he is swiftly followed in his legal battle to gain reinstatement by such other Mexican League jumpers as Max Lanier and Fred Martin.

1971 Negro leagues legend Satchel Paige is nominated for the HOF, but his formal election will take place on June 10 by the new Special Committee on the Negro Leagues.

1972 Angels infielder Chico Ruiz is killed in a car accident in San Diego, CA, at the age of 33.

1995 Outfielder Darryl Strawberry pleads guilty to income-tax evasion and is sentenced to three months in jail.

2000 The Reds deal four players to the Mariners and also agree on a nine-year contract extension worth more than $116,000,000 to acquire Ken Griffey Jr.

10

1916 As part of the peace settlement between the FL and MLB, the FL Chicago Whales sell 10 players to the Cubs, including former Cubs star Joe Tinker, and the St. Louis FL club sells 10 players to the AL Browns, including outfielder Jack Tobin and pitcher Bob Groom.

1920 The minimum adult price for bleacher seats at all ML parks is hiked to 50¢—half the price of grandstand seats.

1924 Washington owner Clark Griffith names his 27-year-old second baseman, Bucky Harris (aka "The Boy Wonder"), the Senators' new player-manager.

1971 Bill White is the first African American play-by-play broadcaster in the bigs when WPIX-TV hires him to join Phil Rizzuto and Frank Messer in the booth for Yankees games.

1990 Samoan native Tony Solaita, a ML first baseman in the 1970s, is shot and killed in his native country during a land dispute with a relative.

11

1900 About to disband after being dropped from the NL, Washington sells outfielders Buck Freeman and Shad Barry and pitcher Bill Dinneen to Boston for $7,500.

1923 Brooklyn shrewdly trades aging outfielder Hy Myers to the Cards for the 1924 NL home-run king, first baseman Jack Fournier, plus infielder Ray Schmandt.

1928 The Pirates dupe the Giants out of future Hall of Famer Burleigh Grimes, destined to lead the NL in victories this season, for Vic Aldridge, who has just four more ML wins left in his arm.

1974 Twins pitcher Dick Woodson is the first player to take his case to arbitration and wins his salary demand of $29,000.

2005 To synchronize with his scheduled appearance on *60 Minutes*, Jose Canseco's inflammatory book, *Juiced*, is released in select markets.

12

1875 In conjunction with his brother Walter, pitcher Al Spalding relocates from Rockford, IL, to Chicago and launches the Spalding Brothers Sporting Goods emporium.

1898 *The Sporting News* reveals that Phils pitcher George Wheeler has been living a double life, married to one wife while also supporting a second under the name of George Heron.

1912 The Braves acquire outfielder Vin Campbell from the Pirates for outfielder Mike Donlin.

1994 Hall of Famer Ray Dandridge, considered by many historians to be the finest third baseman in Negro league history, dies at the age of 80 in Palm Bay, FL.

2002 In a game of switcheroo, MLB owns a team for the first time in more than half a century after purchasing the Expos from Jeffery Loria for $120,000,000, as Loria buys the Marlins from John Henry for almost $160,000,000. The Expos then make Omar Minaya the majors' first Hispanic GM.

13

1911 The Phils swap pitchers Fred Beebe and Jack Rowan, outfielder Dode Paskert, and infielder Hans Lobert to Cincinnati for outfielders Eddie Grant and Johnny Bates and pitchers George McQuillan and Lew Moren.

1914 The Braves sting the Cubs in a swap of second basemen, garnering 1914 NL MVP Johnny Evers for fast fading Bill Sweeney.

1953 The A's rename Shibe Park, calling it Connie Mack Stadium in honor of their former manager.

1970 Paul Edmondson, a rookie pitcher with the 1969 White Sox, is killed in an automobile accident in Santa Barbara, CA, while on his way to spring training.

14

1887 Chicago sells Mike "King" Kelly to Boston for a reported $10,000, the highest figure paid for a player to date.

2001 Umpires are informed by MLB to remove pitchers from the game without warning if they purposely throw at a batter's head.

15

1893 New York acquires second baseman, lawyer, and player organizer John M. Ward from Brooklyn for an undisclosed sum that is rumored to include part of New York's gate receipts for this season.

1910 A new rule mandates that an umpire must announce all substitutes, enabling both spectators and sportswriters in attendance to know when a new player has entered the game.

1916 The A's sell holdout third baseman Frank "Home Run" Baker to the Yankees for $37,500.

1964 Cubs second baseman Ken Hubbs, the 1962 NL Rookie of the Year, is killed in a private-plane crash in Provo, UT, at the age of 22.

1990 A lockout that will last for 32 days begins when owners refuse to open spring training camps without a new Basic Agreement with the Players Association, a move that will delay the opening of the regular season by a week.

1994 Ila Borders is the first female in modern history to pitch in a college baseball game when she helps Southern California College throttle Claremont-Mudd-Scripps College, 12–1.

2002 Padres outfielder Mike Darr is killed in a car accident near the team's Phoenix spring training camp.

16

1895 A machinist by trade, NL umpire Bill Betts invents a new type of indicator, more compact and reliable than the old version, and distributes one to each fellow NL arbiter prior to this season.

1924 Braves third baseman Tony Boeckel is the first active ML player killed in a motor vehicle mishap when he dies of injuries sustained the previous day while helping a friend change a flat tire.

1953 In a four-team deal also involving the Phils and Dodgers, the Redlegs come out on the short end when they hand budding slugger Joe Adcock to Milwaukee and receive only Rocky Bridges and cash.

1961 Charlie Finley buys the remaining A's stock to become sole owner.

1980 Brewers coach Harvey Kuenn has his right leg amputated below the knee to remove a blood clot and recovers to manage the club's first flag winner two years later.

17

1883 At the initial meeting between officials from the NL and the rebel AA, the first National Agreement is drafted, bringing a semblance of peace between the two leagues and increasing the number of players each team is allowed to reserve from 5 to 11.

1891 The AA withdraws from the National Agreement and fires president Alan Thurman after Thurman is branded a "Benedict

Arnold" for having joined with NL mogul Al Spalding in awarding three disputed former AA players from the disbanded PL to NL clubs.

1911 The *Washington Post* explains a new rule for the season that a pitcher cannot go "into his box" unless he has the ball "to render less easy of operation the hidden ball trick."

1971 Left fielder, first baseman, and DH Carl Yastrzemski inks a three-year $500,000 contract with the Red Sox, the largest deal in baseball history to date.

2003 Orioles 23-year-old pitching prospect Steve Bechler dies after a spring training workout, with suspicions linked to the dietary supplement ephedra, which the government bans in 2004.

18

1884 Former ML pitcher Terry Larkin, recently released from prison after shooting his wife and a police officer, is arrested again for threatening to kill his father. Larkin is later institutionalized after challenging his former employer to a duel and then commits suicide in 1894 by slitting his throat with a razor.

1893 Washington swaps second baseman Danny Richardson to Brooklyn for third baseman Bill Joyce and approximately $1,500 but then is unable to sign Joyce, who holds out for the entire 1893 season before acquiescing.

1909 Cleveland sends the Red Sox pitcher Jack Ryan, pitcher Charlie Chech, and $12,500 for pitcher Cy Young.

1916 Ed Irvin, who played with Detroit in the famous 1912 "Strike Game" and went 2-for-3 with two triples, is killed in Philadelphia when he is thrown through a saloon window.

1922 Commissioner Landis resigns his federal judgeship, claiming that both his baseball and bench positions are full-time jobs and that he prefers the former.

1943 New York lumberman William Cox buys the bankrupt Phils from the NL.

1954 The fledgling Baltimore Orioles make their first major trade— and a bad one—sending outfielder Roy Sievers to Washington for outfielder Gil Coan.

1960 Dodgers magnate Walter O'Malley completes his purchase of the Chavez Ravine area in LA by shelling out almost $500,000 for land valued at $92,000.

1967 Softball legend Eddie Feigner strikes out Willie Mays, Willie McCovey, Brooks Robinson, Harmon Killebrew, Roberto Clemente, and Maury Wills consecutively during an exhibition softball game.

1998 Beloved Chicago Cubs broadcaster Harry Caray, renowned for leading Bruins fans in singing *Take Me Out to the Ball Game* during the 7th-inning stretch, dies at the age of 84.

19

1935 After Babe Ruth announces he will only sign with the Yankees again if he is named manager, Lou Gehrig is the new highest-paid Yankee when he inks a contract for $30,000.

1946 Giants outfielder Danny Gardella is the first ML player to jump to the Mexican League and subsequently be declared ineligible to return to the majors by Commissioner Albert Chandler.

1957 The Yankees launch a raid on the A's that by June will bring third baseman Clete Boyer and pitchers Art Ditmar and Bobby Shantz to the Bronx in addition to three players useful to their minor league farm teams for six players whose best days, Yankees GM George Weiss rightly judges, are behind them, and rookie pitcher Jack Urban, who amazingly has a decent frosh season with the A's.

1970 Two-time Tigers Cy Young Award winner Denny McLain is suspended for three months by Commissioner Kuhn for his alleged bookmaking operation.

1983 Dodgers hurler Fernando Valenzuela is the first player to win a $1,000,000 salary via arbitration.

20

1877 The International Association forms in Pittsburgh as a rival of the NL but never achieves enough recognition in its four-year existence to be regarded historically as more than the first minor league.

1884 Altoona, PA, the smallest city to have a ML franchise, is admitted to the UA but disbands on May 31, 1884, and is replaced by KC.

1923 Ailing Christy Mathewson is named Braves president after he, New York barrister Judge Emil Fuchs, and James McDonough buy the Boston NL club for $300,000.

1929 Availing themselves of a new Massachusetts law allowing Sunday baseball in Boston, the Red Sox announce that they will play

Sunday home games, but a local law forces them to use Braves Field temporarily since Fenway Park is too close to a church.

1943 Branch Rickey and Phil Wrigley announce the formation of the All-American Girls Softball League, which switches to using a regulation baseball when the loop proves able to carry its weight financially.

1953 Anheuser-Busch Inc., a St. Louis, MO, brewery, buys all but seven shares of Cardinals stock from recently imprisoned owner Fred Saigh and installs August A. Busch Jr. as club president.

1963 The Cubs end the college of coaches experiment after the team finishes next to last in each of the previous two years and hire Bob Kennedy to be the club's lone manager in 1964. Meanwhile, the Giants' Willie Mays inks a deal for $100,000, making him currently the highest paid player in the bigs.

21

1931 The White Sox and Giants are the first ML teams to play a full game under artificial lighting when they play a night exhibition game at Buffs Stadium, the home of Houston in the Texas League.

1966 The AL announces the hiring of Emmett Ashford, the first African American umpire in ML annals.

1968 Union leader Marvin Miller negotiates the first Collective Bargaining Agreement between players and owners, which includes an increase in the players' minimum salary to $10,000 and the creation of a formal grievance process.

22

1922 Cards catcher Pickles Dillhoefer dies at the age of 26 from typhoid fever, which he contracted in a hospital while recovering from surgery.

2006 Vin Scully's contract is extended through 2008 as he begins his 57th year at the Dodgers' mike.

23

1921 The Braves send shortstop Rabbit Maranville to the Pirates for outfielders Billy Southworth and Fred Nicholson, plus infielder Walter Barbare and $15,000.

1934 Casey Stengel signs a two-year deal to manage the Dodgers.

1954 The Yankees sell Vic Raschi, one of their mound mainstays since 1947, to the Cardinals for $85,000.

1964 The Giants acquire three players from the Nankai Hawks of Japan, including pitcher Masanori Murakami, who will become the first Japanese-born player to appear in the majors.

1996 To speed up play, the Rules Committee announces a series of changes, including the expansion of the strike zone from the top of the knees to the hollow below the knees.

24

1917 Cleveland buys lame-armed pitcher Smoky Joe Wood from the Red Sox for $15,000 and converts him to an outfielder.

1943 The Double A Texas League announces that it will disband for the duration of the war, and other minor leagues soon follow suit, although none except the Texas League is at the Double A or Triple A level.

1948 The Yankees trade catcher Aaron Robinson and pitchers Bill Wight and Fred Bradley to the White Sox for pitcher Ed Lopat.

1966 University of Southern California star Tom Seaver signs with the Braves, but the deal is voided by Commissioner William Eckert, and the Mets later win Seaver's signing rights in a lottery.

1977 The A's deal Ron Fairly to the Blue Jays, making the outfielder, who had previously played with the Montreal Expos, the first big leaguer to appear with both Canadian franchises.

2000 The National Labor Relations Board upholds the decision to abolish the Major League Umpires Association and replace it with the World Umpires Association, ending Richie Phillips's 21-year reign as union chief.

25

1933 Multimillionaire Tom Yawkey purchases the Red Sox from Bob Quinn.

1934 John McGraw dies of prostate cancer at the age of 60.

1957 The pro football NFL's attempt to claim the same protection from antitrust laws that pro baseball receives is rejected by the U.S. Supreme Court.

1972 In a one-sided swap, the Cardinals trade future Cooperstown inductee Steve Carlton to the Phillies for pitcher Rick Wise.

1973 Players and owners settle on a three-year collective bargaining agreement, which includes, among other provisions, a $15,000 minimum salary and salary arbitration.

1981 The Executive Board of the Players Association votes unanimously to strike on May 29 if the free-agent compensation issue remains unsettled, but the deadline is later briefly extended.

1999 MLB hires Frank Robinson for a newly created position to handle on-field disciplinary matters.

26

1873 Cy Bentley, a 22-year-old rookie pitcher with Middletown of the National Association the previous year, dies of consumption in the Connecticut city.

1894 Deciding that scoring has increased too much in 1893 and pitchers need help, the Board of Control decrees that foul sacrifice bunt attempts will count as strikes and introduces the first infield fly rule.

1915 Frank "Home Run" Baker announces that he is quitting baseball rather than accept the Philadelphia A's lowball offer and sits out the entire 1915 season.

1935 Released by the Yankees, Babe Ruth signs with the Boston Braves for $20,000 and a percentage of the club's profits.

1957 The Giants send pitcher Hoyt Wilhelm to the Cardinals for ex-Giant Whitey Lockman.

1992 Red Sox owner Jean Yawkey dies at the age of 83, ending the family's ownership of the team, which began in 1933 when her husband, Tom, purchased the Sox.

2004 Cubs fans' efforts to exorcise their curse reaches its apex when the infamous foul ball Steve Bartman snatched away from Bruins left fielder Moises Alou in Game 6 of the 2003 NLCS is blown to bits at Harry Caray's restaurant in Chicago after the establishment purchased it for more than $100,000.

27

1894 New York acquires pitcher Jouett Meekin and catcher Duke Farrell from Washington for pitcher Charlie Petty, catcher Jack McMahon (who unbeknownst to Washington is terminally ill), and $7,500.

1895   After debating whether to restore the old pitching distance so as to decrease hitting, the NL quixotically votes to reduce the size of fielders' gloves instead so as to increase errors, but a lesser rule change, which charges a batter with a strike on all foul bunts, not just sacrifice attempts, soon creates the desired decrease in batting averages.

1901   The NL introduces a rule that foul balls with less than two strikes are now strikes, but the AL refuses to comply until 1903, accounting for more offense in the AL's first two years of existence.

1908   The sacrifice fly rule is introduced but is rescinded in 1931 and then refined several more times before it becomes a permanent fixture in 1954.

1956   In yet another warning signal that the minor leagues are unable to compete against ML games televised into their areas, the Piedmont League disbands after 37 years in existence, including the period during World War II when the majority of other minor leagues suspended operation.

1989   Washington State University first baseman John Olerud, a Blue Jays draft selection, undergoes surgery for a brain aneurysm after collapsing a month earlier at the conclusion of a workout.

2002   John Henry heads a group of investors who officially purchase the Boston Red Sox. Meanwhile, in the wake of the Enron financial scandal, the Astros buy back naming rights to their new stadium, Enron Field, from the bankrupt company for $2,100,000.

28

1893   The Cleveland Spiders, in recompense for financial aid received from the New York Giants, are coerced into trading coming star George Davis to New York for aging Buck Ewing.

1894   Pete McNabb, an oddball rookie pitcher with Baltimore in 1893, kills himself and his mistress, Louise Kellogg, actress and wife of R. E. Rockwell, former president of the Pacific Northwest League, with a gun at the Hotel Eiffel in Pittsburgh.

1931   One day after his successor, E. S. Barnard, dies unexpectedly at the age of 57, AL founder and longtime president Ban Johnson dies after a long illness.

1986   Commissioner Peter Ueberroth gives seven admitted drug users, including Keith Hernandez, Joaquin Andujar, and Dave Parker, a choice of a year's suspension without pay or hefty fines plus other sanctions, including a 10% garnishing of their annual salaries to fund substance abuse programs.

2000 AL umpire John Hirschbeck is elected the first president of the World Umpires Association.

29

1968 Former big league infielder and manager Lena Blackburne, who introduced a rubbing mud that umpires use to remove the shine from new baseballs, dies in Riverside, NJ, at the age of 81.

1972 Hank Aaron becomes the first $200,000-a-year ML player when he signs a three-year package with the Atlanta Braves.

March

1

1890 *The Sporting News* applauds the "Don Juan of the Diamond," Phillies catcher Harry Decker, a career con man and swindler, after he invents a new type of catcher's mitt and sells the patent to sporting goods magnate Al Reach, who soon has to engage a battery of attorneys when an Illinois man sues, claiming that Decker stole the idea from him. Decker, "a man of many loves and much trouble," is last seen in 1915 walking out the gates of San Quentin.

1919 The Indians fleece the A's of third baseman Larry Gardner, outfielder Charlie Jamieson, and pitcher Elmer Myers for outfielder Braggo Roth.

1947 Cleveland officially opens its first spring training camp in Arizona after owner Bill Veeck, who is planning to sign the first African American player in the AL, orchestrates the move from Florida knowing that the state is among the most tolerant of all races.

1954 In his first spring workout with the Red Sox, Ted Williams breaks his collarbone, idling him until May 15.

1965 A case of malaria forces Pirates star Roberto Clemente to miss a full month of spring training, but he rebounds to lead the NL in batting at .329.

1967 Commissioner Eckert approves the Baseball Writers' Association of America's proposal to choose a Cy Young Award honoree from each league rather than continuing to reward just one ML pitcher each season, the practice since the trophy's inception in 1956.

1969 Mickey Mantle announces his retirement after a .237 season that plummets his career BA below .300 (.298).

1988 Former ML outfielder Luis Marquez, the first Puerto Rican native to play for the Boston Braves, is killed during a family argument in Aguadilla, PR.

1993 Three years after Commissioner Fay Vincent's "lifetime ban" of Yankees owner George Steinbrenner for his relationship with convicted gambler Howard Spira, the tempestuous magnate is reinstated as the team's general partner following Vincent's departure as commissioner.

2

1874 New innovations for the National Association's fourth season unveil the first batters' boxes.

1886 The AA reduces the number of balls needed for a walk to six and adopts the stolen base as an official statistic. Two days later the NL makes the stolen base an official statistic but keeps the number of balls needed for a walk at seven.

1901 Third baseman Jimmy Collins launches a mass exodus of Boston NL stars to the rebel AL when he signs to be the player-manager of the Boston Americans.

1958 Mel Ott, the only slugger to date to clout 500 home runs in the NL, dies in a car accident at the age of 49.

2005 The Congressional Gold Medal, the highest honor Congress can award a civilian, is conferred posthumously on Jackie Robinson with his widow Rachel accepting the tribute, making Robinson the first baseball player so honored.

3

1873 The National Association adopts a standardized ball to be used in all league games.

1927 Babe Ruth signs another three-year deal with the Yankees for $70,000 per annum.

1932 Red Sox pitcher Ed Morris dies during spring training from stab wounds incurred in a fracas at a party in northern Florida given in his honor.

1953 The Browns try to preempt the Boston Braves and move to Milwaukee, but Braves owner Lou Perini, who also owns the Milwaukee minor league club, blocks the Browns and their owner, Bill Veeck, also a former owner of the Milwaukee minor league franchise, by invoking his territorial rights to the city.

1984 Peter Ueberroth, chairman of the Summer Olympic Games in LA, is elected to a five-year term as commissioner of baseball and officially replaces incumbent Bowie Kuhn on October 1.

1998 The Veterans Committee selects four men for the HOF, including Larry Doby, the first African American to play in the AL.

2006 At Tokyo Dome, South Korea's Jae Weong Seo defeats Taiwan 2–0 in the first World Baseball Classic game.

4

1872 The National Association of Professional Baseball liberalizes the pitching rules by allowing a pitcher to snap his wrist when he delivers the ball.

1902 AL clubs agree to adopt a three-tier ticket plan that will charge 25¢ for bleacher seats, 50¢ for grandstand seats, and 75¢ for front center grandstand seats.

1925 John M. Ward, the Players League founder and one of the top players of his era, dies of pneumonia one day after his 65th birthday.

1948 On the eve of putting together one of the finest all-around seasons of any performer in NL history, Stan Musial ends his lengthy holdout and signs with the Cardinals for a reported $31,000.

5

1906 The Cubs acquire third baseman Harry Steinfeldt from Cincinnati for pitcher Jake Weimer and third baseman Hans Lobert.

1966 The players gain their most important ally to date when United Steelworkers Union official Marvin Miller becomes the executive director of the MLB Players Association and eventually helps kick open the doors to free agency.

1973 The term "blockbuster swap" is redefined when Yankees lefties Fritz Peterson and Mike Kekich announce that they have traded wives, children, and dogs, but while Peterson will eventually marry the former Susanne Kekich and have four children, Kekich and Marilyn Peterson part shortly thereafter.

6

1878 After Indianapolis, Milwaukee, and Providence are admitted to the NL, bringing its total number of teams to seven, Louisville joins Hartford and St. Louis in resigning, reducing the floundering NL again to just a six-club circuit.

1922 Babe Ruth signs a three-year deal with the Yankees for $52,000 a year, more than triple what the next highest paid Yankee is getting.

1938 Forever in need of cash to keep his moribund team afloat, Phils owner Gerry Nugent sells first baseman Dolph Camilli to Brooklyn for $45,000 and outfielder Eddie Morgan.

1948 To open a spot at second base for Jackie Robinson, the Dodgers swap Eddie Stanky to the Braves for second baseman Bama Rowell, first baseman Ray Sanders, and $40,000.

1957 The baseball public is first apprised that Dodgers owner Walter O'Malley has been conferring with Mayor Norris Poulson and other Los Angeles public officials regarding a possible move of his club to LA.

2005 Suzyn Waldman is the first female to be a full-time ML color commentator when she joins John Sterling on the Yankees radio station WCBS-AM.

7

1857 The rules committee declares that 9 innings now constitute an official game and formally specifies for the first time that there are nine players to a side.

1893 The last major rule change in baseball history sets the pitching distance at 60'6" after the NL votes for the increase to promote more scoring, and all minor leagues who are members of the National Agreement are forced to comply or forfeit their membership; however, several minor and semipro leagues that are not part of the NA, as well as numerous colleges, continue play at the 50-foot distance for the moment.

1924 Pat Moran, who piloted both the Phillies and the Reds to their first NL pennants, dies at the age of 48 of Bright's disease.

1956 The players, as usual, have little choice but to accept the owners' proposals on the division of the World Series TV pact and to hold the minimum player wage at $6,000.

8

1900 With the season barely a month away, NL owners opt after a winter of dithering to reduce the loop to eight teams by lopping Baltimore, Washington, Louisville, and Cleveland.

1913 The last serious challenge to date to the monopoly on ML status that the National and American leagues have enjoyed since 1901 arises when the FL announces that it is forming as a six-team "outlaw" circuit that will not be bound by OB contract rules.

1923 Overriding the protestations of NL president John Heydler, Commissioner Landis continues his uneven treatment of troublesome players by allowing pitcher Rube Benton, who confessed to having prior knowledge of the 1919 World Series fix, to sign with Cincinnati.

1930 Babe Ruth signs a new two-year deal with the Yankees for $80,000 per annum, and when informed that he is earning more money than President Hoover, he is quoted as saying, "I had a better year that he did."

1941 With World War II imminent, Phils pitcher Hugh Mulcahy is the first MLer to be drafted.

1947 Having temporarily moved their spring training site to racially tolerant Havana, GA, to ease Jackie Robinson's transition to the majors, the Dodgers host the Yankees and win 1–0 in one of several spring games between the two teams that will eventually erupt into a feud among nonplaying members of both clubs and a string of charges and countercharges that force Commissioner Chandler to intervene.

1966 The Special Veterans Committee selects Casey Stengel for Cooperstown less than a year after Stengel's managerial career was ended by a broken hip sustained in a fall during the 1965 season.

1999 Joe DiMaggio dies of lung cancer at the age of 84 in Hollywood, FL.

9

1897 Holy Cross star Louis Sockalexis, a full-blooded Penobscot Indian, joins the Cleveland Spiders, who are more commonly called the Indians during his mercurial stay with the team, a nickname the Cleveland AL club later adopts.

1900 The NL votes to return to the one-umpire system and to make home plate five-sided rather than diamond-shaped so as to ease an umpire's task in determining whether a pitch near a corner is a ball or a strike.

1995 The Tampa Bay Devil Rays and Arizona Diamondbacks are welcomed by ML owners, with each expansion team having to foot a $130,000,000 franchise fee before beginning play in 1998.

10

1857 The National Association of Baseball Players is formed, with William Cott elected its first president.

1934 Jimmie Foxx, one of the last remaining members of the A's 1929 to 1931 AL dynasty, signs with Connie Mack for $18,000 after a bitter holdout campaign.

1993 The Giants hire Sherry Davis as the first female big league public address announcer.

1995 After hitting .202 in Double A ball, Michael Jordan announces that he is leaving the White Sox organization and returning to pro basketball.

11

1892 Cinders O'Brien (aka Darby), an 18-game winner with the Boston Reds in 1891, dies in Boston of pneumonia at the age of 24.

1901 The *Cincinnati Enquirer* reveals that Baltimore's John McGraw has signed a Cherokee Indian, but the deal is rescinded when the player is found to be African American second baseman Charlie Grant.

1941 Former Yankees catcher Pius Schwert, now a second-term New York congressman, drops dead of a heart attack while making an address at a dinner party shortly after proposing a bill calling for a physical fitness plan to aid in national defense, which he dubs "Hale America."

1958 Effective Opening Day in 1958, all AL players are required either to wear batting helmets or protective liners inside their caps.

2002 Outfielder Ruben Rivera is released by the Yankees for swiping Derek Jeter's glove from Jeter's locker and selling it on the black market for $2,500.

12

1902 Outfielder Mike Donlin, the runner-up for the AL batting title in 1901, is forced to miss almost the entire 1902 season when he is sentenced to six months in jail for assaulting actress Minnie Fields. Donlin, a roué with an eye on Hollywood, later marries actress Mabel Hite and plays bit roles in silents.

1907 Former St. Louis Browns pitcher and outfielder Pat Hynes, now with Milwaukee of the AA, is shot to death by a bartender on his 23rd birthday in a saloon near his St. Louis home.

1930 Reginald "Jack" Powell, who pitched in two games for the Browns in 1913, chokes to death in a Memphis, TN, restaurant after betting that he can eat an entire steak in one gulp.

1951 A winter of discontent for Happy Chandler culminates when he is voted out of his commissioner's post by the same 9–7 margin that refused to renew his contract the previous fall.

13

1943 Responding to an edict from the War Department to use cheaper materials, the majors adopt a new ball, with an interior made of reclaimed cork and balata.

1954 Braves outfielder Bobby Thomson, acquired in an off-season trade with the Giants, breaks his ankle sliding in a spring exhibition game, opening a spot in the lineup for rookie Hank Aaron.

1960 Maverick magnate Bill Veeck unveils the new White Sox uniforms, the first to feature last names on the back, making it easier for fans to identify players.

1969 After pitching dominated the 1968 season to the point of absurdity, MLB attempts to rectify the imbalance by shrinking the strike zone and lowering the maximum mound height from 15 to 10 inches.

14

1860 The fourth annual convention of the National Association of Baseball Players draws 62 teams.

1893 After just one season in Philadelphia, slugging first baseman Roger Connor returns to New York in a trade for catcher Jack Boyle, pitcher Jack Sharrott, and cash.

1932 Brooklyn trades outfielder Babe Herman and catcher Ernie Lombardi to the Reds for catcher Clyde Sukeforth, third baseman Joe Stripp, and second baseman Tony Cuccinello.

1961 In the forlorn hope that the Yankees magic will rub off on them, the NL expansion New York Mets name retired Bombers GM George Weiss as team president.

15

1859 At the annual meeting of the National Association of Baseball Players, Rule 36 is amended to state that no player shall be permitted to participate in a game if he is being paid to play.

1925 Cubs shortstop Rabbit Maranville breaks his leg sliding in an exhibition game at LA.

1945 With so many players now in the military, Washington tests one-legged war veteran Bert Shepard as a pitcher while the defending AL champion Browns have already penciled one-armed outfielder Pete Gray, the 1944 Southern Association MVP, into their Opening Day lineup

16

1895 John T. Brush, owner of both the Cincinnati NL team and a minor league team in Indianapolis, introduces the "farm system" when he begins shuttling players back and forth between the two clubs.

1953 The animosity Bill Veeck has incurred as owner of the Indians and Browns impels other AL owners to refuse the Browns' proposed move to Baltimore as long as he remains in control of the team.

1969 San Francisco Giants pitching prospect Nestor Chavez is killed in the worst aviation disaster in history to date, a plane crash outside of Maracaibo, Venezuela, that kills 155 people.

1985 Former Tigers ace Denny McLain is slapped with a 23-year prison sentence upon conviction of extortion, racketeering, and cocaine possession in Tampa, FL, but will only serve 29 months after an appellate court overturns the decision.

1999 Cubs fans are dealt a devastating blow when they learn that NL Rookie of the Year winner Kerry Wood's ligament tear in his right elbow will require surgery, sidelining him for the entire season.

17

1871 The first all-pro league, the National Association of Professional Baseball Players, forms in New York and assesses teams applying for membership an admission fee of $5.00.

1872 Elmer White, an outfielder with the Cleveland Forest Citys the previous year, is the first MLer to die while still active when he expires at his Caton, NY, home.

1884 The UA is the first ML to adopt the percentage system rather than the number of games won in determining its champion.

1886 The oldest sports publication in the United States, *The Sporting News* circulates its first issue in St. Louis.

1965 ABC signs Jackie Robinson as a member of its MLB announcing team, making him the first African American broadcaster to receive a network post.

2005 Retired slugger Mark McGwire is castigated by the press and public after refusing to discuss his past or deny taking performance-enhancing substances during a lengthy Committee on Government Reform hearing concerning the alleged rampant player use of steroids.

18

1910 Cardinals infielder Alan Storke dies at the age of 25 of complications following lung surgery.

1953 The Boston Braves become the first ML team since 1903 to relocate when baseball approves their proposed move to Milwaukee, with the Milwaukee minor league team in the AA moving to Toledo.

1957 The Indians turn down Boston's offer of $1,000,000 for the AL's most prized southpaw at the time, Herb Score.

1985 In a wise public relations move, Commissioner Peter Ueberroth rescinds Willie Mays's and Mickey Mantle's banishment from OB by former Commissioner Kuhn due to their employment as goodwill ambassadors by Atlantic City casinos.

1990 A new collective bargaining agreement is reached that ends the 32-day lockout of spring training camps by ML owners and includes raising the minimum ML salary to $100,000, more than 10 times what it was just 30 years earlier.

19

1898 The Rules Committee tightens the criteria of what constitutes a stolen base, bringing a uniformity among scorers that shrinks player stolen base totals across the board in future seasons.

1998   Media billionaire Rupert Murdoch purchases the Dodgers from Peter O'Malley for a reported $311,000,000, the highest price ever paid at that time for an American sports franchise.

20

1943   Bob Johnson, one of the AL's top outfielders of the past decade, escapes the apathetic Athletics when he is traded to Washington for Bobby Estalella and Jimmy Pofahl.

1973   Roberto Clemente is the first Hispanic American to make the HOF after the mandatory five-year waiting period is waived due to his sudden death.

2000   As part of an interim agreement with the commissioner's office, the emergent World Umpires Association agrees to consolidate all arbiters, making them under the employ of both MLs and able to be assigned to games in either loop.

21

1893   Washington trades pitcher Frank Killen to Pittsburgh for catcher Duke Farrell and $1,500.

1921   Phillies first baseman Gene Paulette is barred from OB for life for his role in fixing games.

1934   Former ML pitcher Pea Ridge Day commits suicide by slitting his throat with a hunting knife after an operation fails to correct his arm trouble.

1959   Cleveland trades Larry Doby to Detroit for Tito Francona, the major surprise of this season when he hits .363 and nearly leads the Indians to the AL flag.

1968   The AL expansion KC franchise announces that it will be called the "Royals" when it begins play in 1969.

1969   Former ML third baseman and manager Pinky Higgins dies of a heart attack the day after he finishes serving a prison sentence for vehicular homicide.

1977   Tigers pitching phenomenon Mark "The Bird" Fidrych tears cartilage in his left knee during spring training, destroying his promising career after earning AL Rookie of the Year honors the previous year.

22

1875 The *New York Times* posits that there are now some 1,500 pro and amateur baseball clubs in America, with a membership of around 25,000.

1877 The NL publishes its schedule for the coming season, marking it the first league-wide schedule ever distributed for public consumption.

1890 Indianapolis sells its franchise to the NL for some $60,000, with the New York Giants picking up much of the tab and the Hoosiers best players, namely pitcher Amos Rusie, shortstop Jack Glasscock, and pitcher-outfielder Jesse Burkett.

1902 Philadelphia police officer Johnny Ryan, a former ML outfielder who debuted with the NA Philadelphia Athletics in 1873 at age 19, is kicked to death while trying to make an arrest.

1936 Spring phenom Joe DiMaggio is severely burned and deactivated until May when a Yankees assistant trainer leaves him unsupervised with his foot receiving treatment in a diathermy machine.

1972 In a notoriously bad trade, the Yankees acquire future Cy Young winning reliever Sparky Lyle from the Red Sox in exchange for fading first baseman/outfielder Danny Cater.

1991 The prized Honus Wagner T-206 tobacco card sells for $451,000 when hockey great Wayne Gretzky and Los Angeles Kings owner Bruce McNall purchase the coveted collectible at Sotheby's in New York.

1993 Disaster strikes the Indians yet again, this time in spring training, as pitchers Tim Crews and Steve Olin are killed and lefty Bob Ojeda narrowly escapes death when the motorboat they are riding in near darkness hits a pier on Little Lake Nellie in Winter Haven, FL.

23

1900 When third baseman John McGraw and catcher Wilbert Robinson refuse to play for Brooklyn after Baltimore is dropped from the NL and its best players are assigned to the City of Churches, they are sold to St. Louis along with second baseman Bill Keister for a reported $16,000. McGraw and Robinson refuse to play for St. Louis as well and do not recant until May 12.

1936 Dizzy Dean ends a bitter holdout by signing with the Cardinals for a reported $24,000, and his brother, Paul, signs the following day for $10,000.

1938 Commissioner Landis resolves the largest cover-up episode in ML history by freeing 78 players in the Cardinals' far-flung minor league system, including Pete Reiser.

1958 The Giants deal first baseman Bill White and ex-Card Ray Jablonski to St. Louis for pitcher Sam Jones.

1992 The NL announces that league president Bill White will step down at the end of his term in 1993, but White remains in his post until March 1994.

24

1911 Cardinals owner Stanley Robison dies, leaving controlling interest in the club to his married niece, Helene Hathaway Britton, making her the first female owner in ML history.

1921 Former ML catcher Larry McLean is slain by a Boston bartender in a barroom scrape.

1933 Blaming the Depression, the Yankees slash Babe Ruth's salary from $75,000 to $52,000.

1961 Funding for what will be known as Shea Stadium is approved by the New York State Senate to the tune of $55,000,000, as the new confine's construction will be built at Flushing Meadows Park in Queens.

1984 The Tigers ship John Wockenfuss and Glenn Wilson to the Phillies for lefty reliever Willie Hernandez and Dave Bergman, with Hernandez the gem in the deal, capturing this season's AL MVP and Cy Young Award after notching 32 saves with a spiffy 1.92 ERA.

25

1878 The NL overrides opposition and votes to retain its 50¢ admission price while restoring the rule that a third strike caught on the first bounce is an out.

1891 Preferring to devote himself to his sporting-goods empire, Al Spalding turns over his position as president of the Chicago NL club to Jim Hart.

1906   Washington shortstop Joe Cassidy (b. Cassady), who set an AL rookie record with 19 triples in 1904, dies at the age of 23 in Chester, PA, of complications from a severe case of malaria.

1910   The National Commission accepts the Chalmers Auto Company's offer to give a new car to the batting titlists in each league, an experiment that will die a swift death when the season features the most controversial batting title race in history.

1962   El Tappe is named the Cubs' first head coach of the season in year two of the team's college of coaches rotation experiment.

26

1936   Coming off a season in which he led the AL in homers and RBI, first sacker Hank Greenberg wins a salary hike to $20,000. Meanwhile, Red Ruffing, who leads the Yankees in wins with 175 during the 1930s, fights for a raise to $12,000 from Bombers GM George Weiss.

1992   Milwaukee trades Gary Sheffield and a minor leaguer to San Diego for pitcher Rickey Bones, outfielder Matt Mieske, and shortstop Jose Valentin. Sheffield wins the NL batting crown for the season and continues to star with several teams for more than a decade.

27

1897   After sitting out the entire 1896 season rather than play for penurious New York Giants owner Andrew Freedman, pitcher Amos Rusie agrees to rejoin the Giants once the rest of the NL owners chip in to pay his 1896 salary to avoid Rusie's threatened lawsuit seeking free agency.

1938   White Sox shortstop Luke Appling, the defending AL batting champ, is yet another spring training casualty when he breaks his leg sliding in an exhibition game against the Cubs.

1973   A former skyrocketing star comes to an ignominious landing when the Braves release 28-year-old Denny McLain, the lone MVP winner to date whose career ended before the age of 30.

1986   MLB's Rules Committee allows a DH to be used in all postseason and All-Star Games played in an AL club's home park, unlike previously when the DH was employed in all games in alternating seasons.

1987   All the Mets need to pry future ace David Cone from the Royals is catcher Ed Hearn plus two minor league chuckers, as Cone goes on to bag 81 of his 194 career victories for the Shea occupants.

1989 Pete Rose's self-imposed nightmare begins when his gambling history is revealed in *Sports Illustrated*.

28

1889 After playing some 28 games abroad, the Spalding world touring teams set sail from Ireland to the United States with Brotherhood leader John M. Ward aboard ready to do battle with the new "Classification" system, the brainchild of Indianapolis owner John T. Brush.

1901 Phillies owner John I. Rogers files for an injunction prohibiting three AL jumpers—Nap Lajoie, Bill Bernhard, and Chick Fraser—from playing for any other team, instigating the most serious legal test of the reserve clause to date.

1907 Named player-manager of the Boston Americans near the close of the 1906 season, outfielder Chick Stahl commits suicide at the team's spring training headquarters in West Baden, IN, for reasons that invite speculation to this day.

1977 Claiming in his defense that his manager, Frank Lucchesi, called him a punk, Rangers second baseman Lenny Randle punches Lucchesi, shattering his cheekbone and evoking a 30-day suspension, a fine, and a trade to the Mets.

29

1907 The day after the suicide of Boston Americans player-manager Chick Stahl, outfielder Cozy Dolan of the Boston NL team dies of typhoid fever in Louisville, KY, leading the team to cancel the rest of its spring training slate.

1932 Former Tigers second baseman Red Downs confesses to the *Los Angeles Times* that liquor has been his downfall, first ruining his baseball career and then turning him into an armed robber who earned a potential life sentence for holding up a jewelry store at the Biltmore Hotel in LA earlier in the month.

1933 Thwarted the previous year by a broken left leg sustained in spring training, Cubs outfielder Kiki Cuyler breaks his right leg in another spring training mishap that keeps him out of action for more than half the season.

1973 A's owner Charlie Finley introduces his newest innovation, the Alert Orange Baseball, in an exhibition game between Oakland and

Cleveland. Despite Finley's claim that the ball will be easier for players and fans to see, it is never used again.

1979 Former Indians first baseman Luke Easter, one of the AL's top sluggers in the early 1950s, is slain by robbers in a payroll heist in a Cleveland suburb.

2000 In the first ML Opening Day contest ever played outside North America, the Cubs inaugurate the regular season at the Tokyo Dome in Japan by beating the Mets, 5–3.

30

1946 Browns shortstop Vern Stephens jumps to the Mexican League and plays a few games south of the border before recanting in the nick of time to avoid Commissioner Chandler's blanket ban on all players who abscond to the Mexican loop.

1955 In the first of countless transactions between the two clubs, the Yankees hand three veteran players with little left—Ewell Blackwell, Tom Gorman, and Dick Kryhoski—to the Kansas City A's for $50,000.

1966 Standout Dodgers hurlers Sandy Koufax and Don Drysdale end their joint holdout after 32 days when Koufax signs for $120,000 and Drysdale agrees to $105,000.

1992 The Cubs acquire outfielder Sammy Sosa and pitcher Ken Patterson from the White Sox for outfielder George Bell, with Sosa exceeding the Bruins' wildest expectations by pounding 545 homers during his 13-year Wrigley stay.

2000 Mets gardener Benny Agbayani hits a pinch grand slam in extra innings on the earliest date in ML history as well as the first four-run jack hit outside the United States when he spoils the ML debut of Cubs reliever Danny Young by going yard in the 11th frame to bring the Mets a 5–1 verdict in the second of the pair of games the two clubs play in Tokyo to open the season.

31

1962 The Professional Baseball Rules Committee votes 8–1 against the PCL's proposal to employ a DH.

1968 The AL expansion club in Seattle chooses "Pilots" as its nickname.

1970 Car dealer Bud Selig heads a group that buys the Seattle Pilots for more than $10,000,000 with plans to move them to Milwaukee.

1979 Former ML pitcher Bob Schultz dies when he is gunned down in a Nashville, TN, bar.

1996 Regular-season action begins in March for the first time when the Mariners defeat the White Sox at the Kingdome 3–2 in 12 innings.

1998 In their inaugural regular-season game, the Tampa Bay Devil Rays lose 11–6 to the Tigers, with starter Wilson Alvarez absorbing the loss. Elsewhere, Andy Benes starts and loses the first game in Arizona Diamondbacks history, 9–2 to the Rockies. After not committing an error in a then record 172 consecutive games, Marlins catcher Charles Johnson makes a wild throw on Opening Day in the 1st inning of Florida's 11–6 win over the Cubs. At Turner Field, the first team in 106 years to change its ML affiliation, the Milwaukee Brewers, after representing the junior circuit since 1970, lose their first game as a member of the NL to the Braves, 2–1.

April

1

1879 The Northwest League forms with four teams in Dubuque, Rockford, Omaha, and Davenport and, unlike the National Association and the IA, refuses to affiliate with the NL under the National Agreement, arguably making it the first true minor league.

1950 The Hollywood Stars of the PCL are the first team to wear a uniform consisting of shorts and a rayon shirt in a regular-season game.

1969 The Seattle Pilots send minor league outfielder Lou Piniella, acquired from Cleveland in the expansion draft, to the Kansas City Royals for outfielder Steve Whitaker and pitcher John Gelnar in a deal that Seattle will regret when Piniella captures the 1969 AL Rookie of the Year Award.

1996 A NL arbiter since 1971, umpire John McSherry dies from a heart attack while working the plate on Opening Day at Cincinnati. Elsewhere, renovations in the Oakland Coliseum bring big league ball to Nevada as the A's lose their season "home" opener 9–6 to the Blue Jays at Cashman Field in Las Vegas.

2

1908 After a purportedly intensive two-year investigation, the Mills committee, headed by Al Spalding and former NL president A. G. Mills, extrapolates from specious evidence that baseball is a wholly American game, invented by West Point cadet Abner Doubleday in Cooperstown, NY.

1931 Jackie Mitchell, a 17-year-old "girl wonder," signs with Chattanooga of the Southern Association and pitches to Babe Ruth, Lou Gehrig, and Tony Lazzeri in an exhibition game with the Yankees.

1933 En route to a spring exhibition game against the Jersey City Skeeters of the IL, the entire Boston Red Sox team has a narrow brush with death when the engine and eight cars on the "Cavalier," the Pennsylvania Railroad express from Norfolk, VA, to New York, derail near Wyoming, DE, killing the engineer and fireman.

1952 Monte Irvin, the 1951 NL MVP, is the Giants' latest spring training casualty when he breaks his ankle sliding in a spring exhibition game against the Indians.

1972 Mets manager Gil Hodges collapses in West Palm Beach, FL, and dies of a heart attack at the age of 47.

1976 A's owner Charlie Finley continues to disassemble his dynasty of the early 1970s, dealing Reggie Jackson and Ken Holtzman, plus a minor leaguer, to the Orioles for Don Baylor, Mike Torrez, and Paul Mitchell.

1995 MLB's lengthiest strike to date ends long after it began the previous August, forcing the majors to adopt a 144-game schedule with many inequities.

2003 Blue Jays shortstop Mike Bordick's record streak for consecutive games played without an error ends at 110 when he flubs a grounder. Elsewhere, a new record is set when Todd Zeile homers for the Yankees to become the first MLer to poke a tater for ten different teams, a mark Zeile extends to 11 clubs when he connects with the Expos later in the season.

2007 Bruce Froemming works the plate for the A's and Mariners opener, tying Bill Klem's ML mark of 37 seasons as an umpire.

3

1888 One year after acquiring Mike "King" Kelly from Chicago for $10,000, Boston purchases Chicago's pitching ace, John Clarkson, for the same sum to give the Hub team baseball's first "$20,000 battery."

1899 On the eve of the season, the Robison brothers, who own Cleveland, also purchase the dilapidated St. Louis franchise and announce the transfer of all of Cleveland's best players to St. Louis.

1974 The Dodgers deal minor league lefty Bruce Ellingsen to Cleveland for prospect Pedro Guerrero, who will hit .309 in 11 seasons in LA, while Ellingsen wins one game before exiting the majors.

1985 Both league championship playoff formats are changed to best-of-seven affairs after having been best-of-five since the two division champions began meeting in 1969.

1987 Dennis Eckersley, a fading starter with the Cubs, is dealt to the A's, where he resurrects his career as a closer and wins the AL Cy Young and MVP awards in 1992.

2005 Tampa Bay outfielder Alex Sanchez is the first MLer to be publicly identified under the majors' tougher steroid policy and is be suspended for 10 days for testing positive for performance-enhancing substances.

4

1937 In a spring exhibition game, Cleveland's Bob Feller beans Giants outfielder Hank Leiber, putting him out of action until August.

1947 The majors announce that a pension plan has been put in place, but for the present it only embraces players active in the majors in 1946 and thereafter.

1974 Babe Ruth no longer stands alone when Braves slugger Hank Aaron poles his record-tying 714th career homer off Cincinnati's Jack Billingham on Opening Day.

1988 The Blue Jays George Bell is the first big leaguer to crank three homers on Opening Day.

1999 For the first time in ML history, baseball's Opening Day is in Mexico, as the Rockies down the Padres at Monterrey Stadium.

2001 In his first start with the Red Sox, Hideo Nomo no-hits the Orioles 3-0 at Camden Yards, joining Don Cardwell as the only two pitchers to date to toss a no-no in their initial appearances after coming over from another ML club.

2005 After 36 years in Canada, the franchise that began as the Montreal Expos plays its first game as the Washington Nationals and loses to the Phillies, 8-4.

5

1925 Heading north from spring training, Babe Ruth collapses with a reported "ulcer" at the railroad station in Asheville, NC, and undergoes surgery that curtails his season to just 98 games.

1934   New Reds owner Powell Crosley, for whom the Cincinnati park was renamed Crosley Field, hires Red Barber to broadcast the Reds' games on WSAI, a radio station owned by Crosley.

1953   San Diego outfielder Herb Gorman, who played one game with the Cards in 1952, suffers a heart attack during a PCL game with Hollywood and dies in the clubhouse.

1972   A player strike delays the start of the MLB season for the first time, with 86 games cancelled before the stalemate ends. Meanwhile, the Mets acquire Rusty Staub from Montreal but at the expense of three prospects—Tim Foli, Mike Jorgensen, and Ken Singleton—who will each play more than a decade in the majors.

6

1958   The IL opens its season in Havana despite the political and social strife in Cuba.

1973   The Yankees' Ron Blomberg makes history as the first DH to bat in a regular-season game and walks with the sacks full against Red Sox ace Luis Tiant.

1989   Seattle's Ken Griffey Sr. and Ken Griffey Jr. are the first father and son teammates to play in the same ML game as Oakland lashes the Mariners, 11–3.

7

1896   A broken wrist that refuses to heal impels Louisville first baseman Pete Cassidy to be the first ML player to try a newfangled medical breakthrough called the "x-ray."

1958   The Dodgers erect a towering 42-foot screen in left field at their temporary home, the Los Angeles Coliseum, since the wall down the left-field line is only 250 feet from home plate.

1969   After becoming an official statistic in 1969, the Dodgers' Bill Singer earns the first bona fide save in MLB history, preserving Don Sutton's 3–2 victory against the Reds.

1971   A U.S. Circuit Court of Appeals upholds the dismissal of Curt Flood's antitrust suit against MLB.

1977   Toronto plays its first regular-season game and defeats the White Sox 9–5, as the Blue Jays' Al Woods is the first MLer to rap a pinch-hit homer in his initial AB on Opening Day.

1979 The Astros' Ken Forsch no-hits the Braves 6–0, making him and his brother Bob, who turned the trick the previous year with the Cards, the first ML siblings to each toss a no-no.

8

1891 The AA opens its final season as a ML two weeks ahead of the NL and thus is the first to implement Section 6, Rule 69, of the revised rulebook, which requires scorers to add a column to each box score that records RBI. But when scorers complain that the new task is too arduous, the experiment is scrapped in May. This stat, which is now such an integral part of the game, is not made a permanent fixture until 1920.

1934 The Phils and A's meet in a preseason exhibition game at Shibe Park in the first legal Sunday ML game ever played in Philadelphia.

1964 Houston reliever Jim Umbricht succumbs to cancer at the age of 33 and is the first member of the club to have his number (32) retired in 1965.

1974 Hank Aaron breaks Babe Ruth's career home-run record by whacking his 715th against the Dodgers' Al Downing.

1975 In his debut as MLB's first African American manager, Cleveland's Frank Robinson blasts a homer in his initial at bat to help his Indians beat the Yankees, 5–3.

1993 Indians second baseman Carlos Baerga is the first big leaguer to switch-hit home runs in the same inning when he blasts a pair from either side in the Tribe's 15–5 thumping of the Yankees.

9

1947 Happy Chandler continues to demonstrate that he will be more than just a figurehead commissioner when he suspends Dodgers manager Leo Durocher for the entire 1947 season for consorting with gamblers.

1956 The Braves acquire outfielder Bob Hazle (soon known as "Hurricane" Hazle for his fantastic partial season in 1957) and pitcher Corky Valentine from Cincinnati for first baseman George Crowe.

1974 Amid San Diego's 9–5 loss to the Astros, Padres owner Ray Kroc commandeers the PA system and howls, "Ladies and gentlemen, I suffer with you . . . I've never seen such stupid baseball playing in my life."

1981 In his first ML start after two wins in relief in September 1980, Dodgers rookie Fernando Valenzuela blanks the Astros 2–0 on Opening Day and eventually strings together 10 consecutive victories at the start of his career—five by shutout—before suffering his first loss.

1982 Starter Francisco Barrios, released by the White Sox the previous September and rumored to have inked a winter deal with the Brewers, dies of a heart attack at the age of 28 in Hermosillo, Mexico.

1985 In a 4–2 win over the Brewers, White Sox hurler Tom Seaver makes his 15th Opening Day start to break the ML mark he shared with Cy Young and Walter Johnson. He extends the total to 16 in 1986.

1990 On Opening Day, the Royals start Bret Saberhagen and close with Mark Davis in the first game in ML history featuring both reigning Cy Young honorees as teammates, with Davis having been signed over the winter after capturing the trophy in Padres garb.

10

1881 Former Boston outfielder Fraley Rogers is the first documented former MLer to commit suicide when he takes his own life with a gun in New York City at the age of 31.

1882 William Hulbert, the primary founder of the NL and its second president, dies while in office and is temporarily replaced by Boston owner Arthur Soden.

1905 A New York magistrate rules that Sunday baseball is legal, but court battles continue for another 27 years before all ML teams begin to host Sunday games.

1947 The Dodgers announce the purchase of Jackie Robinson's contract from Montreal, making him the first documented African American in the majors since 1884.

1953 Caving to political pressure, Cincinnati temporarily changes its team nickname from Reds to Redlegs.

1961 In the first ML game since 1884 played by an expansion club, the new Washington Senators lose to the White Sox 4–3 at Griffith Stadium.

1962 Dodger Stadium, the first ML facility privately financed since Yankee Stadium in 1923, opens in Chavez Ravine. Elsewhere, the expansion era begins in the NL at Colt Stadium, as the Houston Colt .45s' Bobby Shantz goes all the way in an 11–2 blasting of the Cubs.

1976 Don Money seemingly hits a walk-off 9th-inning grand slam to give Milwaukee a 10–9 win over the Yankees, but it is nullified when umpires rule that Bombers first baseman Chris Chambliss was granted a time-out prior to the pitch, forcing Money to bat again and fly out as his team eventually loses 9–7.

1979 Houston's J. R. Richard unleashes a record (since tied) six wild pitches against the Dodgers but fans 13 and wins 2–1.

1983 Pam Postema, a PCL arbiter, is the first female to umpire at the Triple A level.

2007 Forced to postpone their entire season-opening series against the Mariners due to a spring snowstorm in Cleveland, the Indians, with no relief from foul weather in sight and the Angels coming to town, agree to play their "home" opener in Milwaukee.

11

1911 Cleveland pitcher Addie Joss dies at the age of 31 of meningitis. Some 66 years later, the HOF makes an exception to its rule that players must be active a minimum of 10 years in the majors to admit Joss, who died on the eve of his 10th season.

1932 Annoyed by Chick Hafey's holdout, Cards GM Branch Rickey trades the 1931 NL batting king to Cincinnati for pitcher Benny Frey, infielder Harvey Hendrick, and cash.

1954 The Cards swap one of the linchpins of their team for the past 15 years, Enos Slaughter, to the Yankees for three prospects, including outfielder Bill Virdon, who becomes the 1955 NL Rookie of the Year.

1959 The Boston National Association for the Advancement of Colored People (NAACP) requests a probe of the Red Sox organization when the Hub team farms out African American infielder Pumpsie Green to ensure that it will continue to be the only ML team that has yet to integrate.

1966 MLB's first African American umpire, Emmett Ashford, debuts on Opening Day at RFK Stadium.

1969 At Sicks Stadium, veteran Gary Bell brings momentary hope to the Northwest when he blanks the White Sox 7–0 in the first regular-season ML game played in Seattle.

12

1889 After a glass of cider with friends at his KC cigar store knocks him off the wagon and sends him on a weeklong bender, former ML catcher Frank Ringo is so anguished by his lapse that he commits suicide at his parents' home by taking 40 grains of morphine.

1909 Shibe Park, the first all steel and concrete facility to host a ML game, receives its baptism as the Philadelphia A's beat Boston 8–1, but the event is marred when A's catcher Doc Powers dies two weeks later from an intestinal problem that possibly either stemmed from or was exacerbated by an injury he sustained in the game.

1922 For the first time since its inception in 1876, the NL opens the season without any of its eight teams in the hands of a player-manager.

1927 In front of 65,000 fans, the biggest Opening Day crowd to date, the Yankees beat the A's Lefty Grove 8–3 and end the day in a tie for first place, a position they will either share or hold alone until the end of the season. Meanwhile, almost 45,000 fans at Wrigley Field watch the Cubs dismantle Pete Alexander, the 1926 World Series hero, 10–1, and are so enthused that they turn out 1,159,168 strong over the course of the season, making the Bruins the first team in NL history to top 1,000,000 in attendance.

1955 In Kansas City's first game as a member of the AL, the transplanted A's deck the Tigers, 6–2.

1960 The Indians are robbed when they deal future batting champ Norm Cash to the Tigers for third sacker Steve Demeter, who plays just four games with the Tribe before returning to the minors.

1965 The Phils' Dick Allen pelts the first indoor tater in the Astrodome in a 2–0 win over Houston.

1966 Atlanta experiences big league ball for the first time as the Braves play their first game at Fulton County Stadium, losing to the Pirates 3–2 in 13 innings.

1992 Despite hurling 8 no-hit innings, the Red Sox' Matt Young loses 2–1 to the Indians in the first game of a DBH as two of Young's seven walks eventually score. In the nightcap, Roger Clemens whitewashes Cleveland on only two hits, dooming the Tribe to set a ML record for fewest hits in a twin bill.

13

1896 "Harry Wright Day," honoring the recently deceased baseball pioneer and manager, is held in almost every major city east of the Mississippi, with teams at all levels staging exhibition games played under the rules that prevailed in Wright's heyday as a player.

1914 After hastily erecting ballparks in its eight member cities during the winter, the FL plays its opening game in Baltimore, with the home Terrapins defeating Buffalo 3–2 before 27,140 fans.

1921 Cards rookie George Toporcer is the first position player in ML history to wear glasses on the field when he debuts at second base in St. Louis's 5–2 Opening Day loss at Chicago.

1926 Washington's Walter Johnson and the A's Eddie Rommel lock horns in the greatest Opening Day pitching duel ever, with Johnson emerging the victor 1–0 in 15 innings.

1953 The Milwaukee Braves win their inaugural NL game in County Stadium, taking Cincinnati 2–0 behind Max Surkont's three-hitter.

1962 The expansion Mets lose their home debut to the Pirates 4–3 at the Polo Grounds.

1963 Baseball's future hit king, Pete Rose, taps the Pirates' Bob Friend for his first ML safety, a triple at Cincinnati's Crosley Field.

1980 Royals relief ace Dan Quisenberry and catcher Jamie Quirk form the first "Q" battery in ML history as they combine to tame the Tigers.

14

1903 A disgruntled Ed Delahanty rejoins the lowly Washington Senators after a peace agreement between the two MLs nullifies a lucrative three-year contract he signed during the winter with the New York Giants.

1910 William Howard Taft is the first president to throw out the first ball at Washington's home opener and then watches Walter Johnson beat Philadelphia 8–0 but lose a no-hitter when A's third baseman Frank Baker hits a lazy fly ball into the overflow crowd in right field for a ground rule double.

1914 In Walter Johnson's 3–0 Opening Day shutout of the Red Sox, Senators shortstop George McBride ends the day with no hits, no home runs, and no RBI, launching a season in which he is the first ML negative Triple Crown winner—last in his loop among bat title qualifiers in all of the three Triple Crown departments: BA, home runs, and RBI.

1925 The A's unveil a rookie battery featuring two future Hall of Famers, Mickey Cochrane and Lefty Grove, in a 9–8 win over the Red Sox. Elsewhere, Cleveland sets an AL record for the most runs scored on Opening Day in its 21–14 triumph over the St. Louis Browns.

1937 Victors the previous year when Commissioner Landis ignored protests of a cover-up and ruled Bob Feller their property, the Indians lose minor leaguer Tommy Henrich in a similar case, enabling him to sign as a free agent with the Yankees.

1955 Elston Howard is the first African American player to wear Yankees pinstripes in a regular-season game when he replaces ejected left fielder Irv Noren and singles in his first ML AB. Elsewhere, Cards hurler Frank Smith is a force-out victim when he neglects to touch second base on Wally Moon's apparent game-winning single off Milwaukee's Charlie Gorin in the bottom of the 10th frame at St. Louis but is spared infamy as a modern-day "Fred Merkle" when rookie Bill Virdon drills a solo homer in the 11th to give the Birds an 8–7 win.

1967 Red Sox lefty Billy Rohr no-hits the Yankees for 8⅔ innings before Elston Howard singles, consigning a disappointed Rohr to finish with a one-hit, 3–0 win at Yankee Stadium in his ML debut.

1969 In the first regular-season ML game played outside the United States, the Expos nip the Cards 8–7, with lefty Dan McGinn earning the initial win north of the border.

2005 For the first time since 1971, MLB is played in the nation's capital as the Washington Nationals down the Diamondbacks 5–3 at RFK Stadium.

15

1883 The maiden issue of *Sporting Life*, the first weekly paper devoted exclusively to sports, is published in Philadelphia, with Francis Richter as editor.

1906 Brooklyn again circumvents local Blue Laws by charging no admission for a Sunday game against Boston and instead asking spectators to drop contributions in boxes as they enter the park.

1909 Red Ames of the Giants hurls what for many years is deemed the first Opening Day no-hitter in ML history but is no longer viewed as such by MLB because he gave up a hit in the 10th inning before losing 3–0 to Brooklyn in 13 frames.

1930 Les Sweetland's Opening Day gem produces a 1–0 win at Brooklyn and rockets the Phils into a momentary lead in the NL. The Phils lose their next three games to begin a rapid descent to the cellar, and Sweetland surrenders an average of 8 runs per every 9 innings for the remainder of the season to saddle him with an overall 7.71 ERA, the worst ever by a qualifier.

1941 Cubs shortstop Lou Stringer sets a modern record when he makes four errors in his ML debut, but the Cubs still contrive to beat Pittsburgh 7–4 in their season opener.

1946 With World War II over, most ML clubs announce an increase in ticket prices, with an average fee of $2.00 for box seats, $1.25 for general admission, and 60¢ for bleacher seats or standing room.

1947 Jackie Robinson goes hitless in his ML debut with the Dodgers but handles 11 chances flawlessly at first base, his interim position.

1952 Only 4,694 fans attend the Boston Braves' 77th and last home opener as one of the only two remaining original members of the NL (the Cubs being the other) bows 3–2 to Brooklyn.

1954 In the first AL or NL game in Baltimore since 1902, Orioles catcher Clint Courtney raps the first home run in Memorial Stadium as the O's beat the White Sox 3–1 in front of 46,354.

1958 In the first official ML game on the West Coast, the Giants' Ruben Gomez shuts out the Dodgers 8–0 at Seals Stadium.

1968 The Mets and Astros set a ML record for the longest scoreless game before Bob Aspromonte's grounder eludes shortstop Al Weis, allowing the Astros to win 1–0 in the bottom of the 24th inning.

1997 During a 50th anniversary celebration at Shea Stadium of Jackie Robinson's breaking MLB's color line, Commissioner Selig announces that Robinson's number 42 will be retired by every club.

1998 Emergency repair work at Yankee Stadium creates a unique DBH at Shea Stadium when the Bombers shift their game to Queens, with the Yanks beating the Angels 6–3, followed by the Mets downing the Cubs 2–1 in the regularly scheduled night game.

2007 Many players don Jackie Robinson's retired number 42 to celebrate the 60th anniversary of Robinson's ML debut, with the Dodgers being one of six teams whose entire roster bears the number for the day.

16

1887 On Opening Day in the AA, two rookie outfielders, George Tebeau of Cincinnati and Mike Griffin of Baltimore, jointly share the honor of being the first documented players to homer in their first ML at bats.

1913 In Keokuk, IA, Police Chief Jerry Harrington, a former ML catcher, dies of a stab wound he received while trying to break up a barroom brawl on April 1.

1935   Despite freezing temperatures, Braves Field draws a then franchise record Opening Day crowd of 25,000 to watch Babe Ruth make his NL debut with a game-winning two-run homer in Boston's 4–2 victory over the Giants' Carl Hubbell.

1938   The Cards pawn off Dizzy Dean and his suspect arm on the Cubs for $185,000, outfielder Tuck Stainback, and two quality pitchers, Curt Davis and Clyde Shoun.

1940   Cleveland's Bob Feller throws the first universally recognized Opening Day no-hitter in ML history when he beats Chicago's Eddie Smith 1–0 at Comiskey Park.

1959   The Phils' Dave Philley extends his record of consecutive pinch hits to nine when he doubles while batting for catcher Jim Hegan. Philley's streak ends three days later when his long drive to right field off Cincinnati reliever Bob Mabe is caught at the base of the wall by outfielder Gus Bell.

1983   Padres first sacker Steve Garvey plays in his 1,118th straight game, breaking the NL record he shared with Billy Williams.

1997   In losing 4–0 to Colorado, the Cubs break the NL mark for most consecutive defeats to start the season (12) and extend their drought to 14 before beating the Mets four days later.

17

1892   In the first official Sunday game in NL history after the NL and AA merge and the new 12-team league allows each club to decide whether to play home games on the Sabbath, Cincinnati tops St. Louis 5–1 in the Queen City.

1903   Brooklyn stages its first Sunday home game in the 20th century by charging no admission to circumvent local Blue Laws and then requiring fans to buy a scorecard to enter the park and watch Oscar Jones beat Boston, 9–0.

1953   Yankees slugger Mickey Mantle ushers in the era of the tape-measure home run when he hits a 565-foot shot off Washington's Chuck Stobbs in Griffith Stadium.

1960   In a trade that will resonate in Cleveland for decades, Indians GM Frank "Trader" Lane jettisons fan favorite and reigning AL home run champ Rocky Colavito to the Tigers for the circuit's defending batting titlist, Harvey Kuenn.

1976   Mike Schmidt joins an exclusive club when he cracks four homers to help the Phillies erase a 12–1 deficit and beat the Cubs 18–16 in 10 innings.

18

1872   For the second year in a row, the opening game of the National Association season ends in a rare shutout when Baltimore skewers the Washington Olympics 16–0 in the nation's capital.

1888   In the AA season opener at Brooklyn, John Gaffney is the first umpire to move from behind the plate to a position behind the pitcher with men on base. Later that year, Gaffney is also part of the innovative two-umpire system the AA tests in several of its regular-season games.

1899   After refusing to be transferred to Brooklyn with most of his Baltimore teammates, John McGraw makes his managerial debut with the Orioles in a 5–3 win over the New York Giants, the team he will later manage for some 30 years.

1906   A gigantic earthquake in San Francisco followed by raging fires forces the PCL to temporarily suspend operations.

1919   Babe Ruth clubs four home runs in a game for the only time in his career in an exhibition contest between Ruth's Red Sox and the IL Baltimore Orioles.

1922   Third baseman Willie Kamm, the first minor leaguer to be purchased by a ML team for six figures ($100,000), makes his debut with the White Sox in an 6–5 loss to Cleveland.

1923   Yankee Stadium opens with a crowd of 74,217 watching Bombers righty Bob Shawkey, bolstered by Babe Ruth's three-run homer, beat the Red Sox, 4–1.

1945   One-armed outfielder Pete Gray goes 1-for-4 in his ML debut with the Browns, as St. Louis wins its ninth straight Opening Day game, routing reigning AL MVP Hal Newhouser 7–1.

1946   Jackie Robinson debuts with Montreal of the IL, marking the first documented appearance of an African American position player since the 1890s in a league under the umbrella of either the National Agreement or OB.

1949   The first of A's first sacker Ferris Fain's all-time season-record 194 double plays is a 5-2-3 twin killing in a 3–2 loss to Washington on Opening Day.

1950   Sportsman's Park hosts the first ML Opening Day night game as the Cards take the Pirates, 4–2.

1957   New York Parks Commissioner Robert Moses counters Brooklyn owner Walter O'Malley's proposal for a new stadium complex in Brooklyn by proposing a facility with a plastic dome to be built in Flushing Meadows by the Parks Department.

1958   With a then NL single-game record 78,682 fans in attendance, the Dodgers nip the Giants 6–5 in their home opener in the Los Angeles Coliseum.

1959   A monumental flop in his final ML job as Pittsburgh's GM, Branch Rickey still has enough name value to be appointed president of the Continental League, a prospective third major loop.

1966   The Astros and Dodgers play the initial regular-season ML game on artificial turf when LA's future 300-game winner Don Sutton beats Houston 4–2 for his first big league win.

1969   The AA returns to OB as a Triple A circuit after an absence since 1962.

1981   In the longest game in OB history, the IL's Pawtucket Red Sox and Rochester Red Wings are still deadlocked when play is suspended after 32 innings at 4:07 AM. The game resumes on June 23, with the Sox scoring the winning run in the 33rd inning for a 3–2 victory that requires 8 hours and 25 minutes to play.

19

1900   On the minor AL's Opening Day under its new name, Buffalo's Doc Amole tosses an 8–0 no-hitter to spoil Detroit's inaugural game in Bennett Park, named after former Detroit catcher Charlie Bennett who lost both legs in a train mishap.

1915   When Cards right-hander Lee Meadows makes his ML debut, he is the first MLer to wear glasses on the field since Will White left the AA in 1886.

1919   New York governor Al Smith signs a bill legalizing Sunday baseball throughout the state.

1938   The Dodgers' Ernie Koy and the Phils' Emmett Mueller highlight Opening Day in the NL by becoming the first pair of hitters on opposing teams to homer in their first ML at bats in the same game.

1944   Chuck Hostetler, at 40 years and seven months of age, is the oldest rookie position player in AL history when he debuts for the Tigers with an 8th inning pinch single in a 3–1 loss to the Browns' Steve Sundra.

1949 In what will be a rare occurrence for a Yankees pitcher during the season, Ed Lopat gives up just two walks in his 3–2 triumph over Washington in the Bombers' season opener. Even though the Yanks win the AL flag in 1949, their mound staff surrenders 812 free passes (second in ML history only to the 1915 A's with 827), led by Tommy Byrne (179), Vic Raschi (138), and Allie Reynolds (123).

1971 Veteran Giants broadcaster Russ Hodges, noted for his exuberant cry, "The Giants win the pennant!" succumbs to a heart attack in Mill Valley, CA, at the age of 61.

1997 Big league baseball reaches Hawaii for the first time when the Padres, while awaiting stadium renovations, are swept by the Cards in a double dip at Aloha Stadium.

20

1904 Sports promoter Jim Kennedy, purportedly just 23 years old when he managed the AA Brooklyn Gladiators in 1890, which would make him the youngest manager in ML history if true, dies of a heart attack aboard a commuter train in Brighton Beach, NY.

1908 Henry Chadwick, the game's leading writer, critic, and advocate for more than half a century, dies at his home in Brooklyn.

1953 Third baseman Jerry Crosby of Colorado Springs in the Western League is the first player in OB since Nig Clarke in 1902 to homer in four consecutive innings when he tattoos three Pueblo pitchers in frames 4 through 7 of a 20–16 Colorado Springs victory.

1957 In a game against the Braves, Redlegs base runner Johnny Temple purposely lets teammate Gus Bell's ground ball hit him to thwart an otherwise routine double play. When a Redlegs play the following day achieves the same result, a new rule is imposed licensing umpires to award a double play whenever they judge that a base runner has intentionally interfered with a batted ball.

1987 The Milwaukee Brewers win their 13th consecutive game to start the season, tying the 1982 Atlanta Braves record for the best start in NL or AL annals before losing to the White Sox 7–1 the following day.

1988 The Baltimore Orioles drop an 8–6 decision to the Brewers for their 14th straight defeat, setting a new ML mark for the most consecutive losses to start the season, which they will extend to 21 before Mark

Williamson earns the club's first victory in a 9–0 trouncing of the White Sox.

1999   After a controversial 14-year tenure as Reds owner, Marge Schott agrees to sell her controlling interest in the club to a group headed by Carl H. Lindner.

21

1880   George Wright is the first player to tackle the controversial new reserve clause, refusing sign with Providence despite being reserved by the Grays for 1880.

1887   Pittsburgh sends $2,000 and the rights to highly touted West Coast product George Van Haltren to Chicago for pitcher Jim McCormick.

1898   Phillies rookie pitcher Bill Duggleby clouts a grand-slam homer in his first ML AB, a feat that will not be duplicated until the 21st century.

1902   The Pennsylvania Supreme Court reverses a lower court's decision and issues a permanent injunction barring Nap Lajoie from playing in Pennsylvania unless he returns to the Phillies. Lajoie skirts the issue, as do his Philadelphia AL teammates Elmer Flick and Bill Bernhard, by going to Cleveland for token compensation; however, all are enjoined from accompanying the Blues on road trips to Philadelphia.

1946   Cleveland's Frankie Hayes catches his then receiver's record 312th straight game in a 3–2 loss to Detroit before being replaced in the Indians' next contest three days later by rookie Sherm Lollar.

1966   In a multiplayer deal with the Phillies, the Cubs acquire future Hall of Famer Fergie Jenkins.

1967   After 737 consecutive scheduled home games played, the Dodgers experience their first rain out since moving to LA.

2000   Victimizing the Devil Rays, Angels sluggers Mo Vaughn and Tim Salmon hit back-to-back taters in two separate innings, and teammate Troy Glaus adds insult by connecting in the same two frames, marking it the first time in ML history that three teammates homer in the same inning twice in one game.

22

1876   Still pitching under the pseudonym "Josephs," Joe Borden, now with Boston, achieves another significant first when he beats Philadelphia 6–5 in the inaugural NL game.

1897 St. Louis slabster Red Donahue drops a 4–1 decision to Pittsburgh, marking the first of his post–1892 ML season record 35 losses.

1898 Cincinnati's Ted Breitenstein and Baltimore rookie Jay Hughes both hurl no-hitters, the first time in ML annals that two no-nos are tossed on the same day.

1915 Pinstripes first appear on New York Yankees uniforms.

1916 A's hurler Jack Nabors beats the defending champion Red Sox 4–2 before embarking on a ML single-season record 19-game losing streak that sinks his final mark to 1–20, the worst ever by an AL or NL pitcher in a minimum of 20 decisions.

1920 Some 25,000 turn out at the Yankees home opener at the Polo Grounds to watch the Bombers' new strong boy, Babe Ruth. The Yanks set an attendance record for the season of 1,289,422, which remains the standard until the Bombers break their own mark in 1946 with 2,265,512.

1922 Browns outfielder Ken Williams is the first AL performer to hammer three home runs in a game in a 10–7 win over the White Sox. Williams emerges as the year's junior loop's surprise home-run leader with 39 and also swipes 32 bases, making him the lone ML member of the 30/30 club prior to 1955. Elsewhere, Sam Crane plays his final ML game at shortstop before killing his girlfriend and her male companion in a hotel bar, a move that secures him a new position at shortstop on a prison team.

1952 Fred Saigh is indicted for tax evasion by a federal grand jury and is forced to surrender his ownership of the Cardinals.

1956 In the second game of a DBH at Philadelphia, Phils fans rain beer cans and bottles on Giants outfielder Whitey Lockman, triggering legislation allowing beer to be sold only in paper cups at Connie Mack Stadium and prohibiting fans from bringing their own containers of beer to games.

1957 The Phillies are the last NL club to integrate when former Kansas City Monarchs infielder John Kennedy pinch runs for shortstop Solly Hemus in the Phils' 5–1 loss to Brooklyn.

1959 The White Sox score 11 runs in the 7th inning off KC pitchers on just one hit, a single by outfielder Johnny Callison, in blasting the A's 20–6.

1970   Mets stalwart Tom Seaver fans the last 10 Padres he faces to set a ML record and ties the 9-inning whiff mark (since broken) with 19 in a 2–1 win.

1982   The Braves' then ML record for consecutive wins at the start of a season ends at 13 when they lose 2–1 to the Reds.

23

1911   Former Philadelphia A's pitcher George Craig is killed by a burglar at the age of 23 in Indianapolis, IN.

1952   Giants rookie reliever Hoyt Wilhelm gains his maiden victory 9–5 over Boston after going yard in his first ML AB off Dick Hoover for his only home run in his 21-year career.

1954   Hank Aaron hits his first career home run off the Cards' Vic Raschi at Sportsman's Park, helping the Braves to a 7–5 win in 14 innings.

1962   The expansion Mets win their first regular-season game in club history after nine consecutive losses, beating the Pirates 9–1 to end the Bucs' then record-tying 10-game winning streak to open the season.

1964   Houston's Ken Johnson is the first ML hurler to log a 9-inning no-hitter and lose when second baseman Nellie Fox boots Vada Pinson's grounder, allowing the Reds to score the game's only run.

1999   Cards third baseman Fernando Tatis is the first MLer to pound two grand slams in one inning in a 12–5 romp over the Dodgers.

2000   The Yankees Bernie Williams and Jorge Posada are the first teammates to switch-hit a pair of homers in the same game during a 10–7 win over the Blue Jays.

24

1849   The Knickerbocker Club models the first baseball uniform, consisting of blue woolen pantaloons, a white flannel shirt, and a straw hat.

1899   Washington trades third baseman Doc Casey, catcher Duke Farrell, and the rights to pitcher Bill Donovan to Brooklyn for catcher Mike Heydon, first baseman Pete Cassidy, pitcher Dan McFarlan, and around $3,000.

1901   Rain washes out other AL openers, giving Chicago the sole honor of hosting the AL's first game as a ML, an 8–2 win over the Cleveland Blues.

1943 Defenses of the new balata ball in use during the season are so lame that the majors agree to change the ball and utilize the left-over stock of 1942 balls in the interim. With the balata ball, of the first 29 games of the regular season, 11 resulted in shutouts.

1945 Kentucky senator Albert "Happy" Chandler, not even on the short list of candidates the owners are weighing as a replacement for recently deceased Commissioner Landis, wins the job after Yankees coowner Larry MacPhail suggests adding him to the mix.

1951 The St. Louis Browns, a perennial AL doormat, awaken in first place with a 7–1 mark after lefty Bob Cain nips Cleveland's Bob Feller 1–0 the night before in the first double one-hit game in AL history.

1962 At Wrigley Field, Sandy Koufax dominates the Cubs, fanning a then post–1892, 9-inning record-tying 18 batters in the Dodgers 10–2 win.

25

1876 Louisville unveils its revolutionary new gray uniforms in its regular-season opener at Chicago. All teams had previously worn white and were differentiated by their stocking colors.

1901 In its AL opener, Detroit stages the greatest Opening Day rally in history when it tallies 10 runs in the bottom of the 9th to triumph over player-manager Hugh Duffy's Milwaukee Brewers, 14–13. Elsewhere, Cleveland's Erve Beck hits the first home run in AL history off Chicago's John Skopec.

1933 Rookie right-hander Russ Van Atta debuts with the Yankees in spectacular fashion, topping Washington 16–0 and collecting four hits on his own behalf.

1951 Minor league pitcher Jim Prendergast tests the reserve clause in court to no avail when he is traded from the Triple A Syracuse Stars to the Double A Beaumont Texans.

1984 Emerging Mets ace Dwight Gooden is the first teenager to whiff as many as 10 players in a game since the Twins' Bert Blyleven in 1970.

1995 After a strike lasting 257 days, ML baseball returns as the Dodgers edge the Florida Marlins, 8–7.

26

1875 Rookie pitcher/outfielder John Cassidy of the NA Brooklyn Atlantics evens his record at 1–1 when he beats New Haven, 3–2. Cassidy then loses all 20 of his remaining decisions to finish 1–21 with a .045 winning percentage, the lowest season mark ever by a ML pitcher in a minimum of 20 decisions.

1885 Pursuant to Bob Caruthers's 2–0 triumph over Pittsburgh that afternoon, the 1885 AA champion St. Louis Browns go on to win a ML record 27 straight home games over the next three months before Philadelphia's Ed Knouff ends their skein on July 28 when he tops Dave Foutz 8–3 at Sportsman's Park.

1901 Connie Mack begins his record 50-year stint as the manager of the Philadelphia Athletics by watching his club drop its maiden game as a member of the AL 5–1 to Washington's Bill Carrick.

1931 Lou Gehrig loses credit for a home run when he passes Yankees teammate Lyn Lary on the bases, a gaffe that will result in Gehrig finishing the season tied for the AL home-run crown with teammate Babe Ruth instead of winning it outright, and also costing him a RBI, shrinking his AL record total to 184 rather than 185.

1961 The Yankees' Roger Maris begins a belated assault on Babe Ruth's season home-run record by blasting his first tater in the Bombers' 11th game of the season against the Tigers' Paul Foytack.

2005 In a torrid performance, the Yankees' Alex Rodriguez hits three homers and drives in 10 runs in his first three ABs against the Angels' Bartolo Colon, who rebounds to capture the season's AL Cy Young Award.

27

1891 The NL Brooklyn Bridegrooms play their first game at Eastern Park, the former home of the Brooklyn PL club, which is tucked amid a maze of streetcar and railroad lines that oblige fans to dodge their way through to get to and from the park, giving birth to the team's new nickname, the Dodgers.

1909 For the third day in a row, the Browns lose 1–0 to the White Sox when Doc White tops Rube Waddell.

1971 After playing just 13 games with Washington, free-agent trailblazer Curt Flood leaves the big leagues and heads for Denmark to become an artist.

1973 KC hurler Steve Busby pitches the first no-hitter with a DH in the lineup, a 3–0 win over the Tigers.

1983   Houston flamethrower Nolan Ryan seemingly breaks Walter Johnson's career record of 3,508 Ks by fanning Expos pinch hitter Brad Mills, until it is discovered years later that Johnson had one more strikeout than previously credited.

2006   Tampa Bay prospect Delmon Young is suspended indefinitely by the IL a day after hurling a bat that hit an umpire in the chest. Young eventually serves a 50-game suspension, the lengthiest documented penalty in the circuit's 123-year history.

28

1880   Boston catcher Lew Brown is the first casualty of the NL's potent new player control rule when he is suspended for the entire season after endeavoring to play an exhibition game while drunk.

1894   To prevent "mischief" or sensational stories from reaching the ears and eyes of outsiders, especially sportswriters, New York Giants player-manager John M. Ward institutes a rule prior to the Giants' first home game of the season that only players are allowed in the team clubhouse after games.

1900   Walter Plock, whose promising ML career ended abruptly nine years earlier in only his second game when an Amos Rusie fastball broke his jaw, is killed in Richmond, VA, along with three fellow bridge construction workers when a 10-ton girder topples from a crane and crushes them.

1930   Independence, MO, of the Western Association hosts the first regular-season night game in OB history when it loses to Muskogee 13–3 under a network of temporary lights on loan from J. L. Wilkinson, the owner of the Negro league Kansas City Monarchs.

1934   Detroit outfielder Goose Goslin hits into a record four double plays (a record that had since been tied), but the Tigers beat Cleveland nonetheless, 4–1.

1985   Billy Martin assumes the job of Yankees manager for the fourth time, tying the record set by Pirates skipper Danny Murtaugh for the most separate stints as the pilot of one club.

1995   Former ML infielder Gus Polidor is killed during a carjacking in Caracas, Venezuela.

2001   Owing to the regular season starting earlier than in the past, coupled with torrid play, the Mariners win their 20th game, setting a new ML record for the most wins in April.

2007   Yet another eerie incident occurs in Cleveland when the umpiring crew decides in the 6th inning that one of their members, Marvin Hudson, had misapplied a rule back in the 3rd frame and notifies the official scorer to award Baltimore a run 3 innings after the fact that gives the Orioles a 3–2 lead. Elsewhere, closer Trevor Hoffman pitches in his 803rd game for the Padres, breaking Walter Johnson's record for the most games pitched with one club, but unlike the "Big Train," who spent his entire career with the Senators, Hoffman debuted with the Marlins.

29

1877   Outfielder Jack Manning, who has a three-year contract with Boston, is loaned for the balance of the season to NL rival Cincinnati, a type of transaction that the majors allow to continue until the late 1890s.

1916   New Cubs owner Charles Weegham informs his ushers and park policemen that the Cubs will be the first to break with tradition by allowing fans to keep balls hit into the stands.

1930   Suspicions deepen that the ball has been enlivened over the winter to heighten fan interest in the face of the Depression when 14 teams combine to score 123 runs in the seven ML games that day.

1934   Pittsburgh is the last ML city to host a Sunday game when the Pirates beat the Reds 9–5 at Forbes Field.

1948   Cards reliever Ted Wilks is tagged with a 5–4 loss to the Reds in 14 innings, his first defeat in 77 hill appearances dating back to 1945.

1952   Cleveland outfielder Jim Fridley, the 1952 "Cactus League" sensation, helps the Tribe break a four-game skein in which they are shut out three times and held to just one hit twice when he strokes six consecutive singles in support of Bob Feller, who allows 18 hits himself in his complete-game 21–9 win over the A's. Elsewhere, Fort Lauderdale wins its first Florida IL game of the season, beating West Palm Beach 7–4 after beginning the campaign with 29 straight losses.

1981   Phillies ace Steve Carlton is the first left-hander to log 3,000 Ks when the Expos' Tim Wallach goes down on strikes.

1986   Roger Clemens gains national attention for the first time by fanning a ML 9-inning record 20 Mariners in a 3–1 Red Sox win.

2007   Cardinals reliever Josh Hancock is killed while driving intoxicated in St. Louis, MO, at the age of 29. His teammates wear a patch with his number (32) for the rest of the season.

30

1901   En route to a state mental hospital, former ML third baseman Tom Esterbrook plunges to his death from the window of a moving train after years of erratic behavior.

1909   Eighteen days after the A's debut at Shibe Park, Pittsburgh's Forbes Field is the second all-steel and all-concrete facility to open in the majors and gains the distinction that fall of being the first to host a World Series contest when the Pirates snag the NL pennant.

1922   White Sox gardener Johnny Mostil's two acrobatic catches preserve Charlie Robertson's 2–0 perfecto against the Tigers.

1951   Cleveland is stung in a three-way deal with the White Sox and A's that brings the Sox the Tribe's top black Hispanic prospect, Minnie Minoso, and A's outfielder Paul Lehner, while the A's get Dave Philley and Gus Zernial from the Sox, plus Sam Zoldak and Ray Murray from Cleveland. Meanwhile, Cleveland emerges from the transaction with only A's lefty Lou Brissie, who flops as the Tribe's closer.

1952   In his final AB before leaving to serve as a Marine fighter pilot in Korea, Ted Williams belts a game-winning two-run homer to defeat Detroit's Dizzy Trout, 5–3.

1955   The Reds swap outfielders Jim Greengrass and Glen Gorbus plus catcher Andy Seminick to the Phils for catcher Smoky Burgess, pitcher Steve Ridzik, and outfielder Stan Palys.

1961   The Giants' Willie Mays hammers four homers in a 14–4 thrashing of the Braves.

1967   Wildness ruins the Orioles' Steve Barber's solo no-hit bid when he walks 10 Tigers in 8⅔ innings, forcing manager Hank Bauer to bring in Stu Miller to finish the no-no, but the O's still lose, 2–1.

1970   Cubs iron man Billy Williams is the first NLer to play 1,000 consecutive games.

2002   In beating the Diamondbacks 10–1, Mets lefty Al Leiter is the first pitcher to defeat all 30 extant ML teams.

May

1

1878 Cincinnati's Deacon White and his rookie brother, Will, are the first sibling battery to appear together in a ML game as Will tops Milwaukee, 6–4.

1880 A new rule that ends a game immediately when a team scores the game-winning run rather than requiring it to complete its full turn at bat receives a quick baptism when Chicago tallies two runs in the bottom of the 9th on Opening Day to go ahead of Cincinnati 4–3, and both teams then "walk off" the field.

1884 In its season openers, the AA is the first ML to employ a rule giving a batter his base when he is hit by a pitch and also the first ML to hire African American players, as black catcher Moses Walker goes behind the plate for Toledo in a 5–1 loss to Louisville.

1886 Al Atkinson of the AA Philadelphia Athletics is the only ML hurler to date to craft two no-hit games, neither of which is a shutout, when he tops the New York Mets 3–2 in his second career no-no.

1890 Brooklyn third baseman George Pinkney's then ML record consecutive games streak of 577 terminates when he is spiked by Chippy McGarr in the 1st inning of a game at Boston that is rained out before the frame ends.

1920 At Braves Field, Brooklyn's Leon Cadore and Boston's Joe Oeschger duel to a 1–1 tie in 26 innings, the most frames ever played in a ML game, as Cadore faces a single-game record 86 batters. Elsewhere, Washington infielder Joe Leonard dies at the age of 25 of a ruptured appendix.

1953   Boyd Tepler, the author of *In Cub Chains*, loses his suit against the Cubs and OB for ruining his career by forcing him to pitch through an elbow injury suffered on Labor Day in 1944.

1959   ML moguls approve the Players Association's proposal to hold two All-Star Games each year as a way to add revenue to the players' pension fund.

1991   Rickey Henderson breaks Lou Brock's career record by swiping his 939th base in the A's 7–4 win over the Yanks. Elsewhere, 44-year-old Nolan Ryan of the Rangers records his seventh career no-hitter, fanning 16 Blue Jays in the process.

2002   Trevor Hoffman coverts his 321st save with the Padres, surpassing former A's reliever Dennis Eckersley's record for the most saves with one club.

2

1872   The youngest documented pitcher in ML history to hurl a complete game, 16-year-old Jim Britt of the Brooklyn Atlantics loses 8–2 to the Mansfields of Middletown, CT, in his National Association debut.

1876   Chicago second baseman Ross Barnes belts the first home run in NL history, an inside-the-park blow off Cincinnati's Cherokee Fisher.

1883   John M. Ward of the fledgling New York NL entry is the first pitcher in ML history to hit a game-winning walk-off home run when his solo blast in the bottom of the 9th sinks Boston's Jim Whitney, 3–2.

1917   Cubs lefty Hippo Vaughan and Reds righty Fred Toney duel in Chicago's Weegham Park for 9 hitless innings before the Reds break through in the 10th frame to give Toney a 1–0 win, a one-of-a-kind ML "double no-hit" classic; however, MLB later decides that Vaughan's effort was not a no-hitter since he surrendered hits in overtime.

1927   Washington sends infielder Buddy Myer to the Red Sox for infielder Topper Rigney and then connives to recover Myer the following year from the Sox.

1930   Des Moines of the Western League is the first team in OB to host a game played under permanent light standards.

1939   Lou Gehrig volunteers to bench himself, ending his then record consecutive games streak at 2,130 prior to the Yankees' 22–2 rout of Detroit.

1954   Stan Musial belts a record five home runs in a DBH as the Cards and Giants split a pair.

1958   The Yankees threaten to telecast their games nationwide if the NL televises games played by the Dodgers, Giants, and Phillies into the New York area on dates when the Yankees are playing at home.

1968   At Shea Stadium, Phillies reliever John Boozer is tossed by umpire Ed Vargo for throwing spitballs during his warm-up pitches.

1995   The Dodgers' Hideo Nomo is the first Japanese native to play ML ball in 30 years. Elsewhere, former Seton Hall teammates John Valentin and Mo Vaughn blast grand slams in the Red Sox' 8–0 win over the Yankees, the first time in the bigs that two grand slams account for all the runs scored in a game.

2002   Mariners outfielder Mike Cameron homers in each of his first four at bats and joins Bret Boone as the first teammates to belt two taters apiece in one inning during a 15–4 roasting of the White Sox.

2007   The Braves unveil catcher Jarrod Saltalamacchia, owner of the longest last name (14 letters) in ML history.

3

1938   BoSox vet Lefty Grove wins the first of an AL-record 20 consecutive victories in his home park when he tops the Tigers 4–3 in 10 innings at Fenway.

1947   The Phils trade outfielder Ron Northey to the Cards for pitcher Freddy Schmidt and outfielder Harry Walker, who is hitting just .200 but is destined to be the first ML batting champ to play for two teams in the same season when he rips .371 for Philadelphia.

1952   The White Sox trade outfielder Jim Busby to Washington for Sam Mele. Washington also sends outfielder Irv Noren and shortstop Tommy Upton to the Yankees for four players, including former Cal All-American running back Jackie Jensen.

1961   In an IL contest, Toronto's Ellis Burton is the first player in OB history to switch-hit homers in one inning when he belts a two-run shot batting left-handed and a grand slammer from the right side in the 8th frame during the first game of a DBH against Jersey City.

4

1869   The Cincinnati Red Stockings, the game's first admittedly all-professional team, decimate the Great Westerns 45–9 in their season opener.

1871   The inaugural game played by the National Association, the first professional league, occurs in Fort Wayne, IN, between the local Kekiongas and the Cleveland Forest Citys, with Bobby Mathews of the locals prevailing over Cleveland's Al Pratt 2–0 in an extraordinarily well-played game for its time.

1919   The Polo Grounds hosts its first legal Sunday game, with the Giants losing 4–3 to the Phillies.

1951   Recent player suits against OB's reserve clause trigger New York representative Emanuel Celler to announce that the House plans a probe of the game's exclusion from antitrust laws because it has always been ruled a sport and not a business.

1963   Braves chucker Bob Shaw sets a ML record by committing five balks despite lasting just 4⅓ innings before being ejected for arguing balls and strikes.

1966   Willie Mays drills his 512th career homer, breaking former Giants slugger Mel Ott's NL record.

1975   In the opener of a DBH at Candlestick Park, the Astros' Bob Watson races around the bases on Milt May's homer to score the ML's 1,000,000th run just seconds ahead of the Reds' Dave Concepcion's tally against Atlanta in Cincinnati.

5

1887   Ed Flynn debuts with Cleveland AA after conning the Blues into believing he is "Mikado" Flynn, who starred with Topeka in 1886. The ruse is quickly exposed when Flynn hits .185 in his first seven games.

1904   Boston's Cy Young makes the second of his three career no-hitters the first perfect game at the 60′6″ distance as he blanks the Philadelphia A's and Rube Waddell 3–0, with Waddell, as an indication of how much the game has changed, allowed to bat for himself in the 9th and making the last out.

1917   Browns hurler Ernie Koob tosses a 1–0 shutout against the White Sox that is deemed a one-hitter in many papers the following morning, until it emerges that the Browns scorer, John Sheridan, changed Buck Weaver's first-inning single to an error after taking a poll of fellow sportswriters after the game.

1925   Ty Cobb is 6-for-6 with three home runs as he sets a new AL record (since tied) with 16 total bases in the Tigers' 14–8 win over the

Browns. Elsewhere, weak hitting forces Yankees shortstop Everett Scott to the bench, ending Scott's then record consecutive-games streak at 1,307.

1962   The Angels' Bo Belinsky fires the first post–1884 expansion club no-hitter, topping the Orioles 2–0.

1975   Speedster Herb Washington's unique career ends when the A's release him after he played 105 games exclusively as a pinch runner, without ever appearing at bat or in the field in his two seasons up top.

1999   The Rockies are the first ML club since 1964 to score in all nine innings during a 13–6 triumph over the Cubs at Wrigley Field.

2000   Dodgers skipper Tommy Lasorda is named manager of the U.S. Olympic baseball team.

2004   The Mets' Mike Piazza belts his 352nd homer, breaking Johnny Bench's ML record for most career taters by a catcher.

6

1892   In the only ML game ever called because of too much light, Cincinnati's Elton Chamberlain and Boston's John Clarkson battle to a scoreless tie when umpire Jack Sheridan halts play after 14 innings because the "setting sun dazzled the eyes of the batters."

1915   Boston's Babe Ruth collects his first ML home run when he goes deep against the Yankees' Jack Warhop at the Polo Grounds in the 3rd frame of the Red Sox' 4–3 loss to the Yanks in 13 innings.

1917   The Browns no-hit the White Sox on consecutive days when Bob Groom follows Ernie Koob's no-no of the previous day and his own two hitless relief innings in the first game of a DBH with a 3–0 no-no in the nightcap.

1929   The AL discontinues its annual MVP Award, and the NL follows suit after the 1929 season.

1930   The Yankees ignore Red Ruffing's unspeakable 39–96 career record to that point since it has been compiled with abysmal Red Sox clubs and send Boston Cedric Durst and $50,000 in return for the future HOF pitcher.

1941   Brooklyn GM Larry MacPhail lands future HOF second baseman Billy Herman by sending the Cubs two subs and cash.

1951   In his lone ML start, as well as his lone ML decision, Boston Braves rookie George Estock has the ill luck to draw as his mound opponent Pittsburgh's Cliff Chambers, who chooses this day to hurl the first no-hitter by a Pirate since 1907, winning 3–0.

1953 Browns rookie Bobo Holloman no-hits the A's in his first ML start, winning 6–0 in his only complete-game effort before being released later in the season.

1998 Cubs rookie Kerry Wood stages one of the most dominating pitching performances in history by fanning a ML record-tying 20 Astros while allowing just one hit in a 2–0 win.

7

1906 AL umpire Tim Hurst is suspended for five days after he and New York manager Clark Griffith argue a call and he follows Griffith to the Highlanders bench, where he belts him in the jaw.

1933 The Cards trade infielders Sparky Adams and pitchers Paul Derringer and Allyn Stout to Cincinnati for shortstop Leo Durocher and pitchers Dutch Henry and Jack Ogden.

1938 Newark Bears centerfielder Bob Seeds follows a four-homer game on a Friday by hitting three homers off Buffalo pitching on Saturday, giving him seven dingers, 17 RBI, and 30 total bases in consecutive IL contests against the Bisons.

1941 Hank Greenberg, the 1940 AL MVP, plays his last game with the Tigers before beginning voluntary military duty.

1957 Yankees infielder Gil McDougald slashes a line drive that strikes Cleveland southpaw Herb Score in the left eye, forcing his removal on a stretcher. Though Score's sight is preserved, he is never the same pitcher after he is forced to alter his unorthodox delivery to avoid reinjury.

1959 On "Roy Campanella Night," 93,103 fans—the largest crowd in ML history—jam the Los Angeles Coliseum to watch an exhibition game between the Dodgers and Yankees for the benefit of the crippled ex-Dodgers catcher.

1999 For the first time in ML history, two Japanese starters oppose each other when the Yankees' Hideki Irabu squares off against the Mariners' Mac Suzuki.

8

1871 Cleveland's Ezra Sutton hits the first home run in National Association history and adds a second dinger for good measure later in the contest, but the Forest City club still loses 14–12 to Chicago.

1877   Though he goes 2-for-4 in Chicago's season opener, 1876 NL batting champ Ross Barnes soon finds himself hampered by a new rule eliminating his trademark fair-foul hits—balls that land fair but spin foul before passing a base—along with a debilitating illness that haunts him for the remainder of his career.

1878   Providence centerfielder Paul Hines perpetrates what some pundits consider to be the first unassisted triple play in professional history against Boston, but later research casts doubt that the play was unassisted.

1890   Southpaw Willie McGill, still only 16 years old, is the youngest documented pitcher since Jim Britt in 1872 to hurl a complete-game ML win when he leads Cleveland of the PL to a 14–5 win over Buffalo.

1946   After collecting 11 straight hits earlier in the week before being stopped one short of the ML record, BoSox shortstop Johnny Pesky is the first player in AL history to score six runs in a game in a 14–10 win over the Tigers.

1963   The longest offensive drought in ML history ends when Cubs pitcher Bob Buhl slaps his first ML hit in 88 at bats. Elsewhere, the Cards' Stan Musial homers against the Dodgers, giving him 1,357 extra base hits to set a then ML record.

1966   The Giants regrettably send first sacker Orlando Cepeda to the Cardinals for Ray Sadecki, as Cepeda helps the Cards to a world championship the following year and cops the NL MVP.

1968   A's hurler Catfish Hunter tosses a perfect game against the Twins and drives in three of the A's four runs, collecting two singles and a double.

2001   The Diamondbacks' Randy Johnson whiffs a record-tying 20 Reds across the first 9 innings in Arizona's 4–3 victory in 11 frames. Johnson's feat is not initially officially sanctioned because the contest went extra innings, but the *Elias Sports Bureau* later recants.

9

1871   John McMullin is the first documented left-handed pitcher in ML history when he takes the box for Troy of the fledgling National Association and loses 9–5 to Boston's Al Spalding.

1902   Following a DBH loss at Chicago the previous day, Giants manager Horace Fogel has umpire Bob Emslie measure the distance from the pitchers' rubber to home plate prior to the afternoon game in

West Side Park and compels groundskeeper Kuhn to dig up the plate and move it back 13 inches when the distance is found to be too short. Fogel's protest of the twin-bill loss results in both games later being thrown out by NL officials.

1935   Idled by a broken leg all of 1934, Rabbit Maranville returns to action with the Braves, marking his then record 23rd season in the senior loop.

1981   The Mariners' Tom Paciorek is a repeat last-gasp hero when he swats a game-ending homer to defeat the Yanks 6–5 after staggering the Bombers 3–2 with a walk-off solo shot the previous night.

1984   Harold Baines homers in the 25th inning, giving the White Sox a 7–6 win over the Brewers in the longest ML game to date by time (8 hours, 6 seconds).

1999   Florida State second baseman Marshall McDougall breaks the NCAA single-game marks for taters and ribbies when he strokes six straight homers to total 16 RBI in a 26–2 thrashing of Maryland.

10

1884   In his lone big league game, catcher Alex Gardner commits a record 12 passed balls for the Washington AA club.

1909   On a dank Kentucky day, only approximately 300 fans witness a Class D Blue Grass League classic in which Winchester hurler Fred Toney spins an OB record 17-inning no-hitter, stifling Lexington, 1–0.

1934   With screens protecting pitchers and infielders yet to be developed, the Cards' Bill Walker sustains a broken arm when teammate Joe Medwick slashes a batting practice liner through the box.

1939   Bill Klem celebrates his 35th anniversary as a NL umpire by working the plate at Shibe Park in the Phils' 4–3 loss to the Cards' Lon Warneke.

1946   Red Sox lefty Earl Johnson nips the Yankees 5–4 in relief of Joe Dobson to give the Crimson Hose their club record 15th straight win and send them off to a 21–3 start, the best in AL history to that point.

1953   Pirates "bonus babies" Johnny and Eddie O'Brien, former cagers at Seattle University, are the first documented twins to play for the same team in the same game when they both appear as late-inning subs in a 3–2 loss to the Giants.

1970   Future Hall of Famer Hoyt Wilhelm is the first ML pitcher to appear in 1,000 contests when he strolls to the mound for the Braves.

11

1875   In the lowest-scoring pro baseball game to date, Chicago defeats the NA fledgling St. Louis Red Stockings, 1–0.

1887   Former ML third baseman John Ake drowns the afternoon after a game at LaCrosse, WI, when he and teammates Bill Barnes and Billy Earle take a rowboat out on the Mississippi River, where a passing steamer capsizes it, leaving Ake, a poor swimmer, unable to save himself while his teammates swim safely to shore.

1897   Washington catcher Duke Farrell throws out a record eight Baltimore base runners trying to steal in a losing cause as the Orioles win 6–3 despite Farrell's heroics.

1903   In his first start since tossing a perfecto six days earlier, Cy Young tops Detroit 1–0 in 15 innings to extend his string of scoreless innings that eventually reaches a then ML record 45; however, Young surrenders five hits to the Tigers, ending his ML record for the most consecutive hitless innings at 24.

1923   The Phils and Cards combine to smack a then single-game record 10 home runs at the Baker Bowl in a 20–14 Philadelphia win. Elsewhere, former ML pitcher Pete Schneider, now an outfielder, hits five home runs for Vernon of the PCL in a 35–11 win over Salt Lake City.

1929   In the first game in ML history between two teams that both wear numbered uniforms, the Indians defeat the Yankees, 4–3.

1956   The Phils swap pitchers Herm Wehmeier and Murry Dickson to the Cards for pitchers Harvey Haddix, Stu Miller, and Ben Flowers.

1972   Willie Mays ends his lengthy association with the Giants franchise when he is acquired by the Mets for hurler Charlie Williams plus $50,000.

1977   After 16 straight losses, Braves owner Ted Turner tries managing his own team, but the Braves lose again. The NL ends the travesty by removing Turner as skipper after the game.

1984   The Tigers roar through the AL setting a post–1900 ML record for the best 30-game start by improving their slate to 26–4 after defeating the Angels.

1998   The Cubs' Kerry Wood comes within one of Dupee Shaw's 1884 ML record for strikeouts in two consecutive regulation-length games when he follows a 20-K day by fanning 13 D-backs for a total of 33.

1999   For the first time since the Reds' Jack Taylor opposed the Cubs' Jack Taylor on April 16, 1899, two starting ML hurlers with the same name face each other as the Rockies' Bobby M. Jones defeats the Mets' Bobby J. Jones, 8–5.

2001   Arbitrator Alan Symonette orders MLB to reinstate nine of the 22 umpires dismissed in 1999 and also to give them back pay for missed time.

2003   At the age of 72, the well-traveled and much maligned Jack McKeon replaces Jeff Torborg as Marlins skipper and leads Florida to a stunning world championship that fall over the Yankees.

2006   Yankees outfielder Hideki Matsui breaks his left wrist diving for a ball, ending his record-setting consecutive playing streak from the start of his ML career at 518, not including the 1,250 straight contests he had previously appeared in for the Yomiuri Giants in Japan.

12

1884   Philadelphia A's catcher Ed Rowen goes 4-for-4 in a 13–3 loss to Baltimore, setting a record (since tied) for the most hits by a player in his final ML game.

1933   New owner Tom Yawkey begins his frenetic effort to buy the Red Sox a pennant by making the Yankees the recipients of $100,000 for aging pitcher George Pipgras and rookie infielder Bill Werber and then adding $30,000 to Yankees coffers the following day for minor league outfielder Dusty Cooke.

1955   After holding the Pirates hitless through 8 innings, the Cubs' Sam Jones walks the first three batters in the 9th to load the bases and then fans the heart of the Pittsburgh order—Dick Groat, Roberto Clemente, and Frank Thomas—to preserve his 4–0 no-no.

1962   Mets reliever Craig Anderson wins both games of a DBH against Milwaukee but drops his last 19 career decisions before exiting the bigs.

13

1880   Cleveland outfielder Al Hall suffers a career-ending broken leg in a game against Cincinnati and, as per the custom of the time, is immediately released and forced to pay all of his own hospital expenses.

1921 Even though he is acquitted of auto theft charges, Giants out-fielder Benny Kauff is barred for life by Commissioner Landis for having unsavory associates.

1923 Washington yearling Cy Warmoth fans Cleveland shortstop Joe Sewell twice in the same game, a feat that only one other pitcher will accomplish in the eagle-eyed Sewell's HOF career.

1939 The Browns and Tigers complete a mammoth 10-player deal that brings Bobo Newsom and three lesser players to Detroit for six Tigers chattels, including two future members of the Browns' only AL flag winner in 1944, Mark Christman and Chet Laabs.

1942 Braves hurler Jim Tobin is the only ML pitcher to date to blast three consecutive homers in a game when his jacks in the 5th, 7th, and 8th innings boost him to a 6–5 win over the Cubs.

1952 Pirates farmhand Ron Neccai fires a no-hitter for Bristol of the Class D Appalachian League in which he fans all but one batter and 27 total, as one of his victims reaches first on a dropped third strike.

1965 Tragedy strikes the Angels when 25-year-old rookie reliever Dick Wantz dies following brain cancer surgery just one month after making his lone ML appearance.

14

1884 *Sporting Life* reprints a letter to Harry Wright from a fan proposing that three umpires rather than one work each game, but the notion is met with deafening silence for the moment.

1892 Ailing with what turns out to be a terminal case of typhoid fever, Brooklyn second baseman Hub Collins is replaced by pinch hitter Tom Daly, who hits the first pinch homer in ML history off Boston's John Clarkson.

1913 Walter Johnson's then record streak of $55\frac{2}{3}$ consecutive scoreless innings ends when Gus Williams scores in the 4th frame of Johnson's 10–5 win over the Browns.

1943 The Twin Ports League, the only Class E circuit in OB history, is approved for play during the war but is short-lived, disbanding on July 13.

1988 Cards infielder José Oquendo is the first position player in two decades to earn a decision, absorbing a 19-inning loss to the Braves.

15

1862 The Union Baseball Grounds at Marcy Avenue and Rutledge Street in Brooklyn, the first enclosed ball field to charge an admission fee, opens its doors.

1918 Former Cleveland Spiders player-manager Pat Tebeau shoots himself to death in his downtown St. Louis saloon.

1919 A scoreless duel between Cincinnati's Hod Eller and Brooklyn's Al Mamaux ends 10–0 when the Reds explode for 10 runs in the 13th inning, with Mamaux made to endure the entire onslaught.

1922 Detroit's Ty Cobb goes 1-for-3 against the Yankees and reaches once on an error by shortstop Everett Scott according to the box score official scorer John Kiernan publishes in the following day's *New York Times*; however, sportswriter Fred Lieb calls the error a hit in his *Associated Press* box score, leading Cobb to own a .401 BA at the end of the season according to the AP, which is accepted as official even though Cobb really hit only .399.

1933 Both MLs advance the roster cut down date from June 15 to May 15 as a further cost-cutting measure during the Depression.

1941 Joe DiMaggio singles in four at bats against the White Sox Eddie Smith to launch his ML record 56-game hitting streak.

1944 After hurling the first no-hitter of the ML season three weeks earlier, Braves knuckleballer Jim Tobin comes out on the short end in the campaign's second no-no when Cincinnati's Clyde Shoun, normally a reliever, holds the Braves without a safety and wins 1–0 on a solo jack by Chuck Aleno, a .165 hitter in 1944 who never hits another homer in the majors.

1960 In his first game after being dealt to the Cubs by the Phillies, Don Cardwell no-hits the Cardinals.

1973 The Angels' Nolan Ryan hurls the first of a record seven career no-hitters in defeating KC.

1981 At Cleveland, the Tribe's Len Barker spins a perfect game against the Blue Jays.

1998 The Dodgers ship catcher Mike Piazza and third baseman Todd Zeile to the Marlins for Gary Sheffield and four other players, but just a week later, to reduce their payroll, the Marlins deal Piazza to the Mets.

16

1884 A foul tip off the bat of a Detroit player sticks in Boston catcher Mike Hines's face mask and is ruled a catch by umpire Gene Van Court, but NL president Nicholas Young subsequently instructs all arbiters not to call an out for such an occurrence.

1891 In the longest pro game played to date, Tacoma tops Seattle 6–5 in a 22-inning Pacific Northwestern League contest.

1897 Cleveland's effort to introduce Sunday baseball is aborted when police stop the Spiders game with Washington after the 1st inning, forcing team officials to refund 50¢ to each patron.

1937 Browns third sacker Harlond Clift, who finishes the season with a record 405 assists, ties the then AL regulation-length game mark for third basemen with nine assists in a 5–4 loss to Detroit.

1939 Cleveland beats the A's 8–3 in 10 innings at Philadelphia's Shibe Park in the first night game in AL history.

1957 A 29th birthday party for teammate Billy Martin at Manhattan's Copacabana degenerates into a brawl that results in several Yankees being fined and Martin eventually being traded to KC.

1965 Future Orioles Hall of Famer Jim Palmer debuts at the age of 19, earns his first big league victory, and blasts his initial ML homer, a two-run shot off Jim Bouton in a 7–5 triumph over the Yankees.

17

1939 With Bill Stern calling the action, W2XBS in New York City sends a camera to Baker Field in upper Manhattan to capture the first baseball game ever televised, a college contest between Princeton and Columbia.

1956 The Cards send 1955 NL Rookie of the Year Bill Virdon to Pittsburgh for pitcher Dick Littlefield and outfielder Bobby Del Greco.

1970 Braves great Hank Aaron collects his 3,000th career hit, the first player to reach that milestone and also stroke 500 homers.

1978 The Dodgers' Lee Lacy sets a ML record (since tied) by smacking his third consecutive pinch homer in three pinch at bats.

1979 At Wrigley Field, the Phillies and Cubs slug it out until the Phils emerge with a 23–22 10-inning victory.

1998 David Wells authors the Yankees' first perfecto since Don Larsen's World Series gem, baffling the Twins, 4–0.

2000 In Anaheim, Baltimore's Cal Ripken Jr. hits into his 329th career double play, breaking Hank Aaron's former mark. Ripken extends his record to 350 before retiring.

18

1883 The first documented player sale involving teams in rival MLs occurs when Cleveland of the NL sells pitcher/third baseman George Bradley to Philadelphia of the AA.

1888 After finishing his shift at Jones & Laughlin on the rolls, the hottest job in the steel mill, Al Krumm is given a train ticket by Pittsburgh to New York, where he hurls a complete-game 11–7 loss to Tim Keefe of the Giants and then hops a return train to Pittsburgh in time for his next shift at Jones & Laughlin.

1912 When Detroit players strike to protest the suspension of Ty Cobb for going into the stands in New York to fight with a heckler, manager Hughie Jennings is forced to field a team for the day's game in Philadelphia that consists of himself, two coaches, and nine local players, including pitcher Al Travers, a seminary student who goes the route in his only ML game and surrenders a post–1900 single-game record for runs in a 24–2 loss to the A's.

1946 The Tigers get future AL bat king George Kell from the A's for outfielder Barney McCosky, who finishes the season as the only AL regular whom Cleveland's Bob Feller fails to fan.

1956 Mickey Mantle breaks Jim Russell's former ML record when he homers from both sides of the plate in the same game for the third time in his career as the Yankees beat the White Sox 8–7 in 10 innings. On July 1, Mantle extends his record to four in an 8–6 win over Washington.

1968 Senators slugger Frank Howard sets a ML record for homers in a week with a pair of taters against the Tigers' Mickey Lolich, hiking his total to 10 jacks during a six-game hot streak.

2004 At the age of 40, Randy Johnson is the oldest pitcher in ML history to toss a perfect game in leading the D-backs to a 2–0 win over the Braves.

19

1893 Trailing Brooklyn 3–0 in the bottom of the 9th, Boston ties the game after Billy Nash uses an ancient ploy, still legal but never seen anymore, when he rips a seeming two-run homer out of the park but elects to stop at third base, where he can rattle pitcher Ed Stein. Brooklyn still wins 5–4 in 11 innings.

1895 Boston loans rookie outfielder Jimmy Collins to Louisville for $500 and the right to recall him, which Boston exercises later that year after the future Hall of Famer learns to play third base.

1898 Washington acquires outfielder John Anderson from Brooklyn, probably on loan, for when Anderson is leading the NL in slugging percentage, he returns to Brooklyn late in the campaign.

1929 The Yankees cancel the second game of their scheduled DBH with Boston when a torrential rain ends the first game after five innings and send a standing-room crowd in Yankee Stadium's open right field bleachers on a wild stampede that leaves two spectators dead and 62 injured.

1950 In ill health and despondent over losing his job, former Cardinals outfielder Wattie Holm slays his wife, wounds his 13-year-old daughter, and then kills himself.

1962 The Cards' Stan Musial strokes a single off Dodgers reliever Ron Perranoski for his 3,431st hit, breaking Honus Wagner's NL career mark, but years later, Wagner's total is adjusted to 3,420, retroactively making Musial the record setter on May 5.

2004 In a Southern League contest, Cardinals farmhand Brad Thompson breaks Kaiser Wilhelm's 97-year-old minor league mark for consecutive scoreless innings when he hurls his 57th frame for the Tennessee Smokies without allowing an opposing batter to cross the plate.

20

1891 Jim Fogarty, one of the best defensive outfielders in the game but an incurable cigarette "fiend," dies at the age of 27 of lung disease in San Francisco, CA.

1937 Right-hander Joe Kohlman of Salisbury in the Eastern Shore League loses his first start of the season but then wins 25 in a row to finish the campaign with a 25–1 record.

1941 Taffy Wright sets an AL record (since tied by KC's Mike Sweeney) by collecting at least one RBI in 13 consecutive games when he drives home White Sox teammate Joe Kuhel in a 5–2 win over Washington.

1947 A's catcher Buddy Rosar, owner the previous year of the first perfect 1.000 FA by a catcher in a minimum of 100 games, makes his first error since 1945 when he drops a foul pop.

1958 The Cubs trade shortstop Alvin Dark to the Cards for relief pitcher Jim Brosnan, the future author of *The Long Season*.

1999 The Mets' Robin Ventura is the first player in ML history to slug grand slams in both ends of a DBH, helping his club sweep the Brewers.

21

1930 The Giants send pitcher Larry Benton to Cincinnati for second baseman Hughie Critz.

1936 The Phillies reacquire Chuck Klein from the Cubs for pitcher Curt Davis and outfielder Ethan Allen.

1952 Leading off the bottom of the 1st for Brooklyn, Billy Cox is robbed of a hit by Cincinnati second sacker Bobby Adams, but a record 19 consecutive Dodgers then reach base safely, and nearly an hour is consumed before Frank Smith, the Reds' fourth pitcher in the opening frame, finally whiffs Duke Snider to retire the side.

1957 Boston baseball writers join their brethren in New York in maintaining that their job is strictly a male bastion by barring Doris O'Donnell, a reporter with the *Cleveland News*, from sitting with her colleagues in the Fenway Park press box. O'Donnell made history earlier on the Indians' eastern road trip when she was the first female reporter permitted into the press box at Washington's Griffith Stadium.

1970 The Yankees' Mel Stottlemyre walks 11 Senators in 8⅓ innings, but Washington fails to score as reliever Steve Hamilton closes out the 2–0 shutout that ties the record set by fellow Bomber Lefty Gomez in 1941 for the most walks in a 9-inning whitewash.

1981 In first-round action in the NCAA playoffs, St. John's Frank Viola defeats Yale's Ron Darling 1–0 in 12 innings after Darling tosses 11 hitless frames before allowing a scratch single and later a steal of home for the game's lone run.

2000 Giants starter Russ Ortiz beats the Brewers 16–10 despite yielding 10 earned runs, the most by a victorious pitcher since the Pirates' Bob Friend in 1954.

22

1883 Rookie Chicago outfielder Billy Sunday, who later abandons the game to become an evangelist, is the first player to strike out four times in his ML debut.

1893 Louisville inaugurates its new park by beating Cincinnati in a 3–1 pitchers' duel that is "old-fashioned" in every sense, as both teams agree to play the game with the pitching distance set at its former mark of 50 feet.

1913 The Giants acquire pitcher Art Fromme and outfielder Eddie Grant from Cincinnati for pitcher Red Ames, outfielder Josh Devore, $20,000, and third baseman Heinie Groh, whom the New York club spends the next decade trying to reacquire.

1935 Albany of the IL signs prison ball star Alabama Pitts, slated to be paroled from Sing Sing after serving time for armed robbery.

1952 After months of testimony from men in all walks of baseball, Emanuel Celler's House Judiciary Committee reaches a decision, finding that government intervention in the way baseball is run is unnecessary and that the sport is capable of solving its own problems.

1995 The Carolina League Durham Bulls and Winston-Salem Warthogs launch a brawl in which 10 players are ejected, and Warthogs pitcher Glen Cullop is kayoed on "Strike Out Domestic Violence Night."

2003 Arturo Moreno is the first Hispanic to have a controlling interest in a big league team when he purchases the defending world champion Angels from Walt Disney for $184,000,000.

23

1901 To protect a four-run lead with the bases loaded and no outs, Chicago AL player-manager Clark Griffith intentionally walks A's second baseman Nap Lajoie, the first documented instance of a team issuing an intentional walk to a hitter with the bases jammed. Griffith's ploy works as Chicago wins, 11–9.

1945 The Cards pilfer the pitching surprise of the year, Red Barrett, plus $60,000 from the Braves for their rebellious mound ace, Mort Cooper, a holdout when the Cards refuse to raise his salary from $12,000 to $15,000 after he wins 20 games three seasons in a row.

1980 A strike is averted when MLB players and owners announce a new four-year basic agreement, which includes raising the minimum salary from $21,000 to $30,000.

2002 The Dodgers' Shawn Green crunches four homers, a double, and a single for a ML record 19 total bases, plus a record-tying six runs scored against the Brewers.

24

1880 Roger Connor, the career home run record holder prior to Babe Ruth, bangs his first of 138 career jacks as he goes 4-for-5 for Troy in an 8–1 win over Boston's Tommy Bond.

1884 After opening the season with 20 straight wins and ending all semblance of a pennant race in the fledgling UA, the St. Louis Maroons lose their first game, 8–1, to Boston's Tommy Bond.

1906 Boston loses its then AL record 20th straight game, including a then AL record 19 in a row at home, when the White Sox' Nick Altrock beats Cy Young, 7–5.

1918 Philadelphia A's outfielder Ralph Sharman, a late-season sensation in 1917, is the first member of the ill-fated 1915 Ohio League champion Portsmouth team (which included Pickles Dillhoefer and Austin McHenry) to die when he drowns during a training exercise at Camp Sheridan, AL.

1935 Host Cincinnati edges the Phils 2–1 in the first ML night game after Reds GM Larry MacPhail arranges for President Franklin D. Roosevelt to throw a switch in the White House to turn on the lights at Crosley Field.

1936 Yankees second sacker Tony Lazzeri hits three home runs, including two grand slams, and drives home an AL single-game record 11 runs in a 25–2 thrashing of the Philadelphia A's.

1972 After Angels hurler Don Rose strokes a homer in his first ML AB and earns a 6–5 victory, he never connects for another tater or wins another game.

1984 Tigers ace Jack Morris downs the Angels 5–1, earning Detroit's 17th straight road win to tie the 1916 Giants' ML record.

2007 John Smoltz defeats the Mets and former longtime Braves teammate Tom Glavine to become the first pitcher in ML annals to post 200 career wins and 150 saves.

25

1876 Philadelphia and Louisville play the first tie game in NL history when they are knotted 2-all when darkness stops play after 14 innings.

1906 Jesse Tannehill ends Boston's 20-game losing streak, including a then AL record 19 straight losses at home, when he blanks the White Sox, 3–0.

1934 Convinced that fractious sore-armed hurler Wes Ferrell is through, Cleveland foolishly ships him and outfielder Dick Porter to the Red Sox for $25,000, pitcher Bob Weiland, and outfielder Bob Seeds.

1935 Babe Ruth is the first slugger to produce three-homer games in both the AL and NL when he rips a trio of balls over the rightfield wall in Pittsburgh's Forbes Field, the third of which clears the grandstand for his 714th and last career dinger.

1937 An errant pitch from the Yankees' Bump Hadley fractures Tigers player-manager Mickey Cochrane's skull, putting him on the critical list and ending his career.

1946 Unable to get along with the Yankees new GM, Larry MacPhail, Joe McCarthy quits as Yankees manager citing health reasons and is replaced by former Bombers catcher Bill Dickey.

1982 Cubs great Fergie Jenkins fans the Padres' Garry Templeton for his 3,000th career strikeout, making him the first pitcher in ML history to reach that milestone while issuing fewer than 1,000 walks.

1984 The Red Sox trade former 20-game winner Dennis Eckersley and minor leaguer Mike Brumley to the Cubs for former NL batting titlist Bill Buckner.

1989 In what will always be an infamous swap in Ontario, the Expos ship Brian Holman, Gene Harris, and Randy Johnson to the Mariners for Mark Langston and a minor leaguer.

1996 In Las Vegas, NV, a car accident claims the life of ML infielder Mike Sharperson, who is playing with San Diego's Triple A affiliate at the time.

26

1929 For the first time in ML history, two pinch hitters hit grand slam homers in the same game when the Giants' Pat Crawford slugs a four-run jack in the 6th frame and the Braves' Les Bell follows suit an inning later off Carl Hubbell in the Giants' 15–8 win.

1930   The White Sox' Pat Caraway is the second pitcher to fan Cleveland's Joe Sewell twice in a game, but no other AL hurler is able to whiff Sewell even once in a game for the remainder of the season.

1952   Bill Bell, a teammate of Ron Necciai's with Bristol of the Appalachian League, tosses his second consecutive no-hitter in the Class D loop.

1959   Pittsburgh's Harvey Haddix hurls the most remarkable game in ML annals when he is perfect for 12 innings before an apparent game-winning three-run homer off the bat of Joe Adcock in the bottom of the 13th follows an error and an intentional walk to Hank Aaron. Adcock's blow is reduced to a one-run double, however, when he is called out for passing Aaron on the base paths, making Lew Burdette the winner of a 1–0 shutout.

1993   In a play that will forever be a blooper reel highlight, Carlos Martinez's fly ball bounces off Rangers outfielder Jose Canseco's skull and into the stands for a homer as Cleveland edges Texas, 7–6.

2004   The Pirates' Daryle Ward hits for the cycle against the Cards nearly 24 years after his sire, Gary, did so with the Twins, making them the first father and son duo to perform this feat.

27

1931   Will Harridge is named to succeed the late E. S. Barnard as AL president.

1937   Carl Hubbell collects his record 24th consecutive win over a two-year period in relief when Giants teammate Mel Ott homers in the 9th to edge Cincinnati, 3–2.

1955   Though the season is scarcely six weeks old, Giants utility man Bobby Hofman hits his third pinch homer of the year and the ninth of his career in New York's 3–1 win over Brooklyn.

1960   Orioles catcher Clint Courtney uses an oversized mitt designed by his skipper, Paul Richards, to handle Hoyt Wilhelm's elusive knuckleball, but Courtney's flawless performance helps lead to the mitt being banned.

1968   The big leagues expand beyond the United States as the NL announces the inclusion of Montreal plus San Diego in the circuit's fold for the following year.

2001   Barry Bonds hits the 12,000th homer in Giants franchise history during a 5–4 Giants win against the Rockies' Denny Neagle in Pac Bell Park.

28

1928   Connie Mack springs for $50,000 and two players to acquire pitcher George Earnshaw from Baltimore of the IL for his A's.

1930   Cubs pitcher Hal Carlson dies at the age of 38 of a bleeding ulcer.

1951   Willie Mays's first ML hit after a 0-for-12 start is a home run off Braves lefty Warren Spahn.

1957   The other six NL teams approve the proposed moves of the Dodgers and the Giants to the West Coast provided that both clubs make the move at the same time.

1995   At Detroit, the White Sox down the Tigers in a 14–12 slugfest that features a ML record (since tied) 12 homers.

1998   Giants slugger Barry Bonds receives a bases loaded intentional walk against the D-Backs, making him the first such recipient in the majors since the Cubs' Bill Nicholson on July 23, 1944.

2002   Former NL MVP Ken Caminiti, an admitted steroid user, contends in a *Sports Illustrated* article that approximately 50% of current big leaguers use some form of steroids. Caminiti dies some two and a half years later from the long-term effects of substance abuse.

29

1882   In an odd transaction yet to be explained, Worcester of the NL loans pitcher Frank Mountain to Philadelphia of the rival AA and then requests his return in early July.

1888   Phils pitcher/second baseman Charlie Ferguson dies at the age of 25 of typhoid pneumonia.

1915   Umpires Bill Byron and Al Orth halt the first game of a Saturday DBH at Pittsburgh when rain begins after the 5th inning with the Cards and Pirates tied 0–0. After waiting an hour for the rain to stop, the two officials bizarrely call the first game a tie and start the second game, which the Cards win 5–3.

1916   Christy Mathewson's 3–0 shutout of the Boston Braves is the New York Giants' record 17th straight win on the road (tied by the

1984 Tigers). The string ends the following day in Philadelphia when Al Demaree tops Pol Perritt, 5–1.

1922 Dissatisfied with a lower court's decision, officials of the Baltimore FL team pursue their seven-year-old case against the two MLs for giving them the short end in the 1915 peace settlement to the U.S. Supreme Court, which supports the lower court's ruling that baseball is not a form of interstate commerce.

1925 The Fort Worth Panthers score 34 runs in a Texas League game against San Antonio. Managed by former ML second baseman Jake Atz, the Panthers join the 1925 Baltimore Orioles of the IL in setting an OB record when each wins its seventh straight pennant that season.

1939 The Cubs get pitcher Claude Passeau from the Phillies in return for pitchers Ray Harrell and Kirby Higbe and outfielder Joe Marty.

1950 Dr. David Tracy resigns as the Browns' team psychologist when the players lose confidence in him after his attempts at hypnotizing them into improving their play fail abysmally.

1951 Impressed when told that Billy Joe Davidson was coached by his father much like Bob Feller, Indians GM Hank Greenberg signs the prep-school lefty without ever seeing him pitch for a purported $150,000 bonus and is mortified when his pig in a poke never throws a single pitch in top company.

1956 Pirates first sacker Dale Long's new ML record of homering in eight consecutive games is stopped by Brooklyn's Don Newcombe in a 10–1 Dodgers win.

1971 The Giants trade outfielder George Foster to the Reds for shortstop Frank Duffy and pitcher Vern Geishert. Foster will top the majors with 52 homers in 1977 while copping the NL MVP.

1972 Former ML catcher Moe Berg, who distinguished himself as an American secret agent in World War II and an inveterate freeloader afterward, dies in Belleville, NJ, at the age of 70.

1976 Astros moundsman Joe Niekro hits the lone homer of his 22-year big league career against his brother, Phil, in a 4–3 win against Atlanta.

30

1884 In the second game of a DBH at Chicago's tiny Lake Park, where he will hit 25 of his then season record 27 home runs in 1884,

White Stockings shortstop Ned Williamson is the first NLer to hit three dingers in a game as Chicago drubs Detroit, 12–2.

1887 New York Giants rookie Bill George walks a NL-record 16 batters in a 12–11 loss to Chicago (George's NL mark is tied less than a month later by Chicago rookie George Van Haltren).

1894 Boston second baseman Bobby Lowe is the first MLer to hit four home runs in a game in the nightcap of a DBH sweep of Cincinnati at Boston.

1913 On Memorial Day at Washington, Red Sox right fielder Harry Hooper is the first ML batsman to lead off in both ends of a DBH by homering, with his second jack accounting for the only run Ray Collins needs to nip Walter Johnson 1–0 in the nightcap.

1922 Between games of a Memorial Day DBH, Cubs outfielder Max Flack and Cards gardener Cliff Heathcote are traded for each other, enabling each of them to play for both teams in the same day.

1925 Second baseman Rogers Hornsby replaces Branch Rickey as the Cards' manager.

1927 Walter Johnson notches the last of his record 113 career shutouts when he tops Boston, 3–0. Elsewhere, Reading of the IL, headed for a grisly season record of 43–123, ends a 32-game losing streak by whipping Baltimore.

1930 Cubs second baseman Rogers Hornsby breaks an ankle sliding at St. Louis's Sportsman's Park and is idled until September 4, dampening the Bruins' chances to repeat as NL champs.

1935 In his last ML appearance, Babe Ruth exits after the 1st inning in the opening game of a Memorial Day DBH at the Baker Bowl.

1951 After sweeping the Browns in a Memorial Day twin bill, the resurgent "Go-Go" White Sox under rookie skipper Paul Richards are riding a 14-game winning streak and lead the AL by a two-game margin.

1956 Mickey Mantle is the first player in ML history to rap 20 homers before June 1, when he rips a pitch from Washington's Camilo Pascual off the facade at the top of the upper deck at Yankee Stadium, helping the Bombers to a 12–5 win in the second game of a Memorial Day DBH.

1970 For the first time since 1957, fans are allowed to vote for the starting lineup in the All-Star Game as punch-card ballots appear in ballparks and stores across the country.

31

1885 The first documented crowd in ML history of more than 20,000 (20,632) watches Detroit top the New York Giants 4–1 at the Polo Grounds.

1890 George Gore, Buck Ewing, and Roger Connor of the New York PL club lead a 23–3 slaughter of Pittsburgh PL hurler (and future NL president) John Tener, when they become the first trio of ML teammates to hit three consecutive home runs.

1950 Chicago sends infielder Cass Michaels, outfielder John Ostrowski, and pitcher Bob Kuzava to Washington for second baseman Al Kozar, first baseman Eddie Robinson, and pitcher Rae Scarborough.

1964 At Shea Stadium, the Mets and Giants battle for nearly 10 hours in the longest DBH in ML history, which features a 23-inning, 7 hour and 23 minute nightcap won by the Giants, 8–6.

1968 The Dodgers' Don Drysdale hits Giants catcher Dick Dietz in the 9th inning with the bases loaded, apparently ending Drysdale's scoreless innings streak at 44 innings, but plate umpire Harry Wendelstedt invokes a rarely enforced rule by refusing to award Dietz first base for failing to avoid the pitch. A livid Giants skipper Herman Franks is ejected, and Drysdale then gets Dietz to fly out and retires the next two batters to record his fifth straight shutout.

1997 Reliever Ila Borders of the St. Paul Saints in the independent Northern League is the first female in the 20th century to play in the minors as she yields three runs to the Sioux Falls Canaries without retiring a batter, but she rebounds to fan three straight hitters the following day.

June

1

1881 Tommy Bond, winner of 180 ML games before his 25th birthday, is released by Boston with a "used up" arm after a 0–3 start and never wins another game in the NL or AA.

1896 St. Louis sends outfielder Tommy Dowd and catcher Ed McFarland to Philadelphia for second baseman Bill Hallman, catcher Mike Grady, pitcher Kid Carsey, and outfielder Dick Harley.

1913 The Yankees trade bad-boy first sacker Hal Chase to the White Sox for infielder Rollie Zeider and first baseman Babe Borton.

1917 Braves catcher Hank Gowdy is the first ML player to enlist in World War I when he joins the Ohio National Guard and reports for active duty six weeks later.

1925 Lou Gehrig is called off the Yankees bench to pinch hit for shortstop Pee Wee Wanninger, launching his record streak (since broken) of 2,130 consecutive games.

1975 The Angels' Nolan Ryan wins his 100th career game in style by no-hitting the Orioles and tying Sandy Koufax's then record of four career no-nos.

1987 When the Indians' Phil Niekro bags his 314th career win, it gives him and his younger brother, Joe, a sibling record 530 combined ML victories, surpassing Gaylord and Jim Perry.

2001 Cleveland starter C. C. Sabathia earns a victory against the Yankees despite working just four innings when the game is rained out prior to completion, as MLB rules state that in a five-inning game, a starter need not go five full innings to earn a win.

2

1883   Fort Wayne and Quincy, IL, play the first known professional game under electric lighting, with Fort Wayne winning the Northwestern League contest, 19–11.

1885   St. Louis's AA record 17-game winning streak ends with a 7–1 loss to Baltimore's Hardie Henderson.

1924   Jay Hughes, the NL leader in wins and winning percentage in 1899, either accidentally falls or jumps to his death from a railway trestle in Sacramento, CA.

1941   Lou Gehrig dies in Riverdale, NY, less than two years after ALS forces him to leave baseball.

1948   Cleveland trades strikeout-prone slugger Pat Seerey and pitcher Al Gettel to the White Sox for third baseman/outfielder Bob Kennedy.

1995   The Dodgers' Japanese rookie Hideo Nomo beats the Mets for his first ML win.

2000   In interleague play, the Tigers oppose the Cubs in Wrigley Field for the first time since the 1945 World Series as the Bruins win. Elsewhere, on the first occasion that a ML club honors an athlete outside baseball so elaborately, the Expos announce they will don hockey great Maurice Richard's uniform number 9 on their jerseys to commemorate the Montreal Canadiens' legendary star, who died the previous week.

3

1851   The Knickerbocker Club of New York wins its first match of the year, defeating the Washington Club 21–11 under the then rule declaring the first team to score 21 runs the winner unless it is first to bat, in which case its opponent is given "last raps" to try to equal or surpass the leader's total.

1888   Ernest Thayer's immortal poem *Casey at the Bat* first appears in the *San Francisco Examiner*.

1898   Jack Clements, now with St. Louis, is the first and only southpaw to catch 1,000 ML games.

1902   Cardinals pitcher Mike O'Neill hits the first pinch grand slam in ML history when he goes deep in the 9th inning to beat Boston at South End Grounds.

1916   Pitcher Jimmy Claxton, the last documented African American minor leaguer prior to 1946, is released by Oakland of the PCL.

1932   Ailing John McGraw resigns as manager of the New York Giants and is replaced by first baseman Bill Terry. Meanwhile, the Yankees' Lou Gehrig hits four home runs in a 20–13 win over the Athletics, but his feat is eclipsed in the press the following day, especially in New York, by McGraw's departure.

1952   Detroit and Boston engineer the most massive trade to date involving topflight talent as the Tigers get Johnny Pesky, Walt Dropo, Don Lenhardt, Bill Wight, and Fred Hatfield in return for George Kell, Dizzy Trout, Hoot Evers, and Johnny Lipon.

1978   The Phillies' Davey Johnson is the first big leaguer to poke two pinch grand slams in one season.

1995   Expos ace Pedro Martinez works nine perfect innings against the Padres before Bip Roberts leads off the 10th with a double, making Martinez the first ML pitcher since the Bucs' Harvey Haddix to see his bid for a perfecto ruined in extra frames.

2003   Cubs slugger Sammy Sosa is ejected in the 1st inning after umpires spy cork in his shattered bat.

2004   At the age of 45, the Braves' Julio Franco is the oldest ML player to stroke a grand slam, a record he breaks when he connects for another sacks-jammed wallop on June 27, 2005.

4

1953   Pittsburgh trades Ralph Kiner and four lesser players to the Cubs for six players and $150,000.

1964   Dodgers flamethrower Sandy Koufax is the fourth ML hurler to that point to spin three career no-hitters when he victimizes the Phillies.

1968   With his sixth straight shutout, the Dodgers' Don Drysdale breaks the ML record for consecutive scoreless innings with 54 while topping the mark for consecutive complete-game whitewashings.

1972   Hitters are at the mercy of moundsmen as a ML record eight shutouts are pitched in 16 ML games.

1974   Cleveland moronically designates this night's contest with Texas "Ten-Cent Beer Night" and winds up a forfeit loser when drunken fans maul Rangers outfielder Jeff Burroughs with the score tied and the potentially winning Cleveland run perched on third base in the bottom of the 9th.

1986   Future home-run king Barry Bonds blasts his first career tater off the Braves' Craig McMurtry to help Pittsburgh win.

5

1875   After rocketing to a ML record 21–0 start, the Boston Red Stockings suffer their first loss of the NA season, a 5–4 road setback to rookie hurler George Bradley of the fledgling St. Louis Browns.

1914   Pitcher John Cantley, of Opelika in the Georgia-Alabama League, crushes three grand slams and knocks home 15 runs in his own behalf as he drubs Talladega, 19–1.

1937   Pirates first sacker Gus Suhr's NL record (since broken) streak of 822 consecutive games ends when he has to leave the team to attend his mother's funeral in San Francisco.

1949   Confronted with a torrent of legal threats, Commissioner Chandler reinstates all players banned from OB in 1946 for jumping to the Mexican League.

1981   Astros hurler Nolan Ryan breaks Early Wynn's career walk record by issuing his 1,776th free pass, a mark Ryan extends to 2,795.

6

1892   Benjamin Harrison is the first U.S. president to attend a ML game when he watches Washington lose 7–4 to visiting Cincinnati in 11 innings.

1935   Albany rescinds its contract offer to Sing Sing parolee Alabama Pitts when controversy arises as to whether an ex-convict should be allowed to play in OB.

1941   The Giants are the first ML team to wear plastic batting helmets in a DBH loss to Pittsburgh, but the prudent innovation fails to gain support from other ML teams.

1944   The only two ML games scheduled are postponed in commemoration of D-Day. Meanwhile, the Cubs swap Eddie Stanky to Brooklyn for journeyman pitcher Bob Chipman.

1971   Giants great Willie Mays drills his career record 22nd and final extra-inning homer, a 12th-inning blast off the Phillies' Joe Hoerner.

1973   Former ML second baseman Jerry Priddy is arrested by the FBI in California and later sentenced to nine months in prison for trying to extort $250,000 from a steamship company by threatening to put a bomb aboard one of its vessels, the *Island Princess*.

1978 The Braves make Bob Horner, the college player of the year at Arizona State, the first overall pick in the June draft and promote him directly to the parent club.

1982 After working the afternoon White Sox-Rangers game at Arlington Stadium, AL umpire Lou DiMuro is fatally struck by a car while returning to his hotel from dinner. At the time of his death, DiMuro was one of only four umpires who still used an outside chest protector.

2003 Cubs outfielder Sammy Sosa is suspended for eight games despite protesting that his corked bat was used only for thrilling the crowd during batting practice and slipped into an actual game by mistake.

2007 Padres closer Trevor Hoffman is the first reliever to notch 500 saves. Elsewhere, the Twins' Luis Castillo's record errorless streak at second base ends at 143 games, a mark surpassed later in the season.

7

1884 Providence's Charlie Sweeney fans 19 Boston hitters in a NL game to set a ML record that lasts for 102 years.

1885 AA moguls vote to join the NL in eliminating the foul bound rule (meaning that a batter is no longer out if his foul hit is caught on the first bounce) and also to adopt the NL rule licensing overhand pitching.

1893 Baltimore manager Ned Hanlon trades shortstop Tim O'Rourke to Louisville for first baseman Harry Taylor and also—in one of the greatest strokes of luck in history—agrees to accept shortstop Hughie Jennings (hitting a feeble .136 at the time) as recompense for Taylor not being able to report to Baltimore until later in June after he finishes his law school term.

1911 The Pirates log a ML nine-inning game team record 28 assists but still lose to the Giants, 9–4.

1923 The Giants ship pitcher Jesse Barnes and catcher Earl Smith to former Giant Christy Mathewson's Braves for pitcher Mule Watson and catcher Hank Gowdy.

1936 Red Ruffing raps three hits, including a homer, but remarkably fails to strike out a single batter in winning a 16-inning battle over Cleveland's Oral Hildebrand, 5–4.

1940 For the second time in 11 years, the Cards "recall" Billy Southworth from their Rochester farm team to manage the parent club, this time as a replacement for Ray Blades.

1941   Prison-yard baseball legend Alabama Pitts dies after being stabbed by Newland LeFevers when he tried to dance with LeFevers's girlfriend, Mildred Deal, at a Valdese, NC, roadhouse.

1946   Pirates players vote whether to strike in recognition of the newly formed American Baseball Guild one hour before their game with the Giants, but the final tally is short of the required majority for a walkout, stymieing organizer Robert Murphy's efforts to launch a new players union.

1966   The Mets designate catcher Steve Chilcott, who never makes the majors, the overall number 1 pick in the June free-agent draft while passing on outfielder Reggie Jackson, whom the A's snatch with the second pick.

1982   The Cubs have the first pick in the June draft and choose Shawon Dunston, freeing the Mets to later take pitcher Dwight Gooden.

2002   In the independent Northern League, St. Paul Saints owner Mike Veeck gives away seat cushions sporting a likeness of Players Association Executive Director Donald Fehr on one side and Commissioner Selig on the other.

2007   During MLB's initial televised amateur draft, the Devil Rays select Vanderbilt University's David Price first overall.

8

1869   The highest-winning score on record is achieved in a game between two Buffalo, NY, clubs when the Niagaras trounce Columbia, 209–10.

1889   Second baseman Jack Crooks of Omaha in the Western League is the first pro player to hit four home runs in a game and, in addition, drives home 13 runs in Omaha's 19–15 win at St. Paul.

1909   San Francisco's Cack Henley hurls a 24-inning 1–0 shutout in a PCL game.

1920   The Giants swap pitcher Bill Hubbell, infielder Art Fletcher, and cash to the Phils for future HOF shortstop Dave Bancroft.

1923   Browns catcher Pat Collins is the only man in ML history to pinch hit and pinch run in the same game when A's manager Connie Mack agrees to waive the rule that a player removed from a game cannot reenter.

1930   With suspicion growing that the ball has been juiced, Brooklyn's Babe Herman begins the day leading the NL with a .420 BA, while the Dodgers as a unit are hitting .328 and have scored 301 runs in 44 games.

1934   The Reds are the first team to travel by air for a road game when GM Larry MacPhail arranges for all but six players, who demur, to fly from Cincinnati to St. Louis.

1950   After thumping the Browns 20–4 at Fenway Park the previous day, the Red Sox set a then AL single-game record for runs when they take St. Louis to the cleaners, 29–4.

1961   The Milwaukee Braves are the first club to slam four consecutive homers, as Eddie Mathews, Hank Aaron, Joe Adcock, and Frank Thomas blast off in the 7th inning against Cincinnati, but the Braves still lose 10–8.

1965   The A's make Rick Monday the first overall number 1 pick in the initial June free-agent draft, as the Reds choose Johnny Bench in the second round and the Mets select Nolan Ryan after every team passed over him several times.

1968   Don Drysdale's scoreless innings streak ends at 58⅔ when the Phillies' Howie Bedell's sacrifice fly in the 5th frame sends home Tony Taylor.

2005   At the age of 29, Yankees third baseman Alex Rodriguez is the youngest player to join the 400-homer club.

9

1883   Last-place Philadelphia, one of the NL's two new franchises in 1883, is given permission to reduce its admission price from 50¢ to 25¢ so it can compete for fans with the AA Philadelphia Athletics.

1900   At the Stuyvesant House hotel in New York City, the Players Protective Association, an embryonic union designed to act as a voice for players with respect to contract negotiations and proposed rule changes, is launched with Harry Taylor, a former ML first baseman turned lawyer, named the organization's legal adviser, and catcher Chief Zimmer its first president.

1903   The Phils tally a run off rookie Kaiser Wilhelm in the 4th inning at Pittsburgh to break Pirates pitchers' record streak of 56 consecutive scoreless innings.

1963   Houston's sweltering daytime heat induces the Colt .45s and the Giants to play the first Sunday night game in ML history, with Houston winning 3–0.

1966 For the first time in AL history, a club strokes five homers in one inning, as the Twins' Rich Rollins, Zoilo Versalles, Tony Oliva, Don Mincher, and Harmon Killebrew tee off against the A's in the 7th frame.

1972 Former ML first baseman Del Bissonette, who set the then season record for the most home runs by a rookie in 1928, dies of a self-inflicted gunshot wound in Augusta, ME.

10

1880 Boston outfielder Charley Jones, the defending NL home-run king, is the first ML player to hit two dingers in one inning but is jettisoned nevertheless on September 1 when team owner Arthur Soden suspends and then blacklists him for having the temerity to refuse to play until the club forks over the $378 it owes him in back pay.

1898 St. Louis gets outfielder Jake Stenzel and second baseman Joe Quinn from Baltimore for outfielder Ducky Holmes and $2,500.

1944 The Reds' Joe Nuxhall is the youngest documented player in AL or NL history when he takes the rubber 50 days short of his 16th birthday to hurl ⅔ of an inning in an 18–0 loss to the Cardinals.

1951 Otis Johnson of Dothan in the Alabama-Florida League dies from head injuries sustained eight days earlier when he was beaned by southpaw Jack Clifton of Headland, the top pitcher in the circuit.

1954 Giants rookie Bill Taylor's first ML home run off the Braves' Gene Conley is also the first pinch homer in ML history to account for the only run of a game, as New York edges Milwaukee 1–0 in 10 innings.

1959 Cleveland right fielder Rocky Colavito joins Lou Gehrig and Bobby Lowe as the only ML players to date to hit four consecutive homers in a game in sparking the Tribe to an 11–8 win at Baltimore.

2000 The Angels' Darin Erstad collects his 100th hit in his 61st game of the season, making him the fastest to reach 100 hits since Washington's Heinie Manush in 1934.

11

1915 Yankees pitcher Ray Caldwell is the first pinch hitter in AL history to go yard two days in a row when he hits a three-run homer in the 6th inning off Red Faber in a 10–9 win over the White Sox.

1934 The Phils, usually everyone's patsy in the trading mart, swindle the Cubs when they send fast-slipping first sacker Don Hurst west for first sacker Dolph Camilli, plus a wad of cash.

1937 The Giants trade future 200-game winner Fred Fitzsimmons to Brooklyn for Tom Baker, who goes on to win only one game with New York. Meanwhile, Boston sends the Ferrell brothers, Rick and Wes, plus outfielder Mel Almada, to Washington for Bobo Newsom and Ben Chapman.

1938 Trailing the White Sox 13–1 in the 8th, Red Sox pilot Joe Cronin lets rookie pitcher Bill Lefebvre hit for himself and watches Lefebvre homer in not only his first ML AB but also his *only* AB of the season.

1985 In a 26–7 humiliation of the Mets, Phillies outfielder Von Hayes is the first ML player to pole two homers in the 1st inning.

1988 Enamored of his solid stick, the Yanks make Rick Rhoden the first pitcher penciled into the starting lineup as a DH since the inception of the rule in 1973.

1990 At the age of 43, the Rangers' Nolan Ryan is the oldest pitcher to that point to toss a no-hitter, as he extends his ML mark with his sixth career no-no, a 6–0 blanking of the A's.

2003 In a true team effort, the Astros set a record by using six pitchers to no-hit the Yankees when Roy Oswalt, Peter Munro, Kirk Saarloos, Brad Lidge, Octavio Dotel, and Billy Wagner combine to spin the first 9-inning no-no against the Bombers since Baltimore's Hoyt Wilhelm in 1958.

12

1880 Worcester NL lefty Lee Richmond crafts the first perfect game in ML history, edging Cleveland 1–0.

1886 The Detroit Wolverines set a ML record (since broken) when they hammer seven home runs in a 14–7 win over washed-up St. Louis Maroons hurler Charlie Sweeney.

1900 Former ML first baseman Mox McQuery, now a Covington, KY, police officer, is fatally shot by a murder suspect he is pursuing on foot across the suspension bridge between Covington and Cincinnati, OH.

1902 Tim Donahue dies of Addison's disease less than a month after catching his last game with Washington of the AL.

1927 The Braves trade pitcher Larry Benton to the Giants along with catcher Zack Taylor and utility man Herb Thomas for pitchers Hugh McQuillan and Kent Greenfield and infielder Doc Farrell.

1932 The BoSox trade over-the-hill Earl Webb to Detroit for Roy Johnson and Dale Alexander, who becomes the first bat titlist in ML history to split the season between two teams when he goes on a tear after arriving in Boston and raises his BA from .250 to .367.

1940 Cards GM Branch Rickey makes one of his rare bad trades, sending Joe Medwick and Curt Davis to Brooklyn for Ernie Koy, three minor leaguers, and $125,000.

1957 The Cards' Stan Musial breaks Gus Suhr's NL consecutive-game streak record when he plays in his 823rd straight contest, an 8–2 win over the Phillies.

1970 Bucs twirler Dock Ellis no-hits the Padres and later claims in his autobiography that he achieved the feat while on LSD.

1980 Former Brewers outfielder Danny Thomas hangs himself in his prison cell at the age of 29 while awaiting trial for statutory rape.

1997 The Giants defeat the Rangers in the first ML interleague game, as San Francisco's Glenallen Hill is the NL's first regular-season DH and teammate Mark Gardner earns the first interleague win.

13

1915 A's southpaw Bruno Haas goes all the way in his ML debut but loses 15–7 to the Yankees, largely owing to the post-1892, 9-inning record 16 walks he issues.

1938 The Reds obtain a major component of their 1939 and 1940 NL flag winners when they bag pitcher Bucky Walters from the Phillies for catcher Spud Davis, pitcher Al Hollingsworth, and $50,000.

1940 The Cubs and Red Sox meet at Cooperstown's Doubleday Field in the first of what will become an annual exhibition game between rotating ML teams.

1948 The Yankees retire Babe Ruth's number 3 in a ceremony at Yankee Stadium in Ruth's final public appearance before his death.

1973 First baseman Steve Garvey, second baseman Davey Lopes, shortstop Bill Russell, and third baseman Ron Cey play their first game together with the Dodgers in what will be a ML record eight consecutive seasons as the club's regular infield unit.

1984 The Cubs deal Joe Carter and three other players to the Indians for pitcher Rick Sutcliffe and two other players. Sutcliffe goes 16–1 over the remainder of the season, wins the NL Cy Young Award, and spurs the Cubs to the NL East title, while Carter will plate more than 100 runs 10 times in his career.

1999 Astros skipper Larry Dierker is hospitalized after suffering a grand mal seizure in a game against the Padres and soon undergoes successful brain surgery.

2003 In interleague action against the Cards, the Yankees' Roger Clemens wins his 300th game while recording his 4,000th strikeout.

14

1870 After 84 straight wins over a two-year period, the Cincinnati Red Stockings finally taste defeat, bowing to the Brooklyn Atlantics, 8–7 in 11 innings, at Capitoline Grounds in Brooklyn.

1876 Playing second base, Andy Leonard, normally an outfielder and an original member of the legendary 1869 Cincinnati Red Stockings, sets a post–1875 ML single-game record when he makes nine errors for Boston in a 20–6 loss to St. Louis that features a staggering total of 41 miscues by both sides (including a post–1875 single-game team record 24 by Boston) and is deemed by one correspondent dispatching results of the contest, "the worst professional game on record."

1914 Charlie Weber, a one-game pitcher with Washington in 1898 and a deft self-promoter with more nicknames than pitches, is mysteriously shot to death in Beaumont, TX.

1921 Commissioner Landis capriciously bars Reds pitcher Ray Fisher for contract jumping after Fisher announces he is leaving the game to accept a job as head baseball coach at the University of Michigan.

1939 Cleveland sends its career leader in several major batting departments, Earl Averill, to Detroit for pitcher Harry Eisenstat and cash.

1947 The Phils send Cincinnati catcher Hugh Poland and pitcher Ken Raffensberger, who will win the most games of any Reds hurler over the next decade (89), for catcher Al Lakeman, who will hit .159 in parts of two seasons in Philadelphia. Elsewhere, the Red Sox ship first baseman Rudy York to the White Sox for first baseman Jake Jones.

1950 The Indians baffle Tribe fans when they return two-time batting champ Mickey Vernon to Washington for pitcher Dick Weik, who wins only one more ML game and departs as the lone pitcher in a minimum of 200 career innings to surrender more than a walk per inning (237 in 213²/₃ innings).

1953 At Cleveland Municipal Stadium, 74,708 fans agonize as the Yankees sweep a Sunday DBH from the second-place Indians to extend their winning streak to 18 games and take a prohibitive 10½ game lead in the AL even though the season is scarcely two months old.

1956 Frank "Trader" Lane stuns Mound City when he deals long-time favorite second baseman Red Schoendienst, plus catcher Bill Sarni, outfielder Jackie Brandt, infielder Bobby Stephenson, and pitcher Dick Littlefield to the Giants for shortstop Alvin Dark, outfielder Whitey Lockman, catcher Ray Katt, and pitcher Don Liddle.

1965 The Reds' Jim Maloney twirls 10 no-hit innings against the Mets and finishes with 18 strikeouts but loses the game 1–0 by yielding a leadoff homer to Johnny Lewis in the 11th frame.

1978 Cincinnati's Pete Rose slaps two hits against the Cubs to begin his NL record-tying single-season 44-game hitting streak.

1995 Giants infielder Mike Benjamin, the owner of a .229 career BA, defies credibility when he strokes six hits to give him a record-setting total of 14 safeties in a three-game span.

1996 Orioles shortstop Cal Ripken Jr. surpasses Hiroshima Carp third baseman Sachio Kinugasa's world professional record by playing in his 2,216th consecutive game.

2002 For the first time since 1972, a DH is not employed in a full slate of ML games when all of the 15 games that date (14 interleague and one NL contest) are played in NL parks.

2005 The Mariners' Ichiro Suzuki is the first player since the Phillies' Chuck Klein to log his first 1,000 career hits in fewer than 700 games (696), 13 more than it took the Phils slugger.

15

1889 Only six Louisville players show up for a game at Baltimore after the rest of the team strikes in protest of owner Mordecai David-son's miserly supervision, forcing the ragtag Colonels to pull three local players out of the stands to field a nine. They go on to absorb their 20th straight defeat.

1893 Brooklyn outfielder Darby O'Brien dies at the age of 29 of con-sumption at his home in Peoria, IL.

1902   In a Class D Texas League game, short outfield fences at a small park in Ennis rented to skirt local Sunday blue laws help Corsicana catcher Nig Clarke slug an OB single-game record eight home runs in a 51–3 win over the Texarkana Casketmakers.

1925   Called on to mop up in a game that seems hopelessly lost, the A's Tom Glass instead earns his lone ML victory when the Mackmen rally for 13 runs in the bottom of the 8th to beat Cleveland, 17–15.

1928   A's outfielder Ty Cobb, now 41 years old, extends his own ML record when he steals home for the 54th and final time in his career during a 12–5 win over Cleveland.

1938   Reds lefty Johnny Vander Meer is the only ML hurler to date to spin no-hitters in two consecutive games when he follows a 3–0 no-no against Boston on June 11 with a 6–0 gem against Brooklyn in the first night game at Ebbets Field.

1948   Detroit, the last AL team to install lights, tops the A's at Briggs Stadium in the first night game in the Motor City.

1949   Phils first baseman Eddie Waitkus provides the inspiration for Bernard Malamud's *The Natural* when 19-year-old Ruth Steinhagen shoots and seriously wounds him after he responds to her message inviting him to her room at Chicago's Edgewater Beach Hotel. Elsewhere, the Cubs trade Harry Walker and Peanuts Lowrey to the Reds for Hank Sauer and Frank Baumholtz.

1951   The Dodgers seemingly lock up the NL pennant when they garner outfielder Andy Pafko (.292 career BA to that point), lefty Johnny Schmitz, catcher Rube Walker, and infielder Wayne Terwilliger from the Cubs for outfielder Gene Hermanski, infielder Eddie Miksis, lefty Joe Hatten, and catcher Bruce Edwards, but Pafko instead pursues the frequent route taken by stars with a tailender who are traded to a contender when he bats just .249 in the remaining months of the season.

1952   Down 11–0 in the 5th inning, the Cardinals stage one of the most colossal comebacks in ML history when they rally to beat the Giants, 14–12.

1953   Former Yankee Duane Pillette ends both the Bombers' winning streak at 18, one short of their then AL record, and the Browns' team-record losing streak of 14 with a tidy 3–1 win at Yankee Stadium. Meanwhile, Cleveland and Detroit complete an eight-player swap that sends infielder Ray Boone and pitchers Steve Gromek, Al Aber, and Dick Weik to Detroit for pitchers Art Houtteman and Bill Wight, second baseman Owen Friend, and catcher Joe Ginsberg.

1957 The Yankees bundle Billy Martin, outfielder Bob Martyn, and shortstop Woodie Held off to KC for pitcher Ryne Duren, second baseman Milt Graff, and outfielders Harry Simpson and Jim Pisoni.

1958 The Yankees send pitcher Bob Grim and outfielder Suitcase Simpson to the A's for pitchers Virgil Trucks and Duke Maas, while the A's are also busy shipping first baseman Vic Power and shortstop Woodie Held to Cleveland for outfielder Roger Maris, first baseman Preston Ward, and pitcher Dick Tomanek.

1964 The Cards scam the Cubs out of future Hall of Famer Lou Brock and two others for pitchers Ernie Broglio and Bobby Shantz, plus outfielder Doug Clemens.

1965 The Tigers' Denny McLain, working in relief, fans the first seven Red Sox batters he faces, tying a then ML mark, and goes on to total 14 Ks in just 6²/₃ innings.

1973 When Tommie Aaron, Hank's brother, is named pilot of Savannah in the Southern League, he breaks the managerial color line in the Deep South two years *before* MLB hires its first African American skipper.

1976 The Astrodome experiences a surreal rain out when a storm causes flooding that prevents fans, umps, and stadium workers from getting to the domed field. Elsewhere, A's owner Charlie Finley sells three key members of his world champion dynasty teams (Rollie Fingers and Joe Rudi to the Red Sox for $1,000,000 apiece and Vida Blue to the Yanks for $1,500,000), but three days later, Commissioner Kuhn voids Finley's fire sale, contending it is not in the best interests of the game.

1977 In a disastrous public relations move, the Mets deal their first star and future Hall of Famer Tom Seaver to the Reds for Pat Zachry, Steve Henderson, Doug Flynn, and Dan Norman.

1983 The Mets make a key deal for their future 1986 championship season by jettisoning pitchers Neil Allen and Rick Ownbey to the Cardinals for All-Star first baseman Keith Hernandez.

2007 When the Mets' Julio Franco bats against the Yankees' Roger Clemens, their combined age of 93 years and 246 days makes for the oldest batter-pitcher matchup in the majors since the White Sox' Nick Altrock faced the A's Rube Walberg on October 1, 1933.

16

1893 Baltimore trades outfielder/second baseman Piggy Ward and $1,500 to Cincinnati for pitcher Tony Mullane.

1904 The Boston Americans make an ill-advised swap, sending out-fielder Patsy Dougherty to the New York Highlanders for injury-prone infielder Bob Unglaub.

1933 Brooklyn sends former NL batting champ Lefty O'Doul and Watty Clark, a 20-game winner in 1932, to the Giants for first base-man Sam Leslie, whose only distinction is the then ML record for the most pinch hits in a season, with 22 in 1932.

1938 Unable to land a ML manager's job, Babe Ruth reluctantly joins the Dodgers as a coach.

1940 A core of Cleveland players unsuccessfully petitions owner Alva Bradley to remove manager Ossie Vitt, inviting sportswriters else-where in the AL to begin calling the team the "Cry Babies."

1951 A bolt of lightning kills Andy Strong instantly while he is sta-tioned in the outfield for Crowley in an Evangeline League game at Alexandria, LA.

1978 After several near misses, the Reds' Tom Seaver finally pitches his first no-hitter, topping St. Louis, 4–0.

1996 Venerated announcer Mel Allen, who began his work behind a ML mike in 1939 for the Yanks and Giants and was the annual voice in 1950s World Series games, dies at the age of 83.

2001 Mariners first baseman John Olerud hits for the cycle after pre-viously doing the same with the 1997 Mets to join Bob Watson as the only players to "cycle" in both the AL and NL.

17

1880 Just five days after NL lefty Lee Richmond's first-of-its-kind ML gem against Cleveland, Providence's John M. Ward throws a per-fect game against Buffalo, winning 5–0.

1882 Dick Higham umpires his last NL game in Detroit's 8–4 win at Troy. Within the week, the NL will make Higham the only ML umpire ever expelled for crooked officiating, though never formally accusing him of any specific incident of wrongdoing.

1899 In a Western League game at Indianapolis, St. Paul's Chauncey Fisher is thumbed out at second base with two out in the bottom of the 9th when he pauses between first and second to congratulate Eddie Burke, who has just singled to plate the apparent game-winning run, while Indianapolis outfielder George Hogriever retrieves the ball and tags second base. But umpire Al Manassau's groundbreaking force-out call, which almost identically foreshadows the circumstances in the 1908 Merkle game, draws little comment at the time and remains unrecognized by historians for more than a century.

1915 Cubs hurler Zip Zabel replaces Bert Humphries with two out in the 1st inning after Humphries is injured and pitches a record 18⅓ innings in relief to top Brooklyn's Jeff Pfeffer, 4–3 in 19 innings.

1917 The National Commission rules in favor of the Philadelphia A's in a dispute with the Boston Braves over the rights to minor league pitcher Scott Perry, who emerges as a 20-game winner in war-shortened 1918, despite the A's fourth consecutive last-place finish.

1931 Tommy Connolly, an AL umpire since the league's inception in 1901, retires to accept a position as supervisor of junior loop arbiters.

1935 Commissioner Landis allows Albany to sign Alabama Pitts but only to play in official IL games to prevent him from becoming a "carnivallike" gate attraction in exhibition contests.

1943 Boston player-manager Joe Cronin is the first to clout pinch homers in both ends of a DBH when he blasts three-run shots in each game of a twin-bill win over the Browns.

1950 Former White Sox hurler Monty Stratton, whose indomitable refusal to quit pitching since losing a leg in a hunting accident in the fall of 1938 inspired the Hollywood film *The Stratton Story*, returns to pro ball with Greenville of the Big State League after a three-year absence and defeats Austin 11–6 in his latest comeback bid with an artificial limb.

1970 When the Giants' Willie Mays and the Cubs' Ernie Banks homer at Candlestick Park, they become the first members of the 500-tater club to connect in the same game.

1987 Former Royals manager Dick Howser, who led KC to its lone world championship to date in 1985, dies from brain cancer at the age of 51.

18

1877 Unable to meet its payroll, Cincinnati disbands on the eve of a scheduled Eastern trip, but some two weeks later, on July 3, the club is allowed to resume action after reorganizing, the only time in ML history a team is reinstated in the same season after quitting.

1886   The *Cincinnati Enquirer* publishes a letter it claims proves that Reds pitcher Tony Mullane is guilty of throwing games, and though Mullane is eventually exonerated of the charge and goes on to win 30 games for the fourth time in the season, the cloud over him is never entirely lifted.

1940   Just six days after the Cards trade him to Brooklyn, Joe Medwick is beaned by Cards hurler Bob Bowman at Ebbets Field and is never again a major force in the game.

1953   Red Sox rookie gardener Gene Stephens is the first player in AL history to get three hits in an inning when Boston scores 17 runs in the 7th frame in bombing Detroit, 23–3.

1959   The Continental League, a proposed rival ML, rocks baseball speculators when it divulges that franchises in its circuit will sell for $100,000,000 each.

1961   Eddie Gaedel, the 3'7" midget who pinch hit for Bill Veeck's St. Louis Browns in 1951, dies from a heart attack in Chicago, IL, at the age of 36.

1975   The Red Sox' Fred Lynn perpetrates an unprecedented rookie offensive performance by homering three times and collecting 10 RBI against the Tigers.

1977   On national television, after Yankees manager Billy Martin removes Reggie Jackson for loafing in the outfield, the two confront each other in the dugout with fists clenched and are separated by coach Elston Howard.

19

1846   The first recorded baseball game played under the rules sanctioned by Alexander Cartwright takes place in Hoboken, NJ, with the New York Club defeating Cartwright's Knickerbocker Club, 23–1.

1897   After beginning the campaign by hitting safely in 44 straight games to set a universally recognized new ML single-season record, Baltimore's Willie Keeler has his streak stopped by lefty Frank Killen of Pittsburgh. Since Keeler also got a hit in his final game the previous year, his overall streak is actually 45 games, still the second longest overall in ML history.

1916   Former NL infielder John Dodge of Mobile in the Southern Association dies after being beaned by Nashville's Tom "Shotgun" Rogers, who pitches a perfect game in the SA three weeks later.

1927 The Phils' Jack Scott is the last MLer to date to pitch two complete games in one day when he splits a DBH with Cincinnati.

1963 The Tigers' Gates Brown is the first African American in the AL to homer in his initial ML AB.

1972 The U.S. Supreme Court rules against Curt Flood's lawsuit challenging MLB's reserve clause.

1974 In just his second full ML season, Royals starter Steve Busby pitches his second career no-hitter, a 2–0 win against the Brewers.

1977 Cleveland's Frank Robinson, the first African American ML manager, is replaced by Jeff Torborg.

20

1879 Buffalo's rookie first sacker, Oscar Walker, is the first batter to whiff five times in a ML game.

1892 In a 9–3 loss to Boston, Washington shortstop Danny Richardson handles a record 19 chances (since tied), plus one error in a 9-inning game.

1948 Cleveland draws a then record crowd for a regular-season game when 82,781 fans pack Municipal Stadium for a Sunday DBH with the Philadelphia A's.

1965 Jay Dahl, the pitcher in Houston's all-rookie lineup on September 27, 1963, is the youngest former big leaguer to date to die when he is killed in a car crash at the age of 19.

2001 Giants outfielder Barry Bonds poles his 38th homer of the season, establishing a new ML mark for taters before the All-Star Game. Although Bonds has 17 games left to extend the record, he adds just one more before the break.

21

1878 Bill White occupies first base as a one-day fill-in for Providence and more than a century later becomes the first documented MLer with African American heritage when historian Peter Morris confirms that he was a mulatto.

1879 Catcher Alexander Taylor of the semipro Ballston Stars is killed after being struck in the back of the head by a batter's swing while playing up too close to the plate.

1887 In what some consider the greatest single-game strikeout feat in ML history, Louisville lefty Toad Ramsey fans 17 Cleveland hitters under the ephemeral four-strike rule, in effect only this season.

1890 When Chicago PL manager Charlie Comiskey opts to have his team bat first even though it is the home club and Windy City pitcher Silver King is subsequently defeated by Brooklyn 1–0, King becomes the only pitcher ever to lose a regulation-length complete-game no-hitter at home that is not considered a no-hitter by MLB because he failed to pitch 9 innings.

1952 Harrisburg of the Interstate League signs 132-pound stenographer Eleanor Engle as its new shortstop, and minor league chieftain George Trautman swiftly reacts by officially banning all female players from OB.

1957 Fresh out of high school, 18-year-old Von McDaniel, the younger brother of fellow Cardinals pitcher Lindy McDaniel, tosses a two-hit 2–0 shutout win over the Dodgers in his first ML start.

1964 On Father's Day, Jim Bunning flings a perfect game against the Mets, and his batterymate, Gus Triandos, joins Ed McFarland as the only two receivers to that point to catch no-hitters in both the NL and AL. Triandos previously called the signals for Baltimore's Hoyt Wilhelm's gem against the Yanks in 1958.

1968 When they top the Reds 3–2, the Cubs end their scoreless drought at 48 innings after tying the all-time ML mark set by the 1906 Philadelphia A's.

1970 Wearing number 7, Tigers shortstop Cesar Gutierrez lives up to his uniform number as he goes 7-for-7 in a 12-inning, 9–8 victory against the Tribe. Gutierrez later retires with just 128 career hits.

1986 After Tampa Bay made Bo Jackson the number one pick in the NFL draft, the Heisman Trophy winner shocks the sports world by signing a baseball contract with KC instead.

22

1934 Bill Terry and Joe Cronin, managers of the two 1933 pennant winners, launch a still-existing tradition when they are named opposing skippers for the 1934 All-Star Game.

1945 Bill Veeck, son of former Cubs president William Veeck, heads a group that buys the Indians.

1947 Ewell Blackwell just misses duplicating Reds teammate Johnny Vander Meer's feat of nine years earlier when Dodgers second baseman Eddie Stanky deprives him of a second consecutive no-hitter by singling with one out in the 9th of the Reds' 4–0 win.

1984 After having been involved with the Washington/Minnesota franchise for 62 years, Calvin Griffith and his sister Thelma Haynes, the widow of former ML pitcher Joe Haynes, sign a letter of intent to sell their majority ownership of the Twins to Minneapolis banker Carl Pohlad for $32,000,000 at a home-plate ceremony in the Metrodome.

1993 The White Sox' Carlton Fisk breaks Bob Boone's ML record for career games caught when he calls signals for the 2,226th and last time in his 24-year career.

2001 As part of a four-player swap, the Braves unload John Rocker on the Indians more than a year after the controversial *Sports Illustrated* piece appeared in which the reliever blasted immigrants, gays, and other groups, plus New Yorkers as a whole.

2002 Commissioner Selig postpones the scheduled game between the Cardinals and Cubs after 33-year-old Cards starter Darryl Kile is discovered dead in his Chicago hotel room.

23

1889 Behind the "butterfly" slants of southpaw Toad Ramsey, Louisville beats St. Louis 7–3 to end a post-1876 ML record string of 26 straight losses.

1917 Despite entering the game in relief after Red Sox starter Babe Ruth is booted for punching umpire Brick Owens while arguing a ball four call to Washington leadoff hitter Ray Morgan, Ernie Shore is credited with a perfect game (since rescinded by MLB) in his 4–0 win when he retires all 26 hitters he faces after Morgan is caught stealing.

1934 Bill Hallahan earns a 5–4 win over the Dodgers as per today's rules that is given to teammate Dizzy Dean, enabling Dean, the beneficiary of another such scorer's decision in 1934, to be the last NL hurler to date to post a 30-win season.

1938 Red Sox third baseman Pinky Higgins's record string (since tied) of 12 consecutive hits ends when he fans in his first AB in an 8–3 loss to the Tigers' Vern Kennedy.

1950 The Yankees and Tigers join in setting a then ML record when they belt 11 home runs in a 10–9 Detroit win. Elsewhere, two straight pennant losses by a one-game margin induce Joe McCarthy to resign as the Red Sox' pilot.

1959 The Braves introduce the first conveyance to deliver a relief pitcher from the bullpen to the mound when a Harley Davidson "Topper" motor scooter with a sidecar hauls Cards pitcher Hal Jeffcoat from deep in the centerfield pen to replace injured starter Alex Kellner in the 1st inning of Milwaukee's 9–5 win.

1971 In a singular performance, the Phillies' Rick Wise no-hits the Reds and pounds two homers, making him the only ML pitcher to perform both feats in the same game.

1973 Phillies hurler Ken Brett sets a record for moundsmen in a 7–2 win over Montreal by poling a homer in the fourth consecutive game that he pitches.

1988 The revolving door of Yankees managers continues as George Steinbrenner fires Billy Martin for the fifth time, replacing him with Lou Piniella, who previously supplanted Martin in 1986. Martin's goose was cooked two days earlier when Cecilo Guante surrendered a walk-off grand slam in the bottom of the 9th to Alan Trammell, the first batter he faced, giving Detroit an implausible uphill 7–6 win.

2003 Barry Bonds swipes a bag against the Dodgers, making him the first to reach 500 steals and 500 homers.

24

1894 Baltimore accrues another cornerstone for its emergent dynasty when the Orioles front office buys pitcher/second baseman Kid Gleason from St. Louis for the then modest sum of $2,000.

1946 A rickety bus operated by a tired driver slips off a winding mountain road in Washington, killing nine members of the Spokane team in the Western IL, including star shortstop George Risk. But Jack Lohrke, another infielder on the club, is spared when he gets off the bus at its last stop before the accident, evoking the nickname by which he is known for the rest of his baseball days: "Lucky."

1962 Jack Reed hits his only career homer but makes it count in a big way as it gives the Yankees a 22-inning 9–7 win against the Tigers in the longest game ever played in Bombers history.

1964 The Angels sign University of Wisconsin standout Rick Reichardt to the highest signing bonus to date, worth $200,000.

1972   In the New York-Pennsylvania League, Bernice Gera umpires the first game of a DBH between Auburn and Geneva and even tosses Auburn's skipper Nolan Campbell but quits before the second contest, exhausted by the incessant challenges to her authority.

1996   After being released just two days earlier, former Yankees reliever Steve Howe is arrested at Kennedy International Airport for toting a loaded gun in his carry-on.

1997   Seattle's Randy Johnson fans 19 A's to set an AL record, later broken by Johnson himself in the NL, for whiffs in a game by a lefty.

2007   The Yanks' Roger Clemens makes his first regular-season relief appearance in 22 years and 341 days, a new ML record for the longest time between regular-season relief appearances.

25

1885   In an AA contest at Baltimore, Philadelphia A's utility man George Strief bangs a ML single-game record four triples. Strief is released by the A's shortly afterward, having hit only five triples all season and 14 in his five-year career.

1891   In a 13–5 win over Baltimore, Tom Brown and Bill Joyce of the Boston Reds are the first pair of teammates to lead off a game with back-to-back home runs.

1893   In a transaction believed to be the first involving a minor league player under the control of a ML team, Chicago trades holdout pitcher Ad Gumbert to Louisville for pitcher Bert Abbey, who is at the time on loan from Louisville to Macon of the Southern League.

1903   Pitching in front of a Boston home crowd, Wiley Piatt works both ends of a DBH against the Cardinals and allows only one earned run on the day but loses both contests 1–0 and 5–3 to become the last pitcher in ML history to lose two complete games in one day.

1906   Herbert Whitney, a catcher with the Burlington Pathfinders of the Iowa State League, dies from a skull fracture after being beaned by Waterloo pitcher Fred Evans.

1924   Pittsburgh hurler Emil Yde enters a game with the Cubs in the top of the 4th with the Pirates trailing 6–0 and ties the contest in the 9th with a bases-clearing double before winning it in the 14th with a two-run triple.

1937 Augie Galan of the Cubs is the first switch-hitter to homer from both sides of the plate in a NL contest when he goes yard against Brooklyn's Freddie Fitzsimmons and Ralph Birkofer.

1968 Giants prospect Bobby Bonds hits a grand slam in his first ML game (and third AB) off the Dodgers' John Purdin.

1976 The Rangers' Toby Harrah can put his hands in his pockets as he becomes the only shortstop in ML history to go through an entire DBH without a single fielding chance.

1998 Cubs clubber Sammy Sosa homers for the 19th time, breaking a record he shared with Rudy York for taters in a month, and extends the mark to 20 before June is out.

1999 The Orioles' Jesse Orosco makes his 1,051st relief appearance, breaking Kent Tekulve's ML record.

26

1879 Boston catcher Pop Snyder deliberately drops a third strike to engineer a triple play that helps saddle Providence with a 3–2 loss, but a rule eliminating the opportunity for a catcher to perpetrate such a play is not adopted until 1887.

1886 A clandestine "gentlemen's agreement" the previous year between the NL and AA to ban African American players is proven not as yet to extend to the minor leagues when black southpaw George Stovey dons a uniform with Jersey City of the Eastern League.

1893 Pittsburgh gets shortstop Jack Glasscock from St. Louis for shortstop Frank Shugart and $500.

1916 In a game against the White Sox, Cleveland players wear numbers on their sleeves that correspond with numbers in scorecards, the first time in the 20th century a team appears in numbered uniforms, but the experiment fails in part because players are skittish about being numbered like convicts.

1926 The Cards claim 39-year-old Pete Alexander on waivers from the Cubs in what will swiftly prove to be one of the greatest waiver acquisitions ever.

1942 Gene Stack (b. Stachiwiack), an army corporal, is the first player "from the rolls of a major league club" to die in World War II. Stack, who had been recalled by the White Sox from Lubbock of the West Texas-New Mexico League in the fall of 1940, suffers a heart attack after putting a coin in a jukebox at a restaurant where his Fort Custer team has stopped to eat en route back to the base following a 5–2 loss to Michigan City, IN, in a game he pitched.

1947 KC pitcher Carl DeRose, out for the past month with arm woes, returns to action by tossing the first perfect game in AA history in beating Minneapolis, 5–0. His arm throbbing the entire game, De-Rose is able to make only two more hill appearances for the season.

1960 Attempting to expedite the election process, the HOF establishes new rules permitting the Special Veterans Committee to vote annually, rather than every other year, and to enshrine up to two new members per year if so desired.

1962 Red Sox moundsman Earl Wilson is the first African American to fire a no-hitter in the AL and adds icing to the occasion by blasting a homer in downing the Angels, 2–0.

1968 MLB's Executive Council recommends that both leagues be split into two six-team divisions by the 1969 season, a decision that is approved July 10.

27

1876 Philadelphia's Davy Force is the first to make six hits in a NL game when he goes 6-for-6 in a 14–13 win over Chicago's Al Spalding. Force goes on to experience entire months in which he does not make six hits and finishes in 1886 with a .211 career BA over his 11-year span in the NL.

1884 Diminutive Chicago fireballer Larry Corcoran is the first pitcher in ML history to log three no-hitters when he beats Providence, 6–0. Within weeks, Corcoran, destined to toil 516⅔ innings in 1884, engages in a press debate with Chicago president Al Spalding as to whether his arm is being ruined by overwork or he is just a "namby-pamby."

1911 Taking advantage of a new rule in the AL requiring a pitcher to be ready to pitch as soon as the hitter leading off an inning is ready to bat, Philadelphia A's first sacker Stuffy McInnis jumps into the batter's box while the Red Sox are still taking the field, rifles Red Sox hurler Ed Karger's first warm-up toss over second base into the empty outfield, and then tallies an IPHR while his ball rolls unmolested.

1930 A's pitcher Jack Quinn, at the age of 46, is the oldest ML player to date to homer when he pulls the trigger against Chad Kimsey in his 8–3 win over the Browns.

1934   En route to the last 30-win season by a NL hurler, Dizzy Dean is credited with his second specious win of the month when he leaves a tie game in favor of Jim Mooney in the top of the 9th, and the Cards push across a run in the bottom half to beat the Giants, 8–7.

1951   Once-promising lefty Boyd Tepler, who ruined his elbow in 1944 while in the Cubs farm system, sues baseball and the Cubs for $450,000, claiming that the Cubs not only mishandled his injury but refused to release him so that he could mount a comeback elsewhere. Tepler later writes a chilling book about his days in pro ball called *In Cub Chains*.

1955   Budding Red Sox star Harry Agganis dies in a Hub hospital of pneumonia.

1964   Indians third sacker Max Alvis is stricken with spinal meningitis but returns the following year to hit 21 homers and make the AL All-Star squad.

1973   David Clyde, the 18-year-old overall number 1 amateur draft pick, makes his ballyhooed big league debut for Texas, walking seven and fanning eight in a five-inning win against the Twins. Far from ready for the bigs—physically or psychologically—Clyde throws his last ML pitch when he is just 24 years old.

1986   Robby Thompson of the Giants sets a ML record when he is caught stealing four times in a 12-inning victory against the Reds.

1993   The Mets' Anthony Young garners an unenviable ML record in a 5–3 loss to the Cardinals when he sustains his 24th consecutive defeat, breaking the mark he formerly shared with Braves chucker Cliff Curtis (1910–1911).

2002   The Expos deal prospects Grady Sizemore, Brandon Phillips, Cliff Lee, and veteran Lee Stevens to the Tribe for Bartolo Colón and Tim Drew. Already 10–4 with the Cleveland, Colón also goes 10–4 with the Expos to become the first pitcher since Hank Borowy in 1945 to win 10 games or more in both leagues in the same season.

2003   In interleague action, the Red Sox score a ML record 10 runs before making an out in the 1st inning against Florida and also tie the AL mark for the most runs scored in the 1st frame with 14.

2007   Phillies clubber Ryan Howard smacks his 100th career homer, making him the fastest player in big league history to reach that plateau, achieving it in just his 325th game.

28

1871 In the most loosely played game in the National Association's inaugural season, Philadelphia tops Troy 49–33 as the two teams set a record that is tied but never beaten when each scores in all 9 innings.

1896 During St. Louis's 12–1 loss to Cincinnati at Sportsman's Park, Robert Usher, an employee of Browns owner Chris Von der Ahe, is killed when a rowboat he is manning is struck by a boat manned by his brother-in-law rushing headlong down the "Shoot-the-Chutes" ride that Von der Ahe operates while games are in progress.

1907 Washington mercilessly victimizes New York catcher Branch Rickey for a post–1897 record 13 stolen bases in a 16–5 win over the Highlanders.

1939 In their double-dip trouncing of the A's, the Yankees hammer a twin-bill record 13 home runs, with Joe DiMaggio, Joe Gordon, and Babe Dahlgren each hitting three.

1949 After missing the first 65 games of the season while recovering from heel surgery, Joe DiMaggio returns to the Yankees lineup and hits the first of the four home runs he will belt in New York's sweep of a crucial three-game series with the Red Sox at Fenway Park.

1970 The Pirates sweep a DBH from the Cubs in the last games played at Forbes Field.

1987 The Red Sox' Don Baylor breaks the post-1900 career hit-by-pitch mark he shared with Ron Hunt when he is plunked for the 244th time.

1999 Researchers outside baseball's inner circle convince the commissioner's office to credit the Cubs' Hack Wilson with an extra RBI in 1930, upping his season record total to 191, while Babe Ruth is assigned six added walks, raising his then career record mark to 2,062.

2004 The Phillies' David Bell hits for the cycle, joining grandpa Gus Bell as the only grandson-grandfather combo to perform this feat.

2007 Houston's Craig Biggio is the first player to reach 3,000 hits on the strength of a five-hit game.

29

1885 Chicago's Abner Dalrymple is the first MLer to lead off two consecutive games with a home run when he goes deep off Jim Whitney in a 14–10 win over Boston.

1897 Chicago scores in every inning and demolishes Louisville 36–7 to set the still-existing NL and AL record for the most runs scored in a game.

1951 Twin Falls catcher Dick Conway, the Pioneer League home-run leader at the time, is killed at the age of 19 when he is hit over the heart during pregame infield practice by player-manager Don Trower, who throws a ball to him when he is not looking.

1957 After overzealous Redlegs fans respond to a newspaper campaign by stuffing the ballot box and electing eight Redlegs as All-Star Game starters, NL president Warren Giles refuses to allow all eight to start and initiates a proposal that takes voting privileges away from the fans until 1970.

1969 During "Billy Williams Day" at Wrigley Field, the Cubs outfielder breaks Stan Musial's NL record by playing in his 896th consecutive game.

1972 In the first even-up deal involving former MVPs, the A's zip pitcher Denny McLain to the Braves for Orlando Cepeda.

1984 The Reds' Pete Rose plays in his 3,309th ML game, surpassing Carl Yastrzemski's all-time record.

1989 Padres GM Jack McKeon shows no favoritism when he deals his son-in-law, pitcher Greg Booker, to the Twins.

1990 For only the second time in ML history, two 9-inning complete game no-hitters are tossed on the same day when the A's Dave Stewart and the Dodgers' Fernando Valenzuela baffle the Blue Jays and Cards, respectively.

2005 The pitchers' favorite target, Houston's Craig Biggio, breaks Don Baylor's post–1900 record of 267 for being hit by a pitch when he is plunked by Rockies righty Byung-Hyun Kim and retires two years later just two shy of Hughie Jennings's all-time mark of 287.

30

1854 In the first recorded extra-inning game, the Gothams beat the Knickerbockers 21–16, as 16 innings are needed before the Gothams can tally the 21 runs still necessary to win under the rules.

1860 The Excelsiors of Brooklyn embark on the first tour by a baseball club, an ambitious 10-day jaunt that will whirl them over some 1,000 miles of train tracks to play other teams in the state of New York.

1892   Cincinnati's Tony Mullane and Chicago's Ad Gumbert lock horns in the longest ML game to date when they battle to a 7–7 tie in 20 innings.

1894   In a 13–6 loss to Philadelphia's Gus Weyhing, Louisville outfielder Fred Clarke is the first MLer to debut with a five-hit game and finishes the day with a perfect 1.000 BA, but the future Hall of Famer hits only .262 the remainder of this season, far below the league average of .309.

1905   Cleveland's Nap Lajoie is sidelined for the rest of the season by blood poisoning after dye from his stocking leaks into a spike wound on his leg. Elsewhere, former Cleveland hurler Pete Dowling, the AL's leading loser in 1901 with 25, is decapitated when a train hits him after he sets out on a walk from Hot Lake to LeGrande, OR.

1934   Lou Gehrig smokes three triples in the Yankees' first five turns at bat in Griffith Stadium, but his post–1900 record-tying performance is erased when the game is rained out before Washington, trailing 4–1, can bat in the bottom of the 5th.

1938   In the final ML game played at the ancient Baker Bowl, the Phils lose 14–1 to the Giants.

1948   The Braves sign 18-year-old southpaw Johnny Antonelli for $75,000, a then record amount given to a "bonus baby."

1959   In the 4th inning of the Cardinals' 4–1 win at Wrigley Field, a gaffe by home-plate umpire Vic Delmore creates an arbiter's nightmare—two balls in play—and results in a frenzied 10-minute debate among the four umpires working the game to resolve the blunder, followed by Delmore's dismissal by the NL for incompetence.

1978   Larry Doby is the second African American ML manager, replacing the White Sox' Bob Lemon.

1994   Giants outfielder Darren Lewis commits his first miscue in the bigs after a ML record 392 straight errorless games in the pasture.

1997   For the first time since the inception of the DH, a AL pitcher homers in a regular-season game when the Rangers' Bobby Witt connects off the Dodgers' Ismael Valdes in interleague play for a 3–2 victory. Elsewhere, both Canadian ML clubs oppose each other for the first time, with the Expos edging the Blue Jays, 2–1.

July

1

1859   Amherst and Williams play the first intercollegiate game in history at Pittsfield, MA, with Amherst winning, 73–32.

1905   The White Sox' Frank Owen is the first AL hurler to pitch complete-game wins in both ends of a DBH when he corrals the Browns, 3–2 and 2–0.

1916   At the age of 42 and four months, Honus Wagner legs out a gapper off Cincinnati's Elmer Knetzer to become the oldest player to date to hit an IPHR.

1945   Hank Greenberg, the first superstar to leave the game for World War II military duty, is also the first to return to it, as he homers in his first game back off Charlie Gassaway in the Tigers' 9–5 win over the A's.

1951   Bob Feller ties Cy Young and Larry Corcoran for the most career no-hitters when he tosses his third no-no, topping Detroit's Bob Cain, 2–1.

1954   Cards rookie Joe Cunningham is the first since 1889 to rip three home runs in his first two ML games when he goes deep twice in St. Louis's 9–2 win over the Braves.

1957   The only all-Z battery in ML history makes its first appearance when Baltimore rookie Frank Zupo catches reliever George Zuverink in the Orioles' 3–2 loss to the Yankees.

1990   In Chicago, Yankees righty Andy Hawkins throws a no-hitter but loses 4–0 when, with two away in the bottom of the 8th, Mike Blowers boots Sammy Sosa's routine grounder, Hawkins walks two to jam the bases, and outfielders Jim Leyritz and Jesse Barfield drop consecutive flies to allow all four runs to score. Adding insult to injury, Hawkins's no-hitter doesn't officially count because he went only eight innings since the White Sox, the home team, did not have to bat in the 9th.

2005 Rangers pitcher Kenny Rogers is hit with one of the heaviest penalties levied for on-field behavior: a 20-game suspension and a $50,000 fine for shoving two cameramen and sending one to the hospital, in addition to throwing and kicking a camera.

2

1891 In a streak that began on September 27, 1890, third baseman Bill Joyce of the Boston Reds sets a ML record that lasts until 1949, when he reaches base in his 69th straight game before breaking an ankle sliding in a 12–4 win over Washington. Joyce remains out of action until October 3, when he plays part of a game against Washington at first base and ends his skein by going 0-for-2 against rookie Kid Carsey.

1903 Abandoning his Washington AL team in Detroit, outfielder Ed Delahanty boards an eastbound train but is ejected from it for rowdy behavior near Niagara Falls and falls to his death when he tries to cross the railroad bridge over the Niagara River.

1933 The Giants' Carl Hubbell ties a ML record for the longest shutout when he needs 18 innings to top the Cardinals, 1–0.

1945 Former ML catcher and NFL end Frank Grube dies of a shotgun wound he sustained the previous day when he confronted six intruders in his New York City apartment building.

1951 His restaurant business failing in addition to having a recent judgment brought against him for fathering an illegitimate child, former Dodgers relief ace Hugh Casey makes a phone call to his wife. In the midst of the call, he tells her, "I feel just like I was walking out to the pitcher's box—I was never any more calm than I am right now," and then kills himself with a blast from a 16-gauge shotgun.

1956 NBC forks over $16,250,000 to MLB for the television and radio rights to both the upcoming All-Star Game and the World Series, with 60% of the money designated for the players' pension fund.

1963 The Giants' Juan Marichal and the Braves' Warren Spahn duel for 15 scoreless innings before Willie Mays slams a game-ending homer off Spahn in the 16th for a 1–0 victory.

133

1970   For the third time in a month, the Yankees' Horace Clarke singles in the 9th to spoil a no-hitter as the Bombers lose 5–0 to Detroit's Joe Niekro. Clarke earlier spoiled bids by KC's Jim Rooker (June 4) and Boston's Sonny Siebert (June 19).

1993   After three rain delays, the latest-running game in ML history ends at 4:40 AM when reliever Mitch Williams singles home the winning run in the 10th, giving the Phillies a 6–5 triumph over the Padres in the second game of a twin bill.

1995   Dodgers moundsman Hideo Nomo is the first Japanese player chosen for a ML All-Star Game.

2007   Roger Clemens beats the Twins for his 350th career win, making him the first ML pitcher to reach that lofty plateau since the Braves Warren Spahn in 1963.

3

1870   The first organized baseball club in history, the New York Knickerbockers, withdraws from the National Association of Baseball Players to protest the evils the Knickerbockers believe professional players are wreaking on the game.

1890   Jack Fanning, a rookie pitcher with Indianapolis NL in 1889, goes missing, driving his wife to advertise prayerfully in *TSN* for information about his whereabouts. Fanning later turns up on the Pacific Coast, where he again becomes a media darling upon having a falling out with the wife of ML outfielder Sam Dungan after wooing her away with a diamond ring that mysteriously disappears.

1925   Dodgers second baseman Milt Stock sets a modern NL record when he collects four hits in his fourth consecutive game, helping teammate Tiny Osborne to beat the Giants, 6–3.

1958   The newly transplanted Los Angeles Dodgers reach 1,000,000 in attendance in just 35 home dates as they split a DBH with the Cardinals.

1966   The Braves' Tony Cloninger is the first pitcher to rap two grand slams in a game in addition to setting another hurlers' offensive mark with nine RBI in a 17–3 blasting of the Giants at Candlestick Park.

1973   Brothers Gaylord and Jim Perry oppose each other for the only time in their long careers as Gaylord and the Indians lose to the Tigers, 5–4, with Jim getting a no decision.

1994   In a ceremony many baseball observers consider long overdue, the Indians retire Larry Doby's uniform number 14, 47 years after he broke the junior circuit's color line.

4

1873   Leading Elizabeth 11–3 after the New Jersey team's last turn at bat in the 9th inning, as per the rule at the time, Boston is required to bat in the bottom of the frame and scores 21 runs for a 32–3 victory.

1908   Giants southpaw Hooks Wiltse is the first hurler in ML history to lose his bid for a perfect game with two out in the 9th inning when he nicks opposing pitcher George McQuillan of the Phils on a 1–2 count after tossing what appears to be a third strike on the previous pitch in the estimation of everyone near home plate, except umpire Cy Rigler. Wiltse then musters himself and hurls a 10-inning no-hit win.

1923   Tigers catcher Larry Woodall is ejected in the 10th inning by umpire Pants Rowland, forcing manager Ty Cobb to summon 41-year-old coach Fred Carisch to go behind the plate in the bottom of the frame when Detroit has no more available backstops. Cleveland manager Tris Speaker protests the game since Carisch is not on the Detroit roster of eligible players, but the issue is settled when pinch-hitter Glenn Myatt drills a three-run homer to give the Indians' Sherry Smith a 10–7 win.

1932   Buzz Arlett of Baltimore in the IL is the only player in OB history to assemble two four-homer games in the same season when he goes deep four times for the second time in four weeks in a 21–10 win over Reading in the first game of a holiday DBH.

1939   As 61,808 fans "roar tribute" to him at an Independence Day DBH with the Senators at Yankee Stadium, moist-eyed Lou Gehrig proclaims himself "the luckiest man on the face of the earth."

1945   Cleveland is the first team in ML history to play a nine-inning game without logging an assist as Steve Gromek parlays the Tribe's 27 unassisted putouts, including 15 by his outfielders, to top New York, 4–2.

1950   Minutes after arriving at his seat at the Polo Grounds to watch a holiday DBH between his Giants and the hated Dodgers, 56-year-old Barney Doyle is fatally shot by a bullet carelessly fired by a teenage boy from an apartment building rooftop nearly half a mile from the park.

1980 Reds gardener Cesar Geronimo is Houston flamethrower Nolan Ryan's 3,000th career strikeout six years after Bob Gibson made Geronimo his 3,000th victim.

1985 The Mets defeat the Braves 16–13 in a wild battle lasting more than six hours that finishes just before the clock strikes 4:00 AM. The game features a game-tying 18th-inning homer by weak-hitting pitcher Rick Camp, who is forced to bat for himself when the Braves run out of pinch hitters, and closes with fireworks that rudely jolt many of the park's few remaining spectators who are fast asleep.

1987 San Francisco and San Diego engineer a seven-player trade, involving Kevin Mitchell who goes on to win the 1989 NL MVP with the Giants, and Mark Davis, who cops the 1989 NL Cy Young for the Padres.

5

1886 After starting the season 16–0, Chicago's Jim McCormick suffers his first defeat 6–1 at the hands of Boston's Charley Radbourn.

1892 His pay sliced the previous day as part of the NL's massive belt-tightening campaign, Cincinnati's Tony Mullane, the NL's leading winner to date with 20 victories, sulks through a 7–1 loss to Philadelphia. Mullane does not win another ML game during the season after he is suspended for his Philly performance, and he eventually flees in a pique to the Montana State League, where he serves out the campaign in exile from the majors.

1898 Ed Barrow, president of the Paterson, NJ, club in the Atlantic League, signs Lizzy Stroud, a female pitcher, but she has little success, even against minor league competition.

1930 The first Negro league games at Yankee Stadium pit the New York Lincoln Giants against the Baltimore Black Sox in a DBH, highlighted by Sox outfielder Rap Dixon's three home runs.

1935 Tony and Al Cuccinello of Brooklyn and New York, respectively, are the first pair of brothers on opposing teams to homer in the same NL game.

1947 Larry Doby is the first documented African American player in AL history when he bats for Cleveland pitcher Bryan Stephens in the 7th inning and fans against White Sox reliever Earl Harrist.

1952 Detroit hurler Fred Hutchison (2–1 in 12 appearances) is the last pitcher-manager to date when he takes the Tigers' helm from Red

Rolfe, the fourth ML skipper fired since Memorial Day, and proceeds to guide the Motor City entry to its first cellar finish since joining the AL in 1900.

1961   The Yankees' Roger Maris is mistakenly credited with an extra RBI in a game against the Tribe, a blunder that goes unrecognized until 1995 when the reduction makes Maris the 1961 AL co-leader in ribbies with Baltimore's Jim Gentile at 141 rather than the outright leader.

1989   Pittsburgh's Barry Bonds homers, making him and his sire, Bobby, the new father and son record holders with 408 taters, surpassing the mark of 407 the pair previously shared with Gus and Buddy Bell and Yogi and Dale Berra.

1991   NL owners approve expansion clubs in two cities without big league ball, as Miami and Denver are slated to begin play in 1993.

2002   Ted Williams dies of cardiac arrest at the age of 83 in Inverness, FL.

2004   The Diamondbacks end Dodgers closer Eric Gagne's record streak of 84 consecutive saves converted, an astounding run that topped the former mark set by the Red Sox' Tom Gordon (1998–1999) by a whopping margin of 30.

6

1894   In the process of becoming the first ML team to slug four home runs in an inning, Pittsburgh ties the then existing record for dingers in a game with seven in a 27–11 win over Boston rookie Henry Lampe.

1898   After being appointed an army surgeon, Baltimore hurler Arlie Pond returns to the Orioles for one last game and whitewashes Philadelphia 15–0 before leaving for a 32-year career as a medical officer in the Philippines, where he helps rid the islands of leprosy.

1928   His health failing owing to an enlarged heart, pitcher Urban Shocker is released by the Yankees after only one appearance during the season and dies of pneumonia in Denver just two months later.

1932   A spurned paramour shoots Cubs shortstop Billy Jurges in his Chicago hotel room and, when Jurges refuses to prosecute, turns the incident into a brief career as a Windy City nightclub singer billed as "Violet (I did it for love) Valli—the most talked of girl in Chicago."

1933   Comiskey Park hosts the first ML All-Star Game, with the AL winning 4–2 behind Babe Ruth's two-run homer.

1949 Traded to Cincinnati the previous month after landing in Giants manager Leo Durocher's doghouse, Walker Cooper collects six consecutive hits, including three jacks, in a 23–4 win over the Cubs and also scores five runs and bags 10 RBI for the best offensive day by a ML catcher since Wilbert Robinson's seven-hit, 11-RBI game in 1892.

1980 Against the Cardinals, Phillies moundsman Steve Carlton breaks Mickey Lolich's record for the most career strikeouts by a lefty when he fans number 2,833.

1983 In the All-Star Game's 50th anniversary at Comiskey Park, the site of the first Midsummer Classic, the AL trounces the NL 13–3 for its first win since 1971, as the Angels' Fred Lynn blasts the first grand slam in All-Star play off the Giants' Atlee Hammaker.

1986 The Braves' Bob Horner poles four homers, but the Expos prevail, defeating the Braves, 11–8.

1992 Commissioner Vincent's NL realignment plan, which commences in 1994, compels Eastern Division rivals Chicago and St. Louis to switch to the West, but when a third division is created, they both settle in the Central instead.

2000 Cards rookie Keith McDonald is the first big leaguer to pound seat reachers in each of his first two ML at bats since the Browns' Bob Nieman in 1951.

7

1884 Chicago UA hurler Hugh "One Arm" Daily ties Charlie Sweeney's month-old ML record for the most whiffs in a game when he fans 19 in a 5–0 win over Boston, plus a 20th victim who does not count according to the scoring rules of the time because he reaches base safely when Daily's catcher, Bill Krieg, lets a third strike elude him.

1923 Playing at home, the Indians score in every one of the eight innings they bat in a 27–3 massacre of the Red Sox that sets a new AL record (since broken) for the most runs by one team.

1931 The White Sox score in the 12th inning to beat the Browns 10–9 and end the longest documented game in history in which no batter on either team strikes out.

1933 Phils infielder Mickey Finn dies after abdominal surgery.

1936 After three successive defeats, the NL gains its first All-Star Game win, 4–3 at Fenway Park.

1937 In the NL's 8–3 All-Star Game loss, a line drive off Earl Averill's bat breaks Dizzy Dean's toe, resulting in Dean wrecking his arm when he tries to return to action too soon and is unable to put weight on the toe during his delivery.

1939 Forerunning Johnny Cash's visit by several decades, Sacramento and San Francisco play an exhibition game inside the walls of Folsom Prison.

1951 Emmett Ashford, the first African American umpire in OB, makes his pro officiating debut when he works the plate in a Southwestern International League game between Yuma and Mexicali.

1953 The St. Louis Browns lose 6–3 to the Indians, marking their record 20th straight home defeat.

1968 The Cubs' Phil Regan is the first reliever to win two games in one day twice in the same season and for two different teams, having previously bagged a pair on April 21 with the Dodgers.

1971 Commissioner Kuhn and HOF president Paul Kirk announce that former Negro leaguers will be included in Cooperstown's main shrine, not in a separate wing as originally planned.

1991 In Dallas, ML umpire Steve Palermo takes a bullet to the stomach when he comes to the aid of two women during an attempted robbery in a restaurant parking lot.

1996 After firing manager Rene Lachemann, Marlins vice president John Boles replaces him, becoming the first regularly appointed ML pilot with no pro playing experience since Braves owner Emil Fuchs in 1929.

1998 Coors Field is the setting for the highest-scoring game in All-Star history, as the AL beats the NL, 13–8.

2001 Tacoma lefty John Halama, who bagged 14 wins for the Mariners the previous year, pitches the first nine-inning perfect game in PCL history, beating Calgary, 6–0.

8

1902 Baltimore AL third baseman John McGraw finesses his release so that he can sign to manage the NL New York Giants and then begins to strip Baltimore of all its best players, forcing the other seven AL teams to furnish the Orioles with enough warm bodies to finish the season.

1908 Aiming to be the only ML pitcher ever to start a season 20–0, the Giants' Rube Marquard loses 7–2 to the Cubs' Jimmy Lavender, ending his post–1892 record season-winning streak at 19 and his overall string, including two wins to end the 1911 season, at 21.

1941 Hitting .405 at the All-Star break, Ted Williams carries the AL to a 7–5 win in the Midsummer Classic when he homers off Cubs pitcher Claude Passeau with two on and two out in the 9th.

1946 Harvard-trained labor organizer Robert Murphy's attempt to form the American Baseball Guild (a players' union) spawns a meeting between players and owners that generates, among other things, a $5,000 minimum ML salary, a maximum pay cut of 25%, player reps, and an embryonic players' pension fund.

1947 Former Tigers ace Schoolboy Rowe, now with the Phils, is the first player to perform for both leagues in the annual All-Star Game when he pinch hits for Johnny Sain in a 2–1 AL win.

1953 Lou Kretlow ends the St. Louis Browns' ML record skein of 20 consecutive losses at home when he beats Cleveland's Art Houtteman at Busch Stadium I, 6–3.

1960 Havana's IL team relocates to Jersey City after Fidel Castro's Cuban revolution.

1962 At the age of 41, the Cards' Stan Musial is the oldest player to pop three homers in a game in a 15–1 stomping of the Mets.

1976 The Padres' Randy Jones beats the Cubs for his 16th win, setting a NL record for victories at the All-Star break.

1985 Marge Schott, who later comes under fire for her remarks about race and alternative lifestyles, becomes president and CEO of the Cincinnati Reds.

2000 In an unusual twin bill, the Yankees sweep the Mets, with the day game played at Shea Stadium and the nightcap at Yankee Stadium.

2002 The South Atlantic League's Charleston Riverdogs hold "Nobody Night" and bar fans from Joe Riley Stadium for the first few innings to set an OB record for the lowest single-game paid attendance.

9

1885 In perhaps the first player sale for a four-figure sum, Chicago NL purchases pitcher Jim McCormick from the cash-strapped Providence NL club for an amount somewhere between $800 and $1,500.

1936 Long regarded as a Baker Bowl fluke, Chuck Klein gives his critics pause when he rifles four home runs in a 10-inning game at Forbes Field, one of the toughest places in the majors to go yard.

1948 Two days after his purported 42nd birthday, legendary Negro league star Satchel Paige makes his ML debut with Cleveland when he tosses two shutout innings in relief against the St. Louis Browns.

1951 Four-time AL batting king and the radio voice of the Tigers since 1934, Harry Heilmann dies of lung cancer at the age of 56.

1968 At the Astrodome, the NL wins the All-Star Game 1–0 after the Giants' Willie Mays scores an unearned run in the 1st inning of the initial Midsummer Classic played indoors.

1971 The A's beat the Angels 1–0 in 20 innings, the longest shutout win in AL history, as the two clubs combine to saw the air a record 43 times.

1972 The Angels' Nolan Ryan fans an AL-record eight straight Red Sox en route to a 16-strikeout victory.

1988 Chris Speier hits for the cycle to lead San Francisco in a 21–2 skewering of the Cardinals. Speier, who first cycled with Montreal in 1978, is the second performer to date to accomplish the feat for two NL teams, joining Babe Herman (Cubs and Dodgers).

1998 Brewers magnate Bud Selig relinquishes control of his club after the owners officially select him as baseball commissioner, ending his six-year stint as chairman of the Executive Council. Elsewhere, in the Northern League, Duluth's Ila Borders is the first female hurler to start a minor league game, working the first five innings and yielding five hits and three runs in absorbing an 8–3 loss to Sioux Falls.

2002 The All-Star Game ends ignominiously after 11 innings when Commissioner Selig calls the game a 7–7 tie after both leagues run out of pitchers.

2005 It takes more than 11 years, but Coors Field finally hosts a 1–0 game when the Rockies beat the Padres to end the longest drought for a ML venue before it is home to baseball's lowest winning score.

10

1874 Chicago second baseman Jimmy Wood has his right leg amputated above the knee due to infection caused by an accidental self-inflicted knife wound.

1880   After Chicago ties a then ML record two days earlier by winning its 21st consecutive game played to a decision, Cleveland snaps the White Stockings' streak, triumphing 2–0 on Fred Dunlap's two-run homer in the bottom of the 9th.

1911   In a flare up after he is ejected for disputing a called third strike, Phils outfielder Sherry Magee flattens plate umpire Bill Finneran and is at first suspended for the season before NL president Tom Lynch, himself a former umpire, reduces the punishment to five weeks.

1920   Cleveland's Tris Speaker sets a then ML record when he raps 11 straight hits in 11 at bats before being stopped by Washington's Tom Zachary.

1923   Customarily used in relief, Cards rookie Johnny Stuart is pressed into service as a starter in both ends of a DBH with the Braves and responds with two complete-game victories, 11–1 and 6–3, made all the more remarkable in that he fails to notch a strikeout in either game.

1928   Washington's Milt Gaston sets an AL record for the most hits allowed in etching a shutout when he is tagged for 14 safeties in topping Cleveland, 9–0.

1932   A's pilot Connie Mack brings only two pitchers to Cleveland for a Sunday date with the Indians and yanks his starter, Lew Krause, after only one inning, forcing him to stick with veteran Ed Rommel, who gives up a single-game record 29 hits, as the contest lasts 18 innings before Rommel prevails, 18–17. Cleveland gains a measure of satisfaction, however, when Tribe second baseman Johnny Burnett logs a ML single-game record nine hits in a losing cause.

1933   Carl Hubbell highlights the second All-Star Game when he fans five future Hall of Famers in a row, including Babe Ruth, Lou Gehrig, and Jimmie Foxx, but the AL wins 9–7 on the strength of Cleveland righty Mel Harder's five shutout innings in relief.

1945   The All-Star Game, scheduled for Fenway Park, is cancelled for the only time since its inception due to wartime travel restrictions.

1947   Cleveland's Don Black is the first ALer to pitch a no-hitter under artificial light when he tops the A's 3–0 in the first game of a twilight DBH that starts in daylight and is played under the lights for the final six innings after a 45-minute rain delay. Elsewhere, 20-year-old outfielder Stormy Davis of Ballinger in the Longhorn League dies in a Sweetwater, TX, hospital of a beaning sustained a week earlier.

142

1962 At DC Stadium, John F. Kennedy is the only president to date to toss the ceremonial first pitch at an All-Star Game.

1968 Both leagues agree on next year's expansion setup, which features 12 teams in each circuit, split into two divisions, with the winners of each division playing a best-of-five league championship series to determine which two teams advance to the World Series.

1979 The Phillies' Del Unser blasts a homer in his third straight pinch-hit appearance, joining Lee Lacy (1978) as the only two pinch sticks to date to perform the feat.

1984 At the age of 19, hurler Dwight Gooden is baseball's youngest All-Star and demonstrates why he made the squad by working two scoreless innings and fanning the first three batters he faces.

1999 At Leland's auction house, the uniform Lou Gehrig wore during his noted farewell speech on July 4, 1939, is sold for $451,541.

2007 Seattle's Ichiro Suzuki raps the first IPHR in All-Star Game play and is named the contest's MVP, as the AL wins its 10th straight decision.

11

1867 The Nationals of Washington embark by train on the first western trip made by a ball club that eventually covers some 3,000 miles and five states.

1911 Potentially the worst catastrophe in baseball history is averted when Cards manager Roger Bresnahan insists that the cars on the train carrying his team to Boston be rearranged so that his players can sleep in quiet just prior to a derailment near Bridgeport, CT, which plunges the train down an 18-foot embankment and kills 18 passengers from the same part of the train where the Cards' cars were originally located.

1914 Babe Ruth beats Cleveland 4–3 in his ML debut as a pitcher with Boston and fans in his first plate appearance.

1923 Hub fans celebrate when Red Sox owner Harry Frazee, after years of peddling the club's best players to the Yankees to obtain the funds for his Broadway theater projects, sells the club for more than $1,000,000 to a group of Ohio investors.

1934 The Cubs sweep a DBH from the Braves, but their centerpiece off-season acquisition, Chuck Klein, rips a hamstring and is never the same player.

1950   Red Schoendienst's solo homer in the 14th inning off Detroit's Ted Gray at Comiskey Park provides the NL's winning 4–3 margin in the longest All-Star Game to date.

1953   Giants rookie Al Worthington stops the Dodgers' then record NL streak of homering in 24 straight games and ties a record on his own behalf when he blanks Brooklyn 6–0 for his second shutout win in his first two ML starts, marking the only time the Dodgers are white-washed all season.

1961   In the first of two All-Star Games scheduled for the year, gusty winds blow Orioles hurler Stu Miller off the mound in the 9th inning at Candlestick Park, causing him to be charged with a balk. Overcoming his embarrassment, Miller wins the game 5–4 in extra innings.

1967   In the longest All-Star Game ever played, the Reds' Tony Perez homers off the A's Catfish Hunter in the 15th inning, giving the senior loop a 2–1 win.

1978   The Giants' Vida Blue is the first pitcher to start All-Star Games in both leagues in the NL's 7–3 win, after which the Dodgers' Steve Garvey is the first player to bag two All-Star MVP's.

1985   A new standard is set when the Astros' Nolan Ryan fans the Mets' Danny Heep to become the first pitcher to attain 4,000 career strikeouts.

1987   Baltimore's Cal Ripken Sr. is the first father to manage two ML sons, Cal Jr. and Billy.

1998   Sibling rivalry enters a new dimension as Padres closer Trevor Hoffman is the first pitcher to oppose a team managed by his brother, when he saves a game against the Dodgers piloted by older brother Glenn Hoffman.

12

1913   A's hurler Boardwalk Brown walks 15 Tigers before being removed in the 8th inning but nonetheless gains credit for a 16–9 win. Brown's dubious feat still stands as the ML single-game record for the most walks issued by a pitcher who failed to toss a complete game.

1945   Hank Wyse of the Cubs stops Braves outfielder Tommy Holmes's hitting streak at 37 games, leaving him seven short in his bid to overtake Willie Keeler's 1897 NL single-season record skein.

1949 The AL triumphs 11–7 in the first All-Star Game that features African American players, including Larry Doby for the AL and Jackie Robinson, Don Newcombe, and Roy Campanella for the NL.

1979 The most ill-conceived promotion in big league history with the sole exception of Cleveland's 1974 "Ten-Cent Beer Night" results in the White Sox forfeiting the second game of a DBH when thousands of young fans storm the field and refuse to leave during "Disco Demolition Night." The brainchild of White Sox team owner Bill Veeck's son Mike, the event offered 98-cent admission to anyone toting a disco record, all of which were subsequently collected in a huge pile on the field and literally blown up.

1996 The Twins' Kirby Puckett, idle all season, officially retires due to glaucoma in his right eye.

1997 The Pirates' Francisco Cordova spins nine no-hit innings against the Astros, and reliever Ricardo Rincon pitches a hitless 10th, making the pair the first to throw a combined extra-inning no-no in a 3–0 victory.

13

1896 Philadelphia's Ed Delahanty enjoys the greatest hitting day ever in a losing cause, belting four home runs and a single to account for all but one of the Phils' eight runs in a 9–8 loss to Chicago.

1943 In the first All-Star Game under the lights, the AL tops the NL 5–3 at Philadelphia's Shibe Park.

1963 On his eighth try, the Indians' Early Wynn notches his 300th and last win, beating the A's.

1965 For the first time the NL takes the lead in All-Star Games won with a 6–5 victory to forge ahead of the junior loop, 18–17, with one tie.

1971 The AL wins its only All-Star Game between 1962 and 1983, as the A's Reggie Jackson's 520-foot homer off the Pirates' Dock Ellis hits the power generator on Tiger Stadium's right field roof, sparking the junior loop to a 6–4 verdict.

1973 Montreal first baseman Hal Breeden pokes a pinch dinger in both games of a DBH against the Braves, joining the Red Sox' Joe Cronin (1943) as the only players to perform the feat.

1982 For the first time, the All-Star Game is played outside the United States as Montreal's Olympic Stadium hosts the NL's 11th straight victory.

1991 With six hitless frames logged, Baltimore's Bob Milacki is removed from the game after the A's Willie Wilson's smash hits the pitcher's index finger, and O's relievers Mike Flanagan, Mark Williamson, and closer Gregg Olson proceed to preserve the no-hitter.

1997 Seattle and Texas combine for a nine-inning record 31 strikeouts, as the Mariners' Randy Johnson contributes 14 in seven innings during a 4–2 loss to the Rangers.

2004 Selected to the AL as an All-Star Game starter while with the Royals, Carlos Beltran pinch hits and plays center field for the NL after being dealt by the Royals to the Astros in June.

14

1897 Phils slugger Ed Delahanty follows a 9-for-9 performance against Louisville pitching in a DBH the previous day by getting a hit off Louisville's Roy Evans in his first AB to set a new ML record (since broken) of 10 consecutive safe knocks.

1899 Washington sends catcher Deacon McGuire to Brooklyn for catcher Aleck Smith and first baseman Dan McGann, but Smith refuses to play for Washington and is sent to Baltimore.

1903 While his teammates celebrate a 4–3 win over Boston in 12 innings, Cleveland's John Gochnauer has the added distinction of tying Irv Ray's 15-year-old ML record for the longest game by a shortstop with no chances offered.

1910 Jack Horner, a scout for the Tigers and a former ML pitcher, dies after he slips on the marble steps of his hotel bath in New Orleans, fractures his skull, and never regains consciousness.

1919 After being traded by the Cards to the Phillies along with first baseman Gene Paulette for three lesser players, bespectacled hurler Lee Meadows becomes the only pitcher to date since 1892 to lose 10 or more games for two different teams in the same season.

1940 In response to the beanball wars that have marred ML play thus far in the season, *TSN* advertises a rudimentary batting helmet, and though most players disdain the notion, Brooklyn begins to provide cap liners to interested team members the following year.

1946   After Ted Williams crushes three home runs in the first game of a DBH at Boston, in the second game, Cleveland player-manager Lou Boudreau introduces the "Williams Shift," so extreme that it stations everyone but the left fielder on the right side of the diamond.

1967   While in Astros garb, Eddie Mathews hits his 500th career homer off the Giants' Juan Marichal, marking the first time that a future Hall of Famer reaches the hallowed plateau against another future Cooperstown inductee.

1970   When the Reds' Pete Rose crashes into Indians catcher Ray Fosse at the plate to score the game-ending run in the 12th inning of the All-Star Game, the rookie receiver's shoulder is injured so badly that it is never the same.

1972   For the first time in ML history, a game features a catcher and plate umpire who are brothers, as Tigers receiver Tom Haller hears sibling Bill Haller call balls and strikes behind him.

1978   Dodgers hurler Don Sutton is ejected by umpire Doug Harvey after the arbiter discovers three doctored balls thrown by the future Cooperstown inductee.

1987   The BBWAA renames the Rookie of the Year Award in honor of trailblazer Jackie Robinson, who captured the initial trophy in 1947.

1999   The head of the umpires union, Richie Phillips, announces that 57 arbiters will quit on September 2, a decision they later regret when MLB gleefully accepts many of their resignations.

2000   ML owners agree to return to an unbalanced schedule in 2001, with teams playing more games against clubs within their own division to intensify rivalries.

2001   Umpires file a grievance against MLB, contending that the commissioner's office is pressuring them to call more strikes under the pretense of using cameras to track pitch counts, but the arbiters drop their suit when MLB agrees to cease the practice.

2002   Nelson Barrera, the Mexican League's career homer and RBI leader, is electrocuted at the age of 44 while working with metal roofing and high-tension wires.

2005   The Giants beat the Dodgers 4–3 to become the first ML sports franchise to win 10,000 games.

15

1876   St. Louis's George Bradley, en route to posting a record 16 shutouts (since tied), tosses the first NL no-hitter, defeating Hartford's Tommy Bond, 2–0.

1892   For the only time in ML history except for the 1981 strike year, a ML plays a split season, as Boston, the first half winner, and Cleveland, the eventual second half winner, both mark the occasion by losing their opening second half games.

1920   With the season barely half over, Babe Ruth ties his 1919 record of 29 home runs when he goes yard in the 13th inning against the Browns' Bill Burwell to give the Yankees a 13–10 win.

1939   A heated argument following Reds outfielder Harry Craft's fly ball homer down the left-field foul line at the Polo Grounds induces NL president Ford Frick to announce that two-foot screens will be installed inside all NL parks to prevent future ambiguous incidents, and the AL soon follows Frick's lead.

1941   Pitcher Hooks Iott of Paragould in the Northeast Arkansas League sets a single-game OB record when he fans 30 batters in a 16-inning, 1–1 tie with Newport. Less than a month earlier, Iott fanned 25 in a nine-inning win over Batesville.

1942   Responding to criticism that there are no African Americans in OB, Commissioner Landis insists, "There is no rule, formal or informal, against the hiring of Negro players."

1950   The Colonial League sounds an ominous note when it folds, complaining that it can no longer compete with the flood of ML games that are either televised or broadcast into its loop cities.

1952   Lou Sleater gets Tigers first baseman Walt Dropo to foul out to catcher Mickey Grasso in the second game of a twin bill at Washington to end Dropo's ML record-tying consecutive hits streak at 12.

1973   In an overpowering performance, the Angels' Nolan Ryan fires his second no-hitter of the season, fanning 17 Tigers.

1994   Umpire Dave Phillips confiscates Indians slugger Albert Belle's bat, suspicious that it is corked, but Tribe hurler Jason Grimsley perpetrates an ingenious switch. When Grimsley's sleight of hand is uncovered, Belle is made to relinquish another of his bats and is subsequently handed a 10-day suspension, later reduced to seven games and a $7,000 fine.

2000   The most coveted card in sports memorabilia collecting, Honus Wagner's 1909 gem, is sold on eBay for $1,265,000.

2007   The Phillies become the first pro sports club to lose 10,000 games but nevertheless win the NL's Eastern Division for the season.

16

1874   Boston and the Philadelphia Athletics interrupt their National Association season to sail for England, where they remain for more than a month playing a series of cricket and baseball exhibition games in an unsuccessful effort to convince the British public that baseball is the superior sport.

1885   Chicago NL rookie Ted Kennedy starts and wins both ends of a DBH at Buffalo and is forced to pitch an exhibition game the following day against Syracuse. When Kennedy's arm goes dead, he is released by Chicago and never pitches another game in the NL. Later, however, he invents a new type of catcher's mitt and an early-day pitching machine.

1909   Detroit's Ed Summers pitches a complete-game shutout but fails to gain a victory as the Tigers and Browns battle 18 innings in the longest scoreless tie in AL history.

1920   Babe Ruth breaks his season home-run record of 29, set the previous year, when he goes deep for the 30th time in a 5–2 win over the Browns.

1921   Former ML manager and shortstop Arthur Irwin is presumed dead after either having jumped or accidentally fallen overboard while traveling on a steamer between New York and Boston. But when Irwin is later discovered to have been leading a double life, the mystery deepens to include the possibility that he simply elected to disappear and remains unsolved to this day.

1930   Former Pittsburgh pitcher Zeke Rosebraugh takes his own life with a gun in Fresno, CA.

1948   The Giants set New York on its ear when they fire popular ex-Giants outfielder Mel Ott as manager and hire Leo Durocher, who is on equally thin ice in Brooklyn, to replace him.

2000   On eBay, a ball reputedly signed by the infamous 1919 Chicago "Black Sox," which includes the signature of the reputedly functionally illiterate Joe Jackson, is auctioned for $93,666.

2006 The Braves' Chipper Jones ties Paul Waner's 1927 ML record by stroking an extra-base hit in his 14th straight game.

17

1889 Pitcher Nat Hudson is the first player to thwart a trade when he refuses to be sent from St. Louis to Louisville for pitcher Toad Ramsey and winds up instead with Milwaukee of the minor league Western Association.

1899 Cleveland tosser Jim Hughey halts a Spiders' 13-game losing streak when he tops Baltimore 7–2 to lift his season log to 4–14. Hughey then embarks on a 16-game losing streak of his own and finishes 4–30 with a .118 winning percentage, the worst ever by a pitcher in a minimum of 30 decisions.

1914 Pittsburgh's Babe Adams sets a single-game ML record for the most innings pitched without issuing a walk when he goes 21 frames while giving up no free passes in a 3–1 loss to the Giants.

1941 Cleveland pitchers Al Milnar and Jim Bagby Jr., aided by fielding gems from third baseman Ken Keltner and shortstop Lou Boudreau, combine to stop Joe DiMaggio's ML record 56-game hitting streak.

1952 Heading for a mental breakdown that later inspires the film *Fear Strikes Out*, Birmingham outfielder Jimmy Piersall, on assignment from the Red Sox, is suspended by the Southern Association after being ejected from a game for the fourth time in less than three weeks.

1957 Responding to a probe of several recent suspicious deals between the A's and Yankees, A's owner Arnold Johnson perjures himself before the House Judiciary Subcommittee investigating baseball's operations when he denies that he has any links to the Yankees ownership or has favored them in trades.

1961 Ty Cobb, owner of the highest career batting average (.366), dies of cancer at the age of 74 in Atlanta, GA. Elsewhere, with the AL schedule having been increased to 162 games, Commissioner Frick decrees that Babe Ruth's 1927 season record of 60 homers in a 154-game schedule "cannot be broken unless some batter hits 61 or more within his club's first 154 games."

1964 Baseball's first pay cablecast involves the Dodgers and the Cubs in LA, as Subscription Television offers subscribers the game for a fee.

1974 The Cards' Bob Gibson is the first NL hurler to whiff 3,000 batters as he fans the Reds' Cesar Geronimo. Elsewhere, Milwaukee third baseman Don Money commits his first error of the season after 86 games and a record 257 errorless chances.

1978 Yankees manager Billy Martin socks Reggie Jackson with a five-day suspension without pay after the slugger bunts against orders in KC and strikes out on a foul bunt attempt in a tie game that the Bombers go on to lose.

1990 The Twins lose 1–0 to the Red Sox despite becoming the first ML team to turn two triple plays in the same game.

1993 In the PCL, Spokane's Glenn Dishman has his perfect game disintegrate with one out to go when first baseman Jason Thompson, about to take a game-ending throw on a routine grounder, begins celebrating early and commits an error by pulling his foot off the bag before the ball lands in his mitt.

18

1885 The St. Louis Browns' ML record home game winning streak of 27 terminates with an 8–3 loss to Philadelphia A's rookie Ed Knouff.

1913 Cardinals first baseman Ed Konetchy walks in the second game of a DBH with the Giants, halting Christy Mathewson's then record skein of 68 consecutive innings without giving up a base on balls.

1921 Babe Ruth breaks Roger Connor's career home-run record of 138 when he hits his 139th circuit blast into the center field bleachers at Detroit's Navin Field off Tigers rookie Bert Cole. Elsewhere, the "Black Sox" trial of the eight players accused of fixing the 1919 World Series begins in Chicago and results in all eight being barred for life by Commissioner Landis, even though a jury finds them not guilty.

1923 Cards second baseman Rogers Hornsby concludes an all-time ML record skein of 13 straight games in which he notches two or more hits when he collects two safeties in a 6–4 win over the Giants.

1932 Former ML infielder Howard Freigau, now with Knoxville of the Southern Association, dies at the age of 29 on a road trip to Chattanooga, when he dives into an outdoor pool and hits his head on the bottom.

1947 Detroit's Fred Hutchinson blanks the Yankees 8–0 to halt their AL record-tying winning streak at 19 games.

1948 White Sox outfielder Pat Seerey belts four home runs at Shibe Park, including a solo blast in the 11th inning to defeat the A's, 12–11.

1983 Despite being in first place, the Phillies fire manager Pat Corrales and replace him with GM Paul Owens.

1987 The Yankees' Don Mattingly homers in his eighth consecutive game, tying Pittsburgh's Dale Long's 1956 record that will also later be equaled by Seattle's Ken Griffey Jr. in 1993.

1989 At the age of 35, former ML closer Donnie Moore critically wounds his estranged wife and then fatally shoots himself at his home. Friends later claim that Moore never recovered from yielding Red Sox outfielder Dave Henderson's two-run homer in Game 5 of the 1986 ALCS, denying the Angels their first World Series appearance.

1990 Arbitrator George Nicolau rules that all ML owners colluded to squelch competitive bidding for players by keeping a data bank of 1987 salary offers.

1999 On "Yogi Berra Day" at Yankee Stadium, prior to the game, Don Larsen throws the ceremonial first pitch to Berra, commemorating Larsen's World Series perfecto in 1956, which Berra caught, and David Cone follows by throwing a perfect game of his own, handcuffing the Expos, 6–0.

19

1879 The first duel in ML history between two southpaws takes place in Cleveland when the Blues' Bobby Mitchell breezes to an 8–2 win over Boston's Curry Foley.

1909 Cleveland shortstop Neal Ball executes the first documented unassisted triple play in ML history in a 6–1 win over Boston.

1911 Center fielder Walter Carlisle with Vernon of the PCL catches Los Angeles infielder Roy Akin's short fly ball at his shoe tops and races to second base and then to first to complete the first documented unassisted triple play by an outfielder in OB history.

1914 The "Miracle" Boston Braves, occupiers of the cellar at the latest date ever by a preexpansion pennant winner, vacate the basement once and for all for the season when they beat Cincinnati, 3–2.

1924 When Hi Bell tops the Braves 6–1 and 2–1, it marks the second consecutive year that a Cards rookie wins two complete games in one day and the last time to date that a NL hurler starts and wins both ends of a DBH.

1933 In a game between Cleveland and Boston, the Ferrells are the first brothers on opposing teams to homer in the same game when Rick goes yard against his younger sib, Wes, who in turn victimizes Red Sox hurler Hank Johnson.

1942 Brooklyn loses a DBH to the Cardinals when Dodgers center fielder Pete Reiser crashes into the wall in Sportsman's Park chasing Enos Slaughter's long fly in the 11th inning of the nightcap and drops the ball after losing consciousness, allowing Slaughter to circle the bases for an IPHR. Elsewhere, Mike Ryba, a 39-year-old relief pitcher with the Red Sox, catches parts of both ends of a DBH loss to Cleveland at Fenway Park.

1950 The Yankees buy Elston Howard and pitcher Frank Barnes from the Negro league Kansas City Monarchs, but it is another five years before Howard is the first African American to don pinstripes.

1952 Fitzgerald breaks the color line in the Class D Georgia State League when manager Charlie Ridgeway puts an African American batboy, 12-year-old Joe Relford, into the game in the 8th inning of a blowout loss at Statesboro. Relford hits the ball hard in his one AB and makes a sensational catch, but his career is short and sweet as the loop president fires the umpire who let him enter the game, and Fitzgerald owner Ace Adams, a former ML hurler, fires Ridgeway and takes over the club's reins himself.

1955 Tigers reliever Babe Birrer rescues Frank Lary when Baltimore threatens in the top of the 6th, and in the course of finishing the game and saving the win for Lary, Birrer raps a pair of three-run homers off Orioles relievers George Zuverink and Art Shallock. The two jacks and six RBI represent Birrer's career total when he leaves the majors in 1958.

1960 The Giants' Juan Marichal debuts in grand style, pitching no-hit ball against the Phillies for 7⅔ innings, until Clay Dalrymple strokes a pinch single, forcing Marichal to settle for a one-hit shutout.

1974 Cleveland's Dick Bosman no-hits Oakland 4–0 but becomes the only hurler to cost himself a perfect game with his own error when he commits a throwing miscue in the 4th, allowing Sal Bando to become the A's lone base runner on the day.

1975 George Brett's famous "Pine Tar" incident has a precedent when the Yankees' Thurman Munson's RBI single against the Twins is nullified because the tar on his bat handle exceeds the 18-inch limit, allowing Minnesota's Jim Hughes to skate to a 2–1 win over the Bombers.

1982 At the age of 75, Luke Appling takes Warren Spahn deep in the first annual Cracker Jack Old-Timers Classic at Washington's RFK Stadium.

2001 After pounding 32 homers in the bushes, Adam Dunn is summoned by the Reds and goes on to add 19 more seat rattlers for a total of 51 on the season, including 12 in August, a NL freshman record for the most in a month. Meanwhile, in the completion of a suspended game started by Curt Schilling the night before, Arizona's Randy Johnson strikes out 16 Padres in seven innings to break the ML relief K mark set by Walter Johnson on July 25, 1913.

20

1858 An All-Star Game between teams from New York and Brooklyn at Fashion Race Course on Long Island is the first contest in history to charge admission (50¢).

1887 The day after Chicago manager Cap Anson purportedly refuses to let his team take the field in an exhibition game against Newark's star African American southpaw, George Stovey, Newark's loop, the IL, formally bans black players effective at the close of the 1887 season.

1916 The Giants include future HOF outfielder Edd Roush and future HOF manager Bill McKechnie with their fading pitching star Christy Mathewson in a deal with Cincinnati designed to make Mathewson manager of the Reds.

1943 Although the spitball rule has been extant for some 24 years, Browns righty Nels Potter is the first ML hurler to be punished for violating it when he is suspended for 10 days after being banished by umpire Cal Hubbard for moistening his fingers before pitches in St. Louis's 7–3 win over the Yankees.

1947 When the Browns' Hank Thompson and Willard Brown take the field against the Red Sox, it marks the first documented occasion in AL or NL history that two African American players appear in the same lineup.

1965 The Yankees' Mel Stottlemyre is the first pitcher to rap an inside-the-park grand slam since the Bucs' Deacon Phillippe 55 years earlier when he circles the bases against Boston's Bill Monbouquette.

1969 Light-hitting Giants hurler Gaylord Perry raps his first ML homer some 20 minutes after learning that Neil Armstrong has set foot on the moon. The previous year, Perry's skipper, Alvin Dark, had quipped to sportswriter Harry Jupiter, "They'll put a man on the moon before [Perry] hits a home run."

1973 White Sox chucker Wilbur Wood is the last ML pitcher to date to start both ends of a DBH when he loses both games to the Yanks.

1976 The Brewers' Hank Aaron belts his 755th and last career homer, victimizing the Angels' Dick Drago.

2000 Cincinnati debuts Mike Bell, making the Bell family the first to sport three generations to play for the same ML club when Mike joins his grandfather, Gus, and father, Buddy.

2007 The Cuban national team beats the United States for its 10th straight gold medal in the Pan-American Games, while the United States earns the silver for the third straight year.

21

1875 First baseman Joe Start is the first ML player to hit three home runs in a game in leading the New York Mutuals to a 16–13 National Association win over the Philadelphia Pearls.

1938 Winnipeg shortstop Skeeter Ebner is the second Northern League player in three years to die in a Winnipeg hospital after being beaned.

1945 Detroit and the A's set an AL record for the longest tie game when they battle to a 24-frame 1–1 draw in which the Tigers starter, rookie Les Mueller, goes 19²/₃ innings before being removed for Dizzy Trout.

1959 When Pumpsie Green pinch runs for Vic Wertz in the 8th inning of Boston's 2–1 loss at Chicago, the Red Sox are at long last no longer the only ML team to never have an African American player.

1970 The Padres' Clay Kirby no-hits the Mets through eight innings, but manager Preston Gomez, down 1–0, lifts Kirby in the bottom of the frame for a pinch hitter, and Pads reliever Jack Baldschun then blows the no-no in the 9th as the Mets win, 3–0.

1972 Hoyt Wilhelm, the last World War II vet to play in the majors, is released by the Dodgers, ending his career just five days shy of his 50th birthday.

1975   Each of Mets second baseman Felix Milan's four straight singles is quickly erased when teammate Joe Torre ties a ML record by grounding into four straight double plays against the Astros.

2007   At a combined total of 88 years and 307 days, the Padres' David Wells and the Phillies' Jamie Moyer form the second-oldest starting pitching matchup in ML history, trailing only the Angels' Don Sutton and the Indians' Phil Niekro on June 8, 1987, who totaled a combined 90 years and 135 days.

22

1884   Philadelphia Quakers hurler Jim McElroy, so wild that veteran catchers refuse to work on days he pitches, is spared a 0–14 career record when he gains his lone ML win, 10–6 at Providence, after Grays pitcher Charlie Sweeney walks off the field, leaving his team unable to hold a seemingly safe 6–2 lead when it is forced to play the final two innings with only eight men. Afterward, Sweeney jumps to the UA St. Louis Maroons and wins 24 games in the rebel loop, giving him an aggregate season total of 41.

1887   A mysterious new pitcher named Chapman appears with Philadelphia in an AA game against Cleveland. For years, Chapman is believed to be one Fred Chapman, then only 14 years old, which would make him the youngest player in ML history, but the one-game pitcher Chapman is now without a first name.

1911   The Giants send shortstop Al Bridwell and catcher Hank Gowdy to the Braves for infielder Buck Herzog.

1922   The Giants pay high for pitcher Hugh McQuillan, sending pitchers Larry Benton and Fred Toney, plus a minor leaguer, to the Braves, along with $100,000.

1923   Cleveland finishes a club record 32-game home stand (in which all seven other AL teams visit the Forest City) with a 3–1 loss to Washington's Walter Johnson.

1947   In a 6–1 loss to Washington, Detroit first baseman Roy Cullenbine extends his all-time ML record streak of consecutive games receiving at least one base on balls to 22. Cullenbine's skein ends the following night at the hands of the era's greatest streak ender, Washington's Rae Scarborough.

1969   At RFK Stadium in Washington, the All-Star Game is postponed by rain for the first time in OB history.

1993   The 10,000th homer in Tiger Stadium, the first venue to witness that plateau, is poled by the Royals' Greg Gagne off Mark Leiter.

2007   In the Texas League, Tulsa Drillers first base coach Mike Coolbaugh, a former ML third sacker, is killed when a foul line drive struck by Tulsa's Tino Sanchez hits him in the neck.

23

1890   Boston PL outfielder Harry Stovey blasts a 6th-inning toss from rookie Charlie Bartson into the center field stands at the Chicago PL park, marking him the first player in ML history to log 100 career home runs.

1894   First place Baltimore buys lefty Duke Esper from Washington and follows by trading pitcher Bert Inks and $2,000 to Louisville for pitcher George Hemming late the following month.

1922   For the first time since the AL put a team in St. Louis in 1902, both Mound City ML clubs are alone in first place in the morning's standings. Elsewhere, Cubs first baseman Ray Grimes Sr. sets a new ML record when he homers against Brooklyn, giving him at least one RBI in the past 17 games in which he has participated. Meanwhile, the Yankees dupe the BoSox out of third baseman Joe Dugan and outfielder Elmer Smith for $50,000 and four players who do next to naught in the Hub.

1929   The Cards rescind their bizarre off-season managerial switch that sent pennant-winning skipper Bill McKechnie to their Rochester farm and brought Rochester pilot Billy Southworth to St. Louis by ordering the two to swap jobs again.

1955   In a game against KC, the Yankees' Bob Cerv and Elston Howard are the first teammates to hit back-to-back pinch home runs.

1964   Oakland rookie Bert Campaneris ties a ML record by lofting two homers in his debut to help the A's defeat the Twins, 4–3.

24

1887   After taking sick between games of an Independence Day DBH, Pittsburgh first baseman Alex McKinnon dies of typhoid at the age of 30. McKinnon was leading the club with a .340 BA at the time of his death.

1933   The Cards name Frankie Frisch their new player-manager, replacing Gabby Street.

1934 Yankees center fielder Earle Combs fractures his skull and breaks his collarbone crashing into a wall in Sportsman's Park, a pair of injuries that, in conjunction with another major injury he suffers the following year, end his career prematurely.

1948 A bus-truck collision near St. Paul claims the lives of five members of the Duluth Northern League team and the truck driver and leaves 13 players injured.

1968 Rubber-armed White Sox hurler Hoyt Wilhelm surpasses Cy Young's then record for career appearances by making his 907th mound outing.

1978 Billy Martin quits as Yankees manager and is replaced by Bob Lemon, who leads the Bombers to a world championship in the fall.

1979 Commissioner Kuhn slaps outspoken Padres owner Ray Kroc with a $100,000 fine for tampering after Kroc openly declares that he wants to acquire potential free agents Joe Morgan of the Reds and Graig Nettles of the Yanks.

1983 At Yankee Stadium, the Royals' George Brett appears to slam a two-run homer off Rich Gossage, only to have it nullified by home plate umpire Tim McClellan after the Yanks note that the pine tar on Brett's bat handle exceeds the 18-inch limit allowed by the rules. Brett is consequently called out, handing New York a 4–3 victory and triggering an enraged Brett to burst from the dugout and charge toward McClellan before being restrained by teammates. When the Royals protest, for the first time in his tenure, AL president Lee MacPhail, disregarding a precedent (set July 19, 1975) for his umpire's decision, overrules the call, allowing the homer to stand and ordering the game to resume on August 18 at the point when it was hit.

25

1872 The *New York Times* gloomily reports, "Baseball, so far as it can claim to be an American institution at all, is simply a contrivance for gambling that most honest men would cheerfully see suppressed."

1890 In his final minor league appearance before joining Cleveland of the NL, Cy Young tosses a no-hitter for Canton of the Tri-State League against McKeesport, PA, in which he whiffs 18 batters.

1896 Pittsburgh trades first baseman Jake Beckley to New York for first baseman/outfielder Harry Davis, plus $1,000.

1913 Pitching in relief of starter George Baumgardner, Browns lefty Carl Weilman is the first ML player to strike out six times in six at bats, as he and Washington's Walter Johnson duel to a 15-inning 8–8 tie.

1921 Disenchanted with playing for the last-place Phillies, outfielder Irish Meusel is rewarded while serving a suspension for lackadaisical play by being traded to the front-running Giants for catcher Butch Henline, outfielder Curt Walker, pitcher Jesse Winters, and $30,000.

1939 Yankees rookie Atley Donald ties a ML record when he opens his career with 12 straight wins by beating the Browns, 5–1.

1959 IL officials begin plans to move the Havana Sugar Canes franchise to Newark the following year when a wild celebration in the stands of Havana's La Gran Stadium, prompted in part by Fidel Castro's participation in pregame festivities, halts a game between the Canes and Rochester after gunshots wound Rochester third-base coach Frank Verdi and Havana shortstop Leo Cardenas.

1966 During his Cooperstown induction speech, Red Sox immortal Ted Williams argues for the inclusion of Negro league stars in the HOF.

1978 By singling off the Mets' Craig Swan, Pete Rose extends his hitting streak to 38, breaking Tommy Holmes's modern NL mark.

26

1879 Syracuse hurler Harry McCormick homers in the 1st inning and then beats Boston 1–0, marking the only time in ML history that a pitcher wins a 1–0 game by dint of his own 1st-inning homer.

1933 Oakland's Ed Walsh Jr., son of future Hall of Famer Ed Walsh Sr., stops the 61-game PCL batting streak of 18-year-old San Francisco Seals rookie Joe DiMaggio.

1984 Free agent Vida Blue is suspended for the rest of the season by Commissioner Kuhn owing to Blue's conviction on cocaine possession charges the previous November.

1991 Montreal's Mark Gardner runs into tough luck as he pitches no-hit ball for nine innings before LA's Lenny Harris strokes an infield single in the 10th and the Dodgers win, 1–0.

1999 In Philadelphia, big league umps file a suit in U.S. District Court to withdraw their mass resignations. To date, 14 of the 56 umps who threatened to quit have already withdrawn their resignations, and nine of the AL arbiters' resignations have been readily accepted by the league.

2000   After the Phillies deal their ace Curt Schilling to the Diamond-backs for first baseman Travis Lee and pitchers Vicente Padilla, Omar Daal, and Nelson Figueroa, Schilling proceeds to win 45 games and a world championship ring with Arizona over the next two seasons.

27

1893   New York sells Willie Keeler, a 5'4½" bust thus far, to Brooklyn for $800.

1930   Brought in relieve in a 2–2 tie, Ken Ash throws one pitch to the Cubs' Charlie Grimm that ends in a triple play owing to a string of base running gaffes and gains credit for the win, his last in the majors, when Cincinnati scores in its next AB after Ash is removed for a pinch hitter.

1945   In a peculiar waiver deal, the Cubs acquire Hank Borowy, 10–5 to that point with the Yanks, and watch him go 11–2 against NL hitters, making him the first ML hurler since 1884 to win in double figures for two teams in two different leagues in the same season.

1947   When Browns pitcher Fred Sanford intentionally slings his glove at Red Sox first baseman Jake Jones's slow roller along the third base line to insure that it will stay foul, umpire Cal Hubbard properly awards Jones a triple, a rule that is changed in 1954 to apply only to fair balls.

1951   In the game that starts the "Go-Go" White Sox on an irrevers-ible downhill slide for the season, the Yankees lead 3–1 in the top of the 9th and then stall when rain begins to fall, as the White Sox score three runs and load the bases with only one out. After Casey Stengel uses five pitchers in the inning and Gil McDougald is ejected for stall-ing, consuming even more time while his replacement Bobby Brown looks for his glove, the umpires stop play for the second time in the inning and call the game an hour later, erasing the Sox' three runs when the final score reverts to 3–1, where it stood at the end of the 8th frame.

1987   In the Pioneer League, the Salt Lake City Trappers lose 7–5 to the Billings Mustangs, ending their OB record winning streak of 29, which surpassed the former mark of 27 belonging to 1902 Corsicana in the Texas League.

1998   In the Texas League, Arkansas Travelers outfielder Tyrone Horne is the first documented player in OB to "homer for the cycle," smashing a solo, two-run, three-run, and grand slam shot against San Antonio. Elsewhere, against the Rockies, Bucs speedy second baseman Tony Womack goes without hitting into a double play for a ML-record 888 at bats, breaking Pete Reiser's mark of 887 set 52 years earlier. Womack's streak ends at 918 AB when he is doubled up against the Rockies on August 5.

28

1875 Playing as Joe Josephs to conceal from his father that he is playing pro baseball, rookie hurler Joe Borden of the Philadelphia Pearls fires the first recorded no-hitter in the pro game, blanking Chicago, 4–0.

1890 The financially strapped AA Brooklyn Gladiators are forced to forfeit a home game they lead 13–8 in the 8th inning when Columbus's Jack Sneed fouls a ball into the stands and umpire Jim Peoples halts the contest when the ball is not returned because Brooklyn is unable to provide a new ball to replace it.

1928 The Phils pay cash, plus a minor leaguer, to acquire minor league slugger Chuck Klein from Fort Wayne.

1951 Red Sox outfielder Clyde Vollmer singles home the tying run in the 15th inning and then hits a four-run homer the following inning, the latest walk-off grand slam in ML history to date, as Boston tops Cleveland's Bob Feller, appearing in a rare relief role, 8–4.

1976 The White Sox' Blue Moon Odom makes his last ML victory memorable by combining with reliever Francisco Barrios to no-hit Odom's former club, the A's, 2–1.

1989 Cards speedster Vince Coleman's ML record for consecutive stolen bases is halted at 50 when Expos catcher Nelson Santovenia guns him down at second in St. Louis's 2–0 win at Montreal.

1991 The Expos' Dennis Martinez tosses a perfect game against the Dodgers as his backstop, Ron Hassey, is the first receiver to catch two perfectos, having handled Cleveland's Len Barker's masterpiece in 1981. The Dodgers' Alfredo Griffin is also the first to play in three perfect games, having previously appeared in perfectos against the Reds, Tom Browning in 1988 and Barker in 1981.

1993 The Mets' Anthony Young's ML record 27-game losing streak finally ends when he earns a 5–4 victory in relief against the Marlins.

1994 The Rangers' Kenny Rogers is the first southpaw in junior loop history to author a perfect game when he bests the Angels, 4–0.

29

1909 Purportedly no longer able to cope with the pressures of his office, NL president Harry Pulliam commits suicide.

1919 The Red Sox ignore AL president Ban Johnson's order not to trade Carl Mays and send the recalcitrant pitcher to the Yankees for pitchers Bob McGraw and Allan Russell and $40,000.

1928 Cleveland third baseman Johnny Hodapp is the first AL player to get two hits in an inning twice in the same game in a 24–6 whacking of the Yankees.

1957 Whammy Douglas, the last one-eyed player in the majors to date, debuts with the Pirates and goes five innings in his first start, absorbing a 4–0 loss to the Cardinals.

1958 Former MLer Jesse Levan, who later went to Chattanooga in the Southern Association, is barred from OB for life when several fellow players testify that he approached them for help in fixing games.

1973 White Sox hurler Wilbur Wood wins his 20th game of the season, making the knuckleballer the last pitcher to date to bag 20 victories before August 1.

1983 A collision at home plate against the Braves dislocates the Padres' Steve Garvey's thumb, ending his NL record consecutive games played streak at 1,207.

1988 The Orioles deal hurler Mike Boddicker to the Red Sox for Brady Anderson and Curt Schilling. While Schilling does not pay dividends in Baltimore, Anderson goes on to club more than 200 homers and play on three All-Star squads with the O's.

1995 In Millington, TN, Cuban national team pitcher Osvaldo Fernandez defects to play ML ball but goes just 19–26 in four years with the Giants and Reds.

1999 Thirteen NL umps lose their jobs when their July 14 resignations that they misguidedly think are only symbolic are accepted by MLB.

2000 Despite trading closer Bob Wickman to the Indians the previous day for first baseman/outfielder Richie Sexson, the Brewers still stage "Bob Wickman All-Star Poster Night."

2007   Seattle's Ichiro Suzuki raps his 1,500th ML hit in his 1,060th game, marking him the third fastest player to reach that milestone after the A's Al Simmons (1,040) and the Browns' George Sisler (1,048).

30

1906   The New York State Supreme Court rules that Brooklyn is violating the law against conducting a business on Sunday in New York, overriding the Dodgers' argument that they are accepting "voluntary contributions" in lieu of charging admission to their games.

1933   In beating the Cubs 8–2 in the first game of a DBH, Cardinals fireballer Dizzy Dean is the first hurler at the 60'6" distance to fan as many as 17 batters in a regulation-length game.

1947   The Giants nip the Reds 5–4 in 10 innings, ending Ewell Blackwell's Cincinnati franchise record 16-game winning streak.

1952   To prevent the Yankees from perpetrating any more late-season heists of prominent NL players, Commissioner Frick establishes a new waiver rule that puts severe constraints on interleague deals and bars all deals after July 3.

1959   Recalled from Phoenix of the PCL, the Giants' Willie McCovey debuts against the Phillies by going 4-for-4, including two triples, and proceeds to win both the PCL home-run crown, after leading with 29 before his recall, and the NL Rookie of the Year Award. McCovey is still the lone rookie award winner who did not make his first ML appearance until after the All-Star break.

1960   Making his big league debut in a relief role, Phillies righty Art Mahaffey picks off the first batter to get a hit against him (the Cards' Curt Flood) and then nabs the next hitter to reach against him (Bill White). In Mahaffey's second game, he catches the first batter to slap a hit against him napping (the Giants' Jim Marshall), thereby picking off the first three base runners who reach against his slants.

1980   Houston's J. R. Richard suffers a stroke that ends his career after he is rushed to the hospital to remove a life-threatening blood clot from his neck.

1990   Commissioner Vincent orders Yankees owner George Steinbrenner to resign as the club's general partner by August 20 and bans him "for life" after learning of Steinbrenner's $40,000 payment to gambler Howard Spira for damaging information about former Bombers All-Star Dave Winfield. Vincent later rescinds the ban and allows Steinbrenner to resume control of the Yankees on March 1, 1993.

1991 Red Sox reliever Jeff Gray collapses before a game against Texas and is diagnosed with a stroke that takes two years of rehab before Gray becomes a minor league pitching coach in 1994.

31

1896 In an episode typical of the times, Pittsburgh pitcher Frank Killen starts a fistfight on the field with umpire Bud Lally and is arrested for disorderly conduct but is otherwise unpunished when the charges are dropped, and he goes on to become the last southpaw in NL history to win 30 games.

1915 St. Louis FL pitcher Dave Davenport is the only ML twirler to date to be involved in two 1–0 games in one day in which he goes the distance in each when he splits a twin bill with Buffalo.

1932 Cleveland debuts its gigantic new facility, Municipal Stadium, and draws a then record crowd of more than 80,000 to watch the Tribe's Mel Harder lose 1–0 to A's ace, Lefty Grove.

1935 With his club headed for the poorest season record in the NL (38–115) since the 1899 Cleveland Spiders, Braves owner Judge Fuchs declares bankruptcy and forfeits his stock in the team.

1954 Braves first baseman Joe Adcock crushes four home runs and a double for a then ML single-game record 18 total bases in Milwaukee's 15–7 win against Brooklyn at Ebbets Field.

1962 Commissioner Frick's proposal for interleague play in 1963 is rejected by the NL.

1963 The Tigers' Paul Foytack is the first ML pitcher to surrender four straight homers as the Indians' Woodie Held, pitcher Pete Ramos, Tito Francona, and Larry Brown feast on his offerings in rapid order.

1972 In a victory over the Twins, White Sox clubber Dick Allen is the first big leaguer since the Giants' Hank Thompson in 1950 to slap two inside-the-park homers in the same game.

1978 The Reds' Pete Rose singles off the Braves' Phil Niekro to extend his hitting streak to 44 games, tying Willie Keeler's 1897 single-season NL mark.

1981 After 50 days, the longest ML strike to date is settled, with the All-Star Game slated to be the first contest played subsequent to the settlement.

1989   Frank Viola is the first reigning Cy Young recipient to be traded the following season when the Mets acquire him from the Twins for Rick Aguilera and four lesser players.

1997   The Cards ship three pitchers to Oakland for slugger Mark McGwire's services, and although "Big Mac" leads the majors with 58 cumulative homers, he does not have enough taters in either loop to be its leader. Elsewhere, the Red Sox ship reliever Heathcliff Slocumb to the Mariners for prospects Jason Varitek and Derek Lowe, who are major contributors in the Sox' future success.

August

1

1895   Billy Kinlock debuts at third base for St. Louis in a game at Chicago. After a line shot by Bill Lange nearly decapitates him, Kinlock begs team captain Joe Quinn for his immediate release. Quinn assures him that no man alive could have stopped that ball, but Kinlock persists, saying he has a little girl in Denver who won't look good in black.

1896   New York garners slugging infielder Bill Joyce from Washington in return for catcher Duke Farrell, pitcher Carney Flynn, and $2,500.

1903   A's southpaw Rube Waddell holds eight members of the New York Highlanders hitless but loses 3–2 when the ninth Highlander, shortstop Kid Elberfeld, goes 4-for-4 to set an all-time ML record (since tied) for the most hits in a game by a player amassing all of his team's hits.

1918   Pittsburgh and Boston play a then record 20 scoreless innings before the Pirates push across two runs in the 21st frame to prevail 2–0 over the Braves' Art Nehf.

1919   The Giants obtain lefty Art Nehf from the Braves for four players and $55,000.

1925   The Yankees buy second baseman Tony Lazzeri from Salt Lake City of the PCL for 1926 delivery and then merrily watch Lazzeri pound 60 home runs and collect 222 RBI, both figures new OB records.

1945   The Giants' Mel Ott is the first NL performer to collect 500 home runs with a blast off the Braves' Johnny Hutchings into the upper right field stands in a night game at the Polo Grounds.

1951   At a House Judiciary Subcommittee's inquiry into baseball practices, George Trautman, president of the National Association of Professional Baseball Clubs, defends the farm club system against charges that it "might embody evils detrimental to the interests of ball players and the public."

1972   Against the Braves, Padres first baseman Nate Colbert ties a ML record with five home runs in a DBH and sets a new mark (since tied) with 13 ribbies.

1978   The Braves' Larry McWilliams and Gene Garber end the Reds' Pete Rose's NL single-season record-tying hitting streak at 44 games.

1985   Cardinals rookie Vince Coleman snags his 73rd sack to break the ML frosh record set by the Phillies' Juan Samuel the previous year, a mark Coleman stretches to 110 by year's end.

2005   The Orioles' Rafael Palmeiro is suspended and never plays another ML inning when he tests positive for steroids after adamantly denying their use in March before the House Government Reform Committee.

2

1930   In perhaps the first official Negro league game under artificial lighting, Smokey Joe Williams of the Homestead Grays fans 27 and allows only one hit in a 12-inning 1–0 win over Chet Brewer of the host Kansas City Monarchs.

1932   After Rogers Hornsby is fired as manager of the Cubs, first baseman Charlie Grimm assumes control and becomes the first man since Boston's John Morrill in 1883 to pilot a club to a pennant after taking the reins midstream.

1938   Dodgers GM Larry MacPhail portends Charlie Finley when he introduces baseballs dyed dandelion yellow in a DBH at Ebbets Field against the Cardinals.

1960   The Continental League abandons plans to become a third ML when Braves owner Lou Perini proposes that four of the circuit's cities be admitted as expansion clubs with the AL and NL.

1970   Baltimore downs KC for a record 23rd consecutive time over a two-year span.

1975   Billy Martin is named Yankees manager for the first time, replacing Bill Virdon.

167

1979   Yankees All-Star catcher Thurman Munson dies at the age of 32 when the private plane he is piloting crashes at the Canton-Akron Airport, where he is practicing takeoffs and landings.

1982   A's outfielder Rickey Henderson pilfers his 100th base, tying his own AL mark set the previous year.

1997   Houston's Brad Ausmus is the first catcher to provide television fans with a receiver's perspective of a game when he dons a Fox Sports Catcher-Cam atop his mask.

3

1892   Baltimore outfielder Jocko Halligan breaks teammate Cub Stricker's jaw during a poker game altercation and is unofficially black-listed by Orioles manager Ned Hanlon, keeping him out of pro ball until 1898 and out of the majors for the rest of his career.

1914   Yankees backstopper Les Nunamaker nabs an AL record three runners in the same inning trying to steal, but the Bengals still score two runs in the 2nd frame and go on to win, 4–1.

1920   Hal Chase is barred from all PCL parks after allegedly inviting PCL players to throw games.

1923   All ML games are canceled owing to the death of President Warren Harding the previous day, a goodwill gesture repeated for his funeral a week later.

1933   The A's Lefty Grove halts the Yankees' string of 308 consecutive games in which they have scored at least one run when he blanks them, 7–0.

1940   Subbing for injured receiver Ernie Lombardi, Willard Hershberger blames himself for several recent Cincinnati losses and commits suicide in his Hub hotel room while the Reds are at Braves Field splitting a DBH with Boston.

1944   Tommy Brown, at 16 years and eight months, is the youngest player to play two full ML contests in one day when he is at shortstop for Brooklyn in both ends of a DBH with the Cubs.

1960   Indians GM Frank Lane, always looking for a new trade wrinkle, talks Detroit GM Bill DeWitt into swapping skippers, and the Tribe's Joe Gordon and the Tigers' Jimmy Dykes switch dugouts.

1969   The Orioles' Dave McNally's two-year, 17-game winning streak ends when the Twins' Rich Reese smacks a pinch grand slam, making Jim Kaat the victor.

1986 White Sox rookie Russ Morman collects two hits in the 4th inning (a homer and a single), joining the Yanks' Billy Martin as the only two rookies to date to debut with two hits in an inning.

1987 During a game against the Angels, the Twins' Joe Niekro is ejected when he is caught on the mound with a file in his possession. AL president Bobby Brown later suspends him for 10 games.

1989 Cincinnati erupts for the most hits ever in the 1st inning of a ML game, blasting Astros pitching for 16 safe blows in an 18–1 rout.

1990 The Braves trade two-time MVP Dale Murphy to the Phillies for reliever Jeff Parrett and two players named later.

2004 Cards All-Star Albert Pujols is the first player in ML history to hit as many as 30 homers in each of his first four seasons.

4

1897 NL umpire Tim Hurst is hauled from the Cincinnati park in handcuffs after he hurls a beer stein that was thrown at him by an angry fan back into the stands, injuring an innocent spectator.

1909 Tim Hurst, now officiating in the AL, spits at A's second baseman Eddie Collins when Collins questions one of his calls, leading to the pugnacious umpire's permanent banishment from the majors.

1960 After a brushback pitch, the Reds' Billy Martin punches Cubs pitcher Jim Brewer, fracturing the hurler's cheekbone and hospitalizing him for nearly two months.

1979 Braves ace Phil Niekro's knuckleball flutters with a will of its own, as he ties two post-1900 ML records with six wild pitches and four in one inning, leading to a 6–2 loss to the Astros.

1982 In an afternoon game, the Mets' Joel Youngblood strokes a hit off Cubs Hall of Famer Fergie Jenkins and is then traded to Montreal, where he singles that night against another Cooperstown inductee, the Phillies' Steve Carlton, becoming the only ML performer to date to play for two different teams in two different cities on the same day.

1985 Two major milestones occur on the same day when the Angels' Rod Carew reaches the Twins' Frank Viola for his 3,000 career hit and the White Sox' Tom Seaver beats the Yankees on "Phil Rizzuto Day" at Yankee Stadium for his 300th career win.

1989 For the third time in his career, the Blue Jays' Dave Stieb loses a no-hitter with two down in the 9th. Stieb's disappointment is amplified in that he is headed for a perfect game until the Yanks' Roberto Kelly doubles to spoil his latest bid for immortality, and Steve Sax follows with a run-scoring single to deprive the Jays ace of a shutout as well.

1992 Actor Charlie Sheen pays $85,000 for the ball that went through Red Sox first baseman Bill Buckner's legs, culminating the Mets' incredible comeback win in Game 6 of the 1986 World Series.

2007 At 32 years and eight days, the Yankees' Alex Rodriguez is the youngest player to reach 500 career homers.

5

1884 Ed and Bill Dugan are the first brothers to debut as ML battery mates when Ed pitches the Virginia club's opening game in the AA as a replacement for Washington and loses 14–0 to Philadelphia.

1921 Radio station KDKA in Pittsburgh is the first to broadcast a baseball game when Harold Arlin, grandfather of future ML pitcher Steve Arlin, announces a contest between the Phils and Pirates.

1952 Bobby Shantz of the fifth-place A's is the first ML pitcher in 1952 to reach "the charmed circle" when he collects his 20th victory, 5–3 over Boston. The win lifts Shantz's season mark to a sensational 20–3 at that point, while the rest of the A's staff is a weak 31–45.

1953 Four days after setting a then ML record by appearing in eight consecutive games in relief, Red Sox rookie Ben Flowers blanks the Browns 5–0 in what will not only be his first ML start and his lone ML shutout but also his only complete game.

1984 Toronto's Cliff Johnson blasts his 19th career pinch homer off Baltimore's Tippy Martinez to break Jerry Lynch's ML mark for career pinch dingers. Johnson extends the record he still holds to 20 before departing.

1999 When the Cardinals' Mark McGwire takes Padres hurler Alan Ashby deep for his 500th career homer, he is the first slugger to reach that milestone after crashing the 400 barrier only a year earlier.

2001 Trailing the Mariners 14–2 after six innings in a nationally televised game, the Indians stage a stunning comeback and win 15–14 in 11 innings to become just the third ML team to rally from a 12-run deficit.

2007 The Yankees' Mike Mussina beats the Royals 8–5 for his 246th career victory, eclipsing the mark he shared with Dennis Martinez for the most career wins in ML history among hurlers who never bagged at least 20 triumphs in a season.

6

1886   Detroit buys second baseman Fred Dunlap from NL rival St. Louis for a reported $4,700, perhaps the highest sum paid to that point for the acquisition of a single player (some sources contend that Buffalo NL sold pitcher Jim Galvin to Pittsburgh AA for $5,000 in 1885).

1893   Chicago outfielder Jimmy Ryan is lost for the season after he miraculously escapes becoming the only ML player ever killed in a train wreck while on the road.

1930   Waco outfielder Gene Mercantelli (aka Rye) sets an all-time OB record when he goes yard three times in one inning, the 8th, as Waco routs Beaumont 22–4 in a Texas League game.

1942   Former Red Sox pitcher Gordon McNaughton is slain by a jealous husband when he is caught in a tryst at a Chicago hotel.

1949   Giants lefty Adrian Zabala beats the Cards 3–1 after his 1st inning balk cancels St. Louis first sacker Nippy Jones's apparent two-run homer. The obvious injustice to Jones and the Cards later results in a new rule enabling a team at bat to retain a desirable outcome if a balk is called as a pitch is delivered.

1953   Upon returning from military service, BoSox star Ted Williams pops out as a pinch hitter in a loss to the Browns but then rips 37 hits in his remaining 90 at bats, including 13 home runs and 34 RBI.

1962   Reds reliever Johnny Klippstein drills a homer off Don McMahon in the 13th inning to beat the Astros 1–0, marking the latest inning to date that a pitcher has ever won a 1–0 game with a dinger.

1967   The Orioles' Brooks Robinson hits into his record-breaking fourth career triple play.

1969   Twins pitcher Dave Boswell is hospitalized and requires 20 stitches after his manager, Billy Martin, flattens him during a clubhouse dispute.

1981   To rekindle interest after a prolonged strike, ML owners divide the season in half, allowing every team to start over from scratch in an effort to earn a postseason berth in a divisional playoff series.

1985   Big leaguers go on strike for the second time in four years, but the stoppage lasts only two days before owners and players reach an agreement that includes hiking the ML minimum salary to $60,000.

1992   For the first time in his 26-year career, the Rangers' Nolan Ryan is ejected after he hits A's outfielder Willie Wilson with a pitch and the two nearly come to blows.

1999   After the Padres' Tony Gwynn singles off Expos rookie Dan Smith for his 3,000th career hit, Gwynn is greeted at first base by his former college teammate, Kerwin Danley, who is umping at first that day.

2001   The HOF Veterans Committee, established in 1953, is replaced by a group of 90 members, including Hall of Famers, writers, broadcasters, and former Veterans Committee members. The new group is licensed to elect players only once every two years and nonplaying personnel once every four years.

7

1894   Boston outfielder Jimmy Bannon is the first MLer to hit a grand slam homer in two consecutive games when he goes deep with the sacks jammed in the 5th inning of a 19–8 win over Philadelphia's Kid Carsey. Chicago shortstop Bill Dahlen's then ML record 42-game hitting streak comes to a cruel end when he draws the collar while the rest of his mates pile up 18 hits in a 13–11 win over Cincinnati.

1938   Alex Swails of Muskogee in the Western Association sets an all-time OB record when he issues 32 walks in eight innings of a 16–7 loss to Ponca City.

1956   Red Sox outfielder Ted Williams is fined $5,000 by team GM Joe Cronin for spitting at Boston fans who booed him for dropping a fly ball in the 11th inning of the Sox' 1–0 win over the Yankees.

1992   Spendthrift Boston slugger Jack Clark files for bankruptcy, owing more than $11,000,000 despite assets that include 18 cars.

1999   A day after Tony Gwynn joins the list, the Devil Rays' Wade Boggs strokes his 3,000th hit and is the unlikely first member to enter the exclusive club with a homer.

2001   The Braves' Greg Maddux breaks the NL record for the most consecutive innings without allowing a walk (68), shared by the Giants' Christy Mathewson (1913) and the Padres' Randy Jones (1976). Maddux's streak ends at 72⅓ innings in the 2nd frame of his next start.

2007   The Giants' Barry Bonds surpasses Hank Aaron as MLB's all-time home-run king by blasting his 756th round-tripper off Nats chucker Mike Bacsik Jr.

8

1899   Pirates third sacker Jimmy Williams launches a 27-game hitting streak that stands as a rookie record until 1987.

1903   When a section of the leftfield bleachers in the Philadelphia NL park collapses during the 4th inning of the second game of a DBH with Boston, play is immediately halted after 12 people are killed and 282 injured, representing the worst ballpark disaster in ML history.

1921   After replacing Marty McManus at second base in a 16–5 blowout loss to Washington, Browns rookie Luke Stuart achieves all of the following in his lone at bat this day: He collects his only big league hit, collects his only two ML RBI, is the first player in AL history to homer in his first ML AB, and goes deep against none other than Walter Johnson.

1922   Giants manager John McGraw suspends pitcher Phil Douglas, launching a chain of events that culminates in Commissioner Landis barring Douglas for life.

1934   Longtime player and manager Wilbert Robinson dies in Atlanta at the age of 71.

1941   In an apparent double suicide, former ML pitcher Ralph Works slays his wife and then fatally shoots himself.

1946   Three days after Mickey Owen quits the Mexican League, he and former Dodgers teammate Luis Olmo apply for reinstatement in the majors but are rejected by Commissioner Chandler, initiating a flurry of legal actions that eventually grant Owen his wish, but not until the 1949 season is half over.

1949   Dodgers right fielder Carl Furillo awakens in the morning the owner of a lackluster .269 BA in 96 games, but a 2-for-4 day in the afternoon in a 2–1 win over the Giants ignites a remarkable hot streak in which Furillo hits .431 (78-for-181) in the remaining 46 games to lift his final mark to .322 and help Brooklyn cop the NL pennant by a one-game margin.

1952   Bob Neighbors, a member of the 1939 St. Louis Browns, is the only MLer ever to be listed as MIA when he goes missing to this day during a combat mission in North Korea.

1976   White Sox owner Bill Veeck is at it again as he has his players don navy blue Bermuda shorts in the first game of a DBH.

1988   The initial ML night game at Wrigley Field is rained out, and the first official game under the lights is played the next day, with the Bruins downing the Mets, 6–4.

1990   Pete Rose begins serving a five-month sentence for tax evasion in a Marion, IL, federal work camp.

1997   Seattle's Randy Johnson fans 19 White Sox, the first twirler to fan that many twice in one season in a nine-inning game after previously doing it in June.

2002   After years of heel dragging, MLB finally requires mandatory testing for steroids beginning in 2003.

9

1905   A few days before he is sold to Detroit, outfielder Ty Cobb of Augusta in the South Atlantic League receives word that his mother purportedly shot his father to death after mistaking him for an intruder.

1916   The A's halt an AL-record skein of 19 straight road losses when Joe Bush wins 7–1 at Detroit.

1918   Cincinnati manager Christy Mathewson boots first baseman Hal Chase off the Reds when he suspects him of rigging games, but the National Commission rules in favor of restoring Chase after the season ends; Chase leaves the majors at the close of the 1919 season forever suspected of fixing games but is never formally banned.

1946   For the first time in ML history, all of the eight scheduled games at eight different sites on this Friday night are played under the lights.

1956   Washington is the last team in the AL to be licensed to sell beer in its home park, Griffith Stadium.

1976   With his induction to Cooperstown as an umpire, Cal Hubbard is the first man elected to two pro sports Halls of Fame, having been previously inducted to the pro football shrine in Canton, OH, in 1963.

1981   In the first ML game played after a lengthy strike, more than 70,000 fans fill Cleveland's Municipal Stadium to watch the NL win the annual All-Star Game, 5–4.

1998 Braves righty Dennis Martinez wins his 244th career game, topping Juan Marichal as the winningest Latin American hurler, a mark he extends to 245 before retiring.

2001 Colorado's Mike Hampton launches his seventh homer of the season, tying the NL season mark for pitchers.

2007 After struggling unsuccessfully with his control for nearly three years, former Cards pitcher Rick Ankiel returns to the Birds as an outfielder and rockets a three-run homer in his first game back.

10

1901 Washington pitcher Dale Gear surrenders an AL-record 41 total bases in a 13–0 loss to the Athletics.

1938 The Reds acquire shortstop Eddie Miller from the Braves for pitcher Johnny Babich, outfielder Vince DiMaggio, three lesser players, and cash.

1944 The Braves' Red Barrett sets the ML record for the fewest documented pitches needed to hurl a nine-inning complete game when he sets down Cincinnati 2–0 on just 58 deliveries.

1952 Ron Necciai, the phenom who began the season in Class D, makes his ML debut with the Pirates and is blasted for 11 hits in six innings before being removed in his 9–5 loss to the Cubs. Necciai, just 20 years old, makes eight more starts for Pittsburgh after being rushed to the majors by Branch Rickey and then disappears from the show the owner of a 7.08 career ERA and a ruined arm.

1962 Columbus hurler Bob Veale fans an IL record 22 Buffalo batters in nine innings.

1971 Bob Davids gathers a group of 16 baseball researchers in Cooperstown and forms the Society for American Baseball Research.

1980 In losing to Seattle 2–1, Steve McCatty is the fourth different Oakland hurler this season to toss a 14-inning complete game, joining teammates Matt Keough, Mike Norris, and Rick Langford. Manager Billy Martin is later skewered by critics blaming the quartet's subsequent arm woes on overwork.

1981 The Phillies' Pete Rose strokes his 3,631st career hit off Cards reliever Mark Littell to top Stan Musial's NL record.

2002 Cubs slammer Sammy Sosa hits three homers in one game for the sixth time in his career, tying Hall of Famer Johnny Mize's mark.

Elsewhere, the Giants' Barry Bonds breaks Willie McCovey's ML record by drawing his 46th intentional walk. Bonds extends his new standard to 68 before the season ends.

11

1884   In his initial pitching appearance with Washington of the UA, Charlie Geggus sets a ML mark (since broken) for the most K's by a performer in his first game as a hurler when he fans 14 in a 5–3 win over Boston.

1906   Outfielder Tom Burke of Lynn in the New England League dies when surgery to remove a blood clot formed on his brain after Fall River's Joe Jerger beaned him fails to restore him to consciousness.

1929   Babe Ruth hits his 500th career home run in a 6–5 loss to Cleveland's Willis Hudlin.

1941   Yankees ace Lefty Gomez walks 11 men, the most ever in a complete-game nine-inning shutout, as he beats the Browns, 9–0.

1942   A ML rule at that time that no game begun in daylight can end under artificial lights bizarrely results in the first game of a twilight DBH at Cleveland being called by darkness in the 14th inning with the score 0–0 and the lights then turned on prior to the second game, won by Detroit, 3–2.

1946   The Phillies pare the Dodgers NL lead to half a game when they sweep a twinbill at Shibe Park, breaking a record string of 18 consecutive home losses to Brooklyn dating back to May 5, 1945.

1951   The Braves and Brooklyn split a Saturday DBH at Ebbets Field, with the first game marking the initial ML contest to be telecast in color.

1961   The Braves' Warren Spahn beats the Cubs 2–1 to become the first NL lefty to win 300 games.

1970   The Phillies' Jim Bunning is the first pitcher since Cy Young to win 100 games in both leagues after racking up 118 victories with the Tigers prior to moving to the NL.

2001   The Giants' Barry Bonds attains 50 homers at a record rate, gaining the plateau in only his 117th game of the year.

2003   The Cubs' Kerry Wood is the quickest big league pitcher to total 1,000 career strikeouts, reaching the mark in only his 134th hill appearance.

12

1877 Catcher John Quigley of the Poughkeepsie Harlem Clippers dies of injuries sustained in a semipro game at Wappingers Falls, NY, on July 7, when future Hall of Famer Dan Brouthers, at the time a southpaw pitcher with the Wappingers Falls Actives, collided with him near home plate as he was attempting to catch a pop fly bunt.

1929 Outfielder George Quellich of the IL Reading Keys sets an OB record when he collects his 15th consecutive hit over a four-day span before being stopped by Montreal's Elam Vangilder.

1951 The Giants begin the day 13 games behind the Dodgers, but a DBH win over the Phillies in the afternoon launches a comeback that brings the New Yorkers 39 wins in the final 47 games of the season.

1966 After entering the game in the 8th inning, Reds outfielder Art Shamsky hits three home runs, all of which either tie the game or put his team in the lead, but Cincinnati still loses to Pittsburgh 14–11 in 13 innings.

1974 The Angels' Nolan Ryan whiffs 19 Red Sox to eclipse Bob Feller's then AL mark for a nine-inning game.

1987 The Tigers acquire Doyle Alexander from the Braves for the pennant stretch and are pleased when he goes 9–0 with a 1.53 ERA, but only in the short term, as they surrender future Cy Young winner John Smoltz in the deal.

1988 The Red Sox top the A's AL mark, set in 1931, for the most consecutive wins at home by capturing their 23rd straight at Fenway. They extend the figure to 24 the following day before falling 18–6 to the Tigers.

1994 The players begin a costly strike that will not be settled this season.

13

1897 Chicago pitcher Clark Griffith ends the longest skein ever by a ML pitcher before registering his first shutout when he blanks Cincinnati 2–0 for the 104th win of his career.

1906 Jack Taylor of the Cubs is knocked out of the box in the 3rd inning by Brooklyn, ending his string of 188 consecutive complete-game starts.

1932 The Yankees' Red Ruffing is the first ML pitcher since Tom Hughes in 1906 to win a 1–0 game in extra innings with his own home run when he goes deep in the 10th frame at Griffith Stadium to beat Washington's Tommy Thomas.

1945 Branch Rickey and two associates, one of them Walter O'Malley, acquire controlling interest in the Dodgers for $750,000.

1947 Browns outfielder Willard Brown is the first African American to homer in an AL game when he tags an IPHR off Detroit's Hal Newhouser.

1948 Viewed as a publicity stunt when Bill Veeck signed him to a Cleveland contract, Satchel Paige continues to prove anything but as he holds the White Sox to five singles in a 5–0 shutout in front of a Friday night crowd of 51,013 at Comiskey Park.

1949 Frank Wilson of Harlan in the Mountain States League wins his second DBH in two days and fifth of the season when he beats Morristown, 9–8 and 11–3. Three of Wilson's victories are complete games, a post–World War II OB record for the most complete games in a two-day period.

1964 In a sign of future trends, CBS purchases 80% of the Yankees and takes control of the club on November 2, beginning an era of mediocrity.

1969 Reds slugger Johnny Bench hits a grand slam in the 11th against the Expos' Roy Face, dooming the reliever to retire with a ML record 21 extra-frame blasts yielded.

1995 Liver cancer claims the life of Yankees great Mickey Mantle at the age of 63 in Dallas, TX.

2007 Detroit's Placido Polanco plays his 144th consecutive errorless game at second, breaking Luis Castillo's record set earlier in the season.

14

1855 The Atlantic Club of Brooklyn is organized and soon becomes the most dominant team in the game, winning eight of the 10 whip pennants awarded annually between 1859 and 1868.

1888 Chicago rookie Gus Krock stops Tim Keefe's winning streak at 19 games when he beats Keefe's pennant-bound New York Giants 4–2 at the Polo Grounds.

1932 Brooklyn's Jack Quinn, at the age of 49, is the oldest pitcher to date to win a ML game when he tops the Giants in 10 innings, courtesy of Johnny Frederick's record-setting fourth pinch homer of the season.

1940 Former Cubs shortstop Charlie Hollocher shoots himself to death 16 years after walking away from the game at the age of 28 because he thought it was destroying his health.

1947 Former Philadelphia A's pitcher Woody Crowson is killed when his Greensboro team bus collides with a watermelon truck owned by former Dodgers fireballer Van Lingle Mungo as Crowson's club is returning home from Martinsdale after a Carolina League game.

1952 Pitcher Ned Garver rejoices when he is traded by the Browns, a perennial tailender, to the Tigers, a perennial contender, as part of an eight-player deal that brings slugger Vic Wertz to St. Louis, but Garver's black cloud follows him when the Tigers finish last in 1952 for the first time in their history.

1958 Vic Power is the first MLer since 1927 to steal home twice in the same game when he follows his 8th-inning theft with an encore performance in the 10th to bring Cleveland a 10–9 win over Detroit. Power's two swipes not only represent two-thirds of his season total, but the second also marks the only time in an eight-day period that the struggling Indians score after loading the bases.

1968 MLB officially opens its doors to Canada as Montreal joins the NL for 1969.

1984 The Reds reacquire Pete Rose in a trade with the Expos for infielder Tom Lawless and make "Charlie Hustle" the team's player-manager.

1986 Giants reliever Greg Minton surrenders the Reds' Pete Rose's 4,256th and final career hit.

1987 The A's Mark McGwire pounds his 39th homer, setting a new rookie mark that he extends to a whopping 49 by the season's end.

1999 The Rangers' Ivan Rodriguez is the first ML catcher to hit 20 homers and swipe 20 bases in a season.

2007 Umpire Ted Barrett helps put Braves manager Bobby Cox in the ML record book by issuing the fiery skipper his 132nd ejection, eclipsing John McGraw's mark.

15

1885   Atlanta first sacker Louis Henke is the first player in a National Agreement pro league to die from an on-field injury when he expires from a ruptured liver after a first-base collision with Lefty Marr in a Southern League game the previous day.

1886   In addition to hitting three home runs to tie the then-existing ML single-game record, Louisville's Guy Hecker scores an all-time ML record seven runs as he hurls Louisville to a 22–5 win over Baltimore.

1926   Brooklyn outfielder Babe Herman is immortalized when a string of base-running gaffes results in him doubling into a double play in the first game of a DBH with the Braves, but the Dodgers still win the game, 4–2.

1945   Rookie commissioner Happy Chandler dumps the Ford Motor Co., which has been paying $100,000 annually to sponsor the World Series radio broadcast, to ink a new deal with Gillette for $150,000.

1965   Former Cleveland pitcher Stan Pitula takes his own life via carbon monoxide poisoning at the age of 34.

1991   The Yankees' Don Mattingly is benched and fined $250 for refusing to cut his shoulder-length hair.

1996   Pitcher Bobby Seay is the first amateur to be declared a free agent in the same summer he is chosen when the White Sox fail to tender their top pick a contract within MLB's 15-day limit after the draft.

2005   Against the Royals, 18-year-old Mariners hurler Felix Hernandez fans 11, becoming the first teenager to attain a double-figure strikeout total in a game since the Mets' Dwight Gooden in 1984.

16

1870   Before a large crowd at Brooklyn's Capitoline Grounds, 18-year-old Fred Goldsmith from New Haven, CT, demonstrates to sportswriter Henry Chadwick that he can make his pitches curve, but even so, Chadwick, a Brooklyn resident, later successfully champions Brooklyn pitching product Candy Cummings as the inventor of the curve ball.

1890   Chicago's Tom Burns and Mal Kittridge are the first teammates to hit grand slam homers in the same inning as their two four-run blasts off pitcher Bill Phillips spark Chicago NL to a 13-run 5th frame in its 18–5 win over Pittsburgh.

1893 Baltimore's Bill Hawke carves the first ML no-hitter at the 60′6″ distance in blanking Washington, 5–0.

1912 Walter Johnson's record AL single-season win streak (since tied) ends at 16 when he loses a game to the Browns in relief of starter Tom Hughes that under today's scoring rules would have been charged to Hughes.

1920 Cleveland shortstop Ray Chapman is the only unequivocal ML on-field player fatality to date after he is beaned by the Yankees' Carl Mays and dies that night of a fractured skull.

1948 Babe Ruth dies of throat cancer in New York at the age of 53.

1989 The Yankees' Luis Polonia is arrested in his hotel room for having sex with a 15-year-old girl and is sentenced to 60 days in jail.

1996 Padres outfielder Steve Finley is the first ML player to homer in three countries when he connects against the Mets in Monterrey, Nuevo León, Mexico, after previously going yard in the United States and Canada.

2002 At the Little League World Series, 14 members of the 1955 Cannon Street YMCA team from Charleston, SC, are honored after having won the Little League title 47 years earlier by forfeit when white teams refused to play them.

2005 When 87-year-old Bobby Bragan serves as pilot of the Fort Worth Cats in the Central League for one day, he is the oldest person ever to manage in pro ball and quickly shows that he has not lost his spunk by getting tossed for arguing balls and strikes in the 3rd inning.

2006 Veteran ump Bruce Froemming works his 5,000th game, joining Hall of Famer Bill Klem as the only two men in blue to reach the milestone.

17

1882 Providence wins the longest 1–0 game in ML history decided by a home run when the Grays top Detroit on Charley Radbourn's IPHR in the 18th inning.

1894 Headed for a horrendous 7.60 ERA in 22 starts, Louisville's Jack Wadsworth stops off in Philadelphia to hurl a 29–4 loss to the

Phils in which he allows 36 hits and faces a ML nine-inning record 67 batters.

1929 The Yankees buy pitcher Lefty Gomez from San Francisco of the PCL for delivery the following spring.

1933 Lou Gehrig breaks Everett Scott's former ML mark when he plays in his 1,308th consecutive game in a 7–6 loss to the Browns.

1952 One out away from joining the select list of hurlers who have debuted with consecutive shutouts in their first two starts, Cards rookie Stu Miller is betrayed by shortstop Solly Hemus, who makes a double error on Roy McMillan's ground ball, first fumbling it and then throwing wild, allowing Joe Adcock to score the lone Cincinnati run in Miller's 2–1 win.

1990 Carlton Fisk sets two records (both since broken) with one home run: the White Sox career club mark for taters (187) and the leadership in career homers by a catcher (328).

1999 Baltimore reliever Jesse Orosco surpasses Dennis Eckersley's career appearance mark by logging his 1,072nd game.

2002 The Yanks' Alfonso Soriano is the first ML second baseman to hit 30 homers and swipe 30 bases in the same season. Elsewhere, Rangers shortstop Alex Rodriguez is the first infielder to compile five straight 40-home run seasons and eventually extends the mark to six.

18

1893 Dummy Dundon, the first deaf mute in ML history, dies in Columbus, OH.

1902 Rochester first baseman Hal O'Hagan engineers the first documented unassisted triple play in pro history in an Eastern League game against Jersey City.

1952 Borrowing a page from the Yankees trade book, Cleveland garners shortstop George Strickland and pitcher Ted Wilks from Pittsburgh in an interleague waiver deal for outfielder Catfish Metkovich, a minor league pitcher, and $50,000.

1959 Branch Rickey gives up his duties as Pirates chairman of the board to assume his new role as president of the proposed Continental League.

1967 Tony Conigliaro is struck below the left eye by a pitch from the Angels' Jack Hamilton, knocking the popular Red Sox All-Star out of action until 1969.

1983 The resumption of the infamous "Pine Tar Game" takes just 12 minutes to finish, as the Royals win 5–4 with a "throng" of 1,245 fans (admitted for free) looking on.

2001 While pitching for the Bronx, Danny Almonte hurls the first perfect game in the Little League World Series since 1957, but the circuit subsequently forfeits all games won by Almonte's team after discovering that his true age is 14, two years over the limit, and that he did not even attend a Bronx school.

2007 For the first time in ML history, a player homers off a Cy Young winner who copped the award *before* the hitter was even born, as Tigers rookie Cameron Maybin connects against Yankees warhorse Roger Clemens.

19

1918 Working in his season-record 15th extra-inning game, Washington's Walter Johnson tops the St. Louis Browns 3–2 in 14 innings.

1921 Still only 34 years old, Ty Cobb is the youngest player to date to achieve 3,000 career hits when he goes 2-for-5 against Boston's Elmer Myers in the first game of a DBH.

1950 Gillette forks over $800,000 to acquire television sponsorship of the World Series.

1951 The Browns send Bill Veeck's newest promotional stunt, 3'7" midget Eddie Gaedel, up to bat for outfielder Frank Saucier, and Tigers pitcher Bob Cain, unable to control his laughter, walks Gaedel on four pitches. Commissioner Frick later tries unsuccessfully to have Gaedel's name expunged from the record book.

1957 Blaming poor attendance, Giants owner Horace Stoneham sells the team's board of directors on the notion of moving to San Francisco in 1958 by a near-unanimous vote of eight to one.

1965 Reds hurler Jim Maloney spins a 10-inning, complete-game no-hitter against the Cubs after tossing 10 hitless innings in a game earlier in the year before he eventually yielded a homer and lost.

1966 KC rookie Jim Nash suffers his only loss of the season, 7–5 to the Yankees. Despite not joining the A's until July 3, Nash posts a glittering 12–1 mark, tying Perry Werden (1884) for the best record by a ML yearling in more than 10 decisions.

1969 Former ML hurler John Hollison dies in Chicago, IL, at the age of 99, but none of his obits note that he was the last surviving MLer to pitch from a rectangular box 50 feet from the plate 77 years earlier.

1983 The Dodgers ship chuckers Dave Stewart and Ricky Wright to the Rangers for hurler Rick Honeycutt, freezing Honeycutt's AL-leading ERA at 2.42 and enabling him to win the junior loop ERA title.

1992 Seattle's Bret Boone debuts, making him the first third-generation ML player, following his father, Bob, and grandfather, Ray.

20

1886 In the first double one-hit game in ML history, Baltimore rookie Matt Kilroy needs only a 1st-inning run to best Philadelphia's Cyclone Miller 1–0 in front of a sparse home crowd.

1919 Wichita outfielder Joe Wilhoit is stopped by two Tulsa hurlers after setting a new OB record by hitting safely in 69 consecutive Western League games.

1937 Jorge Comellas of Salisbury in the Eastern Shore League is tagged with his first loss of the season after collecting 20 straight wins. Comellas finishes 22–1 and teammate Joe Kohlman 25–1, giving Salisbury the winningest hill tandem in OB history with a combined 47–2 mark.

1938 Lou Gehrig extends his ML record when he tags his 23rd and last career grand slam in the Yankees' 11–3 blasting of the A's Buck Ross.

1945 Dodgers shortstop Tommy Brown sets another youngest-ever mark when he homers at the age of 17 for Brooklyn's only run in a 11–1 loss to Pirates southpaw Preacher Roe.

1948 In front of a crowd of 78,382 at Cleveland Municipal Stadium, the then largest crowd to witness a night game, Satchel Paige hurls the Indians staff's fourth consecutive whitewash and brings the Tribe within two innings of the AL record for consecutive shutout innings when he blanks the White Sox, 1–0.

1961 John Buzhardt ends the Phillies' post–1900 ML record of 23 straight losses, beating Milwaukee's Carlton Willey, 7–4.

1963 In his first ML start, the Mets' 22-year-old Grover Powell blanks the Phils, but he never wins another game after being struck in the face by a line drive in his next start. Forced to change his delivery for his self-protection, Powell injures his arm that winter in Venezuela, ending his career.

1964   After being swept by the White Sox, the Yanks' Phil Linz plays *Mary Had a Little Lamb* on his harmonica in the team bus. When he ignores manager Yogi Berra's order to stop, Berra slaps the instrument from the infielder's hands. The ensuing fight is credited with igniting the Bombers' subsequent pennant stretch run.

1974   California's Nolan Ryan fans 19 Tigers in a 1–0, 11-inning loss, the third time in the season he whiffs that many in a game.

1998   At Shea Stadium, the Cards' Mark McGwire blasts his 50th homer, becoming the first ML player to reach that plateau for three consecutive seasons after totaling 58 in 1997 and 52 in 1996.

2007   White Sox reliever Bobby Jenks's record-tying 41 consecutive batters retired streak ends when the Royals' Joey Gathright slaps a single.

21

1881   To the disgust of fans expecting to see a game between two crack semipro teams at full strength, the Eclipse club of Louisville refuses to allow the visiting Cleveland Whites to play their African American catcher, Moses Walker.

1883   In front of a home crowd, many of them present to watch Rhode Island native Art Hagan pitch for Philadelphia, Providence pounds Hagan and the Quakers, 28–0, for the most one-sided shutout in ML history.

1890   When Jersey Bakely of the Cleveland PL club absorbs a 13–1 shellacking at New York, he earns the distinction of being the only pitcher in ML history to lose 20 or more games in four different leagues. Bakely previously lost 20 or more for teams in the UA, AA, and NL.

1901   To demonstrate that player hooliganism will not be tolerated in his fledgling ML enterprise, AL president Ban Johnson expels Chicago shortstop Frank Shugart from the junior loop "for all time," or so he thinks, after Shugart slugs umpire Jack Haskell in a game against Washington.

1915   In one of the most significant player trades to date, the White Sox receive outfielder Joe Jackson from Cleveland in return for 1915 AL home-run king Braggo Roth, two lesser players, and $31,500.

1932 Cleveland's Wes Ferrell is the first post–1892 ML hurler to reach the 20-win circle in each of his first four full seasons when he beats Washington, 11–5.

1947 Williamsport, PA, hosts the first Little League World Series, won by the Maynard Midgets of none other than Williamsport.

1948 Cleveland sets a then AL record of 47 consecutive shutout innings when Bob Lemon holds the White Sox scoreless through eight frames, only to lose 3–2 in the 9th on home runs by Aaron Robinson and Dave Philley.

1952 The Class D Pony League features the first double no-hit game in OB history that is still recognized as such, when Frank Etchberger of Bradford nips Jim Mitchell of Batavia 1–0, with Bradford scoring the game's lone run in the 8th inning on a walk, a sacrifice, and a wild pitch, followed by a ground out bringing the runner home from third base.

1971 The Reds' Jim Merritt, working in relief, earns his only victory of the season to go with 11 losses, a shocking plummet from the previous year when he bagged 20 victories with Cincinnati.

1975 After the Cubs' Rick Reuschel leaves the game with a blister on his finger without yielding a run to the Dodgers, his brother Paul completes the shutout, marking the first combined whitewash spun by a pair of siblings.

1983 The South Atlantic League's Vince Coleman and the Carolina League's Donnell Nixon both break Rickey Henderson's single-season OB record by pilfering their 131st base. Coleman subsequently finishes with 145, one more than Nixon.

1985 In the Florida State League, Vero Beach skipper Stan Wasiak is the first minor league pilot to notch 2,500 career victories in a 3–2 win over Miami.

22

1891 Chicago NL outfielder Walt Wilmot coaxes six walks from Cleveland pitchers to set a ML single-game record that has since been tied.

1917 The Pirates set a NL record when they play their fourth straight extra-inning game, losing 6–5 to Brooklyn in 22 innings.

1926 The A's host the first Sunday ML game played in the city of Philadelphia and edge the White Sox 3–2, but a court later decrees that the game was illegal, and Sunday ball does not become a staple in Philadelphia until 1934. Elsewhere, Moose Clabaugh of Tyler in the East Texas League hits his 61st home run to break Tony Lazzeri's year-old OB single-season home-run mark of 60 and extends the new record to 62 by the season's end.

1933 Cubs president William Veeck receives little support when he proposes interleague games during the regular season.

1949 The Yankees orchestrate the first of a string of late-season interleague transactions over the next few years that strain credibility when they purchase slugger Johnny Mize from the Giants for $40,000 after Mize somehow passes through waivers.

1957 Stan Musial's then NL-record streak of 895 consecutive games played ends when he injures his shoulder in a game at Philadelphia.

1961 The Yanks' Roger Maris is the first ML player to reach 50 homers in August when he connects against the Angels' Ken McBride.

1965 After tempers flare over brushback pitches, the Giants' Juan Marichal clubs Dodgers catcher Johnny Roseboro over the head with a bat, launching a huge on-field brawl between the two clubs, with Marichal later getting slapped with an eight-game suspension and a $1,750 fine.

1974 In a Carolina League game, Salem outfielder Alfredo Edmead is racing for a pop fly when his head collides with second baseman Pablo Cruz's knee, which is protected by a metal brace, and his skull is fatally crushed.

1989 The Rangers' Nolan Ryan K's Oakland's Rickey Henderson, becoming the first pitcher to fan 5,000 batters.

1999 Cards slugger Mark McGwire is the first MLer to pole 50 homers in four consecutive seasons.

2000 Catcher Brent Mayne works a scoreless relief inning against the Braves as the Rockies win 7–6 in 12 innings, making him the first ML position player to collect a victory since Yankees outfielder Rocky Colavito in 1968.

2007 In the first game of a DBH, the Rangers are the first team to score 30 runs in a game since the Chicago Colts in 1897 when they roast the Orioles 30–9 and follow by scoring nine more runs in the nightcap to break the AL record for tallies (39) in a DBH.

23

1887 Future ML catcher Bill Farmer, while behind the bat for Shamokin in a Pennsylvania League game, riles the crowd when he is observed having a loaded pistol concealed behind his chest protector.

1906 The White Sox set an AL record (since broken) when Roy Patterson gains their 19th straight win by beating the Senators' Cy Falkenberg 4–1 at Washington. The skein ends two days later when the Sox lose both ends of a DBH in the nation's capital.

1914 After occupying the NL cellar scarcely a month earlier, the Boston Braves move into a tie for first place with New York when the Giants lose 3–2 to Cincinnati.

1930 The Yankees mark another promising minor leaguer for delivery the following spring when they obtain shortstop Frank Crosetti from San Francisco of the PCL for cash and infielder Julie Wera.

1931 Lefty Grove's consecutive wins streak is stopped at 16 when A's teammate Johnny Moore botches Ski Melillo's routine fly ball, allowing Fred Schulte to tally the only run that the Browns' Dick Coffman needs to top Grove, 1–0.

1936 In his first ML start, Bob Feller, Cleveland's 17-year-old flame thrower, fans a then rookie-record 15 batters as he beats the St. Louis Browns, 4–1.

1953 Phil Paine and Leo Kiely are the first ex-ML players to play in Japan when each pitches in a Japanese league while serving in the military abroad. Paine and Kiely are also the first performers to return to the majors after playing in Japan when each rejoins his former team, the Braves and the Red Sox, respectively, the following year.

1964 Mets reliever Willard Hunter beats the Cubs in both ends of a DBH, accounting for half of his four career victories.

1970 Pirates outfielder Roberto Clemente is the first big leaguer since Brooklyn's Hy Myers in 1917 to smack five hits in two consecutive games, all of them coming against the Dodgers.

1980 An era in Oakland comes to an end when Charlie Finley agrees to sell the A's for $12,700,000 to the Haas family, owners of Levi Strauss.

1982 After three decades of suspected spheroid hoodoo, Seattle's Gaylord Perry is finally ejected for doctoring a baseball at the tender age of 44.

1989   Dodgers catcher Rick Dempsey homers off Dennis Martinez in the top of the 22nd inning to snap a scoreless deadlock and beat the Expos, 1–0.

1998   The Giants' Barry Bonds homers against the Marlins, making him the first MLer to rap 400 career jacks and snag 400 stolen bases.

1999   Commissioner Selig extends an olive branch by announcing that Pete Rose is invited to the Fall Classic if he is voted to MLB's All-Century Team.

2001   Diamondbacks flamethrower Randy Johnson is the first ML pitcher to fan 300 batters in four straight seasons. Elsewhere, in his 10–0 win against the Mets, Rockies rookie Jason Jennings is the first pitcher in ML history to spin a shutout and hit a homer in his ML debut.

24

1919   Cleveland pitcher Ray Caldwell nearly becomes the first on-the-spot fatality in a ML game when he is leveled by a bolt of lightning with two out in the 9th inning, but he then recovers to retire Joe Dugan and complete a 2–1 win over Philadelphia.

1943   The A's end their AL record 22-game road losing streak when knuckleballer Roger Wolff beats the White Sox 8–1 in the second game of a DBH.

1945   Cleveland's Bob Feller returns from naval duty and demonstrates that he has lost nothing but time as he fans 12 in a 4–2 win over Detroit's Hal Newhouser.

1961   Red Sox star outfielder Jackie Jensen refuses to fly to LA for a series against the Angels, and the Sox announce that they will not pay him for games he misses due to his fear of flying.

1963   For the first time, the Little League World Series is televised as ABC's *Wide World of Sports* covers the championship game, with Grenada Hills, CA, downing Stratford, CT, 2–1.

1967   Phils slugger Richie Allen is shelved for the rest of the year when his hand goes through a headlight while he is pushing his stalled car.

1976   After a poll of local fans, Seattle selects the Mariners as the expansion team's nickname.

1982 By swiping his 31st base, the Royals' John Wathan breaks the White Sox' Ray Schalk's 1916 mark for steals by a catcher. Wathan extends his new mark to 36 by the end of the season.

1983 Orioles southpaw Tippy Martinez picks off three Blue Jays (Barry Bonnell, Dave Collins, and Willie Upshaw) in the top of the 10th inning as Toronto is overzealous in seeking an opportunity to test the arm of infielder Lenn Sakata, who is pressed into an emergency cameo catching appearance. Sakata becomes the hero in the bottom of the inning with a game-ending three-run homer.

1989 Commissioner Bart Giamatti bans Pete Rose from baseball for life for gambling, but while Rose accepts the penalty, he has yet to admit to betting on baseball.

2006 Albert Belle, one of the game's top sluggers in the 1990s, is sentenced to 60 days in Maricopa County (AZ) Superior Court for stalking a former paid escort after putting a tracking device on her car.

25

1922 The Phils compile 26 hits and score 23 runs against five Cubs pitchers but lose 26–23 when they leave the bases loaded in the top of the 9th, as the two teams score a record 49 runs combined.

1939 Yankees third sacker Red Rolfe scores in his 18th consecutive game to set a ML mark (since tied).

1952 Detroit's Virgil Trucks is the second AL pitcher in two years to toss two no-hitters in the same season when he stops the Yankees 1–0.

1956 Yankees shortstop Phil Rizzuto is consulted by team brass as to who on the club should be released to make room for Enos Slaughter, acquired that day from KC, and to Rizzuto's dismay, he discovers that he is the intended victim.

1965 Moonlight Graham, immortalized in W. P. Kinsella's *Field of Dreams* despite having played just one game for the 1905 Giants, dies in Chisholm, MN.

1967 The Eastern League York White Roses are no-hit victims for the fourth time in the season en route to a .217 team BA, which provides York's pitchers with so little offensive support that starter Dick Such, despite owning a fine 2.81 ERA, finishes the season 0–16.

1968 Yankees outfielder Rocky Colavito relieves for 2⅔ innings against the Tigers to earn a 6–5 win and remains the last position player to notch a victory until 2000.

1980   Rangers Canadian-born pitcher Fergie Jenkins is arrested in Toronto after customs officials find nearly $500 worth of cocaine, hashish, and marijuana in his suitcase.

1983   The Louisville Redbirds of the AA are the first minor league team to draw 1,000,000 fans in a season.

1985   By beating the Padres for his 14th straight victory, Mets hurler Dwight Gooden is the youngest pitcher since Willie McGill in 1891 to win 20 games in a season.

1999   While preserving a win against Baltimore, KC's Jeff Montgomery is the first reliever to notch 300 saves exclusively with one team.

2001   At the age of 38, the Yankees' Paul O'Neill hits his 20th homer of the season, becoming the oldest ML player to crank 20 dingers and steal 20 bases in the same campaign.

26

1929   Abraham G. Mills, former NL president and author of both the National Agreement and the original reserve clause, dies in obscurity at the age of 84 and remains there today despite his enormous contributions to the game in comparison to, say, one Morgan Bulkeley.

1930   Cubs gardener Hack Wilson breaks Chuck Klein's year-old NL dinger record when he makes good on a pregame promise to Cubs starter Sheriff Blake and cracks his 44th jack in a 7–5 win over Pittsburgh's Larry French.

1939   W2XBS in New York City hires Red Barber to broadcast the first ML games ever televised, a DBH at Ebbets Field between the Dodgers and pennant-bound Reds.

1947   Brooklyn's Dan Bankhead, appearing in relief, is the first documented ML African American hurler and also the first African American to homer in his first ML AB in a 16–3 loss to Pittsburgh's Fritz Ostermueller.

1955   Cleveland's pennant chances are dealt an irrevocable blow when slugging first baseman Vic Wertz contracts nonparalytic polio and is lost for the season.

1972   Leo Durocher becomes Houston's manager after beginning the season as the Cubs pilot, marking just the second time a skipper guides two NL clubs in the same season. The first was none other than Durocher, who shepherded the Dodgers and Giants in 1948.

1991   The Yanks fill overall number 1 pick Brien Taylor's pockets by inking him to a $1,550,000 deal, the largest sum ever given to an amateur draft choice at that time, but Taylor never makes the majors.

2001   With his 50th homer, Sammy Sosa joins Babe Ruth and Mark McGwire as the only two ML sluggers with four 50-tater campaigns.

2002   The Yankees and Rangers play the first game covered by video streaming on the Internet.

27

1893   Baltimore continues to assemble the pieces of its forthcoming dynasty by purchasing outfielder Steve Brodie from St. Louis for an undisclosed amount after Browns manager Bill Watkins declares that Brodie is not a "winning" player.

1901   Brooklyn pitcher Doc McJames's comeback bid after retiring to practice medicine ends abruptly when he is thrown from a runaway carriage and dies from his injuries at a hospital in Charleston, SC.

1910   Less than two months after it opens for business, Comiskey Park, the White Sox' new home, hosts a night game between two amateur teams under 20 high-powered arc lights.

1918   Christy Mathewson resigns as Cincinnati manager to take an army commission as captain in the chemical warfare division, a decision that results in his suffering permanent lung damage when he is accidentally gassed in a training exercise.

1936   Second baseman George Tkach of Superior dies from head injuries sustained when he was beaned in a Northern League game.

1954   Already in his 12th ML season even though he is just 28 years old, White Sox third baseman Cass Michaels's career is cruelly ended when he is beaned by the A's Marion Fricano in what some who witness the incident feel is a deliberate attempt by Fricano to vent his frustration during an eight-run inning by the Sox.

1958   Washington owner Clark Griffith acknowledges that he has reconsidered and is now open to moving his team to Minneapolis/St. Paul for the right offer.

1982   Oakland's Rickey Henderson breaks Lou Brock's post–1900 season stolen base record with his 119th steal.

2000   The Angels are the first team in AL history to boast four 30-homer men, when Tim Salmon connects against the Indians, joining teammates Mo Vaughn, Garret Anderson, and Troy Glaus.

28

1884   In a 10–2 win over Cleveland at the original Polo Grounds, Mickey Welch of New York NL is the first ML pitcher to fan the first nine batters he faces.

1907   Lefty Tex Neuer begins his brief but meteoric one-month ML career (in which he pitches three shutouts and six complete games for New York AL in six starts) with a 1–0 shutout of the Boston Red Sox.

1909   Washington's Dolly Gray sets two ML records when he walks eight White Sox batters in the 2nd inning, including seven in a row, as he loses 6–4.

1926   Cleveland's Dutch Levsen is the last ML hurler to date to win two complete games in one day when he beats the Red Sox 6–1 and 5–1, despite not striking out a batter in either contest.

1952   The Yankees make another specious late-season, interleague deal, acquiring pitcher Ewell Blackwell from Cincinnati for pitcher Johnny Schmitz, outfielder Jim Greengrass, two lesser players, and $35,000.

1969   In New York, Commissioner Kuhn holds a press conference announcing Macmillan's publication of *The Baseball Encyclopedia*, a tome that opens new frontiers in the game's research.

1983   The Tribe unloads pitcher Len Barker, who fizzles with the Braves, in exchange for pitcher Rick Behenna, $150,000, and two players to be named later—Brett Butler and Brook Jacoby—who combine for more than 3,500 career hits, plus three All-Star appearances.

1989   In the first regular-season pairing ever of reigning Cy Young winners, the Mets' Frank Viola beats the Dodgers' Orel Hershiser, 1–0.

1990   The Cubs' Ryne Sandberg homers, making him the first second baseman to slug 30 homers in consecutive seasons. He finishes with 40 to become the first ML keystoner to lead his loop outright in round-trippers since the Cards' Rogers Hornsby in 1925.

1992   Milwaukee raps Toronto pitchers for 31 hits, setting an AL nine-inning record during a 22–2 romp.

1993   Long Beach, led by former ML slugger Jeff Burroughs's son Sean, defeats Panama to become the first U.S. Little League team to repeat as champs.

2003   At the age of 20, Mets rookie shortstop Jose Reyes is the youngest player in ML annals to swat switch-hit homers in one game.

29

1885 Louisville of the AA initiates what may be the first player trade ever between two teams when it sends pitcher John Connor and $750 to Chattanooga of the Southern League for pitcher Toad Ramsey.

1887 Philadelphia A's third baseman Denny Lyons is held hitless in a 7–5 loss to Cincinnati, ending his 52-game "hitting streak" that includes games in which his only hits were bases on balls. Lyons's skein is unrecognized by MLB today, even though walks were counted as hits in 1887.

1951 In a move the *New York Times* deems "as startling as when they obtained Johnny Mize from the Giants two years ago," the Yankees acquire Braves pitcher Johnny Sain, after he mysteriously clears waivers in the NL, for $50,000 and minor league hurler Lew Burdette, who turns out as the truly startling feature of the deal when he emerges as one of the NL's top pitchers for the next decade.

1966 Robin Roberts, now with the Cubs, earns his last ML victory, which marks him as the only pitcher to beat the Braves in Boston, Milwaukee, and Atlanta.

1972 Giants hurler Jim Barr retires the first 20 Cardinals after nailing the last 21 Pirates who faced him in his previous start, setting a ML mark (since tied) for most consecutive batters retired with 41.

1973 California's Nolan Ryan misses an unprecedented third no-hitter of the season when a 1st-inning pop fly by the Yankees' Thurman Munson drops between two Angels infielders for the Bombers' only hit.

1977 The Cards' Lou Brock swipes two sacks to surpass Ty Cobb's record of 892 career steals. Elsewhere, Indians second baseman Duane Kuiper hits his lone career homer in 3,379 at bats, victimizing White Sox chucker Steve Stone.

1985 The Yanks' Don Baylor is plunked for the 190th time, topping the AL career mark set by Minnie Minoso. Baylor extends his mark to 267 before retiring.

1987 Houston's Nolan Ryan logs his 200th strikeout for a ML-record 11th time and extends his mark to 15 before retiring.

1990 The A's acquire outfielder Willie McGee from the Cardinals for three players, thereby freezing McGee's NL average at .335 and enabling him to cop the senior loop batting crown ex post facto. Elsewhere, Seattle's Ken Griffey Sr. and Ken Griffey Jr. are the first father-and-son teammates in ML history.

1998 The depleted Florida Marlins suffer their 89th defeat, a 7–5 loss to Cincinnati, to surpass the 1991 Reds' record for the most losses by a defending world champ.

30

1905 Ty Cobb makes his ML debut for Detroit in a 5–3 loss to New York's Jack Chesbro and collects his first career hit, a double.

1906 New York's Slow Joe Doyle is the first AL twirler to spin shutouts in his first two ML starts when he calamines Washington, 5–0.

1932 Still furious that he was not manager Roger Peckinpaugh's choice to pitch the inaugural game in Cleveland's new Municipal Stadium on July 31, 20-game winner Wes Ferrell is suspended for insubordination.

1953 Braves outfielder Jim Pendleton is the first African American MLer to hit three home runs in a game as the Braves tie the then ML record by pounding eight jacks in a 19–4 win over Pittsburgh.

1959 The White Sox win a Sunday DBH with the Indians to complete a four-game road sweep that gives them a prohibitive 5½ game lead in their march to their first AL pennant since the 1919 Black Sox Scandal.

1965 Casey Stengel announces his retirement as Mets skipper at the age of 75.

1972 Harold Arlin, who was at the mike in the first live baseball broadcast on August 5, 1921, for Pittsburgh's KDKA radio, is honored by being invited to call the action for a few innings while his grandson, Steve, pitches for the Padres against the Pirates.

1984 Red Sox slugger Jim Rice sets a ML season record by grounding into his 33rd double play and extends that mark to 36 by the campaign's end.

1986 Against Seattle, the Yankees deploy the first more than 40-year-old pitching duo to start both ends of a twin bill in nearly 53 years as Tommy John (43) loses and Joe Niekro (41) wins. The last club to start two more than 40-year-old pitchers in a DBH was the White Sox, with Sad Sam Jones (41) and Red Faber (45), on September 13, 1933.

1990 Red Sox GM Lou Gorman makes a move he never lives down, trading Jeff Bagwell, who will hit 449 homers in a 15-year career with the Astros, for reliever Larry Andersen.

1997   Red Sox rookie sensation Nomar Garciaparra's 30-game hitting streak ends after he broke the former AL freshman mark of 26 set by White Sox outfielder Guy Curtwright in 1943.

31

1903   For the third time in less than a month, New York Giants slabster Joe McGinnity bags two complete-game wins in one day, as he tops the Philadelphia Phillies, 4–1 and 9–2.

1914   White Sox first sacker Jack Fournier's two inside-the-park homers in a 4–3 win over Washington's Walter Johnson make him the first ever to hit two jacks off "The Big Train" in the same game.

1915   Future HOF southpaw Rube Marquard joins the short list of enshrined players waived in the middle of their careers when the Giants let him go to the Dodgers.

1931   The A's set a new AL record when they win their 22nd straight game at home, topping Boston 3–0 behind former Yankees ace Waite Hoyt.

1937   Tigers rookie Rudy York pummels two balls into the seats against Washington to give him 18 dingers in August, breaking Babe Ruth's old mark of 17 in one month (September 1927).

1950   Gil Hodges hammers four homers and a single in Brooklyn's 19–3 blasting of the Boston Braves at Ebbets Field.

1959   Sandy Koufax ties Bob Feller's post–1892 ML single-game record of 18 strikeouts in topping the Giants 5–2 at the Los Angeles Coliseum on the heels of Wally Moon's walk-off three-run "Moon" shot over the short left-field barrier.

1968   Mets rookie Jim McAndrew absorbs a NL record-tying fourth shutout loss this month and also laments that he lost his first four ML starts by whitewashings, commencing on July 21.

1988   In the case dubbed "Collusion II," 12 players are granted no-risk free agency when arbitrator George Nicolau rules that ML owners conspired to downgrade free-agent market salaries after the 1986 season.

1989   The beat goes on as ML owners must fork over $10,500,000 in free-agent collusion damages for 1985 in accordance with arbitrator Thomas Roberts's ruling.

2002   The Mets suffer the worst month at home of any team in NL annals by dropping all 13 of their games at Shea Stadium.

2005   Marlins rookie Jeremy Hermida is the first player since Bill Duggleby in 1898 to drill a grand slam in his first ML AB.

September

1

1872 Brooklyn Atlantics outfielder Albert Thake is the first MLer to die during the season when he drowns after falling out of a fishing boat in the New York harbor.

1902 Joe Tinker, Johnny Evers, and Frank Chance, soon to be immortalized in a poem as the greatest double play trio of their era, appear in the same game for the first time with the Chicago Cubs.

1906 The longest AL game played to a decision without being suspended and later resumed ends with A's hurler Jack Coombs besting Boston's Joe Harris 4–1 in 24 innings.

1913 Fred Thayer, who purportedly introduced the notion of using a fencing mask as the first type of catcher's mask in 1875, dies at the age of 65.

1923 Former ML catcher Frank McManus is found murdered in bed in Syracuse, NY.

1947 Rookie Lucky Lohrke tags the Giants' 183rd homer of the season, surpassing the 1936 Yankees total and setting a new ML team record that is extended to 221 before the campaign is over.

1950 With less than a month to go in the season, the Phillies own a .630 winning percentage and a seemingly insurmountable seven-game lead in the NL after knocking off the Braves, 7–3.

1951 Granite Falls finishes its Western Carolina League season with 33 straight losses and 59 defeats in its final 60 games to reduce its overall record to 14–96.

1954 The third-place White Sox and fourth-place Red Sox split a twin bill, leaving the Pale Hose where they started the day—27 games ahead of Boston in a season that ends with the top three teams in the AL playing at a combined .667 rate, while the remaining five clubs play at a combined .400 pace.

1959 Jack Norworth, Tin Pan Alley songwriter and the coauthor in 1908 of *Take Me Out to the Ball Game*, dies in Laguna Beach, CA, at the age of 80.

2

1880 Two Boston department stores battle to a 16–16 tie at Nantasket Beach, MA, in the first documented effort to play a game at night under artificial lighting.

1889 Boston's Hardy Richardson is the first batsman in ML history to account for a game's only run with a leadoff blast in the 1st inning when his jack beats Indianapolis's Henry Boyle, 1–0.

1918 The ML season comes to a war-abbreviated conclusion on its earliest closing date in history. Elsewhere, the IL, the lone minor league to operate all season, also ends its campaign, with Toronto winning the flag on the final day by two percentage points over the Binghamton Bingos.

1965 The Los Angeles Angels, about to move to Anaheim, change their name to the California Angels.

1969 The Yankees' Ralph Houk inks a three-year deal for $65,000 a season, the top skipper's salary at that time.

1971 When the Red Sox' Sonny Siebert hits two homers and knocks in all three runs in a 3–0 win over the Angels, he is the last AL pitcher to date to go deep twice in the same game.

1972 Cubs starter Milt Pappas is one strike away from a perfect game, but rookie umpire Bruce Froemming calls the next pitch a ball, allowing the Padres' Larry Stahl to walk. A disappointed Pappas then retires Garry Jestadt to preserve his no-hitter.

1979 The Dodgers' Manny Mota collects his 145th career pinch hit to set a new ML mark (since broken).

1990 After several near misses, Dave Stieb at long last spins his first no-hitter, as well as the initial no-no in Blue Jays history, defeating Cleveland, 3–0.

1996 The Red Sox' Mike Greenwell sets a ML record for most RBI in a game (9) by a player accounting for all his team's runs in Boston's 9–8 victory over the Mariners in 10 innings.

2007 Former big leaguer turned Orix Blue Wave slugger Tuffy Rhodes pastes his 400th homer in Japan, making him the first player born outside Nippon to attain that pinnacle.

3

1891 Tom Lovett of Brooklyn NL wins his ML record 24th straight game in his home park in topping Boston, 13–4. Scott Stratton of the AA Louisville club ties Lovett's record on August 3 of the following year.

1901 Just back from a suspension for spitting in AL umpire Tom Connolly's face, Baltimore's Joe McGinnity is the first hurler in AL history to toss complete games in both ends of a DBH, as he blanks Milwaukee 10–0 in the opener and loses the nightcap, 6–1.

1903 Cleveland rookie Jesse Stovall edges Detroit 1–0 in 11 innings to register the longest shutout in AL history by a pitcher making his first ML start.

1927 Given a special day at Braves Field by fans from his Cambridge, MA, home town, Boston leadoff hitter Doc Gautreau is presented with a new automobile and then rewards his followers in spectacular fashion by scoring three runs in the Braves' 4–3 win over Brooklyn and becoming the last NL player to date to steal home twice in the same game.

1928 Ty Cobb collects the last of his then record 4,191 hits (since reduced to 4,189) when he hits a pinch double off Washington's Bump Hadley.

1932 A's first baseman Jimmie Foxx is the second player in ML history to clout 50 homers in a season when he pounds his 50th and 51st jacks off Boston's Gordon Rhodes.

1957 The Braves' Warren Spahn shatters Larry French's record for the most career shutouts by a NL southpaw when he notches his 41st whitewash in beating the Cubs, 8–0. Spahn extends the mark to 63 before he retires.

1961 The Yankees are the only team to date to feature two 50-homer teammates in a season when Mickey Mantle reaches the plateau, joining Roger Maris who already has 53.

1970 The Cubs' Billy Williams voluntarily sits one out, halting his then NL record for consecutive games played at 1,117.

1990 The White Sox' Bobby Thigpen sets a new ML season mark with his 47th save and extends the figure to 57.

1992 Nearly two-thirds of ML owners vote for Commissioner Vincent's resignation, forcing him to step aside a few days later.

2000 Cleveland's Kenny Lofton scores a run in his 18th consecutive game, tying the ML standard set by the Yankees' Red Rolfe in 1939.

2002 The Mets lose to the Marlins in the first game of a twin bill, setting a new NL record with their 15th straight home loss.

4

1877 Seemingly a lock to win the NL pennant only a fortnight earlier, Louisville cedes first place to Boston as rumors reach team owner Charlie Chase that his Grays are intentionally losing games.

1890 Cleveland's Chief Zimmer, the first receiver in ML history to catch 100 straight games, has his skein end at 111 when he is called home by his wife's illness while the Spiders are in Pittsburgh.

1908 In a 10-inning game at Pittsburgh, umpire Hank O'Day, working the contest alone, rejects Cubs second baseman Johnny Evers's appeal that Pirates rookie Warren Gill, who was on first base, left the field without touching second base after Chief Wilson's single gives Pittsburgh an apparent 1–0 win. The following day, a scathing diatribe on O'Day's decision in the *Chicago Tribune* escapes the notice of New York Giants manager John McGraw, even though it is headlined *CUBS WILL FILE PROTEST.*

1916 Christy Mathewson and Three Finger Brown square off in a specially arranged matchup between the Reds and Cubs that concludes both of their careers, with Mathewson winning 10–8.

1933 Minneapolis first baseman Joe Hauser shatters his own OB record (since broken) when he pounds his 64th and 65th home runs off St. Paul hurlers in a Labor Day twin bill, a total he extends to 69 by the season's end.

1941 The Yankees break their own record, set in 1936, for the earliest pennant-clinching date in modern history when they wrap up the AL flag with a 6–3 win over Boston.

1945 Yankees batting practice pitcher Paul Schreiber sets a record for the longest time between ML hill outings when his hitless 3⅓-inning relief stint in the Bombers' 10–0 loss to the Tigers marks his first appearance in a big league game since 1923.

1953 The Tribe gives retiring broadcaster Jack Graney, a former Indians outfielder, a night at Cleveland Stadium to honor his then record 21 consecutive years at the mike of a ML team.

1966 The LA Dodgers are the first club to draw 2,000,000 fans both at home and on the road.

1991 After 30 years of dithering, the eight-man Statistical Accuracy Committee lists Roger Maris's 61 homer season as the undisputed record rather than relegating it in the 162-game category to distinguish it from Babe Ruth's 154-game achievement. The panel also rules that a no-hitter must be a game that ends after nine or more innings without a pitcher allowing a hit, thereby erasing many previously listed hitless performances and perfect games that either failed to include a pitcher facing 27 batters (Ernie Shore) or else were marred by a hit or hits made in extra innings (Harvey Haddix).

1993 The Yanks' Jim Abbott, who was born without a right hand, spins a no-hitter against the Indians.

1998 The Giants' Barry Bonds reaches base in his 15th consecutive plate appearance, setting a new NL record.

2002 After blowing an 11–0 lead, the A's rebound to beat the Royals 12–11 in the 9th frame for their AL record-breaking 20th consecutive win.

5

1871 Boston first sacker Charlie Gould hits the first grand slam homer in ML history in a 6–3 win over Chicago's George Zettlein.

1892 In the first of several deals that transform Baltimore from a tailender into a dynasty, the Orioles trade outfielder George Van Haltren to Pittsburgh for outfielder Joe Kelley and approximately $2,000.

1901 The minor leagues first unite under one umbrella at a meeting in Chicago and dub their new organization the National Association of Professional Baseball Leagues.

1914 Babe Ruth hits his only home run as a minor leaguer when he goes yard for Providence against Toronto's Ellis "Walt" Johnson in an IL game.

1923 Muskogee of the Southwestern League suffers its 38th consecutive loss to set an OB record.

1948 Outfielder Bob Crues of Amarillo in the West Texas-New Mexico League bashes two homers to tie Joe Hauser's then OB season four-bagger record of 69. Crues also finishes the season with a record 254 RBI and a .404 BA.

1950 The Yankees perpetrate yet another controversial late-season interleague heist when they corral first baseman Johnny Hopp (second in the NL with a .340 BA at the time) from Pittsburgh for a never-to-be-disclosed amount of cash.

1952 After logging his third no-hitter of the year on August 27, 18-year-old Bill Bell shares the fate of Ron Necciai, his early-season teammate with Bristol of the Class D Appalachian League, when he is rushed into Bucs livery by GM Branch Rickey and makes his Pirates debut with a 4–0 loss to the Cardinals. Unlike Necciai, who at least wins a game in his short, sad, Rickey-ruined career, Bell never makes another start in the show and exits winless in five appearances.

1954 First baseman Joe Baumann of Roswell in the Class C Longhorn League belts three jacks in a DBH to finish the season with 72 homers, breaking the former OB season record of 69.

1955 The Dodgers' Don Newcombe bags his 20th win in beating the Phillies 11–4 and aids his own cause with his seventh homer of the season, setting a new NL season mark (since tied) for taters by a pitcher.

1960 The oldest rookie in NL history, Pittsburgh's Diomedes Olivo, debuts at the age of 41 and works two scoreless frames against the Braves.

1969 Billy Williams strokes all four hits (two homers and two doubles) the Cubs manage against the Pirates' Steve Blass in a 9–2 loss, tying Kid Elberfeld's 1903 ML record for most hits in a game by a player accounting for all his club's hits.

1998 The Cards' Mark McGwire hits his 60th homer in the team's 142nd game, putting him 12 games ahead of Babe Ruth's 1927 pace and a whopping 17 contests ahead of Roger Maris's in 1961.

2003 Tigers lefty Mike Maroth loses to the Blue Jays 8–6, making him the last pitcher to date to drop 20 games in a season, a figure he extends to 21 by the season's close.

6

1877 A new arrival in Cincinnati from the Champion Citys club of Springfield, OH, Bobby Mitchell is the first southpaw in NL history to start a game as he nips Louisville's Jim Devlin, 1–0.

1883   Chicago scores a ML-record 18 runs in the 7th inning in a 26–6 rout of Detroit, as three White Stockings log a ML record (since tied) three hits in the frame.

1943   A's pitcher Carl Scheib is the youngest player in AL history at 16 years and 248 days when he relieves Orie Arntzen, a 33-year-old rookie more than twice his age, in an 11–4 loss to the Yankees.

1950   In a desperation move, Brooklyn manager Burt Shotton starts Don Newcombe in both ends of a DBH against the front-running Phillies, but after winning the opener 2–0, Newk leaves in the 7th inning of the nightcap trailing Curt Simmons 2–0, only to happily watch his team rally and win 3–2 in Simmons's last start before becoming the first MLer called to military duty in the Korean War.

1995   The Orioles' Cal Ripken Jr. surpasses a record thought unassailable when he plays in his 2,131st consecutive game, eclipsing Lou Gehrig.

1999   Former outfielder Billy Bean shares his trepidations about being a gay MLer in a *New York Times* article.

2000   MLB is permitted to use the URL www.mlb.com after reaching an agreement with the law firm Morgan, Lewis, and Bockis LLP, which had been using it.

2001   Giants slugger Barry Bonds hits his 60th homer of the season in the club's 141st game, bettering Mark McGwire's former record, set three years earlier, by one game.

2002   The Twins' Brad Radke ends Oakland's AL-record 20-game winning streak with a 6–0 victory.

7

1889   Leading Brooklyn 4–2 in the 9th inning, St. Louis captain Charlie Comiskey yanks his team off the field, protesting that it is too dark to continue when the Bridegrooms mount a rally. Comiskey's impulsive act sets off a firestorm of events that results in Brooklyn ending St. Louis's four-year reign as the AA champion and then, to escape having to deal with Comiskey and fractious Browns owner Chris Von der Ahe, deserting the AA to join the NL, a shift that starts the AA on a downward spiral toward extinction.

1908   Washington ace Walter Johnson shuts out New York for the third time in four days, 4–0.

1912 Bugs Raymond is discovered in a Chicago flophouse, dead of a fractured skull. While drunk, the former ML hurler had been beaten mercilessly with a brick several days earlier in a vacant lot where he once played ball and then carried back to his domicile to sleep it off.

1916 The New York Giants begin the day in fourth place before reeling off a ML-record 26 straight victorious decisions but still finish fourth after concluding the campaign by losing five of their last six games.

1923 Red Sox hurler Howard Ehmke is the recipient of a gift no-hitter when his A's mound opponent, Slim Harriss, is called out for missing first base on an apparent double.

1936 Women's basketball star Sonny Dunlap is in right field for Fayetteville in a Class D Arkansas-Missouri League game against Cassville and is the first documented female to play an entire game in OB.

1962 The Dodgers' Maury Wills eclipses the post–1897 NL-season record for stolen bases with his 82nd theft, topping Reds speedster Bob Bescher's 1911 total.

1975 Cincinnati's "Big Red Machine" clinches the NL East title on the earliest date in senior loop annals.

1984 The Mets' Dwight Gooden limits the Cubs to one hit and fans Ron Cey for his 228th strikeout, surpassing the 1911 Phillies' Pete Alexander's post–1892 NL rookie record.

1993 The Cards' Mark Whiten explodes for a record-tying four homers and 12 RBI in the second game of a DBH against the Reds and also equals Nate Colbert's mark of 13 RBI in a twin bill.

1998 Cardinals first sacker Mark McGwire reaches the Cubs' Mike Morgan for his then record-tying 61st homer of the season.

8

1893 In what is his only ML win, Cleveland's Jack Scheible tops Washington 7–0 to become the first ML pitcher to debut with a shutout at the new 60′6″ distance.

1939 Bob Feller, age 20, is the youngest ML 20-game winner since Noodles Hahn in 1899, when the Indians drub the Browns, 12–1.

1946 In a 3–2 win over the Browns, Bob Feller collects his 301st strikeout of the season, a total previously reached only by Rube Waddell and Walter Johnson at the 60′6″ distance. Feller is deemed the post–1892 season record holder when he extends his total to 348, until fresh research uncovers that Rube Waddell had 349 Ks in 1904, not 347, as had previously been thought.

1958   First baseman Rocky Nelson of Toronto wins his second IL Triple Crown in the past four seasons.

1963   For the 13th time in his career, Milwaukee's Warren Spahn bags his 20th victory, tying Christy Mathewson's NL record. In addition, at the age of 42, Spahn is the majors' oldest 20-game winner to date.

1965   A's shortstop Bert Campaneris is the first MLer to play all nine positions in one game.

1988   Owners elect NL president Bart Giamatti to succeed Peter Ueberroth as commissioner the following season.

1995   For the first time since 1954, the Indians clinch a postseason date with a 3–2 win over the Orioles and finish at 100–44, winning the AL Central by a record 30 games over the second-place Royals.

1998   The Cards' Mark McGwire reaches the Cubs' Steve Trachsel for his 62nd homer of the season, topping Roger Maris's hallowed 1961 record.

2002   The Rangers set a ML record by homering in their 26th consecutive game and extend the mark to 27 before it is halted.

2007   The Yankees' Alex Rodriguez belts two homers against the Royals, including his 49th for the season as a third baseman (excluding two he hit as a DH). He closes with 52 at the hot corner to surpass the previous mark by four.

9

1874   The Philadelphia Athletics expel star player John Radcliffe after umpire Billy McLean avers that Radcliffe offered him $175 to see to it that Chicago beat Radcliffe's favored Athletics.

1876   In the first scheduled DBH in NL history, Hartford's Candy Cummings is the initial ML hurler to win two games in one day when he tops last-place Cincinnati, 14–1 and 8–1.

1884   Cincinnati's Will White is the first MLer to log 200 career victories when he drubs the Virginia AA team, 17–3. Elsewhere, Buffalo's Jim Galvin ends Charley Radbourn's 19-game winning streak when he blanks Radbourn's Grays 2–0 at Providence.

1909   Pittsburgh receiver George Gibson breaks Chief Zimmer's 1890 ML record of 111 straight games behind the plate en route to setting a new standard of 140.

1915   Sporting-goods magnate and former star pitcher and club owner Al Spalding dies at the age of 65.

1959   Terry Lyons, a one-gamer with the Phils in 1929, is accidentally asphyxiated by an overdose of gas in a Dayton, OH, dentist's office.

1965   In a mound classic, the Dodgers' Sandy Koufax tosses a perfect game for his fourth no-hitter and beats the Cubs 1–0, while Bob Hendley allows only one hit, a 7th-inning double by Lou Johnson, who also scores the game's lone run in the 5th.

1970   Commissioner Kuhn socks Tigers hurler Denny McLain with his third suspension of the year, this time for toting a gun, as the former Cy Young winner's career continues its descent.

1977   Tigers rookies Alan Trammell and Lou Whitaker debut together in the second game of a DBH and go on to play as teammates with Detroit for a ML-record 19 seasons.

1992   ML owners select one of their own, Brewers magnate Bud Selig, to serve as chairman of the Executive Council until a new commissioner is chosen. Selig continues in the capacity for six years before being officially named to the commissioner's job in 1998.

1993   ML owners vote to split both leagues into three divisions and add a wild-card winner in 1994.

1999   Against the Twins, the Orioles' Cal Ripken Jr. hits into his 324th career double play, surpassing Carl Yastrzemski's AL mark.

2002   The Rangers' Alex Rodriguez breaks his own season homer record for shortstops by blasting his 53rd seat reacher. A-Rod extends that mark to 57 by season's end. Elsewhere, Arizona's Randy Johnson reaches 300 strikeouts for the fifth straight year, extending his own record and also tying Nolan Ryan for the most 300-K seasons with six.

2007   The Tigers' Curtis Granderson is the first ALer to total 20 doubles, 20 triples, 20 homers, and 20 steals in a season, joining the 1911 Cubs' Wildfire Schulte and the 1957 Giants' Willie Mays.

10

1881   In a game played at a neutral site in Albany, NY, with two out in the bottom of the 9th, Troy's Roger Connor tags the first grand slam in NL history to beat Worcester's Lee Richmond, 8–7.

1902 A's southpaw Rube Waddell is the first ML pitcher to win two games in the same day despite starting neither of them when he appears in relief in both ends of a DBH to top Baltimore, 9–4 and 5–4.

1918 Players on the Red Sox and Cubs threaten to strike unless their World Series shares are increased but sheepishly back down when their demands, during wartime, are deemed "un-American."

1933 Host in July to the first annual ML All-Star Game, Comiskey Park also acts as host to the first Negro League East-West All-Star Game, with Bill Foster pitching a complete-game 11–7 win for the West and teammate Mule Suttles tagging the game's lone four-bagger.

1946 Southpaw Bill Kennedy, a Cleveland farmhand with Rocky Mount in the Coastal Plain League, finishes his season with 456 strikeouts to set a new OB record. Kennedy also logs 28 wins in 31 decisions and an ERA of 1.03.

1959 In his ML debut with Cincinnati at Wrigley Field, Jim Bailey and his older sibling, Ed, form the last brother battery to date to start a game, as Jim is charged with a 6–3 loss after being lifted in the 8th frame.

1969 Following seven straight years of abysmal losing seasons, the Mets sit atop the NL East at the latest date in their short history after sweeping the Expos in a DBH.

1974 The Cards' Lou Brock breaks two records in one day, topping Maury Wills's post–1897 season stolen-base mark with his 105th swipe and Max Carey's post–1897 NL career mark with his 739th theft.

1980 The Expos' Bill Gullickson sets a ML rookie record (since broken) for strikeouts in a nine-inning game by fanning 18 Cubs.

1997 The Cards Mark McGwire joins Babe Ruth as the only two ML players to that point to slam 50 homers in consecutive seasons. Elsewhere, Buffalo beats Iowa for the AA crown in the last game played in the loop's lengthy history before it merges with the IL and the PCL in 1998.

1999 Disenchanted with union head Richie Phillips, ML umpires announce plans to form a new union.

2001 The Brewers' Jamey Wright loses to the Cards 8–0 but avoids plunking any batters, ending his modern ML record of hitting a batsman in 10 straight games.

2007 The Rockies' Troy Tulowitzki belts his 20th homer, surpassing Ernie Banks's NL rookie record for shortstops.

11

1882 Louisville's Tony Mullane carves the first no-hitter in AA history when he beats Cincinnati, 2–0.

1902 Jack Malarkey is the only ML hurler ever to win his own game in extra innings with a walk-off homer, which is also the only four-bagger of his career, when he hits a Mike O'Neill toss over the leftfield wall at South End Grounds in the 11th frame to give Boston a 4–3 triumph over the Cardinals.

1912 A's second baseman Eddie Collins steals a record six bases against the Tigers battery of pitcher Joe Lake and catcher Brad Kocher in a 9–6 win at Detroit. Collins repeats his feat 11 days later against the Browns. His mark is tied numerous times afterward but is still the post–1897 single-game theft record.

1923 Bidding to be the first MLer to toss back-to-back no-hitters, Red Sox righty Howard Ehmke is denied immortality when the Yankees' official scorer refuses at the conclusion of Ehmke's 3–0 one-hitter to change the Bombers' lone safety, a scratch single by leadoff hitter Whitey Witt in the 1st inning, to an error.

1927 The Browns prevent the Yankees from being the only ML team to sweep all 22 games from an opponent during the 154-game schedule era when Milt Gaston beats his old teammates 6–2 in the last meeting of the year between the two clubs.

1946 The Dodgers suffer a heavy blow to their pennant chances when darkness ends a 19-inning game with Cincinnati at Ebbets Field, which represents the longest scoreless tie in ML history.

1956 Cincinnati's Frank Robinson ties Wally Berger's still-extant 1930 NL rookie record for home runs when he socks his 38th jack in an 11–5 win over the Giants.

1959 Pirates bull pen magician Roy Face's ML season record of 17 straight wins, all in relief, ends with a 5–4 loss to LA's Chuck Churn when the Dodgers rally for two runs in the bottom of the 9th.

1966 Braves hurler Pat Jarvis is all-time strikeout king Nolan Ryan's first career whiff.

1968 The Mets hand Cubs ace Fergie Jenkins his record-tying fifth 1–0 loss of the season.

1974   The Mets lose to the Cards 4–3 in 25 innings, then the longest game in ML history played to a decision, as two errors on the same play allow Bake McBride to tally the winning run.

1981   The Astros' Cesar Cedeno is fined $5,000 after attacking a fan during a game, even though witnesses claim three men in attendance had been verbally harassing Cedeno's wife by making repeated references to her husband's involuntary manslaughter conviction of a young woman eight years earlier.

1985   The Reds' Pete Rose officially eclipses Ty Cobb's career hit mark by stroking number 4,192 against the Padres' Eric Show.

1998   The Marlins drop their 100th game, making them the first defending world champion to reach the century mark in losses the following season, and the team extends their record to 108 before the season's end.

2001   After the terrorist attack on the World Trade Center, the Pentagon, and Flight 93, all MLB games are canceled and do not resume until September 17. The lengthy postponement forces modern World Series games to be scheduled in November for the first time.

2004   Barry Bonds receives three bases on balls from Diamondback pitchers to become the first MLer to walk more than 200 times in a campaign. Bonds extends his record to 232 by the season's end.

12

1883   At a meeting in Pittsburgh, a new rebel ML, the Union Association, is formed with the avowed purpose of eliminating the reserve clause. Elsewhere, in thrashing Pittsburgh 27–5, Cincinnati's Hick Carpenter and "Long" John Reilly are the first pair of teammates to each stroke six hits in the same game.

1896   Jerry Nops clinches Baltimore's then record-tying third straight NL flag when he tops Brooklyn, 9–5.

1914   Shortstop Roger Peckinpaugh, at the age of 23, is the youngest documented manager in ML history when he replaces Frank Chance at the helm of the New York Yankees.

1930   Brooklyn catcher Al Lopez's shot off Cincinnati's Ray Kolp arouses little attention when it bounces into the centerfield bleachers at Ebbets Field for a three-run homer, but it turns out to be the last such homer in the majors when an off-season rule change renders all subsequent hits like Lopez's doubles.

1954   An ecstatic then record crowd of 86,563 at Cleveland's Municipal Stadium watches the Indians sweep a DBH from the Yankees to move 8½ games ahead of the Bombers and reduce their magic pennant-clinching number to three.

1962   Washington's Tom Cheney sets a ML mark by fanning 21 Orioles in a 16-inning compete-game 2–1 win.

1969   Mets pitchers seize the day when they sweep the Pirates in a DBH, winning both games 1–0 with starters Jerry Koosman and Don Cardwell driving home the lone run in each contest.

1974   Tigers reliever John Hiller notches his 17th relief win against the Brewers, setting an AL record that is later equaled by the Twins' Bill Campbell in 1976.

1982   The Royals defeat the Twins' Terry Felton in his last ML decision, saddling the hapless hurler with a 0–16 career slate, the most losses without a win by any pitcher in ML history.

1984   When the Mets' Dwight Gooden records his 246th strikeout by fanning the Bucs' Marvell Wynne, he eclipses the Indians' Herb Score's post–1892 rookie record set in 1955.

1998   The Cubs' Sammy Sosa slugs his 60th homer to become the fourth MLer to reach that season milestone.

2000   The Dodgers' Dave Hansen hits his record-breaking seventh pinch homer of the year, surpassing Johnny Frederick's 1932 mark.

2006   The Braves' skein of consecutive division titles ends at 14 when the Mets beat the Marlins to clinch the NL East.

13

1887   Chicago's Jimmy Ryan is the only ML position player to earn a pitching win and hit for the cycle in the same game as he goes 6-for-6 in beating the Phils 16–13 after relieving starter Mark Baldwin.

1890   Cincinnati's Jesse Duryea has the humiliating distinction of suffering an 8–6 defeat to Pittsburgh's Dave Anderson, thereupon ending the Smoke City NL entry's ML-record skein of 41 consecutive losses on the road.

1908   Smoke Justis, pitching for Lancaster in the Ohio State League, tosses his OB-record fourth no-hitter of the season as he blanks Marion, 4–0.

1922   Yankees shortstop Everett Scott goes the extra mile to become the first MLer to play in 1,000 consecutive games when he hops an interurban train and then hires a cab for $40 to hurry him to Comiskey Park after the engine of the train he was taking to Chicago from his Indiana home blew out a cylinder head near South Bend.

1927   Miller Huggins wins his fifth pennant, tying him with Connie Mack for the most to that point by an AL manager, when the Yankees clinch their fifth flag in seven years.

1934   Commissioner Landis auctions off the rights to sponsor the World Series broadcast to the Ford Motor Co. for $100,000.

1936   Bob Feller shatters the single-game AL record as well as his own rookie record when he fans 17 in beating the A's, 5–2.

1938   A special committee names two more baseball pioneers, Alexander Cartwright and Henry Chadwick, to the HOF.

1942   Cubs shortstop Lennie Merullo, a Boston native, celebrates the morning birth of his son in a Hub hospital by making a record-tying four errors in one inning in the second game of a twin bill with Boston at Braves Field.

1946   Ted Williams clinches the Red Sox' first flag since 1918 when he thwarts the "Williams Shift" in the 1st inning and loops a ball over the head of Cleveland leftfielder Pat Seerey, playing only a few feet behind what is normally the shortstop position, for the lone IPHR in the Thumper's long career and Boston's only run in a 1–0 win over Red Embree.

1948   Cleveland pitcher Don Black is nearly the second unequivocal on-field player fatality in ML history when he suffers a career-ending cerebral hemorrhage in the 2nd inning after swinging at a fastball delivered by St. Louis Browns lefty Bill Kennedy.

1958   In topping the Cardinals 8–2, the Braves' Warren Spahn is the first southpaw in ML history to bag 20 wins nine times in his career, breaking the mark he formerly shared with Eddie Plank and Lefty Grove.

1989   In the wake of Bart Giamatti's passing, his former deputy, Fay Vincent, is elected commissioner.

1991   The Expos are forced to play their final 13 games on the road after a 55-ton beam hurtles from their stadium into a vacant walkway.

1992 The Indians' Kenny Lofton swipes his 54th base, breaking the AL rookie record set in 1909 by the Tigers' Donie Bush. The speedy Lofton extends the mark to a league-leading 66 steals.

1995 Detroit's Lou Whitaker and Alan Trammell set the junior loop mark for most games played as teammates with 1,915 and add two more games to this total before Whitaker retires at the end of the season.

1996 Blue Jays catcher Charlie O'Brien introduces the hockey-style goalie's mask in a ML game.

14

1900 A paraplegic since a falling beam broke his back in 1897 while he was working as a fireman, Ed Knouff dies in Philadelphia's German Hospital after sitting in a wheelchair for three years at a window overlooking Girard College and the baseball grounds where he had made his ML pitching debut 15 years earlier with the Philadelphia A's at the age of 17.

1905 After Johnny Evers disdains the team carriage and takes a private cab to the park in Washington, IN, for an exhibition game against the local team, he and Cubs teammate Joe Tinker brawl on the field when Tinker chides him for his elitism, and the two allegedly never speak again.

1909 John Heydler, upon replacing the late Harry Pulliam as NL president, announces that the NL will follow the AL's lead in 1910 and assign two umpires to work every game.

1913 Larry Cheney of the Cubs allows 14 hits, the most ever by a NL pitcher tossing a shutout, when he holds the Giants scoreless, 7–0.

1942 Ten games behind Brooklyn at one point in the season, the Cards move into first place, never to be caught, when they split a pair with the Phillies while the Dodgers lose two to the Reds.

1950 Cincinnati's Ted Tappe is the first documented player to homer in both his first minor league and ML at bats when he goes yard as a pinch hitter against Brooklyn's Erv Palica.

1951 Browns rookie Bob Nieman is the first player to homer in each of his first two ML at bats when he takes Boston's Mickey McDermott deep in the 1st and 3rd innings.

1953 The Yankees clinch their ML record (since tied) fifth straight pennant with an 8–5 win over second-place Cleveland.

1955   Cleveland southpaw Herb Score sets a new post–1892 rookie season strikeout record with 235 (later extended to 245) before being removed in the 7th inning of a 3–2 loss to the Senators.

1958   The Yankees clinch their ninth AL pennant since Casey Stengel took over the club's reins in 1949, tying Stengel with Connie Mack for the most junior loop flags won.

1967   Walt Bond, who hit 20 homers for Houston in 1964, succumbs to leukemia at the age of 29.

1968   The Tigers' Denny McLain beats the A's to become the last 30-game winner to date and finishes the season 31–6.

1975   Brewers shortstop Robin Yount plays his 242nd ML game as a teenager, breaking Giants Hall of Famer Mel Ott's precocity mark.

1987   When the Blue Jays hit a ML-record 10 homers in an 18–3 cremation of the Orioles, Baltimore's skipper Cal Ripken Sr. inserts Ron Washington at short in the 8th inning of the blowout, ending his son, Cal Jr.'s, ML record for consecutive innings played at 8,243.

1990   Seattle's two Ken Griffeys, Jr. and Sr., are the first father and son to homer in the same game when they slam back-to-back jacks against the Angels' Kirk McCaskill.

1994   After 34 days of the players' strike, ML teams vote to cancel the remainder of the season, making this the first time since 1904 that a World Series is not played.

1999   The Royals' Mark Quinn debuts in grand style when he smacks two homers and a double against the Angels to join the 1951 Browns' Bob Nieman, the 1964 A's Bert Campaneris, and Charlie Reilly of the 1889 Columbus AA club as the only players to pop a pair of taters in their first big league games.

2002   Boston's Derek Lowe beats the Orioles for his 20th win, making him the first pitcher to reach the charmed circle *after* previously saving 40 games in a season (42 for the BoSox in 2000).

2007   Umpire Bruce Froemming, at age 67 years and 351 days, replaces former umpire Charlie Berry as the oldest person ever to appear in a ML box score.

15

1856   The first recorded baseball game in Canada occurs in London, Ontario, with the local team defeating the Delawares, 34–33.

1884 To avoid paying KC the $60 guaranteed to the visiting team, Wilmington manager Joe Simmons pulls his team off the field when no fans show up and accepts a forfeit loss on the Delaware city's last day as a member of the UA.

1901 The *Chicago Tribune* reports that under pressure from Chicago owner Charlie Comiskey, AL president Ban Johnson has reinstated Chicago shortstop Frank Shugart after expelling Shugart for life the previous month for assaulting an umpire.

1903 Giants rookie Hooks Wiltse sets a new ML record (since tied) for the most consecutive games won at the start of a career when he beats Boston 3–2 for his 12th straight verdict.

1908 Giants ace Christy Mathewson, pitching in relief, bests the Cardinals for a ML record 24th straight time, 5–4.

1909 Dayton infielder Charlie Pinkney dies from a beaning he sustained the previous day in a Central League game.

1921 Babe Ruth breaks his own year-old season home-run record when he goes yard for the 55th time against Bill Bayne in the Yankees' 10–6 win over the Browns. Ruth extends his new mark to 59 by the season's end.

1922 The Phils' Butch Henline is the first NL player since 1897 and the first ML catcher *ever* to loft three home runs in a game, as the Phils beat the Cardinals, 10–9.

1928 The Braves play the last of a ML-record nine consecutive doubleheaders when they split a pair with the Cubs.

1949 Pirates hurler Ernie Bonham dies from complications following a three-hour appendicitis operation six days earlier.

1950 Yankees first sacker Johnny Mize hits three homers in a game for the record (since tied) sixth time in his career, but the Bombers still lose 9–7 to Detroit's Hank Borowy. Elsewhere, the Cards' Red Munger notches a complete-game 6–2 win over Brooklyn's Don Newcombe, even though the start is credited to Cloyd Boyer, who injured his arm while warming up prior to the 1st inning.

1961 The Yankees set a new ML standard for team homers in a season when Yogi Berra boosts their total to 222, breaking the mark held by the 1947 Giants and the 1956 Reds. The Bombers extend their record to 240 (since broken) by the season's end.

1962 The Pirates' Bob Friend beats Jack Sanford, ending the Giants hurler's 16-game winning streak.

1969 The Cards' Steve Carlton sets a then post–1892, nine-inning ML-record by fanning 19 batters but still loses 4–3 as the Mets' Ron Swoboda unloads a pair of two-run shots.

1977 The Yanks acquire slugger Dave Kingman, making him the first MLer to play for all four divisions then in existence in the same season after previously sporting Mets, Padres, and Angels threads.

1978 The Dodgers are the first ML team to draw 3,000,000 fans.

1996 Catcher Mark Parent launches Baltimore's 241st homer of the season, setting a new ML team record (since broken).

1998 The Devil Rays' Rolando Arrojo wins his 14th game, setting a post–1884 record for most wins on a first-year expansion club. His mark is equaled three days later by the Diamondbacks' Andy Benes.

1999 Owners unanimously agree to combine many aspects of both leagues' off-field operations, including the consolidation of umpires and the elimination of league presidents.

2002 Curt Schilling fans his 300th batter, joining D-backs' Randy Johnson as the only teammates to each whiff that many batters in the same season. Elsewhere, the Cubs' Sammy Sosa joins Mel Ott and Willie Mays as the only three NL players to log eight straight 100-RBI campaigns.

16

1885 Detroit buys out NL rival Buffalo for a reported $7,000 to obtain the Bisons' "Big Four"—third baseman Deacon White, shortstop Jack Rowe, outfielder Hardy Richardson, and first baseman Dan Brouthers—but other NL owners prevent Detroit from playing the quartet until the following season.

1905 With regular second sacker Jimmy Williams unavailable, the New York Highlanders station lefty outfielder Willie Keeler at the keystone sack in both ends of a DBH with Washington, marking the last occasion to date that a southpaw occupied a middle infield position in a twin bill.

1917 Nap Lajoie leads the IL in batting with a .380 mark and pilots Toronto to the loop flag, the first time in his 22 seasons of pro ball that he has been on a pennant winner.

1924 As Brooklyn manager Wilbert Robinson watches glumly from the Dodgers dugout, Cards first baseman Jim Bottomley breaks Robinson's 32-year-old single-game record of 11 RBI when he knocks home 12 runs in a 17–3 St. Louis win.

1939   The Yankees become the first AL team to win four consecutive pennants when rookie Marius Russo tops Detroit, 8–5.

1940   Browns rookie switch-hitter Johnny Lucadello's only two home runs this season come in the same game from opposite sides of the plate in St. Louis's 16–4 win over the Yankees.

1957   The Los Angeles City Council approves a site in Chavez Ravine for a new stadium for the Dodgers if they come to LA.

1958   Detroit's Frank Lary cements his status as the ultimate "Yankee Killer" when he tops the Bombers 4–2, making him the only hurler to beat the Yankees seven times in a season since they became the game's most dominant team in the early 1920s.

1968   AL umpires Bill Valentine and Al Salerno are fired by league president Joe Cronin, who claims his decision was based upon their incompetence, but the arbiters cite their involvement in forming an umpires union as the motivating factor.

1972   The Cubs' Glenn Beckert has a day to forget at the plate as he strands a record 12 men in his at bats during the Bruins' 18–5 trouncing of the Mets.

1975   The Pirates' Rennie Stennett ties Wilbert Robinson's 1892 record when he strokes seven hits in a nine-inning game, as the Bucs skewer the Cubs, 22–0.

1987   The Angels' Bob Boone catches his 1,919th ML game, topping Al Lopez's former career mark.

1988   Cincinnati's Tom Browning pitches a perfecto against the Dodgers, striking out eight in a 1–0 win.

1991   Atlanta's Otis Nixon is suspended for 60 days for testing positive for cocaine, causing him to miss the rest of the season. Nixon, who was leading the NL with 72 steals, sees the Expos' Marquis Grissom overtake him and close with 76 to top the senior circuit.

1998   Detroit reliever Sean Runyan logs his 84th game of the year, setting a new rookie mark for appearances that he extends to 88 by the season's end.

2000   Cubs clubber Sammy Sosa pelts his 50th homer, joining Mark McGwire as the only two big leaguers to reach that milestone in three straight seasons.

2007 White Sox DH Jim Thome clouts his 500th career homer to join Frank Thomas and Alex Rodriguez, who reached the landmark earlier in the season.

17

1906 To protect his college eligibility at Columbia University, Eddie Collins resorts to the usual ploy in his day and uses an assumed name, in this case "Sullivan," when he makes his ML debut with the A's against White Sox spitball ace Ed Walsh.

1910 In topping the A's 10–3, the Tigers' Ed Summers is the first performer in the 20th century to hit two home runs in a game while serving as a pitcher.

1931 Red Sox outfielder Earl Webb celebrates his 34th birthday by setting a new ML season record with his 65th double, a mark he extends to 67 by the season's end.

1935 Sent packing by the Dodgers, outfielder Len Koenecke hires a private plane and gets into a fracas with the pilot, who kills him with a blow to the head from a fire extinguisher.

1946 Tony Napoles of Peekskill in the North Atlantic League collects his fourth playoff victory to finish the campaign at 22–0, including going 18–0 in the regular season.

1963 The Dodgers' Sandy Koufax nails his 11th shutout in beating the Cards 4–0 to set a post–1892 ML season record for southpaws.

1979 KC's George Brett strokes his 20th triple, making him the first player since Willie Mays in 1957 to total 20 doubles, 20 triples, and 20 homers in the same season.

1980 A's manager Billy Martin pulls Rick Langford after the hurler yields a homer with two away in the 9th, ending Langford's consecutive complete-games streak at 22, but the move is too late to prevent the arm trouble that eventually short-circuits Langford's career.

1981 The Dodgers' Fernando Valenzuela logs his eighth shutout, tying the post–1892 freshman record shared by Russ Ford (1910) and Reb Russell (1913).

1988 When the Twins' Jeff Reardon notches his 40th save, he is the first to achieve the milestone in both leagues after previously logging 41 with the 1985 Expos.

1993 Angels catcher Greg Myers is Rangers great Nolan Ryan's 5,714th and last career whiff. Elsewhere, the newly minted Rockies are the first ML club to pass 4,000,000 in home attendance.

1998 The longest-lived MLer to date, Chet Hoff, dies at the age of 107, 87 years after debuting with the Yanks and fanning the first batter he faced, Ty Cobb.

18

1893 John Clarkson is the first pitcher in ML history to win his own game in extra innings with a walk-off home run, a 10th-inning blast off Boston's Hank Gastright to give Cleveland a 7–6 verdict.

1899 The downtrodden Cleveland Spiders end their NL record 24-game losing streak when Jack Harper beats Washington 5–4 in 10 innings in the first game of a DBH, only to begin a new 16-game losing streak in the nightcap that gives them 40 losses in their final 41 games as a member of the NL.

1903 The day before Pittsburgh clinches its third straight NL pennant, Pirates owner Barney Dreyfuss agrees to play the Boston AL winner in a best-of-9 series for the overall ML championship.

1922 Joe Bush stops George Sisler's new AL-record hitting streak at 41 in beating the Browns 3–1 and gives the Yankees a 1½ game lead in the AL race that proves prohibitive.

1963 Just 1,752 fans turn out for the last ML game in the Polo Grounds to watch the Phillies beat the Mets, 5–1.

1968 The Cardinals' Ray Washburn exacts revenge against the Giants by no-hitting them the day after the Giants' Gaylord Perry held the Cards hitless.

1977 Boston's Ted Cox raps four hits in his ML debut against the Orioles and strokes two more the following day versus the Yankees, giving him a ML record six straight hits before he makes his first out.

1984 Montreal's Tim Raines is the first ML player since 1897 to post four consecutive seasons of more than 70 stolen bases. Elsewhere, the Tigers clinch the AL East and are the first club in the expansion era to occupy first place every day of the season.

1987 The Tigers' Darrell Evans can boast that he is the first 40-year-old MLer to log a 30-homer campaign two years after becoming the initial slugger to post 40 tater seasons in both leagues.

1996   The Red Sox' Roger Clemens ties his own 1986 record by whiffing 20 Tigers in a 4–0 win.

1999   At the age of 36, former minor league hurler Jim Morris abandons his job as a high school teacher to fulfill a lifelong dream by debuting with Tampa Bay in relief and striking out the Rangers' Royce Clayton. Elsewhere, Cubs slugger Sammy Sosa is the first ML player to power 60 homers twice in his career.

2005   The Rangers set the ML record for round-trippers at home when Rod Barajas connects against the Mariners, giving Texas 150 homers, one more than the 1996 Rockies, as they finish with 153.

19

1901   All ML games are cancelled out of respect for the funeral of President William McKinley.

1931   The A's Lefty Grove is the last southpaw to date to win 30 games in a season when he edges the White Sox, 2–1.

1939   Red Sox' rookie Ted Williams drills his 31st home run off the White Sox' Thornton Lee some 21 years before he homers off Lee's son, Don, in his final ML season at the age of 42.

1970   The Red Sox' Tony and Billy Conigliaro homer in the same game for the second time in the season and finish with a combined total of 54, a season record for sibling teammates.

1977   Paddy Livingston, a catcher with Cleveland in 1901, is the last surviving player from the AL's inaugural season as a ML when he dies at the age of 97 in Cleveland, OH.

1986   The White Sox' Joe Cowley no-hits the Angels in his last ML win.

1995   The Padres' Ken Caminiti drives in eight runs against the Rockies, completing an offensive rampage in which the third sacker is the first to swat homers from both sides of the plate three times in the same season. Elsewhere, Andres Galarraga homers to join Dante Bichette, Larry Walker, and Vinny Castilla in giving the Rockies four players with more than 30 homers, equaling the record of the 1977 Dodgers.

1998   At the age of 23, Seattle shortstop Alex Rodriguez is the first ML infielder to pop 40 homers and snag 40 stolen bases.

2001   Seattle beats the Angels to clinch the AL West after spending the entire season in first place. Elsewhere, the Yankees' Roger Clemens downs the White Sox for his 16th straight win to give him a 20–1 slate that fades to 20–3 after he loses his last two decisions.

2002 In his ML debut, Twins outfielder Michael Ryan strokes two hits, plates two runs, and scores two runs himself, all in the opening frame, but it is for naught when the game is rained out after two innings.

20

1880 Chicago wins its final game of the season to finish at 67–17 and establish a NL record for the highest winning percentage (.798).

1896 Former ML pitcher Ed Crane is found dead in bed from an apparent accidental overdose of chloral. There is speculation that Crane committed suicide after it is learned that just two days earlier he had been talked out of jumping into Genesee Falls in Rochester by two ex-teammates.

1912 After tying Walter Johnson's three-week-old AL record of 16 straight wins on September 17, Boston's Smokey Joe Wood has his string broken in a 6–4 loss to the Tigers.

1931 Cards manager Gabby Street, last active in the majors in 1909 when he caught Walter Johnson, permits St. Louis fans to witness a Johnson and Street battery for one last time when he goes behind the bat for three innings at the age of 49 to handle Birds starter Syl Johnson in a 6–1 loss to Brooklyn and embarrasses Dodgers slugger Babe Herman by throwing him out stealing.

1947 Third baseman Bill Serena of Lubbock in the West Texas-New Mexico League finishes with 70 home runs—57 during the regular season and 13 in 14 postseason playoff contests.

1950 The Phils parlay Jim Konstanty's then record 16th relief win to top the Cubs 9–6 and take a seemingly prohibitive 7½-game lead over the second-place Dodgers with just 11 games left to play.

1951 NL president Ford Frick is elected to a seven-year term as baseball's third commissioner.

1955 Philadelphia's Robin Roberts raises his ML season record total to 40 homers surrendered (later extended to 46 and since broken) in a 6–1 loss to Brooklyn.

1956 Baltimore catcher Tom Gastall dies when his private plane crashes into the waters near Riviera Beach, MD.

1961 The Yanks' Roger Maris belts his 59th homer of the year in the club's 155th contest (including a tie), thereby failing to break Babe Ruth's mark of 60 within the allotted games required by Commissioner Ford Frick to avoid an asterisk.

1984 San Diego hurler Tim Lollar blasts a three-run shot against the Giants, helping the Padres capture their first NL West title since the advent of divisional play.

1988 The Red Sox' Wade Boggs is the first MLer since Willie Keeler to log 200 hits in six straight seasons and joins Lou Gehrig as the only pair to bag 200 hits and 100 walks for three straight years.

1992 Phillies second baseman Mickey Morandini turns the NL's first unassisted triple play since 1927.

1998 The Orioles' Cal Ripken Jr. removes himself from the starting lineup against the Yanks, ending his consecutive games played streak at 2,632.

2002 Baltimore shortstop Mike Bordick sets a ML record by playing his 102nd straight game without a miscue.

2003 The Braves' Marcus Giles homers to join Gary Sheffield, Javy Lopez, Andruw Jones, Chipper Jones, and Vinny Castilla in tying the NL mark for most 20-tater men on the same club with six.

21

1922 The AL reinstates the MVP Award, last given in 1914, but the NL does not resume giving its own league award until 1924.

1934 The Dean brothers blank the Dodgers in both ends of a DBH as Dizzy hurls a three-hitter in the opener, and Paul tops him in the nightcap by tossing a no-no.

1946 Following a 5–3 relief loss to Detroit, Cleveland's Joe Berry departs from the show with 133 hill appearances, the most to that point by a hurler who never made a ML start. Berry's mark is broken the following year by Gordon Maltzberger, but Berry remains the first ML hurler to appear in as many as 100 games without making a start.

1952 In the last ML game ever played at Boston's Braves Field, the home club loses 8–2 to Dodgers Rookie of the Year, Joe Black.

1956 The Yankees strand a nine-inning single-game record 20 base runners in losing 11–7 to the Red Sox.

1958 At Fenway Park, Ted Williams disgustedly flips his bat into a front-row box seat after fanning against Washington's Bill Fischer and strikes Boston GM Joe Cronin's 60-year-old housekeeper, Gladys Heffernan, in the face, immediately bringing him to tears when he realizes what he has done.

1968 Cubs reliever Jophrey Brown never achieves distinction as a ball player, working just two innings and allowing one run in his only ML appearance, but he becomes a Hollywood stuntman and christens the film *Jurassic Park* by getting devoured by a raptor in the opening scene.

1970 Just a month past his 21st birthday, the A's Vida Blue is the youngest AL hurler to spin a no-hitter, blanking the Twins, 6–0.

1973 The Mets beat the Pirates to take first place in the NL East and win the division after being in last place as late as August 31.

1979 Royals switch-hitter U. L. Washington hits his first two career homers in a game against the A's, with each coming from a different side of the plate.

1981 The Phillies' Steve Carlton whiffs his 3,118th career batter, breaking Bob Gibson's NL record.

1984 Baltimore's Jim Traber commemorates his big league debut by singing the national anthem before serving as a DH against the Red Sox.

1987 The Mets' Darryl Strawberry joins Howard Johnson in the 30-homer/30-stolen base club, making them the first teammates to accomplish the feat in the same season.

1998 The Pirates' Jason Kendall snags his 26th sack, breaking the NL season mark for catchers that previously belonged to John Stearns of the 1978 Mets.

2001 The Cards' Albert Pujols homers for his 83rd extra base hit, breaking Johnny Frederick's 1929 NL rookie record of 82. Pujols extends his new loop mark to 88 but falls one short of tying the ML frosh standard set by the Tribe's Hal Trosky in 1934.

2002 Houston catcher Brad Ausmus hits into his 30th double play, tying the 1938 Reds' Ernie Lombardi's NL season record.

22

1870 In a game of such import that for the first time inning-by-inning results are carried nationwide by telegraph wire, the New York Mutuals win the championship for the 1870 season by drubbing the Brooklyn Atlantics 10–4 at Brooklyn's Union Grounds.

1904 In a 7–5 win over Cincinnati that clinches the Giants' first pennant under John McGraw, 52-year-old Jim O'Rourke catches the entire game for New York in his first ML appearance since 1893.

1907 Phils newcomer George McQuillan whitewashes the Cardinals 2–0 en route to a then-record string of 25 scoreless innings by a pitcher at the beginning of his ML career.

1911 Cy Young, finishing his 22-year ML career with Boston NL, edges Pittsburgh's Babe Adams 1–0 to collect his 511th and final career win.

1915 After loaning the Boston Braves Fenway Park to use in the 1914 World Series, the Red Sox arrange to use the Braves' new park, Braves Field, for the 1915 Fall Classic.

1920 In Chicago, a grand jury convenes to examine charges that eight members of the White Sox conspired to fix the 1919 World Series.

1932 After clinching the NL pennant, Cubs players vote to deny Rogers Hornsby a World Series share because he has still not repaid money he borrowed from many of them to bet on horse races.

1953 The Dodgers beat the Pirates 5–4 to end their home season with a 60–17 record, tying the 1942 Cardinals for the then best NL home mark since the schedule was lengthened to 154 games in 1904.

1954 Just recalled by the Dodgers from Fort Worth of the Texas League, lefty Karl Spooner sets a new standard for the most strikeouts by a pitcher in his ML debut when he fans 15 in topping the Giants, 3–0.

1957 In a 7–3 win over the Phils' Robin Roberts, Duke Snider hits two home runs, the second of which is the final home run ever hit in Ebbets Field, and hikes his season total to 40, tying Ralph Kiner's then NL mark of hitting 40 or more home runs in five consecutive seasons.

1959 Vic Power's hot shot with one out in the 9th inning is turned into a quick double play by White Sox keystoners Nellie Fox and Luis Aparicio to give Chicago a 4–2 win that mathematically knocks Cleveland out of the AL race, the last time until 1995 that the Indians remain alive in a pennant chase this late in the season.

1970 The White Sox' Luis Aparicio plays in his 2,219th game, setting a ML record for career games at shortstop that he extends to 2,581.

1980 Raymond Goetz is the first arbitrator to overturn a baseball commissioner's decision when he rules that Fergie Jenkins be reinstated after Commissioner Kuhn suspended Jenkins indefinitely following the pitcher's August 25 drug bust in Toronto.

1997 Atlanta is the first ML team to clinch six consecutive division titles.

2000 Houston's Jose Lima sets a NL season mark by yielding his 47th homer and extends the record to 48 by the campaign's end.

2003 The Tigers drop their 118th game to break the 1916 Philadelphia A's AL record for losses, and the team loses one more before the season ends. Elsewhere, the Yankees' Alfonso Soriano blasts his ML season record 13th leadoff homer.

23

1845 The Knickerbocker baseball club of New York is organized at the behest of Alexander Cartwright and plays by the first set of rules that contain most of the basic elements present in the modern game.

1908 The circumstances of the Cubs' 1–0 loss to Pittsburgh on September 4 of the season are almost exactly replicated, but this time plate umpire Hank O'Day, independent of base umpire Bob Emslie, renders perhaps the most controversial decision in the history of the game when he acknowledges the validity of Cubs second baseman Johnny Evers's appeal and rules Fred Merkle of the Giants out for failing to proceed from first to second base, thereupon erasing Al Bridwell's apparent game-winning single.

1930 Lost amid another 1930 hitting barrage that brings the Cards a 19–16 win over the Phils is outfielder Chuck Klein's 44th assist, the modern season record and second only to Hugh Nicol's 48 in 1884.

1933 The Reds' Paul Derringer loses his 27th game, the most in a season by any ML pitcher since George Bell in 1910.

1936 The Giants' Carl Hubbell logs his 16th straight win as he beats the Phils, 5–4.

1945 The Senators are the last team to go through an entire season without hitting an out-of-the-park home run in their home facility. Washington's lone home dinger in 1945 was an ITPH by first baseman Joe Kuhel.

1957   Hank Aaron's 11th-inning home run gives the Braves a 4–2 win over the Cardinals and clinches the first pennant in ML history by a team representing Milwaukee.

1962   Dodgers speed merchant Maury Wills breaks a new post–1897 record for steals in a season with his 97th swipe, surpassing Ty Cobb's former mark of 96.

1969   When the Dodgers' John Miller homers in his last ML AB after connecting in his first big league trip to the plate with the Yankees three years earlier, he becomes the only player to date to belt four-baggers in both his first and last ML plate appearances. Meanwhile, banished umpires Bill Valentine and Al Salerno sock MLB with a $4,000,000 antitrust suit.

1977   George Foster clouts his 50th homer, making him the first Reds slugger to reach that plateau in a single season and the initial clubber to swat that many since Roger Maris and Mickey Mantle in 1961.

1978   The son of a former Negro league first baseman, Angels outfielder Lyman Bostock is shot to death while riding in his car in Gary, IN. Just 27 years of age, Bostock becomes the first player to earn MVP votes posthumously.

1979   The Cards' Lou Brock purloins his 938th and final base, eclipsing Hall of Famer Billy Hamilton's unofficial career mark, but Hamilton's total is later downgraded to 914.

1983   Dodgers bullpenner Steve Howe's drug problems earn him another suspension after he misses the team's Atlanta flight and then refuses to take a urine test upon his arrival.

1984   The Tigers bag their 100th victory, making their skipper, Sparky Anderson, the first manager to win 100 games in a season in each league, having previously guided the Reds to the century mark twice.

1986   Astros moundsman Jim Deshaies fans the first eight Dodgers to face him, setting a post–1892 ML record for the most consecutive Ks to open a game.

1988   The A's Jose Canseco is the first MLer to hit 40 homers and steal 40 bases in the same season.

1992   OB's first female umpire, Bernice Gera, dies at the age of 61. Meanwhile, the Padres stage "Unemployment Night" and commemorate the occasion by firing skipper Greg Riddoch.

1998   The Cubs' Sammy Sosa hits his 64th and 65th round-trippers of the year against the Brewers, tying the 1938 Tigers' Hank Greenberg's ML-season mark for multihomer games with 11. Elsewhere, Houston's Craig Biggio joins Tris Speaker of the 1912 Red Sox as the only two players to steal 50 bases and slap 50 doubles in the same season.

2000   Tampa Bay first baseman Fred McGriff joins Frank Robinson as the only two players to date to stroke 200 homers in both leagues.

2001   Facing Houston, the Cubs' Sammy Sosa is the first MLer to blast three homers in a game three times in one season.

2002   The last public event in Cinergy Field is a softball game featuring former members of the "Big Red Machine," including admitted gambler Pete Rose, who is allowed to play because the contest is not affiliated with MLB.

2007   Padres outfielder Milton Bradley and umpire Mike Winters have a shouting match at first base. In restraining Bradley, manager Bud Black wrestles him to the ground, and a ligament in Bradley's right knee is torn, ending his season. A few days later, Winters's season is also ended when he is suspended for using profanity during the encounter.

24

1908   NL president Harry Pulliam supports umpire Hank O'Day's ruling of the previous day and declares the "Merkle" game between the Cubs and the Giants a tie, forcing the two clubs to replay the contest deadlocked for first place after the scheduled last day of the season.

1909   Charles Tenhuy of Dayton in the Central League dies of a fractured skull after being beaned by Rip Hagerman of Grand Rapids.

1916   Cleveland's Marty Kavanagh sinks the Red Sox 5–3 when he hits the first pinch grand slam in AL history, a grass cutter that sneaks through a hole in the outfield fence.

1919   Boston's Babe Ruth shatters Ned Williamson's 1884 single-season home run record when his 28th homer of the year off future Yankees teammate Bob Shawkey ties the game 1–1 in the 9th inning.

1926   The Cards clinch the first pennant by a St. Louis NL or AL entry when they beat the Giants, while second-place Cincinnati loses the first game of a DBH to the Phillies.

1929 Yankees hurler Tom Zachary's 5–3 win over Boston gives him 12 victories without a loss, still the ML record for the most wins in a season without a defeat.

1942 White Sox stalwart Ted Lyons stops the Indians 3–1 in the first game of a DBH at Cleveland for his 20th complete game of the season in 20 starts, making him the last ML ERA qualifier to complete all of his starting assignments.

1955 The toast of the Polo Grounds only a year earlier, Giants manager Leo Durocher learns that his contract is not being renewed. Elsewhere, in his last hill appearance of the season, Dodgers lefty Sandy Koufax loses to the Pirates and assures that he will retain his season record for the most consecutive strikeouts in consecutive plate appearances as he fans all 12 times he comes to bat in 1955.

1957 In the final ML game at Ebbets Field, the Dodgers' Danny Mc-Devitt blanks Pittsburgh, 2–0.

1969 Rookie Gary Gentry beats the Cards' Steve Carlton 6–0 to bring the Mets their first NL East title in their eighth year of existence.

1974 Clarence Jones of the Kintetsu Buffaloes is the first American to win a Japanese league tater title when his 38th four-run shot assures him of the Pacific League crown.

1978 The Yankees' Ron Guidry blanks the Indians 4–0 for his ninth shutout, tying Babe Ruth's 1916 AL season southpaw record.

1979 The Phillies' Pete Rose slaps his 200th hit for the 10th season in his career, eclipsing Ty Cobb's previous ML standard.

1980 The Braves are the 12th NL team this season to pass the 1,000,000 mark in home attendance, marking the first time that all teams in one ML have reached the milestone.

1984 The Cubs beat the Pirates to clinch the NL East title and send them to the postseason for the first time since 1945, when Rick Sutcliffe wins his 14th consecutive game, boosting his record to 16–1 since arriving in a June trade.

1993 The Rockies beat the Reds to set a new NL mark for wins by an expansion club with 65, which they extend to 67, three short of the ML mark of 70 set by the 1961 Los Angeles Angels.

1997 Doug Million, the Rockies first pick in the June 1994 draft, dies at the age of 21 in Mesa, AZ, from an asthma attack.

2001   Pirates rookie Craig Wilson poles his seventh pinch-hit homer of the season, tying Dave Hansen's ML record set the previous year. Elsewhere, former MLer Tuffy Rhodes ties Sadaharu Oh's Japanese league season record by blasting his 55th homer with the Kintetsu Buffaloes.

2002   The Yanks' Jason Giambi creams two homers, giving him and his brother, Jeremy, a combined total of 60, surpassing Joe and Vince DiMaggio's 1937 mark for the most by two siblings, which Jason later extends to 61.

2006   Padres reliever Trevor Hoffman preserves a 2–1 win against the Padres to post his 479th career save, eclipsing Lee Smith's old mark.

25

1881   First baseman Chub Sullivan dies of consumption at the age of 25, just a year after playing his final ML game with Worcester. His club is the first on record in ML history to honor the passing of a teammate by wearing a piece of black crepe on their sleeves. Elsewhere, the NL announces that all eight of its teams will return in 1882, a first in pro ball.

1909   Washington's Bob Groom, headed for an AL rookie record of 26 losses, drops his 15th straight decision, 2–1 to the White Sox.

1929   Three days after turning his club over to coach Art Fletcher on an interim basis, Yankees skipper Miller Huggins dies of blood poisoning at the age of 49.

1930   Joe McCarthy resigns as Cubs manager and is replaced by second baseman Rogers Hornsby.

1932   Jimmie Foxx hits his 58th homer, just two short of Babe Ruth's record, but the A's still lose their season finale 2–1 to Washington's Al Crowder, who finishes the year with 15 straight wins.

1936   The Cards' Joe Medwick rips his 64th double to set a NL record that still stands.

1939   Homerless in his first 15 years in the majors, Boston's Johnny Cooney goes yard at the Polo Grounds for the second time in two days—and the final time in his 20-year career—when he reaches the right-field seats against the Giants' Bill Lohrman.

1946   Rookie Ralph Kiner's solo jack off Chicago's Russ Meyer in the 8th frame is his 23rd of the season and not only ties Johnny Rizzo's

Pittsburgh franchise season dingers record but also assures Kiner of the NL home run crown, making him the first freshman loop leader since Braggo Roth in 1915.

1947 Giants first sacker Johnny Mize's 9th-inning blast at Braves Field brings rookie Larry Jansen his 21st victory and ties Mize with Pittsburgh's Ralph Kiner for the NL home-run crown, as both sluggers will finish the season with 51, marking the first time two batsmen have hit 50 jacks in the same season.

1954 The Indians set a new AL record for wins (since broken) when Early Wynn beats the Tigers 11–1 for his loop-leading 23rd victory and the Tribe's 111th triumph.

1960 The Yankees capture their 10th pennant in 12 years under Casey Stengel, as Ralph Terry defeats the Red Sox. Elsewhere, the Pirates clinch the NL flag for the first time in 33 years.

1964 When the Angels' Dean Chance downs the Twins, he is the first member of a post–1884 expansion team to win 20 games and also earns his ML record-tying fifth 1–0 victory of the season.

1965 The A's wheel out 59-year-old Satchel Paige, who spins three relief innings against the Red Sox and surrenders just one hit, a double to Carl Yastrzemski.

1971 The Tigers' Les Cain works six innings for a win against the Yanks but asserts afterward that his manager, Billy Martin, forced him to pitch with a sore arm. Later claiming that Martin ruined his career, Cain wins a landmark suit when the Michigan Bureau of Workman's Compensation orders the Tigers to pay Cain $111 a month for the rest of his life, but a lump sum is subsequently agreed upon.

1974 Medicine takes a quantum leap as Dr. Frank Jobe repairs Dodgers hurler Tommy John's throwing arm by replacing a damaged elbow tendon with a tendon from the lefty pitcher's right wrist, a procedure later dubbed "Tommy John surgery" when John goes on to pitch 14 more years.

1978 Constance Baker Motley, a New York District Court Judge, rules that female sportswriters cannot be banned from locker rooms in the state of New York.

1980 Oakland's Brian Kingman is beaten by the White Sox for his 20th defeat, marking him the last 20-game loser in the 20th century and the first since the Reds' Dolf Luque in 1922 to drop 20 after toiling an entire season with a club that had a winning record (83–79). Else-

229

where, Ozzie Smith and Jerry Mumphrey each snag their 50th base, joining teammate Gene Richards in making the Padres the first NL club to feature three speedsters with 50 steals in a season.

1984 When Rusty Staub clubs a game-ending two-run homer against the Phillies to give the Mets a 6–4 win, he joins Ty Cobb as the only two players to date to swat a jack both as a teenager and at the age of 40.

1986 Mike Scott no-hits the Giants and clinches the NL West title for Houston.

1989 The Red Sox' Wade Boggs is the first ALer to log seven straight 200-hit seasons and also the first to string together four straight seasons with 200 hits and 100 walks.

1992 It's all hands on deck when Seattle beats Texas 4–3 in 16 innings, as the two clubs combine to use a ML-record 54 players.

1998 The Yankees set an AL mark with their 112th win but finish with 114, two shy of the 1906 Cubs' ML mark of 116 (since tied).

2000 Cleveland fans are treated to the first three-club DBH since 1951, as the Indians beat the White Sox in the opener but lose to the Twins in the second game.

2001 The Mariners win their 56th game on the road, setting a new AL record that they extend to 59, just one short of the 1906 Cubs' ML mark of 60. Elsewhere, in a ML first, Pirates rookie Craig Wilson strokes hits off three different Cubs pitchers in the first three innings after rapping hits in each of the final three innings in the previous game off three other Chicago hurlers to give him hits in six straight innings off six different moundsmen. In addition, for the first time in ML history, two teammates blast three homers in the same game as the Brewers' Richie Sexson and Jeromy Burnitz connect against the Diamondbacks.

2003 The Cubs' Sammy Sosa drives in his 100th run for the ninth straight season, breaking the NL mark he shared with Mel Ott and Willie Mays. Elsewhere, Blue Jays slugger Carlos Delgado homers in each of his four trips to the plate, lifting Toronto to a 10–8 victory over the Devil Rays.

2007 At the age of 23, the Brewers' Prince Fielder is the youngest MLer to slug 50 homers in a season and joins with his sire, Cecil, as the only father and son to each reach that milestone in a single season.

26

1878 For the second year in a row, despite a NL schedule calling for only 60 games, Tommy Bond collects his loop-leading 40th win, topping Providence, 4–1.

1896 By making three hits in Cleveland's final game of the season, Jesse Burkett lifts his BA to .410 and not only wins his second straight NL batting title but is the first MLer since Ross Barnes (1871–1873) to hit .400 in two or more consecutive seasons.

1906 The Philadelphia A's end a ML-record 48 consecutive innings without scoring (since tied by the 1968 Cubs) when they tally two runs in the 6th frame while bowing to Cleveland, 5–3.

1908 Cubs right-hander Ed Reulbach is the only pitcher to date to toss two complete-game shutouts in the same day when he blanks Brooklyn in both ends of a DBH, 5–0 and 3–0.

1954 Willie Mays begins the final day of the season third in the NL batting race but wins the crown when he goes 3-for-4 to finish at .345, while fellow Giant Don Mueller is 2-for-6 to reduce his mark to .342 and Brooklyn's Duke Snider draws a 0-for-3 collar to finish at .341.

1955 Detroit's Al Kaline is the youngest batting champ in ML history at the age of 20 when his .340 mark is officially awarded the AL crown over Boston's Ted Williams, who hit .356 but in only 320 at bats.

1961 The Yankees' Roger Maris equals Babe Ruth's season mark by belting his 60th homer, a solo shot in the 3rd off the Orioles' Jack Fisher.

1964 Yankees rookie Mel Stottlemyre excels on the mound and at the plate against the Senators as he fashions a 7–0, two-hit gem while becoming the last pitcher to date to slap five hits in a game.

1971 Jim Palmer beats the Indians to join teammates Pat Dobson, Mike Cuellar, and Dave McNally in making the Orioles the only team other than the 1920 White Sox with four 20-game winners.

1979 Against Houston, the Braves' Phil Niekro wins his 20th game, beating the NL's only other 20-game winner that year, his brother, Joe, as they become the second pair of siblings to date to each bag 20 victories in the same season (joining Gaylord and Jim Perry, 1970) and the first to share a loop lead in wins with 21. Phil added the distinction of notching 20 losses, making him the last pitcher to date to both win and lose 20 in the same campaign.

1981 The Astros' Nolan Ryan garners his record-breaking fifth career no-hitter as he baffles the Dodgers, 5–0.

1984 The Phillies' Juan Samuel pilfers his 72nd base, breaking Tim Raines's ML rookie standard.

1987 The Padres' Benito Santiago hits safely in his 28th straight game, breaking the ML rookie mark he previously shared with Jimmy Williams of the 1899 Pirates. Santiago extends his record to 34.

1993 In their first year of operation, the Colorado Rockies set a ML season home attendance record, drawing 4,483,350 fans.

1997 Against the Marlins, Phillies fireballer Curt Schilling fans his 314th batter to set a post–1892 NL-season record for right-handers that he extends to 319.

1999 Cards bopper Mark McGwire joins Sammy Sosa as the only MLers to date to smash 60 homers twice in a season.

27

1892 Tom Dowse's appearance behind the bat with Washington in an 11–2 loss to Philadelphia marks the first time in ML history that a player has seen action with four different ML teams in the same season. Dowse was previously with Louisville, Cincinnati, and Philadelphia, and though others have since played with four teams in the same season, Dowse remains the only catcher to perform the feat.

1901 Boston Americans hurler Ted Lewis nips the Chicago White Sox, 3–2. The win is not only Lewis's last in the majors before retiring to become an academic but also burdens the AL flag winners with a 0–10 record in Boston, making the 1901 Pale Hose the only ML pennant winner in the 20th century to go winless for an entire season in a rival team's park.

1919 Babe Ruth's homer off Rip Jordan in the first game of Boston's season-ending DBH against the Senators is his record 29th of the season and makes him the first player to homer in every park in his league in one season.

1924 The Giants clinch their NL-record fourth straight pennant when they beat the Phillies, 5–1.

1930 Hack Wilson victimizes Reds lefty Eppa Rixey for his 56th home run, the NL record prior to 1997.

1931 When Jim Bottomley of the Cards bags four hits on the final day of the NL season, while his teammate Chick Hafey and the Giants'

Bill Terry are both making only one safety apiece, less than one percentage point separates the trio at the day's end in the closest three-way batting race in ML history, with Hafey emerging the winner at .3488 to Terry's .3486 and Bottomley's .3481.

1935 The Cubs sweep a DBH with the Cardinals to clinch the NL pennant with a torrid stretch drive that features a 21-game winning streak.

1940 His club two games ahead of the Indians with three to play, Detroit manager Del Baker concedes the first game of the season-ending weekend series at Cleveland to the Tribe's Bob Feller and starts 30-year-old frosh Floyd Giebell, only to receive an astonishing pennant-clinching 2–0 gem from Giebell in what is his last ML decision.

1942 In a 4–3 loss to the Dodgers, Phils left fielder Danny Litwhiler finishes the NL season errorless in 151 games, the first perfect fielding season by an outfielder in ML history; however, Litwhiler's mark is somewhat tainted in that he was charged with an error in an earlier game that was later changed to a hit.

1953 Cleveland's Al Rosen is denied the Triple Crown when he is nipped at first base on his grounder in his last AB of the season in a 7–3 loss to Detroit's Al Aber, leaving him .0011 points behind Washington first baseman Mickey Vernon in the AL batting race.

1954 Final AL figures show Ted Williams with the top BA at .345 but lacking 400 at bats due partly to two stays on the DL, but more to his loop-leading 136 walks, and the AL bat crown goes instead to Cleveland's Bobby Avila, even though Williams has more than enough plate appearances to qualify for the title as per the current rule. The Williams episode represents the only time in ML history that a player was denied a major batting or pitching department lead that he would have qualified for under today's rules.

1959 The Dodgers and Braves finish the NL regular season in a tie for first place (86–68), with the Giants in third at 83–71 after dropping seven of their last eight games.

1961 The Dodgers' Sandy Koufax fans his 268th batter to set a then post–1892 NL-season record for strikeouts, topping the 1903 Giants' Christy Mathewson, and he adds one more for good measure.

1963 The Astros field an all-rookie lineup whose average age is under 20, and though they lose 10–3 to the Mets, four of the frosh (Joe Morgan, Rusty Staub, Jimmy Wynn, and Jerry Grote) enjoy lengthy ML careers.

1973   California's Nolan Ryan sets the post–1892 season whiff record by fanning the Twins' Rich Reese in the 11th inning for his 383rd strikeout, topping Sandy Koufax's former mark by one.

1984   In his only career AB with Cleveland, Jamie Quirk hits a pinch-hit, game-ending solo homer against the Twins' Ron Davis, giving the Tribe a 4–3 victory.

1992   Seattle's Randy Johnson fans 18 Rangers, tying the AL record for left-handers in a 9-inning game (since broken by Johnson himself) first set by the Yanks' Ron Guidry in 1978.

1993   By preserving a victory over the Dodgers, Cubs stopper Randy Myers is the first NL reliever to post a 50-save season.

1996   Baltimore's Roberto Alomar spits in umpire John Hirschbeck's face after being ejected and receives a five-game suspension but is allowed to play the next day and in the postseason after appealing the decision. Elsewhere, the Giants' Barry Bonds is the first NLer to slam 40 homers and swipe 40 bases.

1997   Seattle gift wraps Randy Johnson his 20th victory by having him work just the 5th and 6th innings in relief against Oakland, enabling the "Big Unit" to become the Mariners' first 20-game winner.

1998   The Yankees close the season at 114–48 with a .704 winning percentage, the first ML team since the 1954 Indians to play .700 ball. Elsewhere, for the first time in ML history, two sets of brothers play in the same lineup and in the same infield, as the Reds feature Stephen Larkin at first and his brother, Barry, at short, with Bret Boone at second and his sib, Aaron, at third. Meanwhile, the Cardinals' Mark McGwire creams his 69th and 70th homers to cap his record-breaking season.

2000   The Angels' Darin Erstad posts his 99th RBI from the leadoff spot, eclipsing Nomar Garciaparra's 1997 mark. By the season's end, Erstad extends the mark to 100. Elsewhere, behind the pitching of Ben Sheets, Tommy Lasorda's U.S. Olympic team upsets Cuba to win America's first gold medal in baseball.

2002   Former Braves starter John Smoltz adjusts spectacularly in his first year as the team's closer, setting a NL record by logging his 54th save, which he extends to 55 (since equaled) by the season's end.

2003   Atlanta's Javy Lopez drills his 42nd homer, setting the current ML season mark for taters by a catcher.

2006   The Marlins' Anibal Sanchez beats the Reds for his 10th victory, joining teammates Scott Olson, Josh Johnson, and Ricky Nolasco as the first rookie quartet to win in double figures for one club.

28

1862   Following a 23–11 loss to the Eckfords of Brooklyn, the Mutuals of New York find three team members guilty of deliberately throwing the game and instigate action that results in their being barred from baseball for life; however, all are later reinstated.

1883   Philadelphia A's hurler "Jumping" Jack Jones tops Louisville 7–6 to clinch the AA pennant and then quits baseball to follow in the footsteps of his mother, Emeline, the first female in the United States to open her own dental practice.

1911   The Phils' spectacular newcomer, Pete Alexander, beats Pittsburgh 6–3 to win his post–1892 rookie record 28th game and also sets a new rookie record (since broken) for strikeouts.

1919   In the last ML game played in an all-wooden park, the Cards' Robison Field, Pittsburgh's Jack Wisner goes all the way in his first ML start to beat St. Louis's Frank Woodward, 6–3.

1920   A Chicago grand jury indicts eight members of the White Sox for fixing the 1919 World Series, resulting in their immediate suspension by Sox owner Charlie Comiskey.

1924   Cards second baseman Rogers Hornsby goes 4-for-6 in a season-ending DBH against the Reds to finish with a .424 BA, the highest NL mark since 1894.

1930   In a campaign-ending 12–11 win over Cincinnati, Hack Wilson drives in two runs, his 190th and 191st, to set a still-existing ML season record.

1932   A's manager/GM Connie Mack takes his first major step toward dissolving his 1929–1931 AL dynasty when he peddles Al Simmons, Mule Haas, and Jimmy Dykes to the White Sox for $100,000.

1938   Cubs catcher Gabby Hartnett smacks his famous walk-off "homer in the gloamin'" off the Pirates' Mace Brown to break a 5–5 tie in the bottom of the 9th and put Chicago in first place ahead of Pittsburgh.

1941   Ted Williams begins the day at .3995 (rounded off to .400) but refuses to sit out so he can protect his .400 BA and then goes 6-for-8 in a DBH at Philadelphia to finish at .406, marking the last .400 season to date by a BA qualifier.

1949 Ted Williams's all-time ML record of reaching base in 84 straight games is halted by Washington's ace streak stopper, Rae Scarborough, who holds Boston to just four hits and walks none in winning, 2–1.

1951 The Yankees' Allie Reynolds is not only the first AL hurler to craft two no-hitters in the same season when he sets down the Red Sox 8–0, but the first to clinch the pennant for his team with a no-no.

1952 The Braves' last ML game representing the city of Boston ends in a 5–5 12-inning tie at Ebbets Field marked by Brooklyn reliever Jim Hughes's strikeout of Sid Gordon to give the Dodgers staff 773 Ks, one better than their former NL mark of 772 set in 1950.

1958 At the age of 40, Ted Williams is the oldest batting champ to date after he goes 2-for-4 on the last day of the season against Washington's Pete Ramos to give him the AL crown with a .328 BA.

1974 In the process of spinning his third career no-hitter and downing the Twins 4–0, California's Nolan Ryan also eclipses 200 walks, joining Cleveland's Bob Feller in 1938 as the only pitchers since Cy Seymour in 1898 to do so.

1975 In a ML first, four pitchers combine in a no-hitter as the A's Vida Blue, Glenn Abbott, Paul Lindblad, and Rollie Fingers defeat the Angels 5–0 on the last day of the regular season.

1995 The Expos' Greg Harris is the first hurler since the 1890s to pitch with both hands in a ML game when he faces two Reds batters from his usual right side and two from the left.

1997 The Padres' Tony Gwynn hits .372, tying Honus Wagner's NL record by winning his eighth batting crown.

2007 The Yankees' loop-record reign of nine consecutive AL East titles snaps when the Red Sox capture the crown. Elsewhere, the Cubs clinch the NL Central title as their manager, Lou Piniella, guides his third different club to a division win, including the Reds and Mariners.

29

1880 The independent New York Metropolitans open the first commercial baseball park in Manhattan—a former polo field that is fittingly called the Polo Grounds—by beating the National Association champion Washington club, 4–2.

1881   At a loop meeting, the NL distributes a formal blacklist of players who are barred from the circuit until unanimously voted otherwise and reaffirms its stance that in the event of injury or illness, a player must assume full responsibility for his own well-being, including payment for medical treatment.

1891   After dropping his entire salary in local poolrooms and bookie joints, catcher Bill Wilson deserts the Kansas City Western Association club and abandons his wife, forcing teammates to take up a collection to supply her with funds to get home to Pittsburgh, where Wilson had induced her to leave a convent the previous year. Wilson later becomes involved in organized crime and serves two prison terms before being stabbed to death in 1924 in what police suspected was a hit job.

1895   Out of the majors since 1888 when he debuted with Louisville by fanning a record-tying four times, Herk Burnett goes from the ridiculous to the sublime when he culminates his return to the Kentucky club by going 3-for-5 against Cleveland in his final ML game, including a homer in his last ML AB.

1924   The Senators clinch the first ML pennant in Washington history when they beat the Red Sox, 4–2.

1929   Final NL stats credit the Giants' Bill Terry with a .401 BA, the last .400 season to date in the senior loop, and the Giants with a .319 team BA, the best in the majors since Baltimore's .325 mark in 1897.

1935   Yet another bizarre episode occurs in Cleveland when Washington's Buddy Myer edges Indians outfielder Joe Vosmik for the AL batting title on the last day of the season by going 4-for-5 while Vosmik initially opts to sit out a DBH against the Browns to protect his lead. Alarmed when news of Myer's barrage reaches Cleveland Stadium, Vosmik hastens into action, pinch-hitting unsuccessfully in the first game and going 1-for-3 in the nightcap to finish a fraction of a point behind Myer. Vosmik then learns that if he had remained on the bench all day, he and Myer would have finished in an exact tie for the title with 215 hits in 516 at bats (.349).

1945   Hank Borowy's 21st victory in the first game of a twin bill with the Pirates enables the Cubs to clinch their last NL flag to date and sets them on their way to sweeping a season-record 20 doubleheaders when they also win the second contest.

1946   The Cards and Dodgers both back into a tie for the NL lead on the last day of the regular season when each loses to set up the first pennant playoff in ML history.

1950   The Dodgers sweep a DBH with the Braves, cutting the injury-plagued Phillies' lead in the NL to two games with two head-to-head contests with Brooklyn remaining at Ebbets Field.

1952   The final NL stats show the Phils' Robin Roberts with 28 wins, the most in the senior loop since 1935, and Pittsburgh's Ralph Kiner with his NL-record seventh straight home-run crown, this shared with the Cubs' Hank Sauer.

1953   A syndicate headed by Baltimore mayor Thomas D'Alesandro buys Bill Veeck's interest in the St. Louis Browns for $2,475,000, and the AL immediately approves the Browns' proposed shift to Baltimore.

1954   Willie Mays's storied catch of Vic Wertz's drive to deep center field in the 8th inning of the opening game of the World Series sets the stage for Giants pinch-hitter Dusty Rhodes to lift New York to a 5–2 win in the 10th frame, when he lofts a 260-foot three-run homer off the Tribe's Bob Lemon that travels little more than half the distance of Wertz's blast two frames earlier.

1957   The Giants lose their last home game of the season 9–1 to the Pirates, who have the distinction of providing the opposition in both the last ML game at Ebbets Field and the Giants' Polo Grounds coda.

1958   The Phils' Dave Philley sets a new ML mark when he collects his eighth consecutive pinch hit in eight at bats, breaking Peanuts Lowrey's mark of seven, set in 1952.

1959   The Dodgers bag the NL flag by sweeping the first two games from the Braves of the third pennant playoff series in senior loop history, all of which have involved the Dodgers.

1963   The Colts' John Paciorek (brother of future big leaguers Tom and Jim) goes 3-for-3 with three RBI and four runs scored, plus two walks, in what is his only ML game.

2004   MLB announces that the Montreal Expos are moving to Washington, DC, before the club loses that evening to the Marlins in their final home game at Olympic Stadium.

30

1878   The NL is the first pro loop to complete its entire schedule when all six of its teams play a full 60-game slate.

1879   Though Will White loses 9–6 to Cleveland in Cincinnati's season finale, he finishes with 75 complete games and 680 innings pitched, both records that to date have not been broken. Meanwhile, in an effort to curb rising salaries, NL owners institute an embryonic reserve clause that allows each club to reserve five players from its present roster for the following year.

1894 Leading 16–1 in the bottom of the 6th inning in the season finale, Cincinnati's Frank Dwyer is incredulous when Cleveland rallies to knot the game at 16–all and deprives him of his seemingly certain 20th win of the season after the game ends in a tie.

1897 Boston clinches the NL pennant, its fourth since 1890 under manager Frank Selee, as it finishes the season with a franchise-record .705 winning percentage.

1907 Trailing the front-running Tigers by 1½ games, the A's aim to sweep a DBH but lose their chance to overtake Detroit when darkness ends the first game with the score tied 9–9 after 17 innings, and there is no rule at the time requiring teams involved in a pennant race to make up any tied or unplayed games.

1910 Browns third baseman Ray Jansen bangs four hits, the most ever by a one-game MLer, but also makes three errors, adding up to a 9–1 St. Louis loss to Chicago's Fred Olmstead.

1927 Babe Ruth shatters his own season home-run record when he creams his 60th dinger of the campaign off Washington's Tom Zachary in the 8th inning of a 4–2 Yankees win.

1934 Dizzy Dean clinches the pennant for the Cards when he beats the Reds for his 30th win, while the Giants lose for the second straight day to the Dodgers.

1945 Hank Greenberg's grand slam in the 9th gives Detroit the AL pennant on the final day of the season. Elsewhere, Yankees second baseman Snuffy Stirnweiss singles off Boston's Otie Clark in the 8th inning to win the AL batting crown by one point over Chicago's Tony Cuccinello, who can only wait on events in New York when the White Sox' final game of the season is rained out. In the NL, the Giants' Don Fisher hurls a ML-record 13-inning complete-game shutout in his only big league start to top the Braves 1–0 in the first game of a season-ending twin bill.

1946 The Braves acquire 1947 NL MVP Bob Elliott and catcher Hank Camelli from the Pirates for four players, including Pittsburgh's 1947 player-manager Billy Herman.

1949 In a 3–2 win over the Reds, Pittsburgh's Ralph Kiner, the first NL player to put together two 50-homer seasons, hits his 54th and last jack of the campaign.

1951 With attention riveted on the Giants and Dodgers as both win on the last day of the regular season to create a dead heat in the NL race, the Browns' Ned Garver receives little fanfare when he tops the White Sox 9–5 to become the only hurler in ML history to win 20 for a cellar dweller that loses 100 contests in a season.

1956 Jim Derrington is the youngest hurler in AL history to start a game when he goes eight innings at the age of 16 and 10 months for the White Sox in a 7–6 loss to KC.

1962 The Tigers' Bubba Morton draws a walk off Bill Fischer, ending the A's hurler's ML record string of 84$\frac{1}{3}$ consecutive innings without issuing a free pass. Elsewhere, the Mets' Joe Pignatano hits into a triple play in his last career AB as the Cubs hand the Mets their post–1900 record 120th loss of the season.

1966 The White Sox beat the Yankees 6–5 to assure that New York will finish last in the AL for the first time since 1912.

1968 Arbiters from both leagues form a new Association of Major League Umpires and pledge to strike in the spring of 1969 unless AL umpires Bill Valentine and Al Salerno are reinstated.

1969 Former ML third baseman Hank Thompson dies of a stroke at his mother's home in Fresno, CA, shortly after being paroled from a Texas penitentiary where he was serving 10 years for armed robbery.

1971 In the Senators' final home game before moving to Texas, fans storm the field with Washington up 7–5 with one out to go in the 9th inning, causing the game to be forfeited to the Yankees.

1972 Pirates outfielder Roberto Clemente strokes a double off the Mets' Jon Matlack for his 3,000th and last career hit.

1978 Philadelphia's Randy Lerch powers two homers, and the Phillies snag their third straight NL East title, beating the Pirates and snapping Pittsburgh's 24-game winning streak at home.

1980 Oakland's Rickey Henderson sets a new AL season theft record with his 97th, eclipsing Ty Cobb.

1984 The Angels' Mike Witt pitches the only ML perfect game to date in the final game of a regular season by beating the Rangers, 1–0. Elsewhere, the Yankees' Don Mattingly goes 4-for-5, while teammate

Dave Winfield goes 1-for-4 to give Mattingly the AL bat title, .343 to .340.

1988   President Ronald Reagan throws out the first pitch at Wrigley Field. The former broadcaster later joins Harry Caray in the booth for an inning.

1989   At the age of 42, the Rangers' Nolan Ryan is the oldest pitcher to date to fan 300 batters in a season.

1990   After 80 years in operation, Comiskey Park is home to the White Sox for the final time as they best Seattle in the ancient facility's coda.

1995   Indians outfielder Albert Belle's 50th home run makes him the first player in ML history to rap 50 homers and 50 doubles in the same season.

1998   Dan Quisenberry, at one time the ML season save record holder, dies of brain cancer at the age of 45.

1999   Arizona's Randy Johnson fans 11 Padres, tying Nolan Ryan's 1973 ML season mark for the most double-figure strikeout games with 23.

2001   Colorado's Todd Helton doubles to become the first ML player to belt 100 extra base hits in back-to-back years.

October

1

1887 Brooklyn of the AA purchases the about-to-disband New York Mets for somewhere around $20,000 to gain the rights to the Mets' best players—mainly, first baseman Dave Orr.

1891 Boston overcomes a seemingly prohibitive Chicago lead to clinch the NL pennant and prompts credible accusations from Colts manager Cap Anson and club president Jim Hart that several Eastern teams conspired to throw the NL pennant to the Hub entry.

1903 Pittsburgh's Deacon Phillippe spoils the first "modern" World Series game at Boston's Huntington Avenue Grounds for local fans by topping AL kingpin Cy Young 7–3, as Pirates outfielder Jimmy Sebring hits the first 20th-century postseason home run.

1919 White Sox ace Eddie Cicotte is pummeled for five runs in the 4th inning in Game 1 of a World Series that has already aroused suspicion when Cincinnati, originally an underdog, is puzzlingly the betting favorite.

1922 Rogers Hornsby goes 3-for-5 against three Cubs hurlers on the last day of the NL season to finish with a .401 BA, the first .400 season in the senior loop since 1899.

1924 On the eve of the World Series, Commissioner Landis banishes Giants coach Cozy Dolan and rookie outfielder Jimmy O'Connell from OB for trying to bribe Phils shortstop Heinie Sand to "go easy" on the Giants in the season-ending series between the two teams.

1927 The Yankees extend their new AL season record for the most wins (since broken) when they finish the season with their 110th victory, beating Washington, 4–3.

1932   In Game 3 of the World Series, the Yankees' Babe Ruth belts his second homer of the game into the center-field bleachers at Wrigley Field, igniting an eternal controversy as to whether he "called his shot" prior to Charlie Root's pitch or was merely gesturing.

1944   The St. Louis Browns wrap up their lone AL pennant on the final day of the season when Sig Jakucki tops the Yankees 5–2 to complete an improbable four-game sweep of the defending AL champions, who still had pennant aspirations of their own just two mornings earlier.

1950   Making his third start in five days, the Phils' Robin Roberts prevents the worst collapse ever in the closing days of a season when center fielder Richie Ashburn makes a game-saving throw to nail Dodgers runner Cal Abrams at the plate in the 9th inning, and Dick Sisler follows with a three-run homer in the 10th to bring the Phillies only their second flag in their 68-year history.

1961   The Yankees' Roger Maris breaks Babe Ruth's season mark by belting his 61st homer off the Red Sox' Tracy Stallard, accounting for the game's lone run. Sal Durante, seated 15 rows up in the right-field stands at Yankee Stadium, snags the ball and is offered the stupendous sum of $5,000 for it by a Sacramento, CA, restaurateur.

1973   The Mets beat the Cubs to capture the NL West title as the Bruins' Billy Williams and Ron Santo play in their ML record 2,015th and final game as teammates.

1989   The batting champs in both loops are decided on the final day of the season as San Diego's Tony Gwynn tops San Francisco's Will Clark, .336 to .333, and Minnesota's Kirby Puckett edges Oakland's Carney Lansford, .339 to .336.

1995   The Rockies beat the Giants to become the NL's first wild-card entry in the franchise's third year of existence.

2004   Seattle's Ichiro Suzuki strokes his 258th hit to break the ML season record set by the Browns' George Sisler in 1920 and extends his new mark to 262 by the season's end.

2007   In a one-game play-in, the Rockies beat the Padres 9–8 to win the NL wild card by rallying from a two-run deficit in the bottom of the 13th inning against San Diego closer Trevor Hoffman.

2

1908   In perhaps the greatest pitching duel in ML history, White Sox 40-game winner Ed Walsh allows only four hits but is beaten 1–0 when

Cleveland's Addie Joss twirls a perfect game, putting Cleveland in a near tie for first place with Detroit, while the Sox fall 2½ games back.

1916 Phils ace Pete Alexander beats the Braves 2–0 for his 16th shutout of the season, tying George Bradley's 40-year-old ML record.

1921 Babe Ruth hits his 59th home run off Curt Fullerton to set a new season record, as the Yankees wrap up their first pennant-winning campaign with a 7–6 triumph over the Red Sox.

1936 The Yankees score a single-game World Series record 18 runs in thrashing the Giants, 18–4.

1938 Bob Feller sets a new post–1892 ML 9-inning record when he whiffs 18 in a 4–1 loss to Detroit's Harry Eisenstat.

1947 Yankees sub Yogi Berra hits the first pinch home run in World Series history when he goes yard in the 7th inning at Ebbets Field against Brooklyn's Ralph Branca.

1948 In a scenario eerily reminiscent of 1940 and Floyd Giebell, Detroit starts unheralded rookie Lou Kretlow against Cleveland in the penultimate game of the regular season, but Tribe frosh knuckleballer Gene Bearden puts Cleveland ahead of Boston by one game with only one left to play when he blanks the Tigers 8–0 for his 19th win of the season and seventh since August 31.

1949 For the first time since 1908, both league races are decided on the final day of the season when the Yankees top the Red Sox 5–3 to finish one game ahead of Boston, and Brooklyn needs 10 innings to defeat the Phillies and avoid a pennant playoff series with the Cardinals.

1954 In one of the greatest World Series upsets, the Giants win 7–4 at Cleveland Stadium to complete a sweep of the team with the highest season winning percentage in AL history.

1966 Dodgers ace Sandy Koufax beats the Phillies for his 27th victory and the last win of his career.

1968 The Cards' Bob Gibson dominates the Tigers in Game 1, setting a World Series record with 17 strikeouts in a 4–0 triumph.

1975 Charlie "Dutch" Emig, the last living 19th-century MLer, dies in Oklahoma City, OK, at the age of 100.

1978 The Red Sox are winning their AL East division playoff game 2–0 in the 7th when light-hitting Yankees shortstop Bucky Dent blasts a three-run shot off Mike Torrez, and the Bombers hang on to win 5–4 and advance to the ALCS.

3

1890 After a 3–9 start, Chicago NL twirler Jack Luby finishes 20–9 when he posts his rookie-record 17th straight win in nipping Amos Rusie of the New York Giants, 3–2.

1895 Harry Wright, the player-manager of the legendary 1869 Cincinnati Red Stockings, dies of pneumonia.

1897 On the final day of his 27-year ML career, 45-year-old Cap Anson hits two home runs and steals a base in Chicago's season-ending DBH at St. Louis.

1906 The White Sox clinch the AL pennant and their enduring nickname of "The Hitless Wonders" when they finish the season with a .230 BA, the lowest ever by a ML flag winner.

1915 The Chicago Whales beat Pittsburgh in the second game of a DBH to cop the FL pennant by the slimmest possible margin—one percentage point—while Pittsburgh, which would have won if it had swept the twin bill, drops to third place, three percentage points behind the second-place St. Louis Terriers.

1920 In his lone ML appearance, Cincinnati's Monty Swartz throws a 12-inning complete game, losing 6–3 to the Cards' Willie Sherdel.

1935 Hank Greenberg's postseason ends when he breaks his wrist in Game 2 of the World Series, but the Tigers beat the Cubs without him to win the world championship for the first time in team history.

1937 The Boston Bees are the only team in ML history with two 30-year-old rookie 20-game winners when Lou Fette reaches the charmed circle one day after teammate Jim Turner.

1946 In the first pennant playoff in ML history, the Dodgers lose the best-of-3 affair when the Cards win their second straight game at Ebbets Field, 8–4.

1947 With two out in the bottom of the 9th in Game 4 of the World Series, Yankees righty Bill Bevens loses his bid for the first no-hitter in fall action and, more importantly, the game, when Brooklyn pinch-hitter Cookie Lavagetto slaps a two-run double, giving Dodgers relief ace Hugh Casey his second win in two days, 3–2.

1948 When Boston routs the Yankees 10–5 while Detroit is whipping Cleveland ace Bob Feller, for the first time in AL history the regular season ends in a tie for first place, necessitating a one-game playoff the following day at Fenway Park.

1951 In the decisive third game of the NL pennant playoff series, Bobby Thomson hits his famous three-run "shot heard 'round the world" off Brooklyn's Ralph Branca to give the Giants the NL flag, 5–4.

1962 The Giants advance to the World Series after beating the Dodgers in the deciding third game of the NL pennant playoff, the fourth in the past 17 years, all involving the Dodgers.

1968 The Tigers' Mickey Lolich beats the Cards 8–1 in Game 2 to even the World Series and adds insult by belting the only home run of his long ML career.

1972 Owing to the introduction of the DH rule the following year, until interleague play begins in 1997, the Orioles' Roric Harrison is the last AL hurler to belt a tater in a regular-season game when he goes deep against Cleveland.

1976 On the final day of the regular season, the Royals' George Brett edges teammate Hal McRae in the AL batting race .333 to .332 when his fly ball falls in front of Twins outfielder Steve Brye, leading McRae to allege that Brye purposely let the ball land safely so that a white man would win the crown.

1981 The Expos and Brewers clinch their initial postseason appearances by winning the strike season's second-half division titles, as Montreal beats the Mets to capture the NL East, and Milwaukee downs Detroit to sew up the AL East.

1993 The Blue Jays are the first AL club with a teammate trio that finishes 1–2–3 in the batting race, as John Olerud leads with .363, followed by Paul Molitor at .332, and Roberto Alomar coming in at .326.

2004 The Montreal Expos lose to the Mets in their last game before shifting to Washington in 2005.

4

1884 Sam Kimber of the Brooklyn AA club is the only ML pitcher to date to fail to win a full-length no-hit shutout when he duels Toledo's Tony Mullane for 10 innings before darkness ends the game, 0–0.

1891 St. Louis rookie Ted Breitenstein is the first pitcher in ML history to hurl a nine-inning no-hitter in his initial ML start when he blanks Louisville 8–0 in the Browns' penultimate game as a member of the AA.

1906 The Cubs win their ML record 116th game (since tied) and set a NL mark in the process when the victory comes at Pittsburgh, giving Chicago an .800 (60–15) winning percentage on the road.

1913 In a farcical season finale, Washington manager Clark Griffith uses eight pitchers, including himself, in a 10–9 win over Boston that is credited to Mutt Williams in his only ML start, even though Williams is removed after just four innings. In the lone frame that Griffith pitches at the age of 43, his catcher is his 44-year-old coach, Jack Ryan, making the pair the oldest battery to appear in a ML game.

1924 Giants third baseman Freddie Lindstrom, still nearly two months short of his 19th birthday, is the youngest player to appear in a World Series game, as New York tops Washington in extra innings in the Fall Classic opener.

1925 Washington's Firpo Marberry is the first hurler in ML history to lead his loop in mound appearances without making a start, as he sets a ML season record (since broken) with 55 relief outings.

1937 Brooklyn sends the Cards outfielder Johnny Cooney, third baseman Joe Stripp, and two lesser players for shortstop Leo Durocher.

1948 Cleveland player-manager Lou Boudreau starts lefty Gene Bearden in Boston's Fenway Park on only one day's rest, and the payoff is huge when Bearden dominates the Red Sox 8–3 to capture the AL flag and puncture the Hub's dream of an all-Boston World Series.

1950 Phils skipper Eddie Sawyer gives the ball to relief ace Jim Konstanty in the World Series opener, and though Konstanty allows only one run, the Yankees' Vic Raschi is even better as New York wins, 1–0. Three days later, the Yanks own their 13th world championship after a four-game sweep of the last World Series between two teams that have yet to break the color line.

1955 Johnny Podres blanks the Yankees 2–0 to bring Brooklyn its only world championship in eight tries.

1962 In Game 1, the Yanks' Whitey Ford earns his 10th and last World Series win, beating the Giants 6–2, but his Fall Classic record of 33$\frac{2}{3}$ scoreless innings ends when Jose Pagan's squeeze play plates Willie Mays in the 2nd frame.

1964 The Cards beat the Mets to end the tightest three-way pennant race in NL history when the Phillies slaughter the Reds 10–0, leaving both clubs one game behind the Redbirds following the Phils' unprecedented collapse in which they lose a 6½ game lead with just 12 games to play.

1969   In the first divisional playoff games in ML history, the Orioles down the Twins 4–3 in 12 innings, and the Mets defeat the Braves, 9–5.

1980   The Phillies win their first NL East title as Mike Schmidt's two-run shot in the top of the 11th proves the difference in a 6–4 triumph over the Expos.

1987   The Tigers sweep Toronto in a season-ending three-game series to capture the AL East title and complete the Blue Jays' inexplicable collapse in which they lose their last seven games.

1999   The Mets are the NL wild card when they beat the Reds 5–0 in a postseason play-in game, as Al Leiter tosses a complete-game two-hitter.

2001   The Giants' Barry Bonds slugs his 70th homer, tying Mark McGwire's season mark and extending Bonds's own record for the most round-trippers on the road to 36.

5

1889   The New York Giants win the NL pennant on the final day of the season by beating Cleveland 5–3, while Boston loses to Pittsburgh, 6–1.

1918   Former NL infielder Eddie Grant is immortalized as baseball's greatest World War I hero after he is killed in action in the Argonne Forest in France.

1921   KDKA in Pittsburgh is the first station to broadcast a World Series game when Grantland Rice announces Game 1 between the Yankees and Giants.

1929   On the final Sunday of the season, Phils outfielder Chuck Klein smacks his 43rd homer in the first game of a DBH to break Rogers Hornsby's old NL mark of 42 and then watches his pitchers issue five walks in the second game to Giants gardener Mel Ott, who also began the day with 42 homers, to prevent Ott from catching their teammate.

1941   Brooklyn receiver Mickey Owen's dropped third strike with two out in the 9th gives Tommy Henrich life and ignites a four-run Yankees rally that elicits an improbable comeback victory and their eventual World Series win.

1942   Rookie sensation Johnny Beazley's second World Series win over the Yankees brings the Cards the world championship in one of the greatest upsets in postseason history.

1953   Led by Billy Martin's then record 12 hits in fall play, the Yankees need only six games to take the World Series from the Dodgers and claim their record fifth straight world championship.

1966   In Game 1, Moe Drabowsky sets a World Series relief record by fanning 11 Dodgers as the Orioles win, 5–2.

1980   After trailing the Astros by three games with three to play, the Dodgers complete a three-game sweep of Houston, forcing a one-game playoff that Houston wins the next day to capture the AL West and its first postseason appearance.

1991   On the next to last day of the season, the Braves clinch their first of a remarkable 14 straight NL West titles, excluding the 1994 strike season.

2002   The Angels beat the Bombers 9–5 to clinch the ALDS in four games and end the Yanks' three-year reign as world champs.

2007   The Indians beat the Yankees 2–1 in an ultra bizarre Game 2 of the ALDS when swarms of insects off Lake Erie bombard players and are so thick in the 8th frame that Yanks rookie Joba Chamberlain, who is grotesquely infested with them, throws two wild pitches to allow Grady Sizemore to score the tying run.

6

1845   The first recorded baseball game using rules endorsed by Alexander Cartwright takes place between two groups of members of Cartwright's Knickerbocker Club.

1880   The NL ousts Cincinnati when the club refuses to abide by loop edicts prohibiting member teams from selling alcohol on their home grounds or using the facility to stage Sunday games.

1891   The final game of the AA's 10-year sojourn as a ML is played in Washington, with Baltimore's Kid Madden topping Frank Foreman of the locals, 16–11, in a contest shortened to 5 innings by darkness.

1904   Cards pitcher Jack Taylor sets a post–1892 ML record when he tosses his 39th consecutive complete game of the season.

1908   The AL pennant race is decided on the final day of the season when Bill Donovan beats Chicago, 7–0, lifting Detroit half a game ahead of Cleveland, while the White Sox fall to third place, 1½ games out.

1909 The Cubs win a DBH at St. Louis on closing day of the season to finish with 104 victories, making them the first team in ML history to post a triple-digit win total and not win a pennant.

1912 In Pittsburgh's season finale, Bucs outfielder Chief Wilson extends his ML season record for triples to 36 when he cracks a three-bagger against Cincinnati.

1915 Elmer Myers of the A's sets a new AL record (since tied by Brewers frosh Steve Woodard in 1997) for the most Ks by a pitcher in his ML debut, when he fans 12 in beating the Yankees, 4–0.

1920 Cleveland's Doc Johnston and Brooklyn's Jimmy Johnston are the first brothers to oppose each other in World Series play.

1947 Brooklyn reliever Hugh Casey appears in his then record sixth World Series game in seven days and finishes with two wins, a save and a microscopic 0.87 ERA, but all for naught, as the Yankees win the crucial seventh game 5–2 behind their own relief ace, Joe Page.

1948 Umpire Bill Stewart rules Braves catcher Phil Masi safe at second base on an 8th-inning pickoff attempt, and arguably the most controversial call in World Series history to date, which leads to the lone run in the Fall Classic opener when Tommy Holmes singles Masi home to give Johnny Sain a taut 1–0 win over Cleveland's Bob Feller.

1957 With his team trailing the Yankees in the bottom of the 10th inning of Game 4 of the World Series, Braves pinch-hitter Nippy Jones sparks a three-run rally when he tells plate umpire Augie Donatelli that a pitch hit him on the foot by showing Donatelli a smudge on the ball that he claims is shoe polish.

1963 The Dodgers complete a stunning four-game World Series sweep of the Yankees with help from Frank Howard's homer in the 5th and Willie Davis's sac fly in the 7th to give Sandy Koufax a 2–1 win against Whitey Ford.

1966 At the age of 20, Baltimore's Jim Palmer is the youngest moundsman to toss a shutout in Fall Classic action when he defeats the Dodgers 6–0, with Sandy Koufax absorbing the loss in his last ML game.

1985 Yankees hurler Phil Niekro beats the Blue Jays 6–0 for his 300th career win and, at the age of 46, he is also the oldest pitcher to date to spin a complete-game shutout.

2001 The Mets' Lenny Harris slaps his 151st career pinch hit, breaking the ML mark he shared with Manny Mota. Harris plays four more seasons and extends his record to 212. Elsewhere, the Rockies' Todd Helton is the first MLer to amass 400 total bases in consecutive seasons since the A's Jimmie Foxx (1932–1933).

7

1904 George Stovall hits a three-run homer off his brother, Jesse, in the 1st inning in Cleveland's 8–1 win over Detroit, marking the first time in ML history that a hitter goes yard against his sibling.

1906 Cleveland is the only AL club to date to finish the season as a team Triple Crown winner—the loop leader in batting, fielding, and ERA—and yet not win a pennant.

1919 Smokey Joe Williams, toiling for the Negro league Lincoln Giants, fires a no-hitter in an exhibition game against John McGraw's New York Giants but loses 1–0 on errors by his infielders.

1925 When former Giants star Christy Mathewson dies of tuberculosis at the age of 45 on the day the World Series begins, both the Pirates and the Senators wear black arm bands in his memory during the Fall Classic.

1933 The flag in Griffith Stadium is at half-mast to commemorate the sudden death of Cubs president William Veeck as the Giants defeat the Senators four games to one to gain revenge for their stunning World Series loss nine years earlier.

1947 Under pressure since his spring-training feud with Leo Durocher blemished the Yankees' escutcheon, Larry MacPhail resigns as Yankees GM and is replaced by George Weiss.

1952 Second baseman Billy Martin's last-second grab of Jackie Robinson's pop fly with the bases loaded saves Game 7 of the World Series for the Yankees 4–2 and gives them a then record four straight world championships.

1969 In a multiplayer deal, the Cards ship Curt Flood to the Phillies for Dick Allen, but Flood refuses to be traded and instead sues MLB over the reserve clause that binds a player to a club for as long as that team chooses.

1975 The Red Sox complete a three-game ALCS sweep against the A's, ending Oakland's three-year reign as world champions.

1984 After losing the first two games of the NLCS to the Cubs, the Padres rebound to take the next three, including the 6–3 clincher, and advance to their first World Series.

2001 The Giants' Barry Bonds hits his record 73rd homer of the season against the Dodgers' Dennis Springer.

8

1871 The Rockford team, entrained to Chicago to play the National Association leading White Stockings, turns back home upon finding the Windy City ablaze, a catastrophe that forces the loop leaders to finish the season on the road, where they lose the pennant by one game.

1882 Detroit's Lady Baldwin wins his 42nd game to set a NL season record for the most victories by a southpaw.

1886 Pittsburgh's Ed Morris tops the Mets 9–0 for his 12th shutout of the season, establishing an all-time season record by a lefty.

1894 Baltimore's first ML pennant is marred when the Orioles are swept 4–0 by the New York Giants in the first Temple Cup Series pitting the regular-season champion against the second-place team.

1895 The Temple Cup Series is again a flop as second-place Cleveland routs repeat pennant-winner Baltimore, four games to one.

1896 Baltimore finally redeems itself in Temple Cup play by sweeping second-place Cleveland in four straight games.

1908 The Giants set a new ML season record for attendance with 910,000 but lose the NL pennant when Cubs stalwart Three Finger Brown, working in relief, bests Christy Mathewson, 4–2, in a playoff of the controversial Merkle tie game of September 23. Meanwhile, the Baseball Writers' Association of America is formed, with Joe Jackson of the *Detroit Free Press* the organization's first chairman.

1912 Los Angeles outfielder Heinie Heitmuller, the PCL's leading hitter, dies of typhoid fever while the season is still under way and is awarded the batting title posthumously.

1922 Art Nehf beats the Yankees 5–3 to give the Giants their second straight World Series triumph over the Bombers and becomes the lone pitcher to conclude two consecutive Fall Classics with a complete-game victory.

1929 Howard Ehmke, just 7–2 in the regular season, is Connie Mack's surprise choice to start the World Series opener against the Cubs and makes a genius of Mack with a 3–1 win.

1930 The "rabbit" ball in 1930 notwithstanding, the A's win the World Series with a .197 team BA.

1939 The Yankees sweep the Reds in four games to become the first team to win four consecutive world championships.

1956 Don Larsen makes World Series history when he is perfect in the Yankees' 2–0 win over Brooklyn's Sal Maglie.

1957 Lew Burdette bags his third complete-game World Series win in beating the Yankees 5–0 to bring the Braves franchise its first world championship since 1914.

1959 LA's Larry Sherry is voted the World Series MVP for his relief heroics in the Dodgers' triumph over the White Sox in six games.

1995 Seattle wins the ALDS in five games when Edgar Martinez raps a game-ending two-run double in the 11th inning, lifting the Mariners to a 6–5 win over the Yankees.

9

1885 Mickey Welch blanks the St. Louis Maroons 5–0 on the last day of the season, lifting the Giants to a dazzling .759 winning percentage and the team Triple Crown—first in batting, fielding, and ERA. Yet all their stellar work earns is second place, two games behind Chicago, marking them the only club other than the 1906 Cleveland Blues to win a team Triple Crown and fail to win the pennant.

1889 Columbus AA third baseman Charlie Reilly is the first player to hit two home runs in his ML debut in a 10–6 win over Philadelphia. The following day, Reilly goes deep again, making him the only performer to collect three jacks in his first two games prior to Joe Cunningham in 1954.

1910 The AL bat title appears to be decided on the final day of the season when Cleveland's Nap Lajoie goes 8-for-8 in a DBH with St. Louis, including six specious bunt hits, but he still finishes less than a percentage point behind Ty Cobb. Both men receive new cars from the Chalmers Auto Company, however, which is probably as it should have been, as later research reveals that Lajoie actually had the higher average.

1916 In the longest World Series game to that point, Red Sox lefty Babe Ruth outlasts Brooklyn's Sherry Smith to win 2–1 in 14 innings and launch a then record 29⅓ scoreless postseason frames pitched.

1919 Cincinnati wins the World Series when Lefty Williams of the White Sox manages to retire only one man in the 1st inning before departing in a 10–5 loss to the Reds' Hod Eller.

1924 Cincinnati first baseman Jake Daubert dies in a Queen City hospital after an emergency appendectomy.

1928 The Yankees are the first team to sweep back-to-back world championships when they need only the minimum 36 innings to subdue the NL champion Cardinals.

1934 The Dean brothers win all four of the Cards' victories when Dizzy tops the Tigers 11–0 in Game 7 of the World Series without Joe Medwick, who is removed from the game on Commissioner Landis's order after his hard slide into Tigers third baseman Marv Owen instigates a near riot at Detroit's Navin Field.

1938 The Yankees are the first team in ML history to win three consecutive world championships when they complete a four-game sweep of the Cubs.

1944 Rookie second sacker Emil Verban, who accumulated just 43 RBI in the regular season, drives home all three Cards runs as they claim the last World Series to date to be played entirely in the same ball ground—Sportsman's Park—when Max Lanier tops the Browns 3–1 in Game 6.

1955 Longtime ML hurler Howie Fox is stabbed to death in a bar fight in San Antonio, TX.

1958 By topping the Braves 6–2 in Game 7 of the World Series, the Yankees are the first team in AL history to rally from a 3–1 deficit in games and in so doing give Casey Stengel his seventh world championship to tie him with Joe McCarthy for the most World Series triumphs.

1966 Frank Robinson's solo blast against Don Drysdale accounts for the game's only run as the Orioles sweep the Dodgers in the World Series and keep LA from scoring for a postseason-record 33 straight innings.

1986 Pirates pitcher Bob Moose is killed in an auto accident on his 29th birthday.

1996 In Game 1 of the ALCS, the Yanks are aided in the 8th inning by a 12-year-old fan, Jeffrey Maier, who interferes with a catchable ball hit by Derek Jeter that is mistakenly ruled a homer, tying the game at 4–4. Bernie Williams then blasts a game-ending tater in the 11th to give the Bombers a 5–4 win.

2005 Chris Burke whacks a walk-off homer as Houston wins the NLDS and advances to the NLCS after beating the Cards 7–6 in the longest postseason game to date both by innings (18) and time (5:50).

10

1881 After a series of shadowy meetings in Pittsburgh, a group of baseball parvenus spearheaded by "Hustling" Horace Phillips and Cincinnati sportswriter Opie Caylor announce the formation of a rival ML that calls itself the American Association and operates under the slogan "Liberty to All."

1887 Baltimore AA bulwark Matt Kilroy blanks New York 4–0 for his southpaw season-record 46th win.

1904 The New York Highlanders lose the AL pennant to Boston on the final day of the season when 41-game winner Jack Chesbro wild pitches home the winning Boston run as victorious Bill Dinneen hurls his AL-record 37th complete game.

1915 More than 100,000 fans clog the stadium bowl in Brookside Park, adjacent to the Cleveland Zoo, to watch a semipro championship game between the Cleveland White Autos and Omaha Panhandlers.

1920 Cleveland outfielder Elmer Smith hits the first grand slam homer in World Series play, Cleveland's Jim Bagby is the first pitcher to go yard in a World Series game, and Tribe second sacker Bill Wambsganss turns the only unassisted triple play to date in fall action, as the Indians beat Brooklyn, 8–1.

1924 Washington wins the World Series in seven games on Earl McNeely's 12th-inning ground ball that hits a pebble and hops over Giants third baseman Freddie Lindstrom's head, allowing Muddy Ruel to tally the game-ending run.

1925 With his team trailing Washington 4–3 in the 8th inning of Game 3 of the World Series at Griffith Stadium, Pittsburgh catcher Earl Smith rifles a shot toward center field that Sam Rice leaps for as he topples into the stands. Some 15 seconds elapse before Rice emerges from the crowd and holds the ball triumphantly over his head, convincing umpire Cy Rigler to rule the play a catch and launching a raging dispute that forces Commissioner Landis to confer with Rice, hoping for clear resolution, but Rice only says, "The umpire said I caught it."

1926 Waiver acquisition Pete Alexander brings the Cards the world championship when he follows a complete-game win in Game 6 with a save in Game 7 highlighted by his strikeout of Yankees rookie Tony Lazzeri with the bases loaded in the bottom of the 7th.

1930 Former Cubs pilot Joe McCarthy signs a four-year contract to manage the Yankees.

1945 Cubs starter Hank Borowy is routed in the 1st inning of Game 7 while his hill opponent, Detroit's Hal Newhouser, goes the distance in a 9–3 win that marks the Bruins' last Fall Classic contest to date.

1950 Former ML catcher Paul Richards receives his first opportunity to manage in the majors when the White Sox hire him to bring his dramatic dugout innovations to Comiskey Park in 1951.

1956 In his lone Fall Classic start, Johnny Kucks blanks the Dodgers 9–0 to add another world championship banner to the gargantuan display in Yankee Stadium.

1961 In the first NL expansion draft, the Mets make catcher Hobie Landrith their first choice, and Houston's initial pick is shortstop Eddie Bressoud.

1968 The Tigers' Mickey Lolich beats the Cards' Bob Gibson 4–1 for his third win of the World Series to defeat the defending champs in seven games.

1973 The Mets (82–79) upset the defending NL champion Reds (99–63) behind Tom Seaver's 7–2 victory in Game 5 of the NLCS.

1980 After losing to the Yankees in ALCS action on three straight occasions, the Royals exact revenge when George Brett's three-run shot off reliever Rich Gossage lifts KC to a 4–2 win and a three-game sweep of the Bombers.

1982 Trailing 2–0 in games, the Brewers win and then beat the Angels twice more, capped by a 4–3 victory in the fifth game of the ALCS, to earn their first trip to the World Series.

1990 The A's sweep the Red Sox in the ALCS after Roger Clemens is tossed in the 2nd inning for arguing calls with plate umpire Terry Cooney and is later fined $10,000 and suspended for the first five games of the following season for his tantrum.

1999 The Red Sox set a ML postseason record for runs by whipping the Indians 23–7 to knot their ALDS at two games apiece. Boston wins the series the next day after trailing 2–0 in games.

11

1888   The Giants' Bill George is the last MLer to be the first batter in a game in which he pitches a shutout, as he goes 3-for-6 in his leadoff role while blanking Indianapolis, 13–0.

1899   During its annual meeting at the Great Northern Hotel in Chicago, the Western League changes its name to the American League at the suggestion of Indianapolis owner W. F. C. Golt, and its president, former Cincinnati sportswriter Ban Johnson, announces plans to put clubs in Cleveland and Chicago.

1911   The first MVP Awards in ML history are announced, with honorary new Chalmers cars going to AL winner Ty Cobb of Detroit and NL winner Frank Schulte of the Cubs.

1946   The Indians acquire second baseman Joe Gordon from the Yankees for pitcher Allie Reynolds.

1948   Cleveland's regular-season hero, rookie Gene Bearden, is also the postseason hero when he follows his 2–0 shutout in Game 3 with a save in Game 6 to bring the Tribe its last world championship to date.

1956   AL president Will Harridge blocks Washington's proposed move to the West Coast, saying it first needs the unanimous approval of the other seven AL teams.

1964   Ken Boyer blasts a 6th-inning grand slam that accounts for all the Cards' runs in their 4–3 win over the Yankees in Game 4 of the World Series.

1972   With the Reds down 3–2 in the bottom of the 9th inning against the Pirates in the deciding fifth game of the NLCS, Johnny Bench blasts a game-tying solo shot. Later in the inning, Bob Moose uncorks a wild pitch, sending George Foster home with the run that sends Cincinnati to the World Series.

2006   Yankees pitcher Cory Lidle is killed when his private plane crashes into a Manhattan apartment building.

12

1899   Washington outfielder Buck Freeman hits his NL-leading 25th homer, a figure some purists consider the true pre-Ruth ML season record since it was accomplished in regulation-sized parks.

1911 With the NL pennant already clinched, Giants manager John McGraw calls on quirky team mascot Charlie Faust to hurl the last inning of the regular-season finale against Brooklyn. Faust tosses a scoreless 9th, probably with the Dodgers' complicity, and then, after being hit by a pitch in the bottom of the frame, steals second and third base in rapid order while Brooklyn pitcher Eddie Dent conveniently "look[s] the other way."

1923 Outfielder Casey Stengel hits his second game-winning homer in three days to give the Giants a 2–1 lead in the third straight all-New York World Series, but the Yankees take the next three games to bag their first world championship.

1929 Trailing 8–0 in the 7th inning of Game 4, the A's take 46-year-old starter Jack Quinn off the hook when they stage the greatest rally in World Series history to date and tally 10 runs to win 10–8.

1948 Yankees brass fire Bucky Harris and hire in his stead Casey Stengel, the pilot of the 1948 PCL flag-winning Oakland Oaks, aka "The Nine Old Men."

1949 Blackie Schwamb, a promising but troubled pitcher in the St. Louis Browns chain, while out on bail for robbery, is embroiled in a shakedown that goes awry and ends in a homicide that puts him in the California penal system, where he establishes himself over the next decade as a legendary prison-yard pitcher and hitter.

1967 The Cards win the World Series as Bob Gibson bags the seventh game 7–2, fanning 10 Red Sox and blasting a homer to boot.

1972 The A's grab their first AL flag in Oakland by beating the Tigers 2–1 in Game 5 of the ALCS.

1980 In the deciding fifth game of the NLCS, Garry Maddox plates Del Unser in the 10th inning to beat the Astros 8–7, sending the Phillies to their first World Series since 1950.

1982 The Brewers' Paul Molitor is the first player to smack five hits in a World Series game, as Milwaukee pummels the Cardinals 10–0 in Game 1.

1986 One strike away from leading the Angels to their first World Series appearance, closer Donnie Moore surrenders a game-tying homer to the Red Sox' Dave Henderson, and Boston goes on to win Game 5, 7–6 in 11 innings, and then grabs the next two games as well to win the AL pennant after trailing 3–1 in games.

2005   In Game 2 of the ALCS, with two out in the 9th inning of a 1–1 tie, White Sox catcher A. J. Pierzynski fans, but plate umpire Doug Eddings does not make a palpable call. In the confusion, Pierzynski catches the Angels off-guard and races to first. After pinch-runner Pablo Ozuna steals second, Joe Crede doubles home the winning run and sends the Sox on their way to seven straight postseason wins and the first Windy City world championship in 88 years.

13

1903   Boston wins the first "modern" World Series, five games to three, when Bill Dinneen beats Pittsburgh's Deacon Phillippe, 3–0.

1914   The underdog Boston Braves perpetrate the first World Series sweep in the four-game minimum when Dick Rudolph beats the Philadelphia A's, 3–1.

1915   Harry Hooper's second homer of the game in Philadelphia's Baker Bowl brings the Red Sox a 5–4 win in Game 5 that gives the city of Boston its third world championship in the past four seasons.

1921   The first modern World Series played entirely in one park—the Polo Grounds, home then to both the Giants and Yankees—concludes when the Yankees hit into a double play to give the Giants the championship in eight games.

1953   The Yankees buy the contracts of two black players, Elston Howard and Vic Power, from their KC farm club in the AA.

1960   In Game 7, the Pirates' Bill Mazeroski blasts the first 9th-inning, walk-off homer in World Series history against the Yanks' Ralph Terry for a 10–9 win, as the Bucs cop their first World Championship since 1925.

1971   Bruce Kison wins the first World Series night game when the Bucs beat the Orioles 4–3 in Game 4.

1973   At Shea Stadium, the Mets take a 2–1 lead in games in the NLCS against the powerhouse Reds, winning 9–2 behind Jerry Koosman; however, the contest is best remembered for the benches-clearing brawl in the 5th inning that began when the Reds' Pete Rose slid hard into Bud Harrelson at second and then slammed Harrelson to the ground to earn the wrath of everyone at Shea.

2002   The Angels win their first AL flag, scoring 10 runs in the 7th inning to defeat the Twins 13–5 in the fifth game of the ALCS, as light-hitting second baseman Adam Kennedy belts three homers.

2006   Career minor leaguer Mark Kiger is the first player since the White Stockings' Bug Holliday in 1885 to make his ML debut in post-season action, when Kiger enters in the 8th inning at second base for the A's against the Tigers in Game 3 of the ALCS.

14

1862   In the course of leading his Excelsiors to a 13–9 win over the Unions of Morrisania, pitching star Jim Creighton ruptures his bladder and dies four days later at the age of 21.

1890   Gus Williams, who started the season lid-lifter for the AA Brooklyn Gladiators some six months earlier on April 18, expires at the age of 20 from an upper respiratory ailment.

1905   The New York Giants win the second modern World Series, four games to one over the Philadelphia A's, when Christy Mathewson pitches his third shutout in six days, as every game in the fray results in a shutout by the winning side.

1906   The heavily favored Cubs drop Game 6 to lose the World Series to the crosstown White Sox.

1908   With only 6,210 Detroit fans on hand—the smallest crowd in modern World Series history—the Cubs, behind Orval Overall's 2–0 shutout, crush the Tigers for the second year in a row and bag their last world championship crown to date.

1923   The PCL's 202-game season comes to an end with Salt Lake City outfielder Paul Strand setting an all-time OB season record with 325 hits.

1952   The St. Louis Browns, who can ill afford it, spring for $90,000 and three players to garner minor league shortstop Billy Hunter from the Dodgers.

1953   Despite having won two pennants in a row, Chuck Dressen is forced to resign as Dodgers manager when he refuses to sign a contract renewal for only one year.

1965   The Dodgers beat the Twins in seven games when Sandy Koufax spins his second shutout of the World Series.

1972   In Game 1, the A's Gene Tenace is the first player to homer in his first two World Series at bats, providing Oakland with a 3–2 win over the Reds.

1973   The Mets plate four in the 11th inning to beat the A's 10–7 in Game 2 of the World Series, when Oakland second baseman Mike

Andrews makes an error on two consecutive plays, allowing the last three runs to score. After the game, A's owner Charlie Finley bullies Andrews into signing a statement that he is injured and unable to play so Oakland can substitute Manny Trillo on the Series roster, but the entire club rallies behind Andrews, and Commissioner Kuhn forces Finley to reverse his decision.

1975   With the score tied in the 10th inning of Game 3 of the World Series, Reds pinch-hitter Ed Armbrister's sacrifice bunt attempt is fielded by Red Sox catcher Carlton Fisk, who collides with Armbrister and then throws the ball into center while attempting to force Cesar Geronimo at second. Geronimo advances to third as Armbrister reaches second. Despite heated protests from the Sox, home-plate umpire Larry Barnett rules that there is no interference, and Joe Morgan then singles for a 6–5 win.

1976   The Yanks advance to their first World Series since 1964, when Chris Chambliss blasts a walk-off 9th-inning homer off the Royals' Mark Littell to give the Bombers a 7–6 win in the fifth game of the ALCS.

1992   Canada hosts its first ML World Series games after the Blue Jays beat the A's 9–2 in the sixth game of the ALCS to capture the junior loop flag. Elsewhere, in the bottom of the 9th inning at Atlanta, Braves pinch hitter Francisco Cabrera strokes a two-out, two-run, game-ending single to beat the Pirates and lift the Georgia city to its second straight NL pennant.

2003   The Cubs are ahead 3–0 in the 8th frame of Game 6 in the NLCS, needing just five outs to reach their first World Series since 1945, when Bruins fan Steve Bartman attempts to grab a foul fly hit by the Marlins' Luis Castillo, preventing Cubs left fielder Moises Alou from catching it. Florida goes on to score eight runs and win 8–3.

15

1884   Charley Radbourn of the NL champion Providence Grays concludes the campaign by blanking Philadelphia 8–0 to give him a ML season-record 60 wins as per the rules of his time.

1892   On the last day in ML history that the front line of the pitcher's box puts a hurler only 50 feet from home plate, Cincinnati hurler Bumpus Jones, making his ML debut, no-hits Pittsburgh in a 7–1 win.

1898   Baltimore sets a team record for hit by pitches, as its batsmen are nicked 160 times, led by Hughie Jennings, the all-time individual career record holder for hit by pitches with 287.

1899 Cleveland ends with a ML record 134 defeats after a DBH loss to Cincinnati that marks the only appearance of Eddie Kolb, a cigar boy at Cincinnati's Gibson House Hotel, whose ML pitching aspirations are dashed when the Reds trounce him, 19–3.

1917 Red Faber posts his third victory of the World Series and brings the championship to Chicago's South Side by beating the Giants 4–2 with help from Eddie Collins, who scampers home with a crucial run while Giants third baseman Heinie Zimmerman chases him when the plate is left uncovered.

1925 The Pirates are the first team to overcome a 3–1 deficit in games and triumph in a World Series when they rally against Washington's Walter Johnson in Game 7 to win 9–7.

1946 Aided by Enos Slaughter's mad dash to score from first base on Harry Walker's looping hit to left field, Cards lefty Harry Brecheen gains his third victory in the World Series to send the Red Sox to their first ever defeat in a Fall Classic.

1968 KC and Seattle make their expansion draft picks, with the Royals choosing pitcher Roger Nelson first and the Pilots selecting first baseman Don Mincher as their initial choice.

1981 The Yankees beat Billy Martin's A's 4–0 to complete a three-game sweep of the ALCS and capture their 33rd AL flag.

1986 The Mets clinch the NL pennant by outlasting the Astros 7–6 in 16 innings after rebounding from a 3–0 deficit in the 9th inning.

1988 Hobbled by a knee injury, Kirk Gibson hits a walk-off homer with two outs in the 9th off the A's Dennis Eckersley to give the Dodgers a 6–5 win in Game 1 of the World Series, in what proves to be Gibson's only appearance in the fall affair.

1997 Tony Fernandez homers off Armando Benitez in the 11th inning to hand the Indians a 1–0 victory over the Orioles in Game 6 of the ALCS and send the Tribe to the World Series for the second time in three years.

2001 The Yankees are the first team to win a best-of-five LDS after losing the first two at home when they beat the A's 5–3 in the decisive fifth contest.

16

1909 Pittsburgh defeats Detroit in seven games when the Pirates' Babe Adams is the only rookie to date to win three World Series contests.

1912   The Red Sox win the first best-of-seven World Series that comes down to a decisive seventh game (eighth game officially, since Game 2 ends in a tie) when Giants center fielder Fred Snodgrass muffs a fly ball in the bottom of the 10th inning, opening the door for Boston to score two unearned runs and beat Christy Mathewson, 3–2.

1950   The Brooklyn Dodgers refuse to renew Branch Rickey's contract, leading to his ouster as the club's president and GM.

1962   In Game 7 of the World Series, Yankees second baseman Bobby Richardson spears the Giants' Willie McCovey's 9th-inning two-out liner with runners on second and third to seal a 1–0 win and the Bombers' 20th Series title.

1964   After losing the World Series to the Cards, the Yankees fire their manager, Yogi Berra. Meanwhile, in an ironic turn of events, Johnny Keane, pilot of the champion Cards, quits and assumes Berra's former post three days later.

1969   The New York Mets stun the baseball world by defeating the heavily favored Orioles in five games on Jerry Koosman's 5–3 victory, aided by home runs from World Series MVP Donn Clendenon and the usually light-hitting Al Weis.

1985   In the first year that the LCS expands to a best-of-seven format, KC capitalizes on the change to take Game 7 of the ALCS 6–2 against the Blue Jays and win the junior loop flag after rebounding from a 3–1 deficit in games.

2003   Red Sox skipper Grady Little is vilified for failing to lift his tiring ace Pedro Martinez in the 8th frame in Game 6 of the ALCS, allowing the Yankees to tie the score and setting the stage for Tim Wakefield to surrender Aaron Boone's walk-off 11th-inning shot that hands the Bombers a 6–5 victory and the AL flag.

17

1885   Bug Holliday is the only player to make his ML debut in a World Series game when he plays right field for Chicago NL in a 3–2 loss to St. Louis AA some four years before making his regular-season debut.

1891   Arthur Irwin, manager of the AA champion Boston Reds, speaks for the record in *TSN* when asked if there is any truth to the claim that the 1891 NL pennant race was rigged for Boston to win. He replies, "These charges of crookedness will kill the game unless they are explained away, and they can't be explained away. Simply because they are true, and there is plenty of proof." Irwin's scathing accusations, damning as they are, are subsequently ignored everywhere but in Chicago.

1911   After publicly criticizing a home-run pitch teammate Rube Marquard served to the A's Frank Baker the previous day, the Giants, Christy Mathewson is mortified in Game 3 of the World Series when Baker greets him with a game-tying homer in the 9th inning to earn the nickname "Home Run."

1927   In failing health for several years, Ban Johnson, the AL's only president to date, resigns his office.

1960   Senior loop owners vote to add two expansion clubs that are slated to start play in 1962, one in New York and the other in Houston.

1971   In Game 7 of the Fall Classic, Roberto Clemente, the World Series MVP with a .414 BA, homers off Mike Cuellar as the Pirates beat the defending-champion Orioles, 2–1.

1974   Joe Rudi's homer in the 7th frame proves the game winner, enabling the A's to beat the Dodgers 3–2 and dispatch them in just five games to bring a third straight World Series title to Oakland.

1978   The Yankees grab their second straight world championship, beating the Dodgers in six games.

1979   In the seventh game of the World Series, Willie Stargell's homer helps lift the Pirates to a 4–1 win over the Orioles and make the Bucs champs for the second time in the decade.

1982   Brewers shortstop Robin Yount is the first player to stroke four hits twice in one World Series in leading Milwaukee past the Cards 6–4 in Game 5.

1987   Dan Gladden belts a grand slam in a seven-run 4th inning as the Twins beat the Cards 10–1 in the first World Series game played indoors at Minnesota's Metrodome.

1989   An earthquake devastates the San Francisco Bay area shortly before Game 3 of the Fall Classic between the A's and the Giants, forcing action to be suspended for 10 days before the A's can complete a dominating four-game sweep in which they never trail in any of the contests.

1991   In the seventh game of the NLCS, the Braves beat the Pirates 4–0 behind John Smoltz to capture their first NL flag in Atlanta.

1995 The Indians win their first AL flag since 1954, beating the Mariners 4–0 in Game 6 of the ALCS.

1996 In the NLCS, the Braves rebound from a 3–1 deficit in games to win the NL flag by blasting 17 hits in a 15–0 rout of the Cardinals in the deciding contest.

2000 The Yankees score six runs in the bottom of the 8th inning to beat the Mariners 9–7 and advance to meet the Mets in the first Subway Series in New York since 1956.

18

1925 The PCL season ends with Salt Lake City second baseman Tony Lazzeri leading the loop in homers with 60, RBI with 222, and runs with 202, all of which are new OB records.

1929 George Whiteman retires as an active player after participating in a record 3,282 games in the minors, including 24 seasons in which he played 100 or more games.

1950 Connie Mack retires as manager of the Philadelphia A's and is replaced by Jimmy Dykes.

1960 The Yankees announce the "retirement" of 70-year-old skipper Casey Stengel after he has snared 10 pennants in 12 years at the Bombers' wheel, and they compound the public relations nightmare by claiming the move was mandated by Stengel's age.

1967 A's magnate Charlie Finley receives permission to shift his club from KC to Oakland for the 1968 campaign.

1977 In Game 6 of the World Series, the Yankees' Reggie Jackson earns the nickname "Mr. October" by smacking three straight homers, all on the first pitch, off the Dodgers' Burt Hooton, Elias Sosa, and Charlie Hough, to lift the Yankees to an 8–4 victory and the world championship.

2007 Feeling that he deserves more respect after making the playoffs in each of his 12 seasons at the Yankees' helm, Joe Torre turns down the club's one-year contract offer for 2008, worth up to $8,000,000, plus an option year if the Bombers advance to the World Series.

19

1932 Chuck Klein's Triple Crown season with the Phillies earns the NL MVP Award while Jimmie Foxx, likewise a Triple Crown winner with the A's, is the BBWAA's AL choice.

1949   The White Sox unload catcher Joe Tipton and his .204 BA on the A's in return for rookie second sacker Nellie Fox, a future Hall of Famer.

1978   Larry Doby, the second black skipper in big league history, is fired by the White Sox, who then make shortstop Don Kessinger their player-manager, the last AL pilot to date to function in that capacity.

1981   Rick Monday pelts a 9th-inning shot off the Expos' Steve Rogers to give the Dodgers a 2–1 victory in the NLCS and the NL flag.

1987   Billy Martin assumes the Yankees' managerial post for the fifth and last time, supplanting Lou Piniella, who previously replaced Martin and does so again during the 1988 campaign.

2004   In one of the gutsiest pitching performances in ML history, the Red Sox' Curt Schilling forces a seventh game in the ALCS by beating the Yanks 4–2 while pitching on a visibly bleeding right ankle with three sutures holding a torn tendon in place.

2005   In the final contest played at Busch Stadium, the Astros beat the Cards 5–1 in Game 6 of the NLCS to earn their first World Series berth.

20

1890   The PL gives up the ghost, throwing all of its players and backers into a frenzy of deal cutting with the two veteran MLs.

1896   Cincinnati buys pitcher Ted Breitenstein from St. Louis for an amount that Cincinnati claims is around $4,000 and St. Louis swears is closer to $10,000. Breitenstein is dubbed "The $10,000 Beauty."

1901   Seven St. Louis Cardinals, including the club's top three hitters—Jesse Burkett, Emmet Heidrick, and Bobby Wallace—and half its regular pitching staff, jump to the new AL St. Louis Browns team.

1931   Second baseman Frankie Frisch of the champion Cards wins the first BBWAA NL MVP Award.

1947   Chesterfield pays the Giants $400,000 for the radio-television rights to their games in 1948.

1960   The Yankees name Ralph Houk as Casey Stengel's successor at the Bombers' helm.

1982   The Cards win their first world championship since 1967, rallying from a 3–1 deficit in games to beat the Brewers 6–3 in the deciding contest.

1988   The Dodgers' Orel Hershiser beats the A's 5–2, completing a shocking LA World Series victory in five games over the heavily favored Canseco and McGwire ("Bash Brothers")–led powerhouse.

1990   The Reds sweep the A's in the World Series, capturing the fourth game 2–1, as Oakland's vaunted offense averages just two runs per contest.

1993   The Phillies have leads of 6–3, 12–7, and 14–9, but the Jays rebound each time and win 15–14, as the combatants set a World Series record for most runs scored to date by both teams, with 29 in Game 4.

1996   At the age of 19, the Braves' Andruw Jones is the youngest player to homer in World Series history and joins the A's Gene Tenace (1972) as just the second player to connect in his first two Series at bats.

2000   The Blue Jays first baseman Carlos Delgado signs a then record four-year deal, averaging $17,000,000 per season, on the same day he's selected by baseball broadcasters for the Hank Aaron Award as the AL's top overall hitter.

2002   At the age of 20 years and 286 days, Angels reliever Francisco Rodriguez is the youngest pitcher to date to win a World Series contest, defeating the Giants 11–10 in Game 2. The win for the rookie dubbed "K-Rod" is his fifth of the postseason, but he does not notch his first regular-season victory until 2003.

2004   The Red Sox are the first ML club to win a seven-game postseason series after losing the first three games as they rout the Bombers 10–3 in the ALCS finale.

21

1861   An All-Star Game at Hoboken, NJ, between teams from Brooklyn and New York, attracts some 15,000 fans, as Brooklyn wins 18–6 behind its star pitcher, Jim Creighton.

1925   Just 17 days after pitching his final ML game with Cincinnati, Marv Goodwin is the first MLer to die in an airplane crash when his military plane strikes earth near Houston, TX.

1948   Barney DeFarge, former pitcher-manager of Reidsville, is sentenced to a year in prison for conspiring to throw Carolina League games during the season.

1957   Washington Senators owner Clark Griffith rejects an invitation from the twin cities of Minneapolis and St. Paul to move his team there.

1959   The Players Association approves two annual All-Star Games beginning in 1960. Meanwhile, Continental League president Branch Rickey awards the sixth franchise in the proposed rebel ML loop to Buffalo, leaving two spots still open.

1975   Carlton Fisk prayerfully wills his long fly down the left-field line at Fenway to land fair for a walk-off homer, giving the Red Sox a 12-inning 7–6 triumph over the Reds to force a seventh World Series game.

1976   The Reds beat the Yankees 7–2 to earn a four-game sweep and their second straight world championship.

1980   The Phillies, members of the NL since 1883, win their first World Series by downing the Royals 4–1 in the sixth game.

1995   Greg Maddux pitches a complete-game two-hitter as the Braves take the World Series opener 3–2 against the Indians, with the two clubs joining to tie the record for fewest combined hits (5) by both teams.

2001   The Diamondbacks reach the World Series in just their fourth year of existence, when Randy Johnson beats the Braves 3–2 to win the NLCS.

22

1857   The Atlantics of Brooklyn beat the Eckfords of Brooklyn to take the best-of-three games match that now decides the annual base-ball championship.

1927   Bedridden all of the 1927 season, future HOF outfielder Ross Youngs dies at the age of 30 of Bright's disease.

1928   Baltimore owner-manager Jack Dunn dies of a heart attack while horseback riding.

1929   Phils catcher Walt Lerian is killed near his Baltimore home when a truck hops the curb and levels him.

1972   The A's win their first of three straight World Series titles, beating the Reds in seven games.

1974 The Yanks send Bobby Murcer to the Giants for Bobby Bonds.

1975 Joe Morgan's bloop single in the 9th plates Ken Griffey Sr. with the winning run, as the Reds beat the Red Sox 4–3 in a hard-fought seven-game World Series that many pundits consider the best Fall Classic ever.

1991 Mark Lemke's single with two away in the 12th inning lifts the Braves to a 5–4 win over the Twins in the first World Series game played in Atlanta—or south of the Mason-Dixon line, for that matter.

2000 The Yankees beat the Mets 6–5 in Game 2 to extend their World Series winning streak to 14 straight games, but the contest is marred when the Yanks' Roger Clemens, who beaned Mike Piazza in July, hurls a splintered bat barrel toward Piazza, impelling both benches to empty.

23

1876 The *Chicago Tribune* introduces the notion of dividing a player's at bats by hits and deeming the result his batting percentage.

1886 Curt Welch scampers home on an errant pitch, enabling the St. Louis Browns to edge Chicago 4–3 in 10 innings and become the only AA team to win an undisputed World Series versus the NL.

1920 Four members of the White Sox—Eddie Cicotte, Lefty Williams, Joe Jackson, and Happy Felsch—sign confessions admitting to fixing the 1919 World Series, but all are later repudiated.

1931 Wilbert Robinson is fired as Brooklyn manager, and though management announces that the club will no longer be called the Robins in honor of Robinson, it is several years before Brooklyn becomes universally known as the Dodgers again.

1945 Emboldened now that Judge Landis is no longer commissioner, Brooklyn GM Branch Rickey signs Jackie Robinson, former shortstop for the Negro league Kansas City Monarchs, to play in 1946 for the Montreal Royals, a Brooklyn farm club in the IL, and in January 1946 he also signs African American pitcher John Wright to a Montreal contract.

1952 The PCL adopts a 176-game schedule for 1953 in what will be its second season as a specially designated "open classification" league.

1979 In Minneapolis, battling Billy Martin decks Joseph Cooper, a marshmallow salesman, triggering George Steinbrenner to fire him as Yankees manager five days later.

1993 The Blue Jays garner their second straight world championship, when Joe Carter blasts a game-ending three-run shot off the Phillies' Mitch Williams for an 8–6 victory.

24

1885 The first seven-game World Series in ML history ends unsatisfactorily when both AA champion St. Louis and NL victor Chicago claim the title, as each team won three games with one game ending in a controversial tie that both clubs insist they won.

1927 Garry Herrmann, president of the Reds for the past 25 years and a former chairman of the National Commission, resigns his post with Cincinnati.

1946 The Yankees send former 20-game winner Ernie Bonham to Pittsburgh for reliever Cookie Cuccurullo, who never throws another pitch in a ML game.

1955 His reputation for building ML teams into winners in shreds after the Pirates suffer their fourth straight cellar finish, Branch Rickey cedes his Pittsburgh GM post to Joe L. Brown, son of the actor.

1972 At the age of 53, HOF trailblazer Jackie Robinson succumbs to heart disease in Stamford, CT.

1992 For the first time in ML history, a team based outside the United States wins it all as the Blue Jays down the Braves 4–3 in 11 innings in the sixth game of the Fall Classic.

1994 The Braves' Greg Maddux is the first pitcher to garner three consecutive Cy Young Awards after he posts a 1.56 ERA.

2004 The Red Sox' Curt Schilling beats the Cards 6–2, making him the first pitcher to win a World Series game for three different clubs after notching victories for the Phillies in 1993 and Diamondbacks in 2002.

25

1884 The AA champion New York Metropolitans (aka Mets) lose for the third straight time to NL champion Providence in the first post-season series between two pennant winners played to its conclusion.

1892 Boston ends the only split-season playoff series in ML history for the overall season championship by sweeping Cleveland in five straight games after an 11-inning tie in the series opener.

1955 Cleveland trades outfielder Larry Doby to the White Sox for outfielder Jim Busby and shortstop Chico Carrasquel.

1965 Leo Durocher, inactive as a ML manager since 1955, assumes the Cubs' helm for the 1966 season.

1973 The Cubs ship Fergie Jenkins to the Rangers for third baseman Bill Madlock, who goes on to win four NL batting crowns, and utility man Vic Harris.

1978 The Padres' Gaylord Perry is the first pitcher to bag a Cy Young Award in both leagues, as he earns the NL honor after winning the trophy with Cleveland in 1972.

1986 The Red Sox are one strike away from their first world championship in 68 years when the Mets score three runs in the 9th inning and win 6–5 in 10 frames when Mookie Wilson's grounder scoots through the legs of first baseman Bill Buckner, allowing Ray Knight to score the deciding run and force a seventh game.

1987 The Twins beat the Cards 4–2 in Game 7 to win the franchise's first world championship since the Senators topped the Giants in 1924.

2003 Josh Beckett goes the distance for the Marlins in a 2–0 shutout of the Yanks, giving the Marlins their second world championship in seven games.

2005 Geoff Blum belts a tie-breaking solo shot in the 14th inning of Game 3 to help the White Sox beat the Astros 7–5 in the longest World Series game to date by time (5:41).

26

1903 Former ML pitcher Bill Phyle is expelled from OB for failing to substantiate his charges that several Southern League games played during the season were fixed. Phyle is later reinstated.

1911 Chief Bender pitches the A's to victory over the Giants on the latest ending date for a modern World Series prior to 1989.

1931 White Sox owner Charlie Comiskey dies at the age of 72.

1933 Washington sends player-manager Joe Cronin to the Red Sox for a then record $225,000 and shortstop Lyn Lary, after Cronin marries Senators owner Clark Griffith's niece, Mildred Robertson.

1960 The Senators announce that after residing in Washington since the AL's inaugural ML season in 1901, they are moving to

Minneapolis/St. Paul. Meanwhile, the AL adds two new teams for the 1961 season, in Washington and LA, while extending the season schedule to 162 games.

1977   The Yankees' Sparky Lyle is the first bullpenner to capture an AL Cy Young.

1979   Willie Mays is informed by Commissioner Kuhn that if he accepts a position with Bally's gambling casino, he must sever his ties with MLB. Mays chooses Bally's over baseball.

1982   The Phillies' Steve Carlton is the first hurler to earn four Cy Young Awards after topping the NL with 23 wins and 286 strikeouts.

1985   With the Cards leading 1–0 in Game 6 of the World Series, umpire Don Denkinger rules Royals pinch-hitter Jorge Orta safe at first in the 9th inning (albeit replays indicate that he was out), and KC then plates two runs to win and force a seventh game.

1996   After losing the first two World Series games at home, the Yankees rebound to defeat the Braves in six games and win their first title since 1978.

1997   The Marlins capture their first world championship when Edgar Renteria hits a game-winning single with two away in the 11th inning of Game 7 to beat the Indians, 3–2.

1998   Mets catcher Mike Piazza signs the richest deal in ML history to that point, a seven-year, $91,000,000 package.

2002   Trailing the Giants' Russ Ortiz 5–0, the Angels stave off elimination by scoring three runs in the 7th, plus three more in the 8th to win 6–5 and force a seventh World Series game.

2005   The White Sox beat the Astros 1–0, completing a Series sweep that brings them their first world championship since 1917.

27

1877   The Louisville Grays expel pitcher Jim Devlin, outfielder George Hall, and infielder Al Nichols for throwing games and add Bill Craver to the list on general principals, with Craver the only one of the four denying the charge of conspiring to lose the 1877 pennant to Boston.

1888   Sadie McMahon, soon to become one of the top ML pitchers of his era, is exonerated after a trial in a Wilmington, DE, court for killing a peanut vendor the previous May on the Forepaugh circus grounds.

1924 The Cubs swap pitcher Vic Aldridge and infielders George Grantham and Al Niehaus to the Pirates for shortstop Rabbit Maranville, first baseman Charlie Grimm, and pitcher Wilbur Cooper.

1926 The Yankees and Senators complete a swap begun earlier by sending pitcher Garland Braxton and outfielder Nick Cullop to Washington for pitcher Dutch Ruether.

1965 The Cards deal first baseman Bill White and shortstop Dick Groat, plus catcher Bob Uecker, to the Phillies for outfielder Alex Johnson, catcher Pat Corrales, and pitcher Art Mahaffey.

1985 The Royals win the Series when Bret Saberhagen whips the Cards 11–0 to complete a comeback after being down in games 3–1. Meanwhile, the Yankees can Billy Martin for the fourth time and replace him with Lou Piniella.

1986 In Game 7 of the World Series, the Mets rally after being down 3–0 in the 6th inning to beat the Red Sox 6–5 and capture their first world championship since 1969.

1991 Gene Larkin's 10th-inning single ends a scoreless tie in Game 7 and enables the Twins to beat the Braves for the world championship behind Jack Morris, whose 1–0 complete-game win nets him the Series MVP and is arguably the most masterly pitching performance in post-season history.

1992 Don Baylor is named the first manager of the Colorado Rockies.

1998 President Bill Clinton signs the Curt Flood Act of 1998, a bill overturning the labor relations part of baseball's antitrust exemption established in 1922 but not matters involving relocation, league expansion, or the minor leagues.

1999 The Yankees romp to their second straight World Series sweep, while the Braves lose their fourth Fall Classic of the decade.

2002 The Angels defeat the Giants 4–1 to capture their first World Series, as John Lackey is the first rookie to win the seventh game of a Fall Classic since Pittsburgh's Babe Adams in 1909.

2004 The Red Sox sweep the Cards for their first World Series triumph since 1918.

28

1890 The final NL-AA World Series ends in an unsatisfactory draw when Louisville AA tops Brooklyn NL in front of only some 300 die-hard Brooklyn fans to knot the affair at three games apiece.

1953 Popular Dodgers broadcaster Red Barber quits Brooklyn and signs to broadcast Yankees games.

1954 The A's hopes to remain in Philadelphia fade when ML owners refuse to allow the team to be sold to a local syndicate, enabling Arnold Johnson to purchase the franchise the following week for some $3,500,000 and move it to KC.

1968 The Cards' Bob Gibson earns his first of two Cy Young honors after notching 22 victories with a microscopic 1.12 ERA, plus 13 shut-outs.

1995 Lefty Tom Glavine allows just a 6th-inning single to Cleveland's Tony Pena and combines with closer Mark Wohlers for a 1–0 one-hitter, giving the Braves their first world championship in Atlanta.

2007 The Red Sox beat the Rockies 4–3, completing a four-game sweep and notching their second world championship in four years. Meanwhile, Alex Rodriguez's agent, Scott Boras, announces that A-Rod will exercise his option to void the four years left of his contract with the Yankees and become a free agent. But just a few days later, A-Rod defies Boras and accepts a 10-year, $275,000,000 deal with the Bombers that can potentially earn him millions more if he breaks the career homer record.

29

1889 The NL New York Giants win the first "Subway" World Series when they beat the AA champion Brooklyn Bridegrooms for the sixth time in the best-of-11 affair.

1920 The Yankees resume their assault on Red Sox personnel by pilfering Sox manager Ed Barrow and installing him as the Bombers' business manager.

1928 The Phils acquire Lefty O'Doul, who wins the NL batting title (.398) the following season, and a packet of cash from the Giants for outfielder Freddy Leach, who goes on to hit .290, 108 points less than O'Doul, in his first year in New York.

1931 A's 31-game winner Lefty Grove wins the first BBWAA AL MVP Award.

1959 White Sox righty Early Wynn, at the age of 39, is the oldest Cy Young Award winner to date.

1969 The Mets' Tom Seaver is the first pitcher to win a Cy Young Award for a ML expansion club.

30

1871 The Philadelphia Athletics beat the fire-ravaged Chicago White Stockings, playing in borrowed uniforms, 14–1 at the neutral Unions Grounds in Brooklyn in a game that National Association committee members later declare the contest that decides the first pro league pennant race.

1875 Boston defeats Hartford 7–4 in the final game in the history of the National Association.

1884 Despite finishing second in the 12-team AA race, the financially troubled Columbus, OH, team disbands and sells its players for $8,000 to 10th-place Pittsburgh, which vaults to 3rd the following year.

1922 The Giants give the Baltimore Orioles three players and $65,000 for pitcher/first baseman Jack Bentley and later up the sale price to $72,000. Elsewhere, Detroit sends outfield prospect Babe Herman, pitcher Howard Ehmke, outfielder Danny Clark, pitcher Carl Holling, and $25,000 to the Red Sox for second baseman Del Pratt and pitcher Rip Collins.

1964 Joe Stanka, who pitched two games for the 1959 White Sox, captures the Pacific League MVP with the Nankai Hawks after beating the Hanshin Tigers three times to help his team win the Japanese leagues championship.

1973 The Mets' Tom Seaver (19–10) is the first pitcher to win a Cy Young Award without bagging 20 victories.

2001 Sporting a New York Fire Department windbreaker to honor the September 11 heroes, George W. Bush throws the ceremonial first pitch from the mound at Yankee Stadium, as the Yanks beat the Diamondbacks 2–1 in Game 3 of the World Series.

2005 HOF catcher and manager Al Lopez dies in Tampa, FL, at the age of 97.

2007 Former Yankees catcher Joe Girardi signs a three-year deal for a reported $7,800,000 to manage the Bombers.

31

1942   Billy Hebert, formerly with Oakland in the PCL, is the first OB player to lose his life in World War II when he is killed in a training accident at Henderson Field on Guadalcanal.

1960   The Giants ship infielder Andre Rodgers to the Braves for shortstop Al Dark and make Dark their skipper.

1967   In the first year in which a Cy Young winner is chosen in each league, the Giants' Mike McCormick rides his 22 victories to the NL honor, and the Red Sox' Jim Lonborg earns the AL nod three days later.

November

1

1878 Boston and Providence stage so popular an exhibition game, in which six balls constitute a walk and the first-bounce out on a foul ball is eliminated, that both rule changes are eventually implemented.

1894 Former ML pitcher Charlie Sweeney is convicted of killing Con McManus in a saloon quarrel and sentenced to San Quentin.

1916 Broadway producer and theater owner Harry Frazee buys the Boston Red Sox for a reported $675,000.

1934 The Phils hand shortstop Dick Bartell to the Giants for four players of little account, plus cash.

1937 Despondent when arm trouble ends his ML career, pitcher Benny Frey commits suicide via carbon monoxide poisoning.

1938 Cincinnati's Ernie Lombardi is the lone catcher to win MVP honors and a loop batting title in the same season when he is the NL award winner.

1942 Brooklyn GM Larry MacPhail enters the army, triggering Branch Rickey to leave the Cardinals and take MacPhail's post prior to the following season.

1966 The Dodgers' Sandy Koufax is the first three-time Cy Young honoree. Making his feat even more impressive is that he earned all three unanimously when just one trophy was awarded each season.

1968 Detroit's Denny McLain is the unanimous AL Cy Young winner after going 31–6 for the world champion Tigers.

1982 ML owners vote not to renew Commissioner Kuhn's contract.

1989 The first season of the Senior Professional Baseball Association begins as the list of players (restricted to retired performers age 35 and older) includes future Cooperstown inductees Fergie Jenkins and Rollie Fingers.

1993 After serving a nine-month suspension for making ethnic and racial slurs, owner Marge Schott resumes her everyday operation of the Reds.

1997 The Negro Leagues Baseball Museum, "dedicated to preserving the rich history of African American Baseball," opens its new home in Kansas City, MO.

2001 In the first ML game played in November since the 19th century, the Yankees for the second World Series date in a row tie the contest with two outs in the 9th inning when Scott Brosius clocks a two-run shot off Diamondbacks reliever Byung-Hyun Kim and then win the game on Alfonso Soriano's 12th-inning RBI single.

2007 The Dodgers announce that Joe Torre will be their manager for 2008, signing the former Yankees skipper to a three-year, $13,000,000 deal.

2

1901 *TSN* correspondent Harry Merrill touts a rule change first proposed in the 1890s that would require each team to designate a player otherwise not in the lineup to bat for its pitcher.

1938 BoSox first baseman Jimmie Foxx is the first player to win three MVP Awards as well as the first to win the prize with two different teams (having done it previously with the A's).

1950 The Phils' Jim Konstanty is the first relief pitcher to receive a loop MVP Award.

1960 George Weiss, the Yankees GM since the end of the 1947 season, leaves the Bombers.

1972 Phillies lefty Steve Carlton is selected unanimously as the NL Cy Young winner after bagging an astounding 27 victories for a cellar dweller that totaled only 59 wins for the season. Meanwhile, former Red Sox shortstop Freddy Parent, the last surviving participant in the first modern World Series between Boston and Pittsburgh in 1903, dies at the age of 96 in Sanford, ME.

1974 Atlanta sends Hank Aaron to the Brewers, ending Aaron's 21 years with the Braves franchise.

1988 The A's reap their third straight Rookie of the Year Award winner when shortstop Walt Weiss follows Jose Canseco (1986) and Mark McGwire (1987) to the podium.

1995 The Yankees name Joe Torre their new manager, replacing Buck Showalter.

1996 Toni Stone (born Marcenia Alberga), the first female to play regularly in pro baseball (second base for the 1953 Indianapolis Clowns), dies at the age of 75 in an Alameda, CA, nursing home.

3

1881 The AA elects Pittsburgh's Denny McKnight its first president and, in defiance of the staid NL, proclaims that it will allow liquor to be sold in its parks, charge only 25¢ admission, and play on Sunday in cities where the law permits.

1942 Despite following his .406 season in 1941 with a Triple Crown campaign, BoSox outfielder Ted Williams is again denied the AL MVP as the award goes instead to Yankees second baseman Joe Gordon, who led the AL in batter strikeouts and errors at his position.

1960 Vern Law wins the Cy Young Award and remains the lone Pirate recipient until Doug Drabek in 1990.

1965 Dodgers ace Sandy Koufax is the first two-time Cy Young recipient after setting a post–1892 record (since broken) with 382 strikeouts.

1982 Milwaukee's Pete Vuckovich (18–6) is the first starter to win an AL Cy Young with fewer than 20 victories.

1989 Lou Piniella signs as Reds manager and guides Cincinnati to a world championship in 1990.

1992 The Yankees ship outfielder Roberto Kelly to the Reds for Paul O'Neill, plus a minor leaguer. O'Neill hits .300 in each of his first six years in pinstripes and is a main cog on four world champions.

2001 The Diamondbacks pummel the Yankees for a new World Series single-game record 22 hits in winning 15–2 to force a seventh game.

4

1884 Pitcher Tony Mullane of the disbanded Toledo AA team reneges on a pledge to sign with St. Louis and joins Cincinnati instead, earning a suspension for the entire 1885 season for contract jumping.

1888 A world tour organized by Chicago owner Al Spalding and pitting a team comprised of Chicago players against an aggregate of ML All-Stars is launched in San Francisco when the All-Stars beat Chicago, 14–4.

1897 Texas League pitcher Warren Beckwith, a notorious "lady killer," elopes with Jessica Lincoln, the daughter of Abraham Lincoln's son, Robert.

1948 Former ML outfielder Jake Powell commits suicide by shooting himself while in custody in a Washington, DC, police station.

1953 A rule change for the 1954 season allows a batter to accept the outcome of a pitch if he makes a hit on delivery after a balk is called, but the most significant new rule requires all players to take their gloves with them when they come to bat rather than leaving them in the field.

1959 Cubs star Ernie Banks wins his second consecutive NL MVP Award, the only shortstop to date to be so honored twice, let alone two years in a row.

1976 At the New York Plaza Hotel, the site for the first mass-market free-agent reentry draft, reliever Bill Campbell is the first player to sign, inking a four-year package with the Red Sox totaling $1,000,000.

1980 The Phillies' Steve Carlton wins his third Cy Young, joining Sandy Koufax, Tom Seaver, and Jim Palmer as the only pitchers to that point with three such honors. Carlton adds a then unprecedented fourth trophy in 1982. Elsewhere, in Japan, Yomiuri Giants great Sadaharu Oh retires with 868 homers, still a pro baseball record.

1993 Cliff Young is the third Indians hurler to perish during the year when he is killed in a truck accident in Willis, TX.

1997 Phillies third baseman Scott Rolen ends the Dodgers' five-year domination of the NL Rookie of the Year Award.

1999 Larry Dolan agrees to purchase the Indians from Richard Jacobs for $320,000,000.

2001 Arizona ends the Yankees' three-year reign as world champions by scoring two runs in the bottom of the 9th inning off Mariano Rivera to win Game 7, 3–2. The Diamondbacks are the fastest expansion club to date to win a world title, needing only four seasons to make it to the top.

5

1860   The Excelsiors of Brooklyn notch the first documented shutout, belting the St. George Cricket Club, 25–0.

1869   The Cincinnati Red Stockings beat the Mutual Green Stockings of New York 17–8 to end their season a perfect 60–0.

1889   The Brotherhood, spearheaded by New York Giants shortstop John M. Ward, publishes a "Manifesto" that launches an all-out war between ML players and owners and results in the formation of the PL.

1920   The PCL suspends five players, including former MLers Bill Rumler, Harl Maggart, and Tom Seaton, for conspiring to throw games during the 1919 season. All five are barred from OB the following January, as is former ML pitcher Gene Dale, but Rumler is later reinstated.

1958   Lee MacPhail, the son of Larry MacPhail, is named the new GM of the Baltimore Orioles.

1976   The Oakland A's ship their skipper, Chuck Tanner, to Pittsburgh for catcher Manny Sanguillen, plus $100,000, as Tanner assumes the Bucs' helm. Elsewhere, Toronto chooses infielder Bob Bailor first in the expansion draft, while Seattle makes outfielder Ruppert Jones its initial pick.

1997   The Milwaukee Brewers are the first team to switch MLs since 1889, when they move from the AL Central to the NL Central. Meanwhile, differences with team owner Peter Angelos impel Davey Johnson to resign as Orioles skipper just before receiving AL Manager of the Year honors.

2002   The Diamondbacks' Randy Johnson joins Greg Maddux as the only two pitchers to earn four straight Cy Young honors when he wins the pitching Triple Crown, leading the NL with 24 victories, 334 strikeouts, and a 2.32 ERA.

2003   Rookie Reds outfielder Dernell Stenson is slain at the age of 25 after being kidnapped in his SUV outside a Scottsdale nightclub while playing in the Arizona Fall League.

6

1873 A Henry Chadwick brainchild gets a test run when an experimental exhibition game is staged in Philadelphia between the two brotherly love NA entrants, the Athletics and the Pearls, with 10 men on a side and lasting 10 innings, but Chadwick's proposed innovations are poorly received.

1922 Morgan Bulkeley, the first NL president and later governor of Connecticut and U.S. senator, dies.

1925 Idled by what is misdiagnosed as a gallbladder problem, White Sox infielder Harvey McClellan dies at the age of 30 of liver cancer.

1930 The Pirates send shortstop Dick Bartell (.320 BA in 1930) to the Phils for shortstop Tommy Thevenow (.642 OPS in 1930) and pitcher Claude Willoughby, owner of a woeful 7.59 ERA in 1930 and destined never to win another game in the majors.

1950 Pittsburgh fans rejoice but soon have regret when Branch Rickey is named the Pirates' new GM.

1969 When Detroit's Denny McLain and the Orioles' Mike Cuellar tie for the AL Cy Young Award, to avoid future dead heats, writers in each league start naming three choices, with five points awarded for first place, three for second, and one for third. Each writer previously submitted only his top pitching choice.

1974 The Dodgers' Mike Marshall is the first fireman to win the Cy Young Award, as he sets ML season relief records with 106 outings and 208⅓ innings that are almost certain never to be challenged.

1984 The Tigers' Willie Hernandez garners the AL MVP after winning the AL Cy Young to join Rollie Fingers as the only two relievers to date to capture both honors in the same season. The A's Dennis Eckersley joins this exclusive club in 1992.

1996 For the fifth straight year, the Dodgers sport the NL Rookie of the Year when outfielder Todd Hollandsworth follows Eric Karros, Mike Piazza, Raul Mondesi, and Hideo Nomo, respectively.

2000 At the age of 32, Mariners bullpenner Kazuhiro Sasaki is the oldest AL Rookie of the Year, saving a frosh-record 37 games. Sasaki is far from a unanimous choice, however, as many writers feel the Japanese leagues veteran should not be deemed a rookie.

2007 The Padres' Greg Maddux wins his record 17th Gold Glove, breaking the mark he previously shared with pitcher Jim Kaat and third baseman Brooks Robinson.

7

1891 A special NL meeting to investigate charges lodged by Chicago GM Jim Hart and manager Cap Anson that the 1891 NL pennant race was rigged for Boston to beat out Chicago results in a whitewash of New York Giants who are accused of throwing a five-game series in September to Boston and awards Boston perhaps the most controversial pennant in ML history.

1928 Rogers Hornsby moves to his fourth team in four seasons when the Braves' new manager, owner Judge Emil Fuchs, sends him to the Cubs for a then record $200,000 and five nondescript players.

1951 Representative Emanuel Celler's House Judiciary investigation into the game's practices takes a new turn when Celler announces that his data conflict with Dodgers owner Walter O'Malley's claim his team has been losing money ever since the war and adds that the evidence his committee has unearthed indicates that the reserve clause unfairly limits a player's movements and earning potential.

1963 Yankees catcher Elston Howard is the first African American to win an AL MVP after batting .348.

1967 Cardinals first baseman Orlando Cepeda is the first NL MVP winner selected unanimously after helping the Redbirds to a world championship by hitting .325 with a league-leading 111 RBI.

1973 Little League baseball opens its doors to girls for the first time, with New Jersey leading the way.

1978 Red Sox slugger Jim Rice wins the AL MVP on the strength of the first junior loop season with 400 total bases (406) since the Yankees' Joe DiMaggio racked up 418 in 1937.

1989 The Orioles' Gregg Olson is the first reliever to win an AL Rookie of the Year honor.

1995 MLB fills its growing coffers by signing a five-year, $1,700,000,000, deal with NBC, FOX, ESPN, and Liberty Media.

8

1894 Mike "King" Kelly is the first future member of the HOF to die when he expires from pneumonia in Boston at the age of 34.

1934 NL publicity director Ford Frick succeeds John Heydler as senior loop president.

1941 Hugh "Losing Pitcher" Mulcahy escapes the futile Phillies when he is the first ML player drafted into the military with World War II imminent.

1955 Washington trades Mickey Vernon, Tom Umphlett, Bob Porterfield, and Johnny Schmitz to Boston for five prospects, only one of whom—pitcher Tex Clevenger—pans out.

1966 Baltimore's Frank Robinson is the first to win an MVP in both leagues when he follows his NL selection with Cincinnati in 1961 by capturing the AL honor after achieving the Triple Crown.

1989 Cubs outfielder Jerome Walton receives the NL Rookie of the Year Award with fellow Bruin Dwight Smith second, making them the first senior circuit freshmen teammates to finish 1–2 in the frosh balloting since the Phillies' Jack Sanford and Ed Bouchee in 1957.

2004 Pirates outfielder Jason Bay ends a 57-year drought when he is the initial Pirate to cop Rookie of the Year honors since the award's inception in 1947.

2007 Prompted by the death of minor league base coach Mike Coolbaugh, ML general managers mandate that base coaches must wear head protection.

9

1915 Former Yankees infielder Otis Johnson accidentally kills himself when he stumbles over his own shotgun while chasing a fox in a field.

1925 Slow to mend from the broken leg suffered in spring training, future HOF shortstop Rabbit Maranville is put on waivers by the Cubs and claimed by the Dodgers.

1937 Joe Medwick, the NL's last Triple Crown winner to date, is voted the senior loop MVP.

1993 In his first year with the Giants, Barry Bonds captures his third MVP, posting career bests at that point with 46 homers, 123 RBI, and a .336 BA.

1995 The Dodgers' Hideo Nomo is the first Japanese performer to win a Rookie of the Year Award.

1998 HOF hurler Catfish Hunter announces that he is suffering from Lou Gehrig's disease, an incurable neurological malady that claims his life the following year at the age of 53.

2004 At the age of 42, the Astros' Roger Clemens is the oldest Cy Young recipient to date and extends two of his records, first, by winning the Cy Young for the seventh time, and second, for doing so with his fourth team after previously garnering trophies with the Red Sox, Blue Jays, and Yankees.

10

1870 The New York State Baseball Convention reaffirms its stance that no club in the state with African American players can be admitted to the National Association.

1897 St. Louis trades shortstop Monte Cross, catcher Klondike Douglass, and pitcher Red Donahue to Philadelphia for pitcher Jack Taylor, third baseman Lave Cross, outfielder Tommy Dowd, and catcher Jack Clements. Elsewhere, Pittsburgh and Cincinnati also engineer a seven-player deal, the largest to date, with outfielder Elmer Smith and pitcher Pink Hawley off to the Reds for outfielder Jack McCarthy, catcher Pop Schriver, second baseman Ace Stewart, third baseman Bill Gray, and pitcher Billy Rhines.

1919 Washington manager Clark Griffith becomes president and majority owner of the club after mortgaging his Montana ranch to buy the team.

1948 Desperate for catching help, the Tigers surrender promising southpaw Billy Pierce and $10,000 for White Sox receiver Aaron Robinson.

1978 After winning the Cy Young the previous year, Sparky Lyle is jettisoned by the Yankees in a 10-player deal with the Rangers in which the Bombers receive lefty prospect Dave Righetti, the 1981 AL Rookie of the Year.

1987 Phillies reliever Steve Bedrosian wins the tightest NL Cy Young vote to date, edging the Cubs' Rick Sutcliffe, 57–55.

1992 The Giants are forced to remain in San Francisco after ML owners deny the team's request to move to St. Petersburg, FL.

1997 The Blue Jays' Roger Clemens is the initial AL hurler to receive four Cy Young honors and also the first junior loop twirler to win the pitching Triple Crown since Detroit's Hal Newhouser in 1945, as he leads in wins, strikeouts, and ERA. Clemens goes on to repeat his Triple Crown performance the following season in becoming the first pitcher to collect five Cy Young trophies.

11

1868 The New York State Baseball Convention expels the New York Mutuals for reinstating Ed Duffy, one of their three players banned for life for throwing a game in 1865.

1896 Baltimore sends outfielder Steve Brodie and third baseman Jim Donnelly to Pittsburgh for outfielders Jake Stenzel and Tom O'Brien, second baseman Harry Truby, and pitcher Elmer Horton.

1897 New York swaps third baseman Jim Donnelly, outfielder Ducky Holmes, and $3,500 to St. Louis for catcher Mike Grady and third baseman Fred Hartman.

1920 In *TSN*, John McGraw admits he dropped pitcher Jean Dubuc because of Dubuc's association with gamblers and possible knowledge of the 1919 World Series fix, but Commissioner Landis looks the other way, and Dubuc is allowed to remain in OB until he retires in 1926.

1940 Dodgers GM Larry MacPhail plucks pitcher Kirby Higbe from the Phils for $100,000, two lesser pitchers, and catcher Mickey Livingston.

1949 National Association chieftain George Trautman announces that in 1949 a record 41,872,762 attended minor league games in the 59 loops under the NA's umbrella.

1981 The Dodgers' Fernando Valenzuela is the first rookie to capture Cy Young honors after winning 13 games in the strike-shortened regular season.

1997 After showcasing the NL Cy Young winner six straight seasons (Greg Maddux, 1992–1995; John Smoltz, 1996), the Braves' hammerlock on the award is broken by the Expos' Pedro Martinez, who fans 305 and leads the senior circuit with a 1.90 ERA.

2002 Giants outfielder Barry Bonds extends his ML record when he wins his fifth NL MVP after leading the senior loop with a .370 BA.

12

1886 AA rivals St. Louis and Cincinnati engineer the first overt player trade between two ML teams when outfielder Hugh Nicol goes to Cincinnati in return for catcher Jack Boyle and $350.

1895 Cap Anson debuts in Charles Hoyt's hackneyed stage play *A Runaway Colt* in Syracuse, inducing Windy City sportswriters to begin referring to his team almost exclusively as the "Colts."

1920 Kenesaw Mountain Landis agrees to become baseball's first commissioner only if he can retain his federal judgeship.

1923 The Giants' John McGraw gives his former pitching ace, Christy Mathewson, a present when his swap with the Braves president brings World Series hero Casey Stengel and shortstop Dave Bancroft to Boston for pitcher Joe Oeschger and outfielder Billy Southworth.

1939 The Red Sox buy center fielder Dom DiMaggio from San Francisco of the PCL, making the DiMaggio brothers—Joe, Dom, and Vince—the first sibling outfield trio in the majors since Tom, Mike, and John Mansell in 1882.

1952 Bobby Shantz bags the AL MVP Award after his 24–7 season spurs the A's to break .500 for the final time until 1968, the franchise's first season in Oakland.

1955 The Cards replace Harry Walker with Fred Hutchinson, a move that makes the 1956 season the first in ML history without a single player-manager in either league.

1958 In the closest Cy Young Award vote to date, Yankees World Series hero Bob Turley tops the Braves' Warren Spahn, five votes to four.

1959 Second baseman Nellie Fox is the first member of the White Sox to win an AL MVP Award, as teammates Luis Aparicio and Early Wynn finish second and third, respectively, in the balloting.

1992 Yankees reliever Steve Howe's permanent ban by Commissioner Fay Vincent is overturned by arbitrator George Nicolau as too harsh, enabling the Bombers to re-sign Howe the following month.

2001 The Cardinals' Albert Pujols wins the NL Rookie of the Year after setting senior loop frosh records in RBI (130), extra base hits (88), and total bases (360). Meanwhile, the Mariners' Ichiro Suzuki nabs top AL frosh honors but is denied unanimous selection when Chris Assenheimer of the *Elyria Chronicle-Telegram* in Ohio votes for Cleveland's pitcher, C. C. Sabathia, believing the hurler fits the definition of a rookie, whereas Suzuki previously played nine seasons in Japanese major leagues.

2007 In the closest race since the current voting rules were adopted in 1980, Milwaukee's Ryan Braun edges Rockies shortstop Troy Tulowitzki (128–126) for NL Rookie of the Year.

13

1896   Cincinnati trades shortstop Germany Smith, pitcher Chauncey Fisher, and $1,000 to Brooklyn for shortstop Tommy Corcoran.

1897   The Temple Cup is scrapped at the NL meeting after Baltimore, the previous month, had been the third second place team in the cup's four-year history to defeat the pennant winner, in this case Boston.

1958   When New York Mayor Robert Wagner announces that a third ML will soon become a reality, William Shea, chairman of what comes to be known as the Continental League, avers that the new loop will install a team in New York and raid existing ML rosters for players.

1979   The Cardinals' Keith Hernandez and the Pirates' Willie Stargell are the first players to share a ML MVP Award, as Hernandez tops the NL in batting at .344, and Stargell spearheads the world champion Bucs with 32 homers.

1990   The A's Bob Welch wins the AL Cy Young while notching 27 victories, the most since the Phils' Steve Carlton garnered that many in 1972.

1995   The Braves' Greg Maddux is the first pitcher to snare four straight Cy Young Awards (1992–1995) after topping the NL with a sparkling 19–2 slate and a 1.63 ERA.

1996   The Tribe receives third baseman Matt Williams from the Giants for pitcher Julian Tavarez, infielder Jose Vizcaino, and second baseman Jeff Kent, who embarrasses several teams that gave up on him prematurely with 100 RBI in each of his six seasons in San Francisco, plus an MVP in 2000.

1997   Rockies outfielder Larry Walker is the first Canadian-born player to win an MVP Award after leading the NL with 49 homers while batting a robust .366.

1998   At Lelands, the ball Babe Ruth hit for the first homer in Yankee Stadium history is sold at auction for $126,500 by Mark Scala, who found it two years earlier in his grandmother's home.

2000   The Red Sox' Pedro Martinez is the first pitcher to garner the Cy Young Award unanimously two straight years after winning 18 games with a ML-leading 1.74 ERA.

14

1889   Brooklyn and Cincinnati desert the AA and join the NL, temporarily reducing the AA to six teams and expanding the senior circuit to 10.

1895   In the most active trading day to date in ML history, Boston sends third baseman Billy Nash to Philadelphia for outfielder Billy Hamilton, New York swaps first baseman Jack Doyle to Baltimore for second baseman Kid Gleason and $3,500, and Brooklyn buys outfielder Tommy McCarthy from Boston for approximately $5,000.

1900   The NL rejects an offer from AL president Ban Johnson to treat his loop as a ML, precipitating a war when the AL declares itself outside the National Agreement and refuses to honor NL player contracts.

1929   Braves owner Judge Fuchs sends two players and a chunk of cash to Los Angeles of the PCL for Wally Berger.

1986   Nelson Doubleday and Fred Wilpon purchase the Mets from the Doubleday Publishing Company for $80,750,000, nearly four times what the company paid for it in 1980.

1989   Padres reliever Mark Davis captures the NL Cy Young Award after saving a league-leading 44 games, but he will save just 11 more the rest of his career. Davis's plunge parallels that of the Orioles' Steve Stone, who bagged 25 victories in 1980 and the AL Cy Young but won just four games the following season before exiting the big leagues due to tendonitis.

2001   Lou Piniella wins his second AL Manager of the Year Award after guiding the Mariners to 116 wins, tying the ML record set by the 1906 Cubs.

15

1922   Paul Hines, former two-time NL batting champ and the first Triple Crown winner (1878) in the view of many historians, is arrested in Washington, DC, on a charge of pickpocketing.

1933   The Cards and Phils swap star catchers, with Spud Davis coming to St. Louis and Jimmie Wilson heading to Philadelphia (where he is later named player-manager), along with infielder Eddie Delker.

1951   Yankees' Gil McDougald's selection as the AL Rookie of the Year sets off a firestorm in Chicago, where White Sox yearling Minnie Minoso surpassed McDougald in every major batting department for the season and finished fourth to McDougald's ninth in the loop's MVP balloting.

1961   Yankees outfielder Roger Maris captures his second straight AL MVP, edging teammate Mickey Mantle by just four votes, 202–198.

1979   The Dodgers ink hurler Dave Goltz to a six-year, $3,000,000 pact, but he wins just nine games in parts of three injury-plagued seasons before the Dodgers release him in April 1982.

1981   At the age of 27, Cubs infielder Steve Macko succumbs to cancer in Arlington, TX.

2001   The Yankees' Roger Clemens is the first pitcher to win the Cy Young (his sixth) with three different teams after previously capturing the award with the Red Sox and the Blue Jays.

2004   The Giants' Barry Bonds extends two of his own records by winning his seventh MVP and fourth in succession, and, in addition, is the oldest player to cop the award at the age of 40.

2005   MLB and the Players Association reach an agreement, which must be ratified by players and owners, requiring players to submit to several drug tests each year and imposing lengthy suspensions for steroid, HGH (human growth hormone), and amphetamine use, with third-time offenders suffering a lifetime ban.

2007   The Padres' Jake Peavy wins the NL Cy Young unanimously for his pitching Triple Crown. Meanwhile, baseball is rocked when a grand jury indicts Barry Bonds on perjury and obstruction of justice charges regarding the BALCO steroids scandal.

16

1886   At a joint meeting, the NL and AA abolish the rule permitting a batter to request either high or low pitches and adopt the same rulebook. A plus for the game overall, the agreement also provides a major headache for historians when both loops quixotically decide that in 1887, for what will turn out to be that one season only, four strikes instead of three will constitute a strikeout and a base on ball will be counted the same as a base hit in calculating batting averages.

1887   The Joint NL and AA Rules Committee abolishes the four-strike rule as well as the rule counting walks as hits but refuses to reduce the number of balls needed for a walk from five to four.

1893   New York buys outfielder George Van Haltren from Pittsburgh for $2,500.

1988   A's slugger Jose Canseco wins the AL MVP unanimously after becoming the first ML player to hit 40 homers and steal 40 bases.

2000 San Juan, PR, will host its first Opening Day game when the Blue Jays announce plans to launch the 2001 season there against the Rangers.

17

1893 Cincinnati trades pitcher Mike Sullivan to Washington for outfielder Dummy Hoy.

1933 Pittsburgh gets pitcher Red Lucas and outfielder Wally Roettger from Cincinnati for outfielder Adam Comorosky and infielder Tony Piet.

1947 After trying unsuccessfully to deal shortstop Vern Stephens to Cleveland for Lou Boudreau, the Browns send Stephens and their top pitcher, Jack Kramer, to the Red Sox for six marginal players and a $310,000 chunk of owner Tom Yawkey's fortune, a swap that observers predict will assure the Red Sox of the 1948 AL pennant.

1954 The Yankees and Orioles initiate a record 17-player trade that will be completed on December 1 and bring pitchers Bob Turley and Don Larsen, among others, to New York for outfielder Gene Woodling, shortstop Willie Miranda, catchers Gus Triandos and Hal Smith, and several other players who will help the Orioles.

1960 Former U.S. Air Force lieutenant general William Eckert is named the new commissioner, succeeding Ford Frick.

1971 At age 22 years, 3 months, and 13 days, A's hurler Vida Blue is the youngest player to date to capture the MVP Award, adding it to the Cy Young trophy he earned earlier in the month.

1979 Dan Okrent creates a rough draft for the phenomenon that is dubbed Rotisserie League Baseball in honor of the La Rôtisserie Française restaurant in New York where Okrent first pitched his idea to friends.

1983 The Royals' Willie Wilson, Willie Aikens, and Jerry Martin, plus former teammate Vida Blue, are sentenced to three months in prison for attempting to buy cocaine.

1992 The Rockies' first trade is a success as they ship outfielder Kevin Reimer to the Brewers for outfielder Dante Bichette, who thrives in Colorado's thin air, swatting 201 homers and batting .316 in his seven-year Denver stay.

2005 ML owners unanimously vote to approve the stricter steroids policy agreed upon by the Players Association.

18

1947 The Red Sox make their second major deal with the Browns in two days, acquiring pitcher Ellis Kinder and infielder Billy Hitchcock for three players and $65,000. Elsewhere, the Braves send first baseman Johnny Hopp and second baseman Danny Murtaugh to Pittsburgh for catcher Bill Salkeld, outfielder Jim Russell, and pitcher Al Lyons.

1958 Milwaukee's Red Schoendienst is found to be suffering from tuberculosis.

1966 Bowing to the pain in his arthritic left elbow, Dodgers ace Sandy Koufax announces his retirement at the age of 30.

1980 Royals third baseman George Brett receives the AL MVP after hitting .390, the highest ML season average to that point since the Red Sox' Ted Williams swatted .406 in 1941.

1981 The Phillies' Mike Schmidt is the first third baseman to win consecutive MVP Awards after leading the NL during the strike-shortened season with 31 homers and 91 RBI.

1987 Cubs outfielder Andre Dawson is the first player to win an MVP with a cellar dweller, as he leads the senior loop in homers with 49 and RBI with 137, while the Bruins finish last in the NL East.

1997 The Expos make a wretched deal, sending Pedro Martinez to the Red Sox for pitchers Carl Pavano and Tony Armas Jr. Martinez posts a 117–37 mark in Sox threads with two Cy Young Awards and a world championship ring. Elsewhere, Tampa Bay makes Astros prospect Bobby Abreu their sixth pick in the expansion draft but then deals him to the Phillies for shortstop Kevin Stocker. Abreu hits more than 200 homers in Philadelphia with five 100-RBI seasons. Meanwhile, Arizona taps lefty Brian Anderson as its first pick in the expansion draft, while southpaw Tony Saunders is Tampa Bay's initial choice.

1998 The Indians pay dearly for lefty reliever Ricardo Rincon, sending the Pirates outfielder Brian Giles, who cranks 35 or more homers in each of his first four seasons in Bucs garb.

2007 The *New York Times* reviews a book written by Babe Dahlgren's grandson that all but incontrovertibly establishes that the first baseman who inherited Lou Gehrig's spot on the Yankees was unjustly accused of drug use, first by Yankees manager Joe McCarthy, followed by Dodgers GM Branch Rickey and scout Ted McGrew. After leaving the majors under a cloud in 1946, Dahlgren spent the remaining 50 years of his life trying to clear his name and found many sympathetic ears, but none that would step forward and openly acknowledge the grievous wrong three of the most revered baseball men of his era had done him.

19

1891 Ernie Hickman, a pitcher with Kansas City UA in 1884, shoots his wife during a drunken quarrel and then takes his own life.

1895 In a deal that takes several days to complete because it involves the largest number of players traded to date, Cincinnati sends third baseman Arlie Latham, pitcher/outfielder Tom Parrott, catchers Morgan Murphy and Ed McFarland, plus cash, to St. Louis for catcher Heinie Peitz and pitcher Red Ehret.

1928 Cleveland garners PCL star Earl Averill from San Francisco for $5,000 and two minor leaguers.

1956 The Cards snare slugging outfielder Del Ennis from the Phils for outfielder Rip Repulski and infielder Bobby Morgan.

1962 The Cards ship pitcher Don Cardwell and shortstop Julio Gotay to the Pirates for 43-year-old lefty Diomedes Olivo and shortstop Dick Groat, who is an All-Star Game starter in each of the next two seasons and a key member of the 1964 world champions Redbirds.

1975 Joe Morgan is the first NL second baseman to win the MVP since the Dodgers' Jackie Robinson in 1949. The following year, Morgan is the first second sacker to cop the honor in consecutive seasons.

1979 The Astros sign free agent Nolan Ryan to a four-year package worth $4,500,000, making Ryan the first MLer to earn $1,000,000 annually.

1984 Mets moundsman Dwight Gooden, who won 17 games and fanned a post–1892 freshman record 276 batters, is the youngest player to date (20 years, three days) to win the Rookie of the Year Award. The following year, Gooden wins the pitching Triple Crown and becomes the youngest hurler to date to cop Cy Young honors at 21 years, two days.

1986 Phillies third baseman Mike Schmidt wins the NL MVP, tying a ML record for the most to date with his third such honor.

1993 The Expos ship second baseman Delino DeShields to the Dodgers for Pedro Martinez, who goes on to win 55 games over the next four years with Montreal, including a Cy Young, before departing for Boston.

1996 Albert Belle is the first player to eclipse $10,000,000 annually when he inks a five-year deal with the White Sox valued at $55,000,000.

2001 Barry Bonds's record 73-homer season helps make him the first to win four MVP Awards.

20

1888 The Joint Rules Committee finally reduces the number of balls needed for a walk to four, commencing the four-ball, three-strike rule that has remained in effect since.

1897 The *Chicago Tribune* lists the 1897 leaders at each position in chances received per game and contends it is a better way to gauge a player's defensive prowess than his fielding average.

1957 Billy Martin, Gus Zernial, and four other Kansas City A's head for Detroit, while six Tigers set sail for Missouri, including outfielder Bill Tuttle and two former highly touted Bengals' "bonus babies"—outfielder Jim Small and catcher Frank House.

1958 Cleveland swaps relief aces Ray Narleski and Don Mossi, plus a minor leaguer, to Detroit for second baseman Billy Martin and pitcher Al Cicotte.

1962 The White Sox release Early Wynn, even though he needs just one victory to reach 300, but he eventually signs with the Indians and wins his 300th there before retiring. Elsewhere, the Red Sox deal last year's AL Rookie of the Year winner, pitcher Don Schwall, and catcher Jim Pagliaroni to the Pirates for first baseman Dick Stuart and pitcher Jack Lamabe.

1989 Milwaukee outfielder Robin Yount wins his second MVP after copping his first as a shortstop in 1982, making him the first performer to win the honor at both of these positions.

2001 Seattle's Ichiro Suzuki joins former Red Sox outfielder Fred Lynn as the only two players to date to capture the MVP and Rookie of the Year in the same season.

21

1887 The first multiple-player trade in ML history brings shortstop Bill Gleason and outfielder Curt Welch from St. Louis to the Philadelphia Athletics in return for catcher Jack Milligan, outfielder Fred Mann, infielder Chippy McGarr, and $3,000.

1888 Cleveland is the second team in two years to desert the AA when it joins Pittsburgh in defecting to the senior circuit.

1933 The cash-poor Phils peddle 1933 Triple Crown winner Chuck Klein to the Cubs for $125,000 (some sources say only $65,000) and three players.

1949 Bill Veeck sells the Indians for $2,200,000 to a group headed by Ellis Ryan, and they name Hank Greenberg the club's new GM.

1956 Brooklyn's Don Newcombe wins the first Cy Young Award, a new honor originated by Commissioner Frick the previous July, as well as the NL MVP Award to add to his 1949 NL Rookie of the Year Award and make him the first MLer to win each of the top three honors at least once.

1959 The opening day of the new interleague trading period brings the first such swap as Cubs first baseman Jim Marshall and pitcher Dave Hillman head for Boston in return for first baseman Dick Gernert.

1980 Yankees skipper Dick Howser, after guiding the Bombers to 103 wins, resigns and is supplanted by Gene Michael.

2002 The A's and Mariners agree to the earliest scheduled ML season opener to date, as they plan to square off on March 25, 2003, in Tokyo, Japan.

22

1888 The NL adopts Indianapolis owner John T. Brush's salary classification plan that limits a player's annual earnings to $2,500, causing an inferno within the Brotherhood, a nascent players' union started by New York Giants shortstop John M. Ward, among others, some two years earlier.

1917 Former ML infielder Danny Shay is acquitted of the charge that he shot and killed an African American waiter in an Indianapolis hotel during an argument over whether there was enough sugar in a sugar bowl.

1921 In return for pitcher Jimmy Ring and outfielder Greasy Neale, the Phils send pitcher Eppa Rixey to Cincinnati, where he labors with little recognition for the remaining 13 years of his career and becomes the first southpaw in ML history to lose 250 games.

1932   An errant shot shatters the leg of the Cards' Charlie Gelbert while he is hunting, reducing one of the top shortstops in the game to a part-timer when he is able to return to the majors three years later.

1934   The Cubs send pitchers Guy Bush and Jim Weaver, plus outfielder Babe Herman, to Pittsburgh for third sacker Freddie Lindstrom and pitcher Larry French.

1957   After becoming the oldest batting champion to date with a .388 mark in 1957, Boston's Ted Williams also nearly becomes the oldest MVP to date before losing the honor to the Yankees' Mickey Mantle by just 24 votes.

1960   The AL suggests that both leagues expand to nine teams in 1961 and begin interleague play, but while each circuit grows to 10 clubs by 1962, interleague play does not commence until 1997.

1983   Donald Fehr is named executive director of the Players Association after his predecessor, Kenneth Moffett, is fired. Elsewhere, former White Sox outfielder David Short's body is found beaten to death in the trunk of his car in Shreveport, LA.

2000   In a true rarity, White Sox shortstop Jose Valentin chooses to remain with the Pale Hose despite being offered more money by three other clubs, signing a three-year pact worth $5,000,000 per season.

2002   Astros outfielder Richard Hidalgo is shot during a carjacking in Venezuela but nonetheless strokes .309 with 28 homers the following season.

2004   The relocated Washington club announces that it will be known as the Nationals.

23

1870   The first shutout between two crack teams takes place at Dexter Park in Chicago when Netherlands native Rynie Wolters of the New York Mutuals bests the local White Stockings 9–0, an event so unprecedented that the word "Chicagoed" immediately becomes a synonym for a shutout.

1898   Walter "Mother" Watson, who pitched two games with Cincinnati 10 years earlier, is shot to death in Gardner's Saloon outside Pomeroy, OH, by Louis Schreiner, who becomes the object of an international manhunt when he flees the country.

1943 Commissioner Landis bars Phils chieftain William Cox, a rookie owner in every sense, from baseball for life for betting on his own team, a NL cellar dweller in five of the past six seasons.

1977 The Yankees ink free-agent reliever Rich Gossage to a six-year, $2,750,000 contract even though they already have closer Sparky Lyle, the season's AL Cy Young recipient, but the following season Lyle is the odd man out, saving only nine games, with Gossage bagging a league-leading 27.

1990 In Caracas, Venezuela, Bo Diaz, a former catcher with the Red Sox, Indians, Phillies, and Reds, is adjusting a satellite dish on his rooftop when the dish falls on him, ending his life at the age of 37.

2007 ML hurler Joe Kennedy dies at the age of 28 of a heart ailment at his in-laws' home where he and his family are spending the long Thanksgiving weekend.

24

1877 An unknown writer on the staff of the *New York Mercury* pens with eerie prescience, "The base ball mania is getting so bad that every city will soon have a mammoth structure like the Roman Coliseum to play in. This will be illuminated by electric lights so that games can be played nights, thus overcoming a serious objection at present existing."

1891 Lawrence Farley, an outfielder with Washington of the AA in 1884, is sentenced to life in prison after fatally shooting saloonkeeper Michael Minnaugh in Alton, IL, but Farley is pardoned six years later owing to extenuating circumstances.

1897 Harvard University unveils a cage 130 feet long, 60 feet wide, and 30 feet high built for $15,000 and designed to be used for indoor baseball practice.

1953 The Dodgers name minor league skipper Walter Alston as their new manager.

1997 Toronto hires Tim Johnson to replace Cito Gaston as manager, but on March 17, 1998, the Jays fire Johnson after learning that his inspiring combat tales of his days as a U.S. Marine in Vietnam are fallacious and that he had been no more than a Marine Corps reserve.

25

1889 Shortstop Jack Glasscock is the first to renege on a signed contract with the newly formed PL and return to the NL. Glasscock's betrayal of the Brotherhood, in the scheme of things, probably denied him any chance of admission to the Baseball HOF when he still had sufficient name recognition.

1941   Shortstop Lou Boudreau so surprises Indians owner Alva Bradley when he applies to replace Roger Peckinpaugh as Tribe pilot that Bradley names him the second youngest documented player-manager in ML history to none other than Peckinpaugh himself 28 years earlier.

1944   Kenesaw Mountain Landis, baseball's only commissioner to date, dies at the age of 78 of a heart attack.

1947   Sam Breadon, a member of the Cards family since 1917, sells the Redbirds to Postmaster General Robert Hannegan and Fred Saigh for a then record $4,000,000+ in a transaction that turns over not only the ML club but also its vast minor league empire.

1949   Despite losing what would have been his third Triple Crown when Detroit's George Kell edges him for the AL bat crown, .3429 to .3428, Ted Williams finally wins the AL MVP Award.

1981   The Brewers' Rollie Fingers is the first reliever to win the AL MVP, but more significantly, he is also the initial bullpenner to win the award in either league while capturing the Cy Young in the same season.

1985   White Sox shortstop Ozzie Guillen cops the AL Rookie of the Year and 20 years later guides the Pale Hose to their first world championship since 1917.

2002   The Red Sox ink Theo Epstein as their GM. At the age of 28, the Yale graduate is the youngest GM ever hired to date in ML history.

2003   The Cubs deal first baseman Hee-Seop Choi and a minor leaguer for first sacker Derrek Lee, who in 2005 clubs 46 homers while leading the NL in batting at .335.

2004   Nintendo's U.S. subsidiary now owns 50% of the Mariners after spending $67,000,000 to acquire its former president's shares.

2005   The Marlins cut roughly $27,000,000 from their payroll when they ship Carlos Delgado to the Mets for first baseman Mike Jacobs and two prospects, following a blockbuster deal the previous day in which Josh Beckett, Mike Lowell, and Guillermo Mota went from Florida to the Red Sox for shortstop Hanley Ramirez, plus pitchers Anibal Sanchez, Harvey Garcia, and Jesus Delgado.

26

1887 Brooklyn purchases pitching ace Bob Caruthers from St. Louis for $8,250, a transaction that many observers predict will shift the balance of power in the AA from the Mound City to the City of Churches.

1950 Gillette signs a six-year contract for $1,000,000 per annum for the television and radio sponsorship rights to the World Series.

1961 An attempt to legalize the spitball is soundly trounced by an 8–1 vote with only NL supervisor of umpires Cal Hubbard supporting the idea.

1974 In New York City, pitcher Catfish Hunter and A's owner Charlie Finley haggle at the American Arbitration Association over whether Finley breached Hunter's contract to the tune of $50,000. The following month, arbitrator Peter Seitz rules in Hunter's favor, making the plum starter baseball's first modern-era free agent.

1975 Following his earlier choice as the AL Rookie of the Year, Red Sox pasture man Fred Lynn is the first freshman to cop the MVP after hitting .331 with 105 RBI and 103 runs for the junior loop flag winner.

1979 Toronto's shortstop Alfredo Griffin and Twins' third baseman John Castino tie for the AL Rookie of the Year. To avoid future deadlocks, in 1980 the writers adopt the system used for Cy Young candidates in which scribes make three choices, ranked by a 5–3–1 point scale.

1996 Owners approve interleague play for the 1997 season.

27

1922 Cards outfielder Austin McHenry, a .350 hitter in 1921 who was incapacitated midway through the 1922 season, dies of a brain tumor.

1941 Joe DiMaggio is named AL MVP, even though his .406 BA during his record 56-game hitting streak for the season was lower than Ted Williams's .408 BA over the same stretch and Williams outhit him by 57 points on the season.

1947 Impartial AL fans are incensed when the Yankees' Joe DiMaggio (.315, 20 homers, and 97 RBI) is named the AL MVP (albeit by just one vote) despite Ted Williams having won the Triple Crown (.343, 32 homers, and 114 RBI).

1951 The White Sox snare catcher Sherman Lollar and two lesser players from the Browns for five players, including outfielder Jim Rivera and pitcher Dick Littlefield.

1967 The Senators trade manager Gil Hodges to the Mets, where he assumes the helm as well, in exchange for pitcher Bill Denehy and $100,000.

1972 The Indians GM Gabe Paul engineers a deal obtaining outfielders Charlie Spikes and Rusty Torres, catcher John Ellis, plus infielder Jerry Kenney from the Yankees for third baseman Graig Nettles and catcher Jerry Moses, which acquires a taint when scarcely six weeks later Paul jumps ship to the Bombers' front office, where Nettles goes on to star on four flag winners and two straight world champions.

1974 George Steinbrenner is slapped with a two-year suspension by Commissioner Kuhn due to the Yankees owner's conviction for illegal campaign contributions to Richard Nixon and other politicos.

1997 Hall of Famer Buck Leonard, who anchored first base for the Homestead Grays' nine straight pennant winners from 1937 to 1945, dies at the age of 90 in Rocky Mount, NC.

2001 Commissioner Selig's contract is extended by ML owners through 2006.

28

1859 The Eagle Club of San Francisco is the first baseball club to form on the West Coast.

1927 The Pirates trade future Hall of Famer Kiki Cuyler to the Cubs after he clashes with manager Donie Bush, receiving only infielder Sparky Adams and backup outfielder Pete Scott.

1944 For the only time in history to date, two pitchers on the same team finish 1–2 in MVP balloting when Hal Newhouser gathers four more votes for the AL prize than fellow Tiger Dizzy Trout.

1958 The AL reveals that its 1959 schedule calls for the season to open on April 9, the earliest starting date by a ML to that point.

1966 Completing an October deal, the Bucs acquire hurler Juan Pizarro from the White Sox for knuckleballer Wilbur Wood, who notches at least 20 wins each year with the Pale Hose from 1971 to 1974.

1972 The Angels send pitcher Andy Messersmith and third baseman Ken McMullen to the Dodgers for Frank Robinson, Bill Singer, and three others. Messersmith wins 20 games for LA in 1974, plus 19 more contests the following season, and Robinson belts 30 homers in 1973, while teammate Bill Singer bags 20 victories.

1978 After winning four pennants and two world championships, Reds manager Sparky Anderson is fired following a season in which the Reds finished just 2½ games behind the Dodgers in the NL West.

2005 Free agent B. J. Ryan inks the biggest contract to date by a reliever, a five-year, $47,000,000 deal with the Blue Jays.

29

1887 Seemingly bent on disassembling his AA dynasty in St. Louis, owner Chris Von der Ahe sells Brooklyn pitcher Dave Foutz for $5,500, thereupon bestowing his two best pitchers, Foutz and Bob Caruthers, and his best catcher, Doc Bushong, on his chief AA rival in the space of 10 days.

1926 Less than four weeks after Ty Cobb quits as Tigers player-manager, Tris Speaker resigns his same post with Cleveland, kicking off an incendiary December in which both stand accused of making a hasty exit to avoid being banned for fixing games.

1962 After four years of playing two All-Star Games each season, ML officials and player reps agree to stage just one Midsummer Classic in 1963.

1966 Cubs pitcher Jim Brewer is awarded $100,000 in damages by a Chicago circuit court jury for his on-field fight with Billy Martin in 1960.

1971 In a one-sided deal, the Indians ship Sam McDowell to the Giants for shortstop Frank Duffy and pitcher Gaylord Perry, the AL Cy Young recipient the following season and owner of 64 victories in his first three years in Cleveland, while the fast-slipping McDowell notches just 11 wins in parts of two seasons with San Francisco. Elsewhere, in an equally lopsided swap, the Reds trade Lee May, Tommy Helms, and Jimmy Stewart to the Astros for Cesar Geronimo, Ed Armbrister, Denis Menke, Jack Billingham, and Joe Morgan, who goes on to win two straight MVP Awards in Cincinnati that help carry him to Cooperstown.

1976 The Yankees and Reggie Jackson begin their stormy relationship when the future "Mr. October" signs a five-year, $3,500,000 deal to play in the Bronx.

1990 Claude Brochu heads a group of Canadian investors that buys the Montreal Expos from Charles Bronfman for a reported $85,000,000.

1992 The *New York Times* quotes Reds owner Marge Schott as saying that Adolf Hitler was initially good for Germany and downplays her slurs against African Americans and the Japanese.

30

1932 The Cubs acquire Babe Herman from the Reds for pitcher Bob Smith, catcher Rollie Hemsley, and outfielders Johnny Moore and Lance Richbourg.

1948 Cleveland player-manager Lou Boudreau is selected the AL MVP after producing a .987 OPS, the highest ever to date by an AL shortstop.

1952 Bitter relations between the Yankees and Dodgers extend beyond the field of play when Brooklyn's Jackie Robinson bluntly accuses the Yankees on a New York television station of being racist for still refusing to put an African American player in pinstripes, and Yankees GM George Weiss calls the charge ridiculous.

1959 Baltimore acquires outfielder Jackie Brandt, catcher Roger Mc-Cardell, and pitcher Gordon Jones from the Giants for pitchers Billy O'Dell and Billy Loes.

1972 The Royals deal Roger Nelson and Richie Scheinblum to the Reds for Wayne Simpson and Hal McRae, who plates more than 1,000 runs in 15 seasons with KC.

1998 Arizona inks free-agent lefty Randy Johnson to a four-year, $53,000,000 contract.

1999 In the wake of the ML umpires' mass resignation disaster, arbiters agree by vote to form a new union. Meanwhile, Pete Rose explores new venues for reinstatement by starting a website that allows fans to put their names on a petition calling for his return.

December

1

1930 After their sixth consecutive basement finish, the hapless Red Sox hire former ML outfielder Shano Collins to manage the club, which "miraculously" rises to sixth in 1931 under the rookie pilot.

1962 The structure of minor league baseball changes when classifications B, C, and D are eliminated, and many of those circuits are now designated Class A. The South Atlantic and Eastern loops move from Class A to AA, and the Appalachian League shifts from Class D to the newly created Rookie classification.

1964 Responding to objections by the Colt Firearms Company to the Colt .45s' sale of items carrying its name, Houston officially changes its nickname to Astros.

1998 Mike Piazza's arrival via trade frees the Mets to send former All-Star catcher Todd Hundley along with a minor leaguer to the Dodgers for outfielder Roger Cedeno and catcher Charles Johnson, who is then dealt to the Orioles for closer Armando Benitez. Elsewhere, Rafael Palmeiro brokers a deal, without his agent, for a five-year, $45,000,000 pact to stay with the Rangers, while rejecting Baltimore's offer that would have paid him $5,000,000 more. Meanwhile, Baltimore inks Albert Belle to a five-year contract worth $65,000,000, but a degenerative hip condition ends Belle's career after just two seasons in Orioles garb.

2002 Former Orioles hurler Dave McNally dies of lung cancer at the age of 60 in Billings, MT, 27 years after playing his final season without a contract, as per a decision by arbitrator Peter Seitz that granted McNally free agency and opened the door to players seeking the highest bidder for their services.

2

1916   Years of pressure from players finally bear fruit when ML owners agree to pay an injured player for the duration of his contract rather than the previous required period of 15 days before either releasing or suspending him.

1927   The Tigers send first baseman Lu Blue and future HOF outfielder Heinie Manush to the Browns for pitcher Elam Vangilder, shortstop Chick Galloway, and outfielder Harry Rice.

1937   Detroit peddles Gee Walker, Marv Owen, and Mike Tresh to the White Sox for Vern Kennedy, Tony Piet, and Dixie Walker. Meanwhile, Boston ships the Browns pitcher Bobo Newsom, outfielder Buster Mills, and shortstop Red Kress for outfielder Joe Vosmik.

1958   Cleveland acquires center fielder Jimmy Piersall from the Red Sox for first baseman Vic Wertz and outfielder Gary Geiger.

1963   Two franchises far to the east of the Rocky Mountains, the Arkansas Travelers and the Indianapolis Indians, are transferred from the IL to the PCL.

1971   The Dodgers deal Dick Allen to the White Sox for lefty Tommy John and infielder Steve Huntz.

1974   The MLB Rules Committee permits baseballs to be made of cowhide rather than horsehide as a cost-cutting measure.

2002   The Phillies sign Indians first baseman Jim Thome to a six-year, $85,000,000 pact after Thome sets a new Indians season mark with 52 homers.

3

1879   The NL launches a three-day meeting in Buffalo to hammer out the details of the first reserve clause, several lasting rule changes, and one draconian change that permits any of its member clubs to suspend a player at will for drunkenness or insubordination.

1891   Led by Denny Lyons, Red Bittman, Jack Boyle, and Lefty Marr, pro players residing in Cincinnati stage the "Owl Club Ball," a benefit dance for former ML catcher Frank Bell, who was slain in a bar fracas several months earlier and buried in an unmarked grave. The proceeds from the dance are converted into a "monument fund" to give Bell a proper headstone.

1957 The ChiSox get Billy Goodman, Tito Francona, and pitcher Ray Moore from Baltimore for pitchers Jack Harshman and Russ Heman, outfielder Larry Doby, and first baseman Jim Marshall.

1958 The Giants trade pitcher Ruben Gomez and catcher Valmy Thomas to the Phils for former NL Rookie of the Year Jack Sanford, who wins 24 games four years later when the transplanted Giants win their first pennant in San Francisco.

1968 To stimulate offense and increase run production, the MLB Rules Committee lowers the pitcher's mound from 15 inches to 10 inches and shrinks the strike zone. Meanwhile, Democratic National Committee treasurer Bob Short purchases the Washington Senators for $10,000,000 and names himself GM.

1969 The Mets ship outfielder Amos Otis and pitcher Bob Johnson to the Royals for third baseman Joe Foy, who plays one dismal season in Queens, while Otis makes five AL All-Star squads with KC.

1974 The Mets anger their fans by trading popular ace reliever Tug McGraw and two others to the Phillies for catcher John Stearns, outfielder Del Unser, and a minor leaguer.

1980 Don Sutton, the Dodgers' career record holder for wins, losses, strikeouts, and innings, leaves after 15 seasons, signing a four-year, $3,500,000 agreement with the Astros.

2001 Despite filing for bankruptcy, the Enron Corporation plans to continue making payments on its 30-year, $100,000,000 agreement to retain the company's name on the Astros' new park, Enron Field, but Houston buys back the remaining years on Enron's contract for just $2,100,000 in February 2002 and sells the naming rights four months later to the Minute Maid Company in a 28-year deal for some $170,000,000.

2007 The Veteran's Committee elects managers Billy Southworth and Dick Williams, plus executives Barney Dreyfuss, Bowie Kuhn, and Walter O'Malley, to the HOF.

4

1878 The NL, in addition to admitting franchises in Syracuse, Buffalo, and Cleveland for 1879 to replace Indianapolis and soon-to-be-jettisoned Milwaukee, adopts many new rules, but the only lasting one requires the first batter in a new inning to follow the batter in the order that was last to bat in the previous inning rather than the last to make an out.

1940 Dodgers GM Larry MacPhail gives the Cardinals $65,000, backup receiver Gus Mancuso, and a minor league pitcher for catcher Mickey Owen.

1946 The Reds snare outfielder Augie Galan from Brooklyn for pitcher Ed Heusser.

1952 Detroit swaps pitchers Virgil Trucks and Hal White, plus outfielder Johnny Groth, to the Browns for rookie slugger Bob Nieman, second baseman Owen Friend, and "bonus baby" flop Jay Porter.

1957 ML owners agree to abolish the bonus rule and raise the minimum ML salary to $7,000. Meanwhile, Cleveland sends pitcher Early Wynn and outfielder Al Smith to the White Sox for third baseman Fred Hatfield and outfielder Minnie Minoso.

1958 The Dodgers trade outfielder Gino Cimoli to the Cardinals for pitcher Phil Paine and outfielder Wally Moon, who earns fame the following year for his "moon" shots over the short left-field screen in Los Angeles Coliseum.

1964 Washington ships pitcher Claude Osteen, infielder John Kennedy, and $100,000 to the Dodgers for outfielder Frank Howard, third baseman Ken McMullen, and two pitchers, plus a player to be named later. Meanwhile, ML owners agree to begin a free-agent draft in January, the selections to be made every four months by teams based upon the inverse order of the previous year's standings.

1968 Houston blunders by sending Mike Cuellar and two prospects to Baltimore for outfielders Curt Blefary and John Mason, as Cuellar shares the AL Cy Young in 1969 and wins 20 games four times with the Orioles.

1974 The Expos ship two future stars, outfielder Ken Singleton and Mike Torrez, to the Orioles for fading pitcher Dave McNally and two lesser players.

1975 Ted Turner enters a tentative agreement to buy the Atlanta Braves from Bill Bartholomay and officially makes the purchase in January 1976 for a reported $12,000,000.

1976 Tigers third baseman Aurelio Rodriguez wins the AL Gold Glove, ending Baltimore's Brooks Robinson's uninterrupted 16-year reign as the junior loop's hot corner fielding honoree.

2004 Ron Williamson, the first player picked from the state of Oklahoma in the 1971 ML draft, dies in an Oklahoma nursing home after spending 11 years on death row for a murder that DNA evidence eventually established had been committed by one of the witnesses against him at his trial.

2007 The Marlins trade third baseman Miguel Cabrera and pitcher Dontrelle Willis to the Tigers for outfielder Cameron Maybin, pitcher Andrew Miller, catcher Mike Rabelo, and three prospects.

5

1878 The NL supplements its rule changes of the previous day by eliminating first-bounce outs on both foul balls and third strikes. The old rule on fouls is later restored before being permanently dropped.

1926 The Cards' Bob O'Farrell is the first catcher to receive a league MVP Award and receives a further bonus when he is named the Birds' manager, replacing the recently traded Rogers Hornsby.

1956 The Tigers acquire four players from the A's, including first baseman Eddie Robinson and third baseman Jim Finigan, in return for pitchers Virgil Trucks and Ned Garver, first baseman Wayne Belardi, a minor league pitcher, and $20,000.

1957 The Cards garner outfielders Curt Flood and Joe Taylor from Cincinnati for pitchers Willard Schmidt, Marty Kutyna, and Ted Wieand.

1963 Detroit sends Jim Bunning with catcher Gus Triandos to the Phillies for outfielder Don Demeter and hurler Jack Hamilton.

1969 Chub Feeney is named the new NL president, succeeding Warren Giles.

1973 When the Cubs' Ron Santo nixes a deal to the Angels, he is the first player to invoke the new 10-and-5 rule, allowing veterans with at least 10 years in the majors and the last five spent on the same club to veto a trade; however, Santo consents to a swap to the White Sox six days later. Meanwhile, the Dodgers deal outfielder Willie Davis to the Expos for reliever Mike Marshall, who wins the 1974 NL Cy Young.

1978 After 16 years in Reds garb, Pete Rose signs a four-year, $3,200,000 deal with the Phillies.

1984 In a seven-player deal, the A's send Rickey Henderson to the Yankees but save his uniform, as the speedy outfielder returns to Oakland a record four more times during his lengthy career.

1988 The Rangers and Cubs swing a nine-player deal, highlighted by the Bruins shipping outfielder Rafael Palmeiro and lefty Jamie Moyer for reliever Mitch Williams.

1989 Cleveland obtains infielder Carlos Baerga, future AL Rookie of the Year Sandy Alomar, and outfielder Chris James from San Diego for RBI machine Joe Carter.

1990 The Padres trade second baseman Roberto Alomar and outfielder Joe Carter to the Blue Jays for first baseman Fred McGriff and shortstop Tony Fernandez.

2007 Despite dropping more than 100 points off his slugging average from the previous season and belting 25 fewer homers than two years earlier, Braves free agent Andruw Jones reaches a preliminary agreement with the Dodgers worth $36,200,000 for two years.

6

1877 The NL meeting in Cleveland concludes with William Hulbert reelected loop president and Hartford and St. Louis resigning as members of the league, soon to be joined by Louisville, leaving the struggling two-year-old circuit with only three of its eight original teams—Chicago, Boston, and Cincinnati.

1882 A. G. Mills is elected NL president, replacing interim officer Arthur Soden.

1920 A court of appeals upholds baseball's reserve clause and rules that because the game is a sport, it is neither subject to interstate commerce nor antitrust laws.

1921 The Giants procure third baseman Heinie Groh from Cincinnati in return for outfielder George Burns, catcher Mike Gonzalez, and $150,000.

1938 Shortstop Dick Bartell is the centerpiece of a major trade for the third time in the 1930s when the Giants swap him, Gus Mancuso, and Hank Leiber to the Cubs for shortstop Billy Jurges, outfielder Frank Demaree, and catcher Ken O'Dea.

1939 Dick Bartell is on the move again, this time from the Cubs to Detroit for shortstop Billy Rogell.

1946 The Yankees pick up catcher Sherman Lollar, the 1945 IL batting champ, and veteran second baseman Ray Mack from Cleveland, for outfielder Hal Peck and two minor leaguer pitchers, one of which is 1948 rookie sensation Gene Bearden.

1954 The White Sox send former two-time AL batting champ Ferris Fain to Detroit along with pitcher Leo Crisante and first baseman Jack

Phillips for first baseman Walt Dropo, pitcher Ted Gray, and outfielder Bob Nieman.

1958   Washington swaps third baseman Eddie Yost, shortstop Rocky Bridges, and outfielder Neil Chrisley to Detroit for infielders Reno Bertoia and Ron Samford and outfielder Jim Delsing.

1959   Cleveland garners first baseman Norm Cash, catcher Johnny Romano, and third baseman Bubba Phillips from the White Sox for outfielder Minnie Minoso, catcher Dick Brown, and pitchers Jake Striker and Don Ferrarese.

2002   The Indians engineer a coup, sending catcher Einar Diaz and pitcher Ryan Drese to the Expos for Travis Hafner, who pounds 42 homers and a season record-tying six grand slams in 2006.

7

1937   Five of the game's pioneers—Connie Mack, John McGraw, Morgan Bulkeley, Ban Johnson, and George Wright—comprise the third group of electees to the HOF.

1939   In a special balloting, Lou Gehrig is elected to the HOF less than six months after his official retirement.

1995   On his 28th birthday, Seattle's Tino Martinez is packaged with relievers Jeff Nelson and Jim Mecir to the Yankees for third baseman Russ Davis and pitcher Sterling Hitchcock.

8

1880   The NL breaks with its custom of accepting only established professional teams to fill vacancies when it accepts Detroit as a replacement for the recently ejected Cincinnati franchise, even though the Michigan city as yet has no team to represent it.

1886   Pittsburgh purchases second baseman Sam Barkley from AA rival St. Louis, triggering a controversy over whether Barkley belongs to Pittsburgh or Baltimore that culminates in the ouster of AA president Denny McKnight.

1899   Barney Dreyfuss, part owner of both the Louisville and Pittsburgh franchises, perpetrates the third and final major syndicate ownership heist in a 12-month period when he earmarks most of Louisville's top players, including manager Fred Clarke and Honus Wagner, for delivery to Pittsburgh.

1914 Amid a massive dismantling of his Philadelphia A's dynasty that has won four AL pennants in the past five years, club manager Connie Mack peddles the loop's reigning MVP, second baseman Eddie Collins, to the White Sox for $50,000.

1947 The Dodgers give outfielder Dixie Walker and pitchers Hal Gregg and Vic Lombardi to the Pirates for third baseman Billy Cox, infielder Gene Mauch, and pitcher Preacher Roe.

1954 The Cards pay high for one of the first relief specialists, Frank Smith, sending the Reds pitcher Gerry Staley and third sacker Ray Jablonski.

1959 With Continental League president Branch Rickey twittering at him mockingly, AL president Joe Cronin continues to report that expansion plans for his loop are indefinite, even as Rickey's rebel loop announces that a franchise will be installed in Atlanta.

1966 Roger Maris is shipped to the Cardinals for third baseman Charley Smith after hitting just 13 homers for the last place Yankees.

1983 The Mets rob the Dodgers by peddling utility man Bob Bailor and reliever Carlos Diaz for starter Sid Fernandez and a prospect. Meanwhile, former Yankees third baseman, cardiologist Dr. Bobby Brown, is elected AL president.

1991 In Barquisimeto, Venezuela, Brewers reliever Julio Machado is arrested for slaying a woman after a car accident in which she was a passenger. In 1996, Machado is sentenced to 12 years in prison.

1992 Free agent Barry Bonds signs a then-record six-year, $43,750,000 contract with the Giants.

1994 Darryl Strawberry and his agent, Eric Goldschmidt, are indicted on federal tax evasion charges for failing to declare income from card and autograph shows. Strawberry compounds his plight two months later by testing positive for cocaine, earning a 60-day suspension from MLB and a pink slip from the Giants.

2005 Just one season after signing shortstop Edgar Renteria to a four-year, $40,000,000 pact, the Red Sox trade him to the Braves for minor leaguer Andy Marte.

9

1867 At their annual convention, the National Association of Baseball Players bans African Americans from all teams for "political" reasons.

1868 The National Association of Baseball Players bows to the inevitable at its 12th annual convention and agrees to allow its clubs to use players who are paid to play.

1880 The NL, in the course of its annual meeting, adopts several new rules, all of them ephemeral, though one, which moves the front line pitcher's box from 45 feet to 50 feet, endures until 1893.

1913 Former ML pitcher John Tener is elected NL president, adding to his already full plate, which includes serving as the governor of Pennsylvania.

1923 Former ML pitcher and manager Bill Donovan is killed in a train wreck after swapping berths with future Yankees GM George Weiss, who escapes with minor injuries.

1925 Under pressure for several years to resign, AL president Ban Johnson instead has his contract extended to 1935 and his salary hiked to $40,000.

1931 To cut costs during the Depression, ML owners vote to shave the roster limit from 25 to 23.

1936 In a swap of quality third basemen, the Red Sox trade the AL's top stolen base threat, Billy Werber, to the A's for Pinky Higgins.

1942 Charles Mears, reportedly the first to make a career of automobile advertising and the owner of "probably the most extensive collection of baseball literature in existence," dies in Cleveland at the age of 68.

1947 Cleveland acquires infielder Johnny Berardino, soon to become the star of the soap opera *General Hospital*, from the Browns for an eventual price of $65,000.

1953 The Red Sox send pitcher Mickey McDermott and outfielder Tom Umphlett to Washington for outfielder Jackie Jensen. Meanwhile, the majors raise the minimum player salary to $6,000 but are still loath to add broadcast revenues from the World Series and All-Star Games to the player pension fund.

1955 Brooklyn acquires third baseman Randy Jackson and pitcher Don Elston from the Cubs for outfielder Walt Moryn, pitcher Russ Meyer, and third baseman Don Hoak.

1959 The Phils obtain outfielder Johnny Callison from the White Sox for third baseman Gene Freese.

1965 The Reds front office unwisely acquires pitchers Milt Pappas and Jack Baldschun, plus outfielder Dick Simpson, from the Orioles for Frank Robinson, who pays immediate dividends by leading Baltimore to a world championship in 1966 while also copping the Triple Crown and AL MVP. Meanwhile, Branch Rickey dies in Columbus, OH, at the age of 83.

1977 The A's and Reds announce that Vida Blue is going to Cincinnati for first baseman Dave Revering, plus $1,750,000, but Commissioner Kuhn blocks the deal in January, claiming that the large amount of money involved will create a competitive imbalance amongst ML clubs.

1980 The Cubs swap ace reliever Bruce Sutter to the Cardinals for Leon Durham and Ken Reitz.

1981 Dodgers righty Rick Sutcliffe is dealt with second baseman Jack Perconte to the Indians for Jorge Orta and two prospects. Elsewhere, the Yankees announce that former manager Gene Michael is replacing Bob Lemon in 1983 one day after publicizing that Lemon, who replaced Michael during this past season, will remain in 1982.

1992 The Braves ink Cubs free agent Greg Maddux to a five-year contract worth $28,000,000. Maddux goes on to win Cy Young honors in each of his first three seasons in Atlanta and 194 games overall with the Braves.

1996 The Marlins sign free agent Alex Fernandez to a five-year, $35,000,000 deal, but after winning 17 games in 1997, Fernandez is diagnosed with a torn rotator cuff during the NLCS and garners only 11 more career victories over the next two years.

2000 Five days after the Rockies sign southpaw Denny Neagle to a five-year, $51,000,000 pact, they ink lefty Mike Hampton to a $121,000,000 agreement over eight seasons, but Colorado gets just two undistinguished years from Hampton (21–28, 5.75 ERA) and three from Neagle (19–23, 5.57 ERA).

2003 The Mets sign Japanese shortstop Kaz Matsui to a three-year, $20,100,000 deal, but the former Nippon star flops and is injury-riddled before being dealt in June 2006.

10

1876 At the close of a loop meeting in Cleveland, newly elected NL president William Hulbert announces that New York and Philadelphia, the two largest cities in his fledgling enterprise, are being expelled for refusing to make their last western trips of the 1876 season.

1897 Washington trades pitcher Doc McJames, shortstop Gene DeMontreville, and first baseman Dan McGann to Baltimore for pitcher Doc Amole, first baseman Jack Doyle, and second baseman Heinie Reitz.

1918 John Heydler, long the NL secretary, is elected senior loop president.

1919 NL officials vote to ban all pitchers who are not established MLers from using the spitball.

1924 A new World Series system is adopted, slated to begin the following year, with the two leagues alternating which will host four games and which will host the remaining three.

1935 Connie Mack dissolves the last remnants of his 1929 to 1931 A's dynasty when he sells Jimmie Foxx to the Red Sox along with pitcher Johnny Marcum for $150,000 and two lesser players and then peddles Al Simmons to the White Sox for $75,000 and two lesser players.

1936 The Indians get the worst of a three-way deal when they ship future 20-game winner Thornton Lee to the White Sox, with Jack Salveson moving from the Sox to the Senators and aging Earl Whitehill coming from Washington to Cleveland.

1950 The IL strikes an ominous note when it announces that its Jersey City franchise is moving to Ottawa, Canada, in 1951, marking the second New Jersey IL club in the two years to quit trying to compete with ML games from New York being televised in the Garden State.

1951 The Phils garner catcher Smoky Burgess and two lesser players from Cincinnati for catcher Andy Seminick, outfielder Dick Sisler, and two lesser players.

1956 Frank Lane makes one of the few good trades in his tenure as the Cards GM when he bags pitcher Sam Jones and three lesser players from the Cubs for four players the Cards never miss.

1971 The Mets make a "slight" error by dealing Nolan Ryan, plus three others, to the Angels, for third baseman Jim Fregosi, who fizzles in Queens while Ryan exits with 324 wins and a record 5,714 strikeouts.

1972 The AL votes unanimously to adopt the DH rule for a three-year experiment and two years later makes it a permanent fixture. Meanwhile, MLB codifies the first rules governing saves.

1975 After leading a group that purchases 80% of the White Sox from John Allyn, maverick magnate Bill Veeck opens shop in the hotel lobby at the winter meetings and starts dealing by sending Jim Kaat, a 20-game winner in each of the past two seasons in Pale Hose garb, plus a prospect to the Phillies, for pitchers Dick Ruthven and Roy Thomas and utility man Alan Bannister.

1976 Rangers shortstop Danny Thompson dies of leukemia at the age of 29 in Rochester, MN.

1981 In a multiplayer deal on both sides, the Cards come out a winner by acquiring future HOF shortstop Ozzie Smith from the Padres for Garry Templeton.

1984 The Mets add a key piece to their 1986 world championship club by snaring Expos catcher Gary Carter for infielder Hubie Brooks, outfielder Herm Winningham, catcher Mike Fitzgerald, and minor league hurler Floyd Youmans.

1991 Former George Steinbrenner crony Howard Spira is sentenced to two and a half years in jail for attempting to extort $110,000 from the Yankees owner.

1993 The Colorado Silver Bullets, an all-female baseball team sponsored by the Coors Brewing Co., announce that they will play some 50 exhibition games against men's minor league, semipro, and college clubs, with some contests scheduled at ML parks.

1999 An Associated Press panel votes Babe Ruth as player of the 20th century, with Willie Mays coming in second.

11

1884 The AA votes to refuse to adopt the NL rule allowing overhand pitching and to continue to allow a batter to be retired on a foul ball caught on one bounce, but the loop rescinds both archaic statutes on June 7, 1885.

1911 The Eastern League, the oldest existing minor league, changes its name to the IL and elects Ed Barrow loop president.

1917 Phils owner Williams Baker, pressed for cash, saddens his clientele when he sells Pete Alexander and Bill Killefer, the NL's top battery, to the Cubs for $55,000 and two lesser players.

1928 At the NL winter meeting, President John Heydler proposes that a DH bat in place of the pitcher, contending that fans dislike watching weak-hitting hurlers make an almost automatic out.

1931 The Cubs swap 1931 bust Hack Wilson to the Cardinals along with pitcher Bud Teachout for the often-traded Burleigh Grimes.

1934 The NL is alone in voting to permit any of its teams that install lights to play a maximum of seven night games a year, as the AL refuses to play under artificial lighting until 1937.

1935 Cleveland sends pitchers Steve Sundra and Monte Pearson to the Yankees for pitcher Johnny Allen.

1938 With the apparent complicity of the other seven AL teams, Washington pulls off an interleague deal that sends first baseman Zeke Bonura, the Senators' top slugger in 1938, to the Giants for $20,000 and two minor leaguers.

1939 Led by Russian-born pitcher Victor Starfin, the Yomiuri Giants clinch their first of four consecutive Japanese league pennants.

1941 The Giants cheaply pick up slugging first baseman Johnny Mize from Branch Rickey, forking over three expendable players and a mere $50,000 to the Cardinals GM.

1950 ML moguls vote 9–7 not to renew Happy Chandler's contract as commissioner.

1951 Joe DiMaggio officially retires from the Yankees. Meanwhile, the Cards acquire their 1952 player-manager, Eddie Stanky, from the Giants for lefty Max Lanier and outfielder Chuck Diering.

1956 The Cards trade four players to the Cubs, including pitcher Tom Poholsky, for pitchers Sam Jones and Jim Davis, utility man Eddie Miksis, and catcher Hobie Landrith.

1957 U.S. Congressman Emanuel Celler threatens ML baseball with antitrust action if it goes ahead with its plan to televise a weekend Game of the Week into minor league sectors.

1959 The Yankees garner Roger Maris from KC in a seven-player deal that nets the A's Hank Bauer, Norm Siebern, and Don Larsen, along with backup first baseman Marv Throneberry.

1970 The Braves' Rico Carty, the NL's defending bat titlist at .366, suffers a knee injury in the Dominican Winter League, shelving him for the entire 1971 season after he misses all of 1968 with tuberculosis.

1975   The Yankees help build their next dynasty by sending pitcher Doc Medich to the Pirates for second baseman Willie Randolph, plus pitchers Dock Ellis and Ken Brett. Meanwhile, the Bombers also acquire hurler Ed Figueroa and outfielder Mickey Rivers from the Angels for Bobby Bonds.

1991   The Mets ship outfielder Kevin McReynolds and infielders Gregg Jefferies and Keith Miller to the Royals for Bret Saberhagen and shortstop Bill Pecota.

2000   The Rangers sign Alex Rodriguez to the richest deal in sports history to date, a ten-year pact worth $252,000,000.

2001   In an eight-player deal with the Indians, the Mets receive Roberto Alomar, but the All-Star second baseman flops and is dealt to the White Sox in July of the following campaign.

12

1866   The 10th annual convention of the National Association of Baseball Players adopts rule changes that include the introduction of called balls as well as strikes and of a rectangular pitcher's box measuring 6' by 4'.

1903   The Cards stumble by trading rookie hurler Three Finger Brown and catcher Jack O'Neill to the Cubs for pitcher Jack Taylor and catcher Larry McLean.

1913   Pittsburgh sends pitcher Hank Robinson, infielders Dots Miller and Art Butler, and outfielders Chief Wilson and Cozy Dolan to St. Louis for first baseman Ed Konetchy, pitcher Bob Harmon, and third baseman Mike Mowrey.

1922   Jake Ruppert buys out his partner, Til Huston, and gains full control of the Yankees.

1924   Convinced that pitcher Stan Coveleski is washed up, Cleveland deals him to Washington for two players who contribute nothing to the Indians and watches its former ace wins 20 games for the Senators in 1925 and leads the AL in winning percentage and ERA.

1928   The Pirates buy pitcher Larry French, one of the top southpaws in the 1930s, from Portland of the PCL.

1930   New rules abolish both the sacrifice fly and counting balls that bounce into the stands as home runs.

1933   Connie Mack continues the decimation of his former A's dynasty by peddling catcher Mickey Cochrane to the Tigers for catcher

Johnny Pasek and $100,000 and then sending Lefty Grove, Max Bishop, and Rube Walberg to the Red Sox for $125,000, infielder Rabbit Warstler, and pitcher Bob Kline and, finally, bestowing pitcher George Earnshaw and newly acquired Pasek on the White Sox for $20,000 and catcher Charlie Berry.

1935 Brooklyn sends infielder Tony Cuccinello, catcher Al Lopez, and rookie pitcher Bobby Reis to the Boston Bees for outfielder Randy Moore and pitchers Ed Brandt and Ray Benge.

1940 Cleveland sends catcher Frankie Pytlak, pitcher Joe Dobson, and infielder Bad News Hale to the Red Sox for pitcher Jim Bagby Jr., catcher Gene Desautels, and outfielder Gee Walker.

1941 The Pirates trade shortstop Arky Vaughan to Brooklyn for pitcher Luke Hamlin, catcher Babe Phelps, infielder Pete Coscarart, and first baseman Jimmy Wasdell.

1948 The Yankees send the Browns catcher Sherman Lollar and $100,000 for pitcher Fred Sanford, catcher Roy Partee, and two lesser players.

1949 The rules committee shaves the strike zone from a batter's shoulders to the knees to the distance between the armpits and the knees, a seemingly odd response to a season that produced a record number of bases on balls in the AL.

1966 The U.S. Supreme Court preserves baseball's antitrust laws by refusing to review Wisconsin's suit to prevent the Braves from moving to Atlanta.

1968 The first trade in Kansas City Royals history involves a future Hall of Famer, as relief great Hoyt Wilhelm is shipped to the Angels for Ed Kirkpatrick and a minor leaguer.

1969 The Twins ship third baseman Graig Nettles, outfielder Ted Uhlaender, plus pitchers Dean Chance and Bob Miller, to the Indians for hurlers Luis Tiant and Stan Williams.

1970 At the age of 25, Twins outfielder/pinch runner Herman Hill drowns in Valencia, Venezuela, where he has been playing winter ball.

1975 The Mets trade fan favorite Rusty Staub and a minor leaguer to Detroit for 13-year Tigers veteran Mickey Lolich.

1980 The Brewers acquire two future Cy Young winners in one swap when they send Sixto Lezcano, David Green, Dave LaPointe, and Lary Sorensen to the Cardinals for Rollie Fingers and Pete Vuckovich, who capture the trophy in 1981 and 1982, respectively, for Milwaukee.

1985   The Yankees send hurler Joe Cowley and catcher Ron Hassey to the White Sox for southpaw Britt Burns and two prospects, but a degenerative hip condition prevents Burns, who won 18 games in 1985, from pitching again in the majors.

1998   Kevin Brown inks baseball's first nine-figure contract when he signs a seven-year, $105,000,000 deal at the age of 33.

13

1907   The Giants obtain shortstop Al Bridwell, first baseman Fred Tenney, and catcher Tom Needham from the Boston Doves for pitcher George Ferguson, first baseman Dan McGann, shortstop Bill Dahlen, catcher Mike Bowerman, and outfielder George Browne.

1910   Former ML first baseman Dan McGann is found dead in his Louisville hotel room with a bullet in his chest and a revolver in his hand. The death is ruled a suicide when McGann's associates attest that he was despondent over the recent tragic deaths of several family members, but his two sisters insist that he was murdered for a valuable diamond ring missing from his body.

1927   Washington owner Clark Griffith is given permission for the Senators to open the AL season a day ahead of the rest of the league, the start of a long tradition for Griffith's franchise.

1928   The Cards swap shortstop Tommy Thevenow to the Phils for shortstop Heinie Sand and $10,000.

1934   Cincinnati acquires minor league first baseman Johnny Mize from the Cardinals, only to return him the following April when he brings a gimpy knee to spring training.

1941   Washington snatches promising outfielder Stan Spence from the Red Sox along with pitcher Jack Wilson in return for outfielder Johnny Welaj and pitcher Ken Chase.

1943   The A's send pitcher Roger Wolff to Washington for pitcher Bobo Newsom.

1949   The A's package four players and $100,000 to the Browns for outfielder Paul Lehner and third baseman Bob Dillinger.

1956   Giants pitcher Dick Littlefield is involved in his third trade in less than seven months when he is sent to Brooklyn along with $30,000 for Jackie Robinson, but only temporarily, as the deal is rescinded when Robinson chooses to retire rather than join the hated Giants.

1961   After Mickey Mantle clubs 54 homers, the Yankees reward him with an $82,000 contract for 1962.

1966   The Giants swap outfielder Cap Peterson and pitcher Bob Priddy to the Senators for Mike McCormick, who captures the 1967 Cy Young honor with San Francisco.

1996   After 13 years with the Red Sox, Roger Clemens signs a three-year deal with the Blue Jays worth nearly $25,000,000.

2000   The Red Sox lure free-agent outfielder Manny Ramirez away from the Indians with an eight-year, $160,000,000 pact.

2001   The Yankees ink free agent Jason Giambi to a $120,000,000, seven-year deal, after he averages 38 homers over the previous three seasons with the A's, but the slugger's career soon bottoms out when he publicly admits to using steroids and injecting human growth hormones.

2007   Former Senate Majority Leader George Mitchell releases a 409-page report on the use of steroids and performance-enhancing drugs in baseball. The document identifies 85 names, in varying degrees of severity, featuring seven MVPs, two Cy Young Award winners, and 31 All-Stars, with Jose Canseco mentioned most often (105), closely followed by Barry Bonds (103). Other players listed include Roger Clemens, Andy Pettitte, Gary Sheffield, Jason Giambi, Rafael Palmeiro, Miguel Tejada, Troy Glaus, and Eric Gagne.

14

1864   The eighth annual meeting of the National Association of Baseball Players adopts the "fly" game, abolishing the old rule that declared any ball struck fair that is caught on the first bounce an out.

1882   The AA is the first ML to hire a permanent staff of umpires for the coming season that will be scheduled, paid, and overseen by the league rather than by individual teams.

1898   Washington makes its best trade during its tenure in the NL, sending second baseman Heinie Reitz to Pittsburgh for outfielder Jimmy Slagle, second baseman Dick Padden, and outfielder Jack O'Brien.

1901   Searching for a strong leader to combat the AL, four NL owners oust Nick Young and select Al Spalding as president, but the senior league is forced to appoint an interim committee instead to assist Young when a court overturns Spalding's election two days later.

1906   The Braves swap second baseman Ed Abbaticchio to Pittsburgh for former NL batting champ Ginger Beaumont, second baseman Claude Ritchey, and pitcher Patsy Flaherty.

1911   Pittsburgh owner Barney Dreyfuss proposes a new dispersal of the annual World Series gate that eventually results in every first division finisher in both leagues receiving part of the postseason money.

1917   The BoSox send the A's sore-winged Vean Gregg, two other players, and $60,000 for catcher Wally Schang, pitcher Joe Bush, and outfielder Amos Strunk.

1922   In an action stemming from the Yankees' unpopular late-season acquisition of third baseman Joe Dugan from the Red Sox, both MLs approve a ban on nonwaiver trades after June 15.

1932   The Senators put in a busy day, trading five players and $20,000 in two separate deals for Earl Whitehill, a 22-game winner in 1933; former Washington star Goose Goslin; and two other players.

1938   The NL, in recognition of baseball's 100th anniversary, launches a new tradition when it grants Cincinnati the right to open the season a day ahead of the rest of the senior loop in honor of having had the first professional team, the 1869 Red Stockings.

1945   The Indians foolishly trade outfielder Jeff Heath to Washington for former AL stolen-base king George Case, whose legs are nearly gone.

1948   The world champion Indians ship first baseman Eddie Robinson and pitchers Ed Klieman and Joe Haynes to Washington for former batting champ Mickey Vernon and future 300-game winner Early Wynn. Elsewhere, the Cubs send pitcher Hank Borowy and first baseman Eddie Waitkus to the Phils for pitchers Monk Dubiel and Dutch Leonard.

1949   The Giants acquire the Braves' keystone combo of Alvin Dark and Eddie Stanky for Willard Marshall, Sid Gordon, Buddy Kerr, and Sam Webb. Elsewhere, Detroit sends $100,000 and pitcher Lou Kretlow to the Browns for second baseman Jerry Priddy.

1960   In baseball's first-ever expansion draft, two Yankees pitchers are made each fledgling club's initial pick when the new Washington Senators choose Bobby Shantz and the Angels select Eli Grba.

1961   Despite his record-breaking 61-homer season, Roger Maris's request for a $75,000 salary is denied by Yankees GM Roy Hamey.

1976 The dismantling of the A's dynasty continues as the Padres sign free agents Rollie Fingers and Gene Tenace, two key figures in Oakland's three-year world championship run from 1972 to 1974.

1985 Lung cancer claims Roger Maris at the age of 51 in Houston, TX.

2001 Nine of the 22 umpires dismissed after a misguided mass resignation two years earlier must be rehired by MLB after U.S. District Court judge Harvey Bartle III upholds most of arbitrator Alan Symonette's decision.

15

1900 Amos Rusie, a holdout for the second time in his career, goes from the New York Giants, after being idle for two full seasons, to the Cincinnati Reds for a pitcher the Reds drafted just two weeks earlier from the Giants—one Christy Mathewson—in a Machiavellian deal orchestrated by Cincinnati owner John T. Brush, who expects to soon buy a controlling interest in the Giants.

1905 After losing a post–1900 record 29 games in 1905, future HOF hurler Vic Willis is rescued by the Pirates from the lowly Braves in return for third baseman Dave Brain, first baseman Del Howard, and pitcher Vive Lindaman. Elsewhere, the Cubs acquire outfielder Jimmy Sheckard from Brooklyn for third baseman Doc Casey, outfielders Billy Maloney and Jack McCarthy, pitcher Buttons Briggs, and $2,000.

1912 The Cubs send Reds pitcher Grover Lowdermilk, catcher Harry Chapman, and shortstop Joe Tinker, who becomes Cincinnati's player-manager, for five players, including pitcher Bert Humphries, third baseman Art Phelan, and outfielder Mike Mitchell.

1920 Ed Barrow, the Yankees' new trade chieftain, plucks future Hall of Famer Waite Hoyt, catcher Wally Schang, and two lesser players from his former team, the Red Sox, in return for four players who never do anything of note in Boston. Elsewhere, the Reds swap pitcher Dutch Ruether to Brooklyn for pitcher Rube Marquard.

1928 A year after acquiring future infield star Buddy Myer from Washington, the Red Sox return him to the Senators for five players, including pitchers Milt Gaston and Hod Lisenbee and shortstop Bobby Reeves.

1932 ML owners overrule Commissioner Landis when he tries to curtail the type of "chain store" farm system a number of teams, most notably the Cardinals, are now operating.

1933 Years of bickering that the AL ball is substantially livelier than the NL brand end when both MLs agree to use the same ball.

1938 The Tigers trade pitchers Eldon Auker and Jake Wade and outfielder Chet Morgan to the Red Sox for third baseman Pinky Higgins and pitcher Archie McKain.

1951 Former Ohio State Heisman Trophy winner Vic Janowicz signs with Pittsburgh for $25,000, making him the first victim of a new bonus rule passed on December 7, which stipulates that any free agent signed by a ML team for more than $4,000 must spend two years with his parent club before becoming eligible to be farmed out or else must be put on irrevocable waivers for $1.

1959 The Cards trade second baseman Don Blasingame to the Giants for outfielder Leon Wagner and infielder Daryl Spencer. Elsewhere, Cleveland ships first baseman Gordy Coleman, pitcher Cal McLish, and second baseman Billy Martin to Cincinnati for second baseman Johnny Temple.

1960 In one of the "biggest" swaps in ML annals, the Red Sox deal 6'6" hurler Frank Sullivan straight up to the Phillies for 6'8" chucker Gene Conley.

1961 Charlie Comiskey's grandson sells his 46% of the White Sox to a group of investors headed by Bill Bartholomay, ending the Comiskey family's ties to the Pale Hose that date back to the team's charter membership in the AL.

1969 The National Labor Relations Board rules that the case of fired umpires Bill Valentine and Al Salerno is subject to its jurisdiction. Although the two arbiters ultimately lose in federal court, NLRB's decision gives baseball unions the leverage they previously lacked by providing an impartial arbitrator to whom they can now appeal.

1980 Free agent Dave Winfield signs the biggest contract in OB history to date, a 10-year pact with the Yankees worth $16,000,000.

1983 Convicted drug users Willie Wilson, Willie Aikens, and Jerry Martin of the Royals and the Dodgers' Steve Howe are suspended for one season without pay by Commissioner Kuhn, but these penalties are lifted by an arbitrator on May 15; however, all three Royals, along with teammate Vida Blue, who was also convicted, eventually serve 90 days in jail.

2004 The Mets formalize a four-year, $53,000,000 pact with Pedro Martinez.

16

1877 The *Chicago Tribune* prints a letter from banned pitcher Jim Devlin to Louisville owner Charlie Chase implying that the previous season's scandal ran deeper than suspected and accusing NL umpire Dan Devinney of favoring Louisville in games he worked. Devinney, noted for whistling *See That My Grave Is Kept Green* while he officiates, never umpires another game in the NL.

1926 Kenesaw Mountain Landis is given a new seven-year term as commissioner along with a healthy raise to $65,000, more than any player, except Babe Ruth, will make in 1927.

1953 The Yankees swap six players to the A's, including 1954 rookie star Jim Finigan and first baseman/outfielder Vic Power, for first sacker Eddie Robinson, former AL Rookie of the Year Harry Byrd, and three lesser players.

1957 The Redlegs snag southpaw Harvey Haddix from the Phillies for outfielder Wally Post.

1976 The Reds deal first baseman Tony Perez, who had six 100-RBI seasons in Cincinnati, and reliever Will McEnaney to the Expos for hurlers Woodie Fryman and Dale Murray.

1982 After an absence of more than four years, Tom Seaver returns to the Mets from the Reds for pitcher Charlie Puleo, utility man Lloyd McClendon, and a minor leaguer.

1983 Yankees manager Billy Martin is fired for the third time by owner George Steinbrenner and replaced by Yogi Berra.

17

1889 After being officially launched the previous day, the PL breaks with tradition by adopting the two-umpire system, a rudimentary infield fly rule, and an increase in the pitching distance to 57½ feet, but the league rubberstamps the NL rule forbidding Sunday games and the unwritten rule enforcing the "color ban."

1891 The AA surrenders after its 10-year run as a ML, and a new 12-team ML is formed called "The National League and American Association of Professional Base Ball Clubs," after the four most solvent AA clubs—St. Louis, Louisville, Washington, and Baltimore—are absorbed by the NL.

1920 Both MLs agree to allow all established ML pitchers who use the spitball to continue using it for the remainder of their careers.

1924 The Yankees acquire pitcher Urban Shocker from the Browns in return for hurlers Joe Bush, Milt Gaston, and Joe Giard.

1928 Though John Heydler's recently proposed designated-hitter-for-the-pitcher rule is backed by several influential NL figures, the idea dies when the AL vetoes it at a joint ML meeting.

1932 After nearly winning the NL batting title in 1931, Cards first baseman Jim Bottomley brings the only NL loss leader, Ownie Carroll (19), and outfielder Estel Crabtree (.274) in a trade with Cincinnati.

1959 In a hearing to establish how much child support he should pay, Ted Williams reveals that his reported salary from the Red Sox of $100,000 was deliberately exaggerated and that he was actually only paid $60,000 by the club for the past season.

1964 After 18 years behind their mike, television and radio legend Mel Allen is fired by the Yankees.

1996 The Yankees ink lefty David Wells to a three-year, $13,500,000 contract.

18

1918 The Yankees send pitchers Ray Caldwell and Slim Love, catcher Roxy Walters, outfielder Frank Gilhooley, and $15,000 to the Red Sox for outfielder Duffy Lewis and pitchers Ernie Shore and Dutch Leonard.

1920 On his 34th birthday, Ty Cobb accepts a $32,500 annual salary to act as both player and manager of Detroit.

1950 The Yankees' Tommy Henrich retires after playing on eight pennant winners and seven world championship teams in his 11-year career.

1956 Phil Rizzuto swallows his bitterness at being released by the Yankees the past season and accepts a post in their broadcast booth, where he remains for some 40 years.

1973 The Yankees sign A's skipper Dick Williams despite Oakland's owner Charlie Finley's demand that he be compensated for the loss of his skipper since Williams still had a year left on his contract; however, AL president Joe Cronin nixes the Bombers deal, resulting in their inking Bill Virdon to guide the club.

1980 Although Fergie Jenkins is convicted on cocaine possession charges in a Canadian court, Judge Gerald Young overturns the decision.

19

1908   Reddy Foster, the first player in ML history to see action exclusively as a pinch hitter, commits suicide on the bank of the James River in Richmond, VA, by sticking a double-barreled shotgun in his mouth and pulling the trigger with his big toe.

1934   The Yankees complete a deal begun on November 21, when they send cash and three players to San Francisco of the PCL for Joe DiMaggio with the proviso that he remain with the Seals for another year of seasoning.

1986   Though Detroit free agent pitcher Jack Morris agrees to salary arbitration with the Tigers after he suspiciously fails to draw interest from any other club, he eventually accuses ML owners of collusion.

1991   Yankees pitcher Steve Howe is arrested again, this time in Montana, on a cocaine possession charge.

2002   The Yankees lure Japan's premier slugger, Hideki Matsui, from the Yomiuri Giants with a three-year, $21,000,000 contract, and he responds in his first ML season by plating 106 RBI and capturing the 2003 AL Rookie of the Year Award.

20

1903   Boston garners pitcher Jesse Tannehill from the New York Highlanders for pitcher Tom Hughes.

1904   The Pirates send first baseman Kitty Bransfield, infielder Otto Krueger, and outfielder Moose McCormick to the Phils for first baseman Del Howard. Elsewhere, the Phillies trade pitcher Chick Fraser and third baseman Harry Wolverton to the Boston Braves for pitcher Togie Pittinger.

1921   When the AL votes for the World Series to return to a best-of-seven affair and the NL prefers to keep the current best-of-nine setup, Commissioner Landis casts the deciding vote, siding with the AL. Meanwhile, the Yankees continue looting the Red Sox by snagging pitchers Joe Bush and Sad Sam Jones and shortstop Everett Scott for shortstop Roger Peckinpaugh and pitchers Rip Collins, Bill Piercy, and Jack Quinn.

1926   In arguably the most pivotal player trade to date, the Cards send second baseman Rogers Hornsby to the Giants for second baseman Frankie Frisch and pitcher Jimmy Ring.

1933 One year to the day after he had been reacquired by the Senators, Goose Goslin is sent to Detroit for outfielder John Stone, a favorable deal for Washington until Stone's career ends abruptly when he contracts tuberculosis.

1940 Connie Mack buys controlling interest in the "apathetic" A's from the Shibe family for a paltry $42,000.

1960 Charlie Finley gains majority control of the Kansas City A's when he purchases 52% of the late Arnold Johnson's estate.

1978 Sports cartoonist Willard Mullin, creator of the Brooklyn Bum, dies at the age of 76 in Corpus Christi, TX. Elsewhere, former ML second baseman Don Blasingame is the first American not of Japanese ancestry to manage a team in Japan when he signs with the Hanshin Tigers.

1993 The Indians deal first baseman Reggie Jefferson and shortstop Felix Fermin to the Mariners for shortstop Omar Vizquel, who goes on to win eight Gold Gloves in 11 years with the Tribe.

2001 The partners of the Jean Yawkey Trust (whose family has owned the Red Sox since 1933) announce that they are selling 100% of the club for more than $600,000,000 to a group headed by Marlins owner John Henry.

21

1944 Cards shortstop Marty Marion nips Cubs slugger Bill Nicholson to win the NL MVP Award by a single vote.

1960 Cubs owner Phil Wrigley announces that the Bruins will not hire a manager for the following season but rather will employ a "college of coaches" who will rotate between the majors and minors.

1977 Free agent Ross Grimsley signs with the Expos and goes on to win 20 games in 1978, making him the only pitcher to enter the charmed circle during the franchise's 36-year stay in Montreal.

1999 After signing third baseman Adrian Beltre at the tender age of 15, the Dodgers are fined $50,000 and banned from scouting any Dominican Republic players for one year.

22

1915 The FL's war with the two established MLs ends when a peace treaty brings FL owners $600,000 as part of the agreement and the right to auction their players to the highest bidder.

1959   Continental League president Branch Rickey awards the rebel loop's eighth and final franchise to Dallas/Fort Worth.

1980   The Boston Red Sox tender contracts to stars Carlton Fisk and Fred Lynn on December 22, two days after the Basic Agreement deadline, making the pair eligible for free agency. Lynn agrees to be dealt to the Angels in January, but Fisk becomes a free agent and signs with the White Sox in February.

1983   The Phillies' Pete Rose is awarded a tax refund of more than $36,000 after winning his lawsuit against the Internal Revenue Service.

1995   Although *Forbes* magazine values the Cardinals at more than twice the purchase price, Anheuser-Busch sells the Cards for approximately $150,000,000 to a Southwest Bank investment group after the buyers agree to keep the club in St. Louis.

23

1915   The Giants buy outfielder Edd Roush for $7,500 from Newark of the disbanding FL.

1958   The Dodgers trade second baseman Sparky Anderson to the Phillies for outfielder Rip Repulski and two minor league pitchers.

1975   Arbitrator Peter Seitz rules that pitchers Andy Messersmith and Dave McNally, who refused to sign new contracts with their present teams, are free agents, thereby opening the floodgates to escalating player salaries.

24

1921   The Indians pay high for first baseman Stuffy McInnis, sending the Red Sox three quality performers in first baseman George Burns, outfielder Elmer Smith, and first baseman/outfielder Moon Harris.

1930   Serving life in the Ohio State Penitentiary after slaying a fellow police officer in Xenia, OH, former ML catcher Tacks Latimer is pardoned by Governor Meyer Cooper on Christmas Eve for his role in helping guards stop a prison break in 1926, followed by his heroism the previous April in the worst disaster in Ohio penal history—a fire that killed 322 inmates.

1940   Cleveland sheds tempestuous outfielder Ben Chapman by dealing him to Washington for pitcher Joe Krakauskas, who wins just three games with the Tribe.

1967 Red Sox Cy Young winner Jim Lonborg tears ligaments in his left knee while skiing in Lake Tahoe. Though he continues pitching until 1979, Lonborg never regains his old form.

2002 After the Yankees and Cuban defector Jose Contreras agree to terms on a four-year, $32,000,000 pact, Red Sox club president Larry Lucchino, whose team had also actively courted the hurler, refers to the New York Yankees as an "evil empire," a nickname that sticks with Boston fans.

25

1898 Cincinnati pays Washington $5,000 for outfielder Kip Selbach.

1957 Buoyed by the support of New York congressmen Emanuel Celler and Kenneth Keating, the minor leagues seek recompense from the majors for televising games into their territorial rights.

1989 Fiery former player and manager Billy Martin dies in a car accident in Johnson City, NY, at the age of 61.

26

1914 The Phils send Sherry Magee to the Braves for cash, Possum Whitted, and Oscar Dugey.

1934 Commissioner Landis denies the Dodgers the rights to teenage southpaw Johnny Vander Meer, freeing him to sign with Cincinnati.

1953 The Braves land Pirates second sacker Danny O'Connell for $100,000 and six players, led by pitcher Max Surkont, outfielder Sid Gordon, and former NL Rookie of the Year Sam Jethroe.

1990 Poor attendance and other financial problems doom the Senior Professional Baseball Association and cause it to fold in the midst of its second season.

27

1984 Free-agent hurler Ed Whitson enters a Faustian bargain by signing a five-year, $4,400,000 deal with the Yankees. The hurler breaks the arm of his manager, Billy Martin, in a fight in 1985 and is hooted relentlessly at home for his poor performances until the Yankees send him back to San Diego, where he regains his form.

2003 Former ML outfielder Ivan Calderon dies in a bar in Loaiza, PR, after being shot seven times in the head in a suspected mafia killing.

2004   The Giants sign free agent Moises Alou, making him the first MLer to play for his father twice, as Felipe Alou, San Francisco's skipper, previously guided his son on the Expos from 1992 to 1996.

28

1887   *Sporting Life* reprints an article from the *Detroit Free Press* titled "A Loss to the Game" that decries how "colored players" are being kept out of the majors through prejudice.

1901   About to board a train for Arizona in desperate search of a cure for his terminal pulmonary trouble, former Chicago outfielder Dibby Flynn changes his mind because he wants to die among friends and starts homeward. He dies within 10 minutes after his lungs begin hemorrhaging.

1957   The Redlegs trade first sacker Ted Kluszewski to the Pirates for first baseman Dee Fondy.

2001   Four days before leaving office, New York City mayor Rudy Giuliani announces that the Mets and Yankees have forged a tentative bargain with the city to build two $800,000,000 retractable-roof ballparks.

2007   Former big leaguer Jim Leyritz is arrested on charges of DUI and killing a female driver after his car crashed into hers in Fort Lauderdale, FL. Leyritz refused a Breathalyzer test and initially rebuffed police when asked to give blood, even after learning of the woman's death.

29

1969   The *New York Times* reveals that former Cardinals outfielder Curt Flood, who had written a letter to Commissioner Kuhn several days earlier refusing his trade to the Phillies, plans to sue MLB over the reserve clause that binds players to their clubs in perpetuity.

30

1903   Former ML shortstop Dan Leahy, now in the minors, is shot and killed at the age of 33 in a Knoxville, TN, saloon quarrel.

1926   The *Chicago Tribune* gives the hot stove league fresh fodder when it runs a story that Detroit threw a four-game series to the White Sox in 1917 to assure that the AL pennant would go to Chicago rather than Boston or Cleveland.

2004 Relief supplies originally planned for Nicaragua are sent to the earthquake and tsunami victims of South Asia after Roberto Clemente Jr. postpones his trip to honor the 32nd anniversary of his father's death.

31

1914 The New York Yankees, under shady ownership since their inception in 1903, in answer to the prayers of AL president Ban Johnson, are sold for $460,000 to Jake Ruppert and Til Huston.

1966 Future Cooperstown inductee Eddie Mathews, who spent 15 seasons with the Braves that included two franchise shifts, is packaged with two others to Houston for pitcher Bob Bruce and outfielder Dave Nicholson.

1972 Pirates standout Roberto Clemente perishes at the age of 38, when the plane flying him to bring relief supplies for earthquake victims in Managua, Nicaragua, crashes in the Atlantic Ocean.

1974 Newly minted free agent Catfish Hunter signs a five-year, $3,750,000 contract with the Yankees, tripling the salary of any other active player to date.

2005 In memory of his father's ill-fated plane trip 33 years earlier, Roberto Clemente Jr. announces his plans to travel to Nicaragua to give humanitarian assistance.